CW01034070

THE BOY GENERALS

George Custer, Wesley Merritt,
and the Cavalry of the Army of the Potomac

Adolfo Ovies

SB

Savas Beatie

California

Library of Congress Cataloging-in-Publication Data

Names: Ovies, Adolfo, author.
    Title: The Boy Generals: George Custer, Wesley Merritt, and the Cavalry of
        the Army of the Potomac / by Adolfo Ovies.
    Other titles: George Custer, Wesley Merritt, and the Cavalry of the Army of
        the Potomac
    Description: El Dorado Hills, CA : Savas Beatie LLC, [2020] | Includes bibliographical references and
index. | Summary: "The first installment in a remarkable trilogy that examines the strategy, tactics, and
relationships of the leading Union army's mounted arm and its influence on the course of the Civil War in the
Eastern Theater. This volume is a rich and satisfying study that exposes the depths of one of the most
dysfunctional and influential relationships in the Army of the Potomac, and its long-lasting impact."
— Provided by publisher.
    Identifiers: LCCN 2020039841 | ISBN 9781611215359 (hardcover) | ISBN 9781611215366 (ebook)
    Subjects: LCSH: United States. Army of the Potomac. Cavalry Corps—History.|
        Custer, George A. (George Armstrong), 1839-1876. | Merritt, Wesley, 1834-1910. |
        United States—History—Civil War, 1861-1865—Cavalry operations. | United States.
        Army—Cavalry—History—Civil War 1861-1865. | Generals—United States—Biography. |
        United States. Army—Biography.
    Classification: LCC E470.2 .O93 2020 | DDC 355.0092/2 [B]—dc23
    LC record available at https://lccn.loc.gov/2020039841

First Edition, First Printing

SB

Savas Beatie
989 Governor Drive, Suite 102
El Dorado Hills, CA 95762
916-941-6896 / sales@savasbeatie.com / www.savasbeatie.com

All of our titles are available at special discount rates for bulk purchases in the United States. Contact us for information.

Proudly published, printed, and warehoused in the United States of America.

God bless the Irish!
There is no doubt in my mind that my wife, Juliet Ovies Sullivan,
would have shouldered her musket and stood in the firing line with the
greatest of that warrior race. Faugh a Ballagh! This was the motto inscribed
on the regimental flags of the Irish Brigade, and is translated as "Clear the Way!"
She not only cleared the way for this work, but for the course of my life.

I owe her everything.

Table of Contents

List of Maps

Photographs and illustrations have been distributed
throughout the book for the convenience of the reader.

The Hussar and the Dragoon

STUDENTS OF NAPOLEONIC CAVALRY operations know the French armies of the early nineteenth century featured three types of mounted soldiers: heavy cavalry, which contained armored horses and men (a paradigm never adopted in the United States), dragoons, and hussars. Dragoons were trained to fight equally effectively mounted and dismounted. Hussars were that era's fighter pilots: devil-may-care warriors riding into battle with a saber in one hand and a pretty girl in the other. Dragoons were stodgy; Hussars were flamboyant. There was an obvious fundamental tension between these two different philosophies of how to conduct mounted operations.

This tension carried over into nineteenth-century American military doctrine. The antebellum United States Army also featured three types of mounted units: two regiments of dragoons, a regiment of mounted infantry, and two regiments of light cavalry. The dragoons were much as they had always been: trained to fight equally effectively whether mounted and dismounted. Mounted infantry used their horses to move from place to place and then dismounted to use infantry weapons and infantry tactics. Light cavalry typically carried only sabers and pistols. It was not designed to fight dismounted. Rather, its primary purpose was to perform the traditional role of cavalry: scouting, screening, and reconnaissance. In short, the light cavalry served as the eyes and ears of the army, a more modern incarnation of the hussars of the Napoleonic era.

Advances in technology, however, soon made these artificial distinctions obsolete. The introduction and widespread use of rifled muskets and breech loading carbines meant that there was little need for hussars in a United States military largely designed and trained to fight Native Americans. With the coming of civil war in 1861, the powers in charge of the U.S. Army realized this fact, and did away with the distinctions between dragoons, mounted infantry, and light cavalry, re-designating them with the catch-all name of "cavalry." All of these Regular cavalrymen had been trained to act as dragoons—that is, they could fight effectively mounted or dismounted, *and* they had been taught how to scout, screen, and reconnoiter, critical roles traditionally reserved for light cavalry. In short, all mounted soldiers serving in the U. S. Army were to become its eyes and ears, not just the light cavalry. The units were re-designated in the order of their seniority: the 1st Dragoons became the 1st Cavalry; the 2nd Dragoons became the 2nd Cavalry; the Regiment of Mounted Rifles became the 3rd Cavalry; and the 1st Cavalry—a light cavalry regiment—became the 4th Cavalry. The 2nd Cavalry, a veritable all-star team of antebellum officers who later achieved prominence during the Civil War (including, but not limited to, Albert Sidney Johnston, Robert E. Lee, John Sedgwick, and John Bell Hood), became the 5th Cavalry. A new unit of light cavalry authorized and raised in 1861, and originally known as the 3rd Cavalry, was soon re-designated as the 6th Cavalry.

As the Army set about the grim task of putting down the rebellion of the Southern states, it did so with a newly unified command of mounted soldiers led by the so-called "Father of the U.S. Cavalry," Brig. Gen. Philip St. George Cooke, a stuffy old Regular who had led the 2nd Dragoons for years before the Civil War. Though he was a career dragoon, Cooke's tactics reflected those of a hussar and not a dragoon. He quickly discovered that the new era of mounted operations had passed him by.

The ending of the artificial distinctions among the army's mounted units, however, did not end the fundamental debate about their proper role; indeed, that debate continued into the twentieth century, with no less than the future World War II hero George S. Patton, Jr., serving as the most vociferous proponent of the hussar school of thought. Others strongly advocated the dragoon theory, which was embodied by the most famous of all of the dragoons the Army produced: Maj. Gen. John Buford, the hero of Gettysburg. When Buford died of disease in December 1863, his protégé, Brig. Gen. Wesley Merritt, picked up the mantle and carried it into the twentieth century. Only the end of the horse cavalry in the 1930s and the advent of armored cavalry using tanks ended the debate for good.

Wesley Merritt was the quintessential dragoon. He was quiet, competent, and a hard-fighting career Regular. Nobody would ever describe him as flamboyant or as hell-bent-for-leather. Instead, he was solid and dependable. Like his mentor Buford, Merritt believed that cavalrymen needed to be equally proficient at fighting as well as at the less glamorous roles of the cavalry. His soldiers admired and respected him, but they did not love him. Merritt was something of a martinet, and did not have a charismatic personality. He was, however, a great soldier, and he ended his career after 40 years of service as the second highest ranking officer in the Army.

By contrast, George Armstrong Custer was the ultimate hussar. Flamboyant, handsome, with his long, curly blond hair streaming behind him, nothing thrilled Custer quite so much as leading a mounted charge, his saber glinting in the afternoon sunshine while waiting to be brought to bear against some unfortunate foeman. The men in the ranks loved George Custer. They called him the "Boy Soldier with the Golden Locks," and they would follow him anywhere he led them. There is no better description of Custer than to call him a hell-bent-for-leather trooper, just the sort of fellow the young Georgie Patton desperately longed to be. Custer had no particular talent for the traditional roles of cavalry, and if given a choice, he preferred the saber to dismounting and fighting with a carbine. He always led from the front.

While it is easy to dismiss Custer because of the end he met at Little Big Horn, doing so is a tragic mistake, and one I fell into for many years. After carefully studying his nearly unprecedented record of accomplishment in the Civil War while simultaneously disregarding the events of June 1876, I came to regret that mistake a great deal. Custer was an extremely capable cavalryman, particularly during the Civil War, where he made a meteoric rise from captain to brevet major general and division commander in a span of about three years. He was an expert horseman and a charismatic leader. Tall and handsome and seemingly bulletproof, he embodied the stuff that legends are made of, at least in part because of the spectacular record of success he accumulated in putting down the Southern rebellion.

These two young men—Merritt and Custer—were a year apart at West Point and ought to have been friends. Both were career cavalrymen, and both left indelible marks on the mounted service during the Civil War. And yet, they became bitter rivals and even enemies. In short, their personal relationship was a microcosm of the tension between the hussars and the dragoons. There were only so many opportunities for advancement, and only so many opportunities for glory, and both gained their fair share of each. Somewhere along the way their relationship deteriorated to the point of open warfare, particularly when Merritt ascended over Custer as commander of the Army of the Potomac's First Cavalry Division.

In *The Boy Generals: George Custer, Wesley Merritt, and the Cavalry of the Army of the Potomac*, author Adolfo Ovies closely examines the relationship between Custer and

Merritt. His study, a detailed and comprehensive trilogy, demonstrates how that cordial relationship broke down, grew into a fierce rivalry, and eventually turned into bitter enmity. The result is a monumental and unprecedented study of how these two men—seemingly so unlike in personality and temperament—cast such a long shadow over the United States Cavalry during the second half of the nineteenth century. Along the way, Ovies addresses their respective Civil War campaigns in great detail and demonstrates how each man exemplified the paradigms they represented: Merritt the dragoon, and Custer the hussar. Much like the friction between these two disparate schools of military doctrine, the respective dissimilar personality traits of Merritt and Custer eventually brought them into outright conflict, with Custer being openly insubordinate to the former friend who became his commander. No other study of either man, or of Civil War cavalry operations, has ever addressed these issues, let alone in the detail tackled by Ovies.

Of course, the career paths of both men deviated in the postwar army. Custer never advanced beyond the rank of lieutenant colonel and met a horrific death along the banks of the Greasy Grass River in Montana on June 25, 1876, along with nearly 300 troopers of his vaunted 7th Cavalry. Merritt, by contrast, found glory in commanding the expedition that captured Manila during the Spanish-American War, and lived well into old age. The irony of Merritt belatedly leading a column of the 5th Cavalry to rescue Custer's 7th Cavalry is striking. At the same time, it also represents a closing of the circle begun during the Civil War. Theirs is the story of the ultimate ascendance of the dragoons over the hussars. George Armstrong Custer was the last hussar.

There are lessons to be learned here, and we have Adolfo Ovies to thank for taking the time and trouble to teach them to us.

Eric J. Wittenberg
Columbus, Ohio

Following the Guidons to Glory

1959 WAS A WATERSHED year in Cuba. Fidel Castro's guerrillas were in open revolt in the Sierra Maestra mountains on the island's easternmost reaches. Turmoil gripped the capital of Havana. Students from the University of Havana protested angrily in the streets of the historic city, battling in bloody mêlées with the regime of Fulgencio Batista's police and armed forces. Occasionally, the heavy thump of an explosion reverberated through the still and heavy tropical night air of the ancient capital. Upper-class adults would inevitably act as though they had heard nothing.

Despite the ongoing *Revolución*, the monied classes pretended everything was normal. They tried to shield their children from the violence that blanketed the city; to shield them from the fact that life at that moment was especially precarious. The silvery screen of the television provided the parameters of my life. The broadcast of American movies continued unabated, symbolic of a normalcy that no longer existed.

At just seven years old, I had already become an enthusiastic fan of American war movies, and definitely knew what a detonating explosive sounded like. The roguish, dashing Errol Flynn was my hero, and when he portrayed George Custer in "They Died with Their Boots On," Custer, by extension, became my hero as well. Though decades removed from my first viewing, Flynn's mesmerizing portrayal of Custer never ceases to amaze me. I was struck by the dichotomy of how such a historically inaccurate movie could so perfectly capture the elusive nature of Custer's buoyant personality.

In 1960, destiny beckoned. My father managed to arrange our escape to New York from communistic Cuba. Luckily, his mother was married to an American. "Abuelo Jack," as we called him, was a former captain in the U.S. Army and had landed on the beaches of Normandy on D-Day. The Bronze Star awarded for his part in the invasion is still one of my most prized possessions. My grandparents had made a good life for themselves in Connecticut, and after landing at New York's

Idlewild Airport, we moved in with them. Unlike many Cuban refugees who relocated to Miami, Florida, and maintained their Cuban customs, I became a New England Yankee, immersed in American culture.

I was 12 when my father took the family to Gettysburg. It turned out to be one of the most memorable vacations of my childhood. To see firsthand the layout of the hallowed ground where so many soldiers had given their lives fighting for their beliefs was an inspiration to me. The "bug" bit me deeply, and I have to this day embraced the rich heritage of the American Civil War.

Custer's entire life fascinates me. My literary journey began with Quentin Reynolds's *Custer's Last Stand*, a part of the Landmark Series of history books for children. I continued to read as much as I could about the cavalryman. When I was a young teenager, Abuelo Jack gave me a copy of Jay Monaghan's *Custer: The Life of General George Armstrong Custer*. This book was a real eye-opener for me. For the first time I fully realized Custer's career could be divided into two main periods: the Civil War, and the Indian Wars. In the years that followed, I learned that many dedicated scholars were writing groundbreaking material on the Indian Wars in general, and on the Battle of the Little Big Horn, in particular. By this time I had moved to Miami and was far removed from that Montana battlefield. I came to realize there was no chance I would ever be able to match their research. I turned my attention exclusively to Custer's Civil War career.

Anyone who has studied the Civil War knows at least the outline of the story. Captains George Custer, Wesley Merritt, and Elon Farnsworth were part of a class of staff officers who were promoted to higher rank by the commander of the Cavalry Corps, Maj. Gen. Alfred Pleasonton. Their elevation to brigadier general just days before the battle of Gettysburg put each in command of a brigade. Lamentably, Farnsworth was killed on the last day of Gettysburg. At the time, it was understood that a spirited rivalry existed between Custer and Merritt. In fact, there was nothing friendly about this competition between the two young and ambitious officers.

Elizabeth Bacon "Libbie" Custer was aware of the true nature of the relationship that existed between her husband and Merritt. To her, it seemed as if "every upward step" of her husband's career "was contested by enemies."[1] In truth, George Custer had no greater adversary than Wesley Merritt. With their careers inextricably meshed for the duration of the war, their interactions

---

1 Arlene Reynolds, *The Civil War Memories of Elizabeth Bacon Custer* (Austin, TX, 1994), 38-39.

would—battle by battle, campaign by campaign—degenerate into open rancor, bitterness, and eventually, on Custer's part, outright insubordination.

The story of the Army of the Potomac's cavalry has been told by many capable men I admire and from whom I have learned much. These acclaimed writers, however, have largely omitted the narrative of the interpersonal relationship between Custer and Merritt that so impacted the actions of the cavalry during its storied history. They did not explore or even acknowledge that Custer's tactical vision of mounted cavalry stood in sharp contrast with Merritt's views of dismounted cavalry. Merritt, a man of which so little has been written, is barely mentioned in the Custer story, but you cannot understand George Custer without considering and appreciating the influence of Wesley Merritt.

At its core, my study *The Boy Generals: George Custer, Wesley Merritt, and the Cavalry of the Army of the Potomac* is about the contest for the tactical supremacy of the cavalry. It is about Custer's mounted shock tactics versus Merritt's dismounted, tenacious style of attack. It is about the hussar versus the dragoon. Each battle, each campaign, added nuances to the deterioration of their personal relationship. The basic framework of *The Boy Generals* relies on the *Official Records of the War of the Rebellion*, but I flesh out the narrative through the words of those who knew Custer and Merritt—the men who fought alongside them, messed with them, shared the camaraderie of Army life with them, and bore the pain of the loss of a friend. It is a story told, as much as possible, through the eloquent words of those who were there. Though thoroughly researched in the narrative, the military maneuvering serves more as a backdrop against which these two men battle for the soul of the cavalry. Few students realize they fought each other as hard as they fought the enemy.

The study of each man presented unique challenges. Historian John M. Carroll's *Custer in the Civil War* lists close to 600 bibliographic entries for the cavalry officer. More than 140 years after Little Big Horn, the story of Custer's life—and spectacular death—continues to grip the imaginations of both historian and buff with unabated interest. Any study of Custer's Civil War experience is complicated by the ongoing controversy surrounding the latter part of his career as an Indian fighter, and the dramatic events of his demise at the hands of the Sioux and their Cheyenne allies. Particularly damaging to Custer's place in history were the charges of rashness and impetuosity that were inevitably leveled at him—which had always been leveled at him—and which his death, and those of every soul with him, seemed to serve as proof positive. Almost every examination of Custer in the Civil War is tainted by the tragedy that unfolded under an unblinking Montana sky in June 1876 on the bloodstained slopes of what is now known as Custer Ridge.

The great majority of the evidence suggests that the apex of Custer's military career was not in the badlands of the Old West. His greatest victories—his real claims to fame—were attained on the battlefields of the Eastern Theater of the Civil War, beginning with his tenure as a brigadier general in command of the famed Michigan Cavalry Brigade. After meritorious service in the Shenandoah Valley in 1864, Custer was promoted to major general, commanding the 3rd Cavalry Division.

Many of these accounts struggle to understand the essence of the man. Too often they get it wrong. *The Boy Generals* goes beyond the platitudes—"reckless," "gallant," "impetuous," etc.—to get a clear understanding of how Custer achieved his victories, as well as how he suffered his defeats; how he interacted with his men in the daily give and take of military life; and how he was presented to the American reading public by members of the press corps. These intrepid correspondents were drawn to Custer's mess tent like moths to a flame, for he made them all welcome. One thing is certain: Custer was either loved with an intensity bordering on idolatry, or despised with a fervor that for some men would be stilled only by the coldness of the grave.

Wesley Merritt is an enigma. He was a great soldier. His career spanned 40 years, from his graduation from West Point in 1860 to his retirement in 1900. He fought against the Indians, the Confederates, and, late in his career, against the Spanish in the war of 1898. His real accomplishments surpassed the battlefield. He was superintendent of West Point and had the honor of serving as the military governor of the Philippines. His legacy to the U.S. Army he loved, however, was the founding of the *Journal of the United States Cavalry Association* (JUSCA). In Merritt's view, the Army had significantly evolved since the days of the Indian frontier, and he used *JUSCA* as a forum to press his vision of a military force capable of taking on the European powers.

While hundreds of books have been published on Custer, finding material on Merritt is a different challenge altogether. Only one writer is known to have produced a full-fledged biography about him, but even that book is bereft of personal papers; it is almost as if the correspondence of a lifetime had been completely wiped out. There are no letters to and from friends and colleagues, no love notes to fiancées and wives, no communications with his family. Where are Merritt's personal papers? Maybe a musty old trunk full of his personal writings waits in some cobweb-filled attic and will fall into the hands of the right researcher. Until then, Merritt will remain little more than an enigma. Despite the scarcity of primary and even secondary material on Merritt, *The Boy Generals* pulls together a variety of sources from his contemporaries that, when combined with Merritt's extensive writings for public consumption like veteran's organizations and professional journals, adds depth and tone to a man who has been treated as a one-dimensional individual in the historiography of the war.

Understanding this man is a subjective process. Some glimpses do not paint a pretty picture of a soldier renowned for his imperturbability in combat, rectitude in his social dealings, and his reputation for fairness. Merritt's courage was never doubted, his sagacity rarely questioned, and his honor never blemished. He was respected and obeyed. His low-key persona gave rise to the accusation, especially compared to Custer, that he lacked "color." Some maintain that he was a stickler for detail, preaching obeisance to regulations for the sake of regulations. In the prewar days of fighting Indians on the frontier, the roster of the 2nd Dragoons included many martinets. Merritt, as much as he was mentored by cavalry greats like Philip St. George Cooke and John Buford, also learned from these martinets. Merritt had a reputation for being haughty and autocratic in his official capacity, and stand-offish and sometimes prickly in his unofficial relations.

In the eyes of the American public during the Civil War, Merritt relegated himself to the second tier of leadership. His obstinate resistance to recognize the crucial role of the printed media in the grand scheme of things proved to be his Achilles heel. In the long run, his distaste for publicity was hurtful to the morale of his commands. While it is certain that Merritt, who scorned adulation, never craved the limelight for himself, his men thirsted for recognition. They all read the newspapers and gossiped around the campfires with other soldiers. They were sick and tired of always hearing about Custer's commands. Merritt's veterans had pulled Custer's chestnuts out of the fire on multiple occasions, and they were deeply bothered that their sacrifices and achievements were not placed front and center before the American public. Merritt, however, did not see the value of publicity and thus grew to despise Custer with a passion. Custer's amiable relationship with the press went against Merritt's grain. And therein lies the difference between my work and everything that has come before it.

*   *   *

The story will be told in three parts. In your hands is the first installment. *On the Cusp of Glory* lays out the background of the hatred that developed between Merritt and Custer. It begins with their tenures as cadets at West Point, moves through George McClellan's Peninsula Campaign, and continues on to Brandy Station, where inklings of tension between the two officers becomes visible. During the battles of Aldie, Middleburg, and Upperville, their careers took divergent roads.

Destiny guided them on dissimilar paths to the sanguinary fields of Gettysburg. Merritt's actions on South Cavalry Field and Custer's participation at East Cavalry Field set the groundwork for their blossoming adversarial relationship.

The second installment, *The Stars Weighed Heavy On Their Shoulder Boards*, follows their respective brigades as they battled with the defeated and retreating Rebels down the face of the rugged Blue Ridge Mountains during the weeks following Gettysburg. After Maj. Gen. Philip H. Sheridan replaced Maj. Gen. Alfred A. Pleasonton as commander of the Cavalry Corps, the tension between Merritt and Custer ratcheted up several notches. The hard-fought battles of the Overland Campaign exposed their differences under the harsh light of a new kind of war, and at Trevilian Station their rupture became part of the official record. In August 1864, Sheridan's troopers were transferred to the Shenandoah Valley. There, the relationship between Custer and Merritt—already strained and tension-filled—deteriorated rapidly. The infamous episode in which several of Col. John Singleton Mosby's partisan rangers were shot and hanged serves as but one example. The blame for the deaths was placed on Custer, though it was Merritt's men who had affected the captures. The ramifications would rankle Custer for more than a decade.

In *Good God Man! Is There No Chivalry Left?*, the third and final installment of this study, the situation between them spiraled from bad to worse as the Shenandoah Valley Campaign rumbled southward up the valley. The dysfunctional relationship finally erupted into public view following the Battle of Cedar Creek on October 19, 1864. Thereafter, there was no hope of reconciliation. The glory of the Appomattox Campaign would be forever tarnished by Custer's insubordinate behavior to Merritt. Their acrimony spilled over into the postwar army and their return to the western frontier.

Acknowledgments

A work of this scope is not a one-man project, and let me pay obeisance to those who have contributed immeasurably to what I have written.

First and foremost is Eric J. Wittenberg. The circumstances under which I met Eric would best be described by the ancient Saxon/Norse concept "wyrd." It should not be misconstrued as fate, with its negative connotations of predetermination, but as the resultant consequences of one's own actions. After back-and-forth emails, we finally agreed to meet for a weekend at Gettysburg. That was more than 20 years ago. We established a warm friendship that has been renewed each year on many Eastern Theater battlefields. Eric has given *The Boy Generals* his unstinted support, provided input from his vast wealth of knowledge, and soaked my effort with the goodness of his heart. It is doubtful this work could have been completed without his mentorship. The one concept Eric banged into me was that it was impossible to understand the flow of battle without having been on the actual field, without having trekked in the paths of those stalwart horsemen.

I have done religiously followed his advice by attending the Chambersburg Civil War Seminars, directed by the late Ted Alexander and supported by the incredible logistical skills of Lark Kennedy, Scott Anderson, and the "Gunny," Dave Kelvington. Thanks to them, I can safely say that I have tramped across just about every battlefield covered in this narrative. Led by top-notch guides and intermixed with superb speakers in the classroom sessions, Ted and his gang have given me access to vistas which, in many cases, are still enshrouded with the reek of battle, unchanged and untrammeled since the 1860s. They were perfect hosts in every respect.

It was during the course of my attendance at these seminars that I made the acquaintance of the incomparable Edwin C. Bearss. The unique cadence of his voice and the vast wealth of knowledge of his steel trap mind will remain with me until my dying days. I will never forget the night he sat with my wife and I at the dinner table at the Golden Corral, regaling us with stories enhanced by his irrepressible sense of humor. Ed passed away recently, but I will never forget him or the knowledge he imparted.

Of all of my visits to these storied battlegrounds, I cannot recall any I enjoyed as much as the one guided by Robert E. L. Krick, Jr., of the National Park Service, during the Chambersburg seminar to the Richmond area of operations. At one point, Krick discovered that I, like him, was a cigar aficionado. As we began trekking to the crest of Malvern Hill, he offered me a cigar. We fell behind the group so as not to engulf them in the fragrance of secondhand smoke and I enjoyed one of the most pleasurable conversations of my long association with the Chambersburg series.

I particularly want to thank J. David Petruzzi, whose knowledge of the cavalry's actions at Gettysburg is exceeded, in my opinion, by no one. He took me on a personal tour, beginning with Buford's truculent stand at McPherson's Ridge, to East Cavalry Field, and over South Cavalry Field. It has been a while since J. D. and I last got together. I can't wait to meet with him again and personally thank him for the manner in which he brought these far-flung battles into one cohesive narrative. Hopefully, that day will not be too far in the future.

In rectifying my ignorance of the details of the development of Civil War tactics, I had the help of two gentlemen, Bob O'Neill and Andrew German. Thank you so much for that, and for the lively—and practical—discussions we had on the development of cavalry tactics over the course of the war. I took all of their comments to heart, and they had a tremendous influence on the development of the manuscript, particularly during the Sheridan years.

One of my most memorable tours was that of Brandy Station. The battlefield was opened up to us like never before by the efforts of Clark B. "Bud" Hall. Mr. Hall had previously served as the chief investigator for the congressional inquiry into the Iran-Contra scandal, and with my Cuban background, we found a unique bond over drinks discussing subjects such as the Bay of Pigs and the Cuban Missile Crisis. But I digress. No tour could have been better managed.

It was my unique pleasure to spend the day with former U.S. Army officer Donald C. Caughey, who specializes in the history of the Regular Cavalry. I spent the next day touring the Cedar Creek battlefield with him. His 2013 book on the battles of the U.S. Cavalry (*The 6th United States Cavalry in the Civil War*) was instrumental in developing Merritt's side of the story. Thanks for a great couple of days!

What can I say about Professor Gregory J. W. Urwin? His *Custer Victorious: The Civil War Battles of General George Armstrong Custer* is, and always be, my bible. Despite his busy schedule as one of the nation's great historians, he made time to read my manuscript from cover to cover. His detailed critique of my work directed much of the final product. To Jeffry Wert, I can confidently say "Fear not." Your writings on Custer in particular, and the Civil War in general, place you at the top of my list of favorite historians.

Frederic C. Wagner, III, a former U.S. Army officer who served during the Vietnam War and an acknowledged expert on the battle of the Little Bighorn, also read the entire manuscript. Mr. Wagner is the administrator of several Custer discussion groups on Facebook. His unique perspective on time and movement served to steer the direction of my work. His conclusion that *The Boy Generals* falls into the rare category of "Must Read" warms the cockles of my heart.

I cannot thank artist Bruce K. Lawes enough for graciously allowing me to use his spectacular painting "Custer Before the Storm" for the cover of my book. It is like a photograph in time, so rich are the details. Moreover, he has consented to provide the artwork for the two remaining volumes. To paraphrase an old saying, "If you can't judge a book by its cover, you better read it at the bookstore." Bruce, thank you, thank you. Thank you!

No battlefield historian ventures onto a contested field without a good map. Cartographer Mark Moore has created more than 20 gorgeous maps to accompany the text for this trilogy. Thank you, Mark, for your excellent work. More importantly, Mark also gave me sage advice. "The publishing process is long," he warned me. "Be patient." Mark, you were right.

I want to thank Theodore P. Savas of Savas Beatie for giving me the opportunity to present my work to the Civil War community. His faith in my work has been outstanding—everything an author would wish for from his publisher. Special thanks are also due to the incredible SB ladies on his staff: Sarah Keeney, Lisa Murphy, Donna Endacott, Sarah Closson, and Lois Olechny. Each in their own way have worked tirelessly to make sure my book is widely available. Ted, thanks for taking a chance on a fledgling author. Ted had Craig Robertson read the manuscript and offer helpful ideas for changes that made it better, and the unerring eye of Joel Manuel performed similar work and corrected my tendency to lapse to the passive voice. Joel's passion for the subject matter is evident on every page. Lee Merideth provided the excellent index in record time. Thank you, all.

In addition to the many individuals who assisted me are the countless organizations that contributed unstinting assistance to this opus. To name all their staff members would be to write an additional chapter. On the government side, I want to laud those who helped me in the two weeks I spent rummaging through their collections. Kudos to the archivists at the library of Gettysburg National Military Park, the National Archives and Records Administration for their access to the Wesley Merritt papers, and the U.S. Army Heritage and Education Center at Carlisle, Pennsylvania. There was so much primary source material that I could have written a couple more volumes!

Enough praise cannot be given to the university collections of the state of Michigan. Of particular note are the Bentley Historical Library at the University of Michigan, the University of Central Michigan, and Michigan State University for all their material on George Custer. Every request I made of them was answered promptly.

Special thanks are also due to the Cincinnati Historical Society, which granted me access to the writings of Roger Hannaford, a member of Custer's 3rd Cavalry Division. A prolific writer, his comments on the years he spent under Custer's command are an integral part of the volumes yet to come.

The articles of the *Journal of the United States Cavalry Association*, the organization founded by Wesley Merritt, provided a rich insight into not just the man himself, but into the men who fought with him and came to honor and respect him. Although it never approached the level of adoration that Custer's men had for him, if you are ever going to understand just what a great soldier Merritt was, the evidence will be found in the countless articles he wrote, or were written about him, in the *JUSCA* volumes.

We live in the modern digital world, and I cannot help but thank the many members of the various Civil War and Custer groups I belong to on Facebook. Reading their posts is a part of my daily life, and their insights are integral to the story I am telling. I cannot mention them all due to space restrictions. The following are among my favorites: Shelby Foote and the American Civil War, The Original Civil War Buff, The General George A. Custer History Forum, and Clinton Richardson's American Civil War Group.

Though many of the photographs included in the manuscript came from the Library of Congress, I must mention the contributions of Eric Duncan of Cowan's Auctions for his unprecedented access to several of the very rare images in their collection. Many thanks to Charmaine Wawrzyniec of the Monroe County Library for the use of an 1882 portrait of Libbie Custer.

Of special note is Drew Gruber, the executive director of Virginia's Civil War Trails. Our conversation was instrumental in helping to develop my understanding of the siege of Yorktown and the battles around Williamsburg.

There are so many other organizations from which I have sought that it seems a crime not to mention them all. For that, I am truly sorry. Particularly, I want to thank the staff of the Handley Library in Winchester, Virginia, the Montana Historical Society, and the *Kansas Historical Quarterly*, which provided much interesting material on Custer's life after the Civil War and his interactions with Wesley Merritt. The Historical Society of Pennsylvania supplied important access to the papers of William Brooke Rawle of the 3rd Pennsylvania Cavalry. Dartmouth College sent me a copy of the Civil War diary of Eri Woodbury. Finally, The Virginia Historical Society provided me with a copy of the incredible autobiography of St. George Tucker Brooke. To all of them I owe my undying gratitude.

Finally, there is no doubt that errors have crept into the final manuscript, as they always do, and the responsibility rests with me as the author, and no one else.

Glory Was Their Destiny; Rancor Was Their Legacy

THE JANUARY GALES WORKED their way down the length of Lake Michigan, whipping the sluggish waters into whitecaps that slammed into the city of Chicago on its southern shore. Driven by the biting winds, snow swirled in front of the gray and monolithic Palmer House Hotel in the heart of downtown at Monroe and State streets.[1]

The Palmer House aspired to the greatness offered by the best of European hospitality, with over-sized rooms and high-vaulted public spaces decorated in "the tortured grandeur of the Victorian Age." That ever-so-proper Englishman, Rudyard Kipling, once had the misfortune of testing the Palmer House's hospitality and came away appalled by the spectacle he had witnessed. "They told me to go to the Palmer House," he lamented:

[It] is a gilded and mirrored rabbit-warren, and there I found a huge hall of tessellated marble, crammed with people talking about money and spitting about everywhere. Other barbarians charged in and out of this inferno with letters and telegrams in their hands, and yet others shouted at each other. A man who had drunk quite as much as was good for him told me that this was "the finest hotel in the finest city on God Almighty's earth."[2]

---

1 "Palmer House, Chicago," 1873, lithograph, American Oliograph Company, The Great Chicago Fire and the Web of Memory, www.greatchicagofire.org/queen-of-west-once- more/ bricks-and-mortar.

2 John Upton Terrell and George Walton, *Faint the Trumpet Sounds: The Story of Major Marcus A. Reno* (New York, 1966), 234-235; Rudyard Kipling, "American Notes, Chapter Five: Chicago" (Boston, MA, 1899), 92.

The Palmer House was the site of the much-awaited Reno Court of Inquiry of 1878, which delved into the aftermath of the battle of the Little Bighorn. *American Oliograph Company 1873*

Elizabeth Bacon Custer, bundled to the neck in furs to ward off the harsh chill, swept into the chaos like a shot of hot pepper sauce into a boiling gumbo. Now in her late thirties, she remained a striking woman, presenting a vivacious, articulate, and determined façade. It served to mask the deep sadness that would permeate the rest of her long life, for she would outlive her beloved husband by more than 50 years. As befitted her status as a grand dame, she was accompanied by her entourage and a stack of luggage that tested the bell staff to the utmost. Libbie, as she was known to all, settled into one of the Palmer House's palatial suites along with her aunt, Loraine Richmond; her close friend, cousin, and confidant, Rebecca Richmond; and her sister-in-law, Maggie Calhoun.[3]

---

3 Shirley A. Leckie, *Elizabeth Bacon Custer and the Making of a Myth* (Norman, OK, 1993), 199. Libbie never remarried. In her later years, she would write three highly acclaimed books about life on the frontier and the happy years she spent alongside her husband. In the process, she stole the hearts of the American reading public and shaped their perspective of the battle of the Little Bighorn. Despite her determination to secure his legacy in the pantheon of American heroes, Libbie's depiction of George Custer has been greatly tarnished over the years. None of

This photo of Elizabeth Bacon Custer, taken in 1882, shows very little change in her appearance since the Reno Court of Inquiry in 1878. She would remain clothed in the black vestments of bereavement until her dying day. *Monroe County Library*

Despite the Palmer House's proximity to shopping, theaters, and the city's renowned restaurants, Libbie had more serious business on her mind. The United States Army, finally succumbing to a multitude of pressures, had officially ordered a board of inquiry into the events surrounding her husband's death and the crushing defeat of the 7th U.S. Cavalry Regiment at the battle of the Little Bighorn.

On June 25, 1876, Lt. Col. George Armstrong Custer led his vaunted cavalry regiment on what many have condemned as an ill-advised and reckless attack on a village populated by the largest gathering of Northern Plains tribes ever witnessed on the North American continent. Thousands of Sioux, Cheyenne, and Arapaho warriors moved against Custer, cut him off, surrounded him, and in one dust-choked hour—an hour that must have seemed like an eternity to those encircled unfortunates—overran and slaughtered Custer and the five companies of troopers that accompanied him. Not a single man survived, and only one wounded horse was found wandering aimlessly over the bloody battlefield. The blaring headlines that appeared atop the July 6 issue of the *New York Times* stunned the entire nation: "Gen. Custer and Seventeen Commissioned Officers Butchered in a

___

her accomplishments, however, managed to ease her sense of loss. To her close friend, Marguerite Merington, she would write, "When I heard the news [of his death] I wanted to die." Unburdening herself further, she acknowledged that she "had to live—a hero's widow—to the end of my appointed time, worthily."

Battle on the Little Horn . . . Three Hundred and Fifteen Men Killed and Thirty-one Wounded . . . The Battle-field Like a Slaughter Pen."[4]

Frederick Whittaker's *A Complete Life of General George A. Custer*, published in 1876 in a rush-to-print job, blasted Custer subordinates Major Marcus Reno and Capt. Frederick Benteen, whose detached companies had survived the battle. Whittaker accused Reno of cowardice and Benteen of deliberately sacrificing Custer's command. In May 1878, Whittaker wrote to his friend, W. W. Corlett, the delegate to the United States Congress from the Territory of Wyoming. "I desire to call to your attention . . . the necessity of ordering an official investigation into the conduct of the United States troops engaged in the battle of the Big Horn."[5]

In 1872, Whittaker had published a treatise on cavalry tactics based on his short-lived stint as a brevet captain in the 6th New York Volunteer Cavalry, grandiloquently entitled *Volunteer Cavalry: The Lessons of the Decade by a Volunteer Cavalryman*. An abridged version had appeared in the *Army and Navy Journal*. Regardless of its size, the mere fact of its publication established, at least in Whittaker's mind, his tactical bona fides.

Whittaker detailed his charges in a six-point letter to Corlett, and had it published to keep it from being swept into the dustbin of other legislative rubbish. He alleged that, "[o]wing to such cowardice, the orders of Lieut. Col. Custer, commanding officer, to said Reno, to execute a certain attack, were not made," and the result was fatal:

> . . . the failure of this movement, owing to his cowardice and disobedience, caused the defeat of the United States forces on the day in question; and that had Custer's orders been obeyed, the troops would probably have defeated the Indians.[6]

On November 25, 1878, the war department, responding to congressional pressure, issued the necessary orders to convene a board of inquiry, to be held at the Palmer House in January 1879. Whittaker wrote to Libbie in his bombastic style. "[The board of inquiry will] clear the General of the charge of rashness and leave him with his laurels unstained by the shadow of a slur. That is my object, and

---

4 "Massacre of Our Troops," *The New York Times*, July 6, 1876.

5 Terrell and Walton, *Faint the Trumpet Sounds*, 229.

6 Ibid., 230.

will be accomplished in God's good time. I am glad, all things considered, that you knew nothing of all this till the papers informed you."[7]

The board of inquiry would be composed of three senior officers, with Col. John H. King of the 9th Infantry serving as its president. Two cavalry officers made up the rest of the board: Lt. Col. William B. Royall of the 3rd U.S. Cavalry Regiment, and Col. Wesley Merritt of the 5th U.S. Cavalry Regiment.[8]

After graduating from West Point in 1860, Merritt reported to the 2nd Dragoons—soon to be re-designated the 2nd U.S. Cavalry—in the Utah Territory. With the outbreak of the Civil War, the regiment traveled back east, where Merritt's meteoric rise through the ranks began.

Just days before the start of the battle of Gettysburg, Maj. Gen. Alfred Pleasonton promoted Merritt to brigadier general and gave him command of the Reserve Cavalry Brigade. Merritt's leadership and gallantry during the Overland campaign of 1864 so impressed Maj. Gen. Philip H. Sheridan that Sheridan named him head of the 1st Cavalry Division at the start of the Shenandoah Valley campaign later that year. When Sheridan set off down the valley in February 1865, he promoted Merritt to the command of the Cavalry Corps of the Army of the Shenandoah. Merritt was tireless in the pursuit of Lee's Army of Northern Virginia to Appomattox Court House in the early days of April 1865.

Merritt mustered out of the volunteers in February 1866 and reverted to his Regular rank of lieutenant colonel. While others jockeyed for the few officer positions available in the postwar army, Merritt inexplicably set off on a European excursion. When he returned, he took an assignment with the 9th U.S. Cavalry, a regiment composed of African American troopers that would become legendary as the "Buffalo Soldiers." Given the state of army politics at the time, this was not considered a plum assignment. Merritt stayed with the 9th Cavalry until 1876, when he took command of the 5th U.S. Cavalry.

A palpable tension existed between Merritt and Royall, dating back to their service together in the aftermath of the Custer disaster. Fifty-six days after his defeat by the Indians at the battle of Rosebud Creek, Maj. Gen. George Crook was ready to go back into the field in order to avenge Custer; the resulting actions became known as the Big Horn and Yellowstone campaign. The core of Crook's 2,000-man force consisted of Merritt's 5th Cavalry, ten companies strong, and the

---

7 Leckie, *Elizabeth Bacon Custer*, 221.

8 William A. Graham, *The Reno Court of Inquiry* (Harrisburg, PA, 1953), 3.

entire 3rd Cavalry under Royall. Their task was to comb the Big Horn Mountains and the Yellowstone River for the elusive Sioux and their Cheyenne allies.

On August 4, 1876, Crook appointed Merritt as his chief of cavalry. The mounted columns were to move fast, and Crook ordered his men to get rid of all unnecessary equipment. Each trooper carried rations for four days, one overcoat, one blanket, and 100 rounds of carbine ammunition. All other supplies and accoutrements were carried by the mules of the pack train. Merritt's primary duty during the campaign was to conserve the command's horses and supervise the march discipline of the cavalry columns. He proved admirably suited for this task.

The columns moved out early on August 5, but the hot, dry weather turned nasty soon after their departure, with a cold rain slashing at the scantily equipped troopers. The men suffered horribly from the inclemency, and their fruitless pursuit of the enemy came to be known as the "Mud March." As a result, Crook earned the disgust of the veteran soldiers, officers and enlisted men alike.

During this campaign, Merritt quickly became disenchanted with Royall, blaming him for the slack camp discipline of the 3rd Cavalry. Merritt could be a bit of a martinet, and he believed in the strict enforcement of cavalry procedures. The notorious disciplinarian berated Royall, and a heated argument between the two men was easily overheard by the regiment's officers, who had gathered within earshot of the commanding officer's tent. Two and a half years later, the rancorous feelings between the two men still simmered as they gathered for the board of inquiry.

The "Reno Board of Inquiry," as it came to be known, convened on January 13, 1879. For the next 25 days, survivors of the 7th Cavalry squirmed in the witness chair and addressed, to the best of their recollection, the tumultuous events of that disastrous day. Like buzzards, the investigator and defense teams picked away at the desiccated shell of what had once been the proud "Garryowen Regiment." Elizabeth Custer heard every word. Day after day, she sat attentively in the audience, holding out for the vindication of her husband. In truth, however, she would settle for the condemnation of Reno and those officers of the 7th Cavalry she thought were complicit with him. In her naiveté, Libbie looked to Merritt, as a past comrade-in-arms, to lead that effort. She was to be sadly disappointed.

First Lieutenant Jesse M. Lee of the 9th Infantry was appointed as the court's recorder. Lee, serving for all intents and purposes as the prosecutor, was not an attorney by training, and he openly admitted that he did not aspire to a career in law. He was ill-equipped to handle the duties of the government's chief court official, especially given the fact that at Col. King's direction, the court would "expect to go over the whole ground. The recorder will proceed in his own way to prove whatever matters he chooses to allege against Major Reno."[9]

Reno was represented by 33-year-old Lyman D. Gilbert, Pennsylvania's assistant attorney general. With his reputation as a shrewd and competent lawyer already established in his home state, Gilbert sought a big case to catapult him into national notoriety. Seeing the Reno inquiry as that case, he offered to represent the beleaguered major for a nominal fee. His forceful and knowledgeable cross examinations of witnesses were fueled by his belief that he had an airtight case. Gilbert was so confident, in fact, that he cancelled his plans to call defense witnesses and simply put Reno on the stand to tell his side of the story. To that point, his defense had been very impressive.[10]

After summations by the opposing counsels, the members of the court retired to a private room to begin their deliberations. They emerged on February 1 and handed down their decision, which was a shocker. "The conduct of the officers throughout was excellent," read Lee in conclusion, "and while subordinates in some instances did more for the safety of the command by brilliant displays of courage than did Major Reno, there was nothing in his conduct which requires animadversion from this Court. It is the conclusion of this Court that no further proceedings are necessary in this case."[11]

Libbie was stunned. From her privileged seat, she must surely have been staring directly at the court and focused on Wesley Merritt. In all probability, her eyes reflected the betrayal she felt. Merritt, ever the professional soldier, would not have flinched under her withering gaze.

The members had deliberated over every aspect of the battle. Merritt stood completely behind the court's decision, but he must have been a little uncomfortable. Airing the fractious political relationships of his beloved United States Army to the public went very much against his grain. Merritt privately believed that the witnesses had not told the entire truth, and he felt the court had not been harsh enough when it had "damned Reno with praise."[12]

Whittaker, who had stormed out of the proceedings, launched a strident attack on the court's decision in the *New York Sun*, calling it a "Mockery of Justice," and "a

---

9 Terrell, *Faint the Trumpet Sounds*, 235.

10 Ibid., 235-236.

11 Don E. Alberts, *General Wesley Merritt: From Brandy Station to Manila* (Columbus, OH, 2001), 268; Leckie, *Elizabeth Bacon Custer*, 223.

12 Alberts, *General Wesley Merritt*, 269.

complete and scientific whitewash." He charged that Reno had "sneer[ed] at Custer for his Civil War record, an appeal to the old rivalry between Custer and Merritt, now one of the court." Mincing no words, Whittaker placed the blame squarely on Merritt's shoulders. He accused Merritt of closeting himself privately with Lieutenant Lee, and in the space of a few hours, doing "most of the work of the decision, the Recorder having no voice save to present the case on trial." Whittaker claimed that Maj. Gen. Sheridan, the commander of the military district, had tried to influence the testimony of several witnesses in Reno's favor by supplying them with "ladies of pleasure."[13]

By the time the members of the court filed out of the hushed assemblage, Libbie Custer realized that there was a strong foundation to the rumors she had heard about tension between her husband and Wesley Merritt; there should be no doubt that as she departed the mahogany-paneled meeting room, she had become Merritt's enemy. When defending her husband's reputation, Libbie was an implacable foe, as Merritt would soon learn. They were to clash openly—bitterly—in the near future. The basis of their confrontation could be traced to the events surrounding the placement of a statue of General Custer at the United States Military Academy.

Not long after the Reno inquiry, Libbie learned that a committee had been formed for the purpose of erecting a monument to her husband at West Point. Despite renewed interest due to the national coverage of Custer's interment at the Academy, the committee had only managed to raise just under $10,000, making an equestrian statue out of the question. The relatively low commission only drew two artists' designs, of which the one by J. Wilson McDonald was chosen. Libbie made her objections known at once; she did not think much of McDonald's reputation as a "self-taught sculptor." Bluntly, she asked the committee how the artist and design had been chosen, and implicit in her letter was the question of why she had not been consulted at the outset of the project. She was astounded to learn that the work had progressed to the point where McDonald had already drawn the first part of his commission.[14]

In early August 1879, Libbie was informed that the statue had been unveiled in a private ceremony and had been "much admired by all who had seen it." Brusquely she was told that the "statue is completed, the stone for the pedestal on the ground, and everything in readiness to place" it. The matter of a monument to George

---

13 Leckie, *Elizabeth Bacon Custer*, 223; Alberts, *General Wesley Merritt*, 268.

14 Leckie, *Elizabeth Bacon Custer*, 224.

Armstrong Custer at West Point apparently was a done deal. The date of the official unveiling ceremony was set for August 30, 1879. Unfortunately, the committee chose the wrong person to ignore, and Libbie chose to ignore the committee. Her absence, and that of anyone closely associated with her, was noted by all. "The bronze is a figure eight feet in height, and is an accurate likeness of the dead soldier," wrote a reporter for the *New York Herald*:

> The dress is a colonel's uniform. The attitude is a spirited one, the left foot being advanced, and the motion of a charge on foot being forcibly expressed by the position. The sword is gripped firmly in the right hand and held well down, while the pistol is in the left hand which is held across the breast and forward. . . . The features are set in the sternness of battle, and one looking at the statue can well imagine the moment of the gallant hero's struggle.[15]

Libbie was aghast, for no rendition of Custer could have been further from the mental image she cherished of her husband in his greatest moments of glory. Hers was of a hardened warrior, at a full gallop astride one of his warhorses, saber pointed directly at the enemy, with his trademark red necktie streaming in the wind. She was further outraged when she read in the pages of the *Detroit Free Press* the comments of some of Custer's contemporaries. "Several of them sneered at the statue and said it was a ridiculous one," reported the newspaper. "That no soldier ever held sword and pistol in that way and that Custer was a hero made by the newspapers and said that military men did not look on him as did the general public." Writing to Lawrence Barrett, the famous actor and Custer's intimate friend, she bemoaned, "The whole costume is incongruous and incorrect. . . . [He was] armed like a desperado in both hands—while some of General Custer's most brilliant charges, were made without a firearm about him." To her friend, the sculptress Vinnie Ream, she was equally vehement, declaring, "I was never consulted and did not even know about it until it was done. The bitter disappointment I feel is such a cross for me to bear it seems to me I cannot endure it. I shall not."[16]

---

15 Leckie, *Elizabeth Bacon Custer*, 224-225; Minnie Dubbs Millbrook, "A Monument to Custer," in Paul L. Hedren, ed., *The Great Sioux War, 1876-77: The Best from Montana: The Magazine of Western History* (Helena, MT, 1991), 273, 274.

16 Millbrook, "A Monument to Custer," 274.

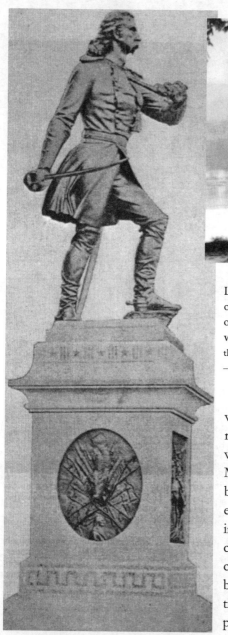

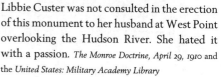

Libbie Custer was not consulted in the erection of this monument to her husband at West Point overlooking the Hudson River. She hated it with a passion. *The Monroe Doctrine, April 29, 1910* and the *United States: Military Academy Library*

For three fruitless years, Libbie waged a war to have the hated statue removed. Then, in 1882, Wesley Merritt was appointed superintendent of the Military Academy, and Libbie—like a pit bull gnawing on a bone—intensified her efforts; unwittingly, Merritt had stepped into another of those Custer controversies that seemed to dog his career. Merritt arrived at West Point with big plans. High on his list was a desire to tighten up the discipline of what he perceived to be a very slack Corps of Cadets, including an end to the practice of hazing. But most of all, he was determined to leave his mark on the curriculum that would be used to train the next generation of American military officers. Merritt wanted to drag the army out of the "dark ages" and into the modern world of war as practiced by the European powers. In the grand scheme of things, the controversy over the Custer statue was an unwanted distraction left over from the previous administration.

To Libbie, toppling the ludicrous rendition of her husband was an essential first step in her crusade to perpetuate Custer's memory, and, perhaps, to end the process of bereavement and get on with her life. She wasted no time, going straight to the top of the U.S. Army: its commanding general, William Tecumseh Sherman. A wily survivor of the army's political wars, Sherman ushered Libbie out of his office and sent her to Secretary of War Robert Lincoln. Like a hot potato, she was passed on to Gen. Oliver O. Howard, the incumbent superintendent at West Point, whose departure was imminent. Howard gladly handed the matter off to Merritt when he arrived to assume his new posting. Exasperated by the continuous shunting around, Libbie again addressed Sherman. "It frightens me dear General Sherman, because this vital matter to me rests so much in other hands," she wrote, using her feminine wiles shamelessly to tug on the heartstrings of the old warrior. "I tell you frankly," she continued,

> I do not believe that General Merritt will interest himself to aid the Secretary of War in hiding that statue unless you ask him to do it, dear General Sherman. A wife's love sharpens her eyes and quickens her instinct, and years ago I knew (not from my husband) that General Merritt was his enemy. On the plains we entertained him and he seemed to have conquered his enmity and jealousy that was so bitter in the Army of the Potomac. But when he was placed at the head of the Court of Inquiry that sat to investigate Col. Reno's conduct at Chicago—I saw all through the trial how General Merritt still felt toward his dead comrade.[17]

The statue was still in its place of honor—or perhaps "dishonor," if viewed from Libbie's position—when Sherman retired in November 1883.

Finally, in November 1884, Robert Lincoln directed Superintendent Merritt "to cause the statue to be removed from its pedestal and to be securely boxed and stored at the Post." Libbie would later claim that she had "literally cried it off the pedestal." Historian Minnie Millbrook wryly noted that they were tears that "had to be applied in the right places—and judiciously."[18]

Later that year, the pedestal that had supported the ill-fated statue of Custer that Libbie so detested replaced the original headstone. The marble pedestal was

---

17 Millbrook, "A Monument to Custer," 278-279.

18 Marguerite Merington, *The Custer Story: The Life and Intimate Letters of General Custer and His Wife Elizabeth* (New York, 1950), 327; Millbrook, "A Monument to Custer," 280.

The pedestal of the monument utilized the base of the West Point statue Libbie Custer so detested, and was enhanced, in 1905, by the addition of an obelisk. *James Nesterwitz*

six feet tall with bronze panels on each side. The front featured a representation of Custer on horseback, and buffalo heads adorned the two side panels. The rear panel was inscribed with Custer's name, rank, and the details of his death. In 1905, an obelisk would be added to the base.

Somewhere in time, the crated statue disappeared, gobbled up in the vastness of a musty army warehouse filled with relics from the nation's wars. Maybe someday, many years from now, it will be found by a warehouse clerk with time on his hands and spurred on by a curious nature; or by some nameless historian, who, in the course of his research, stumbled onto a clue as to its whereabouts.

Ironically, with the removal of the statue, Wesley Merritt's Custer problems disappeared for the rest of his career.

Chapter One

A Cadet's Soul Must Be Malleable

SOLDIERS HAVE BEEN BURIED at West Point as far back as the Revolutionary War. The earliest known grave belongs to Ensign Dominick Trant of the 9th Massachusetts Infantry, who died on November 7, 1782, at the age of 21. Trant was "a young Irish gentleman who had come over in 1780 and warmly espoused the American cause," wrote Dr. James Thacher, a surgeon with the Continental Army from the start of the Revolution to its close. While serving at West Point, the doctor tended to the ailing young ensign. Dr. Thacher had come to admire Trant's "fortitude and resignation" and deeply lamented his passing. "His remains were decently interred in the garrison at West Point," he observed with a touch of pride, and they "were followed to the grave by His Excellency General Washington, and a very respectable procession."[1]

Other soldiers soon joined Trant as they succumbed to wounds or disease and were buried nearby. Many of their headstones bore the simple word "Unknown." In 1802, with the Revolution a memory and America a free country, Congress created the United States Military Academy, which was established at the impregnable position high atop the bluffs overlooking the Hudson River. In 1817, a site along the campus's northern edge was designated as a national cemetery and the soldiers in the existing graves, including Ensign Trant, were disinterred and reburied there.

In some ways, this revered cemetery is where the "long gray line" truly begins. Throughout the following years, the rolls of honored dead grew as more brave

---

1   A. B. Berard, ed., *Reminiscences of West Point in the Olden Time* (East Saginaw, MI, 1886), 23.

souls gave their lives for their country and their freedom. Two particularly distinguished West Point alumni rest close to one another, much as their military careers had intertwined and intersected in life. In fact, nothing may be more indicative of the differing personalities of Wesley Merritt and George Custer than the contrast between their funerals and grave sites at West Point.

There's No Sound in a Tomb

Brevet Major General George Armstrong Custer reached his final resting place on October 10, 1877, after a circuitous journey that began with his disinterment on Last Stand Hill the previous July 28. His remains had traveled to Fort Lincoln, North Dakota, on to Chicago and then Poughkeepsie, New York, where Libbie stored the body until a full military funeral could be arranged at West Point in the fall.[2]

The Academy was the one place, wrote Libbie, "that he loved . . . better than any place on earth. Its traditions were dear to him. He followed the careers of his

2   Arlene Reynolds, *The Civil War Memories of Elizabeth Bacon Custer, 50; Lawrence A. Frost, General Custer's Libbie* (Seattle, WA, 1976), 234, 241-242; Leckie, *Elizabeth Bacon Custer*, 218. A year after the battle of the Little Bighorn, at Libbie's behest, an expedition led by Col. Michael Sheridan visited the battlefield in order to collect the remains of Custer and several of his officers. Under the strictest military protocol, Custer's body was exhumed and sent east for proper burial. Reporters accompanying the expedition sent back graphic photographs of the battlefield, clearly showing the exposed bones of some of the hastily buried troopers and horses. Troubled by the lurid images, Libbie dreamed of buzzards and coyotes feasting on the savaged flesh of her husband and other loved ones. Forlornly she wrote, "The wind now sighs through the prairie grass waving above the scattered stones on a Montana plain, and moans over the sod that covers the bones of the men who fell because they were deserted by their comrades." Libbie was pained by the scurrilous and often spiteful allegations that the remains in the casket were just the bones of some luckless trooper who had not merited a deep enough grave in the hard scrabble of the battlefield, and whose body had subsequently been unearthed by scavenging animals. Colonel Sheridan wrote to Libbie, assuring her that Custer's remains had been positively identified "without the slightest difficulty" and had been escorted for the entire trip by Maj. Joseph Tilford of the 7th Cavalry, who had "personally superintended the transfer of the remains from the box in which they came from the battlefield to the casket which conveys them to West Point." Of equal import to Libbie was a thoughtful gesture by Tilford, detailed in a reassuring letter dispatched on his arrival at Fort Lincoln. "I enclose you a lock of hair taken from the remains which are so precious to you," he wrote in great sympathy. "I also kept a few hairs for myself as having been worn by a man who was my beau ideal of a soldier and honorable Gentleman." To Libbie, it was proof positive that the remains were indeed those of her beloved "Autie." "Who else in the command had hair like her husband's?" Jay Monaghan, *Custer: The Life of General George Armstrong Custer* (Lincoln, NE, 1959), 399.

classmates, both at the North and South, with admiration and love, and finally asked to lie there when 'Taps' should sound in his ear for the last time."[3]

Much to the dismay of Superintendent John McAllister Schofield, who would have preferred a more private ceremony, Libbie Custer insisted on a funeral befitting a major general, complete with the resplendent turnout of the full Corps of Cadets. Her deliberate postponement of the burial guaranteed that all the cadets would be back from the summer camp that introduced plebes to their new life at West Point. It also ensured that Schofield could not shirk his duty, and that he would "be better able to pay the honor he wishes to the heroic dead."[4]

On October 2, the superintendent issued the necessary orders, beginning with a suspension of all academic duties after 1:00 p.m. "The funeral of the late Brevet Major General George A. Custer, Lieutenant Colonel of the 7th Cavalry," read General Order No. 24, "will take place from the Chapel, at 2 o'clock P.M., Wednesday, Oct 10, 1877." While he hoped for the best, Schofield prepared for the worst. The funeral notice drew requests for attendance from a legion of Custer adherents wishing to pay their final respects. The Connecticut Cavalry Association planned to attend and parade en masse, "dressed in dark material, a knot of crepe upon the left arm, and 'The Custer Tie' (the flowing necktie introduced by the general, and [that] was used by the Third Division as a distinctive badge)."[5]

Custer's funeral abounded in pure drama from start to finish. Schofield had the body transported across the Hudson River aboard the steamer *Mary Powell*, which was draped from stem to stern in black bunting and flying the national colors at half-mast. Reports indicated that more than 1,500 people took passage on the ship in order to file in tribute past the flag-draped casket. Although dangerously overcrowded and on the verge of capsizing, she chugged neatly and safely up to the dock at the foot of the daunting bluffs. "Nature had done her best to make the day the most perfect of the season," wrote a correspondent with *The Christian Union*—a reference to the grounds of the Academy ablaze with autumn colors. Hundreds of sailing craft used the incoming tidal waters to lazily drift upriver. "The sun bathed the noble height of the Storm King in warm light, and threw shadows across the

---

3   Reynolds, *The Civil War Memories of Elizabeth Bacon Custer*, 35.

4   Millbrook, "A Monument to Custer," 271.

5   Bob Novak, "General Custer's West Point Funeral," *Little Big Horn Associates Newsletter* (February 2005), Vol. 39, No. 1, 4-5.

blue river, where sails changed from dark to white and back again in magical variety."[6]

Shortly after noon, the Academy's cavalry detachment took charge of Custer's remains and conveyed the casket to the Old Chapel. There, it lay in state under a guard of honor, which had been turned out in immaculate dress uniforms. The grieving widow, dressed in black from head to toe, arrived on the arm of Gen. Schofield. A coterie of relatives, friends, and old comrades-in-arms followed. A host of others never made it inside the Old Chapel, which had exceeded its capacity.[7]

Custer's casket rested in the middle of the aisle, covered with the flag that had once belonged to Capt. Louis M. Hamilton, late of the 7th Cavalry. Hamilton's death in battle against the Sioux at the Washita River would forever remain controversial, and not to Custer's advantage. Custer's sword and plumed dress helmet lay atop the flag. The helmet added yet another point of irony, for he never wore the overly ostentatious trapping of rank. "The casket's only floral arrangement," wrote western historian Minnie Millbrook, "was a major general's shoulder strap, two feet long and eight inches wide, the background woven of geraniums, the stars of tuberoses."[8]

The post chaplain, Pastor John Forsyth, delivered the solemn funeral rites of the Episcopalian Church. The choir chimed in with the sweetness and serenity of Psalm 39: "LORD, let me know my end and the number of my days, so that I may know how short my life is." Libbie just sat there, staring at a photograph of her

---

6   "West Point in October, *The Christian Union*, October 17, 1877, Vol. 16," *Little Big Horn Associates Newsletter* (October 2004), Vol. 38, No. 8, 8.

7   Anson Mills, *My Story* (Washington, DC, 1918), 44; Morris Schaff, *The Spirit of Old West Point, 1858-1862* (New York, 1907), 127-128. Completed in 1837, the Old Cadet Chapel became a memorial for generations of fallen heroes. The great generals of the Revolution and the dead of the Mexican War are immortalized in black memorial tablets embedded in its walls. *Peace and War*, a painting by Robert Walter Weir, who taught drawing at the Academy for over 40 years, adorns the wall above the altar. One former cadet declared that the painting was "one of the things that impressed me most during my stay at the academy. . . . [It] was so beautiful and the sentiments so inspiring that it impressed me all my life." The inscription, he remembered, said "Righteousness exalteth a nation; but sin is a reproach to any people." Cadet Morris Schaff, class of 1862, understood the chapel's allure. "The secret of the precedence of the old chapel over the other buildings in the affections of the cadets does not seem mysterious to me," wrote Schaff in retrospect. "Weir's great suggestive painting, its sky mounting with a sense of infinite space over the chancel . . . transport him beyond the domain of drums, and there is established between him and the chapel a companionship that lasts."

8   Millbrook, "A Monument to Custer," 271; Frost, *General Custer's Libbie*, 242.

A *Harper's Weekly* woodcut depicting Custer's funeral procession. *LOC*

husband displayed on his casket, tears flowing quietly and unabated down her cheeks.

After the service, the battalion of cadets received the body, wheeled into columns of companies, and with arms reversed marched to the gravesite. Muffled drums beat out the ceremonial cadence. Morris Schaff, one of Custer's old classmates, described the ceremony, unchanged since the dedication of the cemetery. "I can see the caisson with the coffins, the stars in the flag lying on them, and immediately behind them, led by a soldier, the horse in full equipment, a trooper's boots in the stirrups pointed to the rear." It was beautiful in its simplicity, stark in its finality.[9]

The Academy had chosen the perfect spot for Custer's burial place. "There is a jetting out of land at West Point," recounted Libbie, "where a battery is placed commanding a fine strategic situation, and love for the great mountain opposite was doubtless because it seemed [my husband's] only friend when he was walking his demerits the only free afternoon of the week." As the coffin was lowered, the

Three ceremonial volleys were fired over the grave by the Cadet Honor Guard,
as depicted in this *Harper's Weekly* woodcut. *LOC*

"battalion of three hundred cadets fired three volleys over the grave." "Crow Nest echoed the volley," wrote Schaff, touched by the forlorn atmosphere of the ceremony. "The smoke billowed over, and up, and disappeared."[10]

Major General Wesley Merritt followed Custer to the slopes above the Hudson more than three decades later. His funeral was scheduled for the daylight hours of December 6, 1910, but the winter weather wreaked havoc with the planned pageantry of the ceremonies. The special car detailed to transport the body to West Point encountered numerous delays on its journey north from Washington, and it missed its connection at Weehawken, New Jersey. A special locomotive arrived to carry Merritt's coffin the final distance, but the mournful cargo did not arrive at West Point until well past five o'clock of the day scheduled for the funeral. When the Corps of Cadets finally assembled into parade formation on the drill field, it was pitch dark. "The wind," recalled one participant, "was as a knife, and as it cut across the level sweep of the drill grounds it drove the powdered snow in stinging flurries."[11]

10 Reynolds, *The Civil War Memories of Elizabeth Bacon Custer*, 38; Leckie, *Elizabeth Bacon Custer*, 219; "Funeral of General Custer," *Harper's Weekly*, October 27, 1877; Schaff, *The Spirit of Old West Point*, 118-119.

11 "Buried by Lamplight," *The Washington Post*, December 7, 1910.

As the weather rapidly deteriorated, officials decided to cut the ceremonial honors short. For Merritt, there would be no service in the Old Cadet Chapel. The fife and drum corps fell in at the front as the flag-draped coffin was transported across the drill field. "The fifers' breath," wrote the *Washington Post's* correspondent, "froze on their instruments as they shrilled the slow measures of the dead march." The full cadet corps fell in behind and the procession headed straight for the cemetery. A battery of artillery preceded the coffin, its customary clanking muffled by the snow. A group of pallbearers, mourners, and other civilian attendants brought up the rear. As the procession stepped off, 13 guns began booming their salutes at one-minute intervals. The *Post* reported that "[l]anterns guided the procession to the grave, and there, while the mourners stood bareheaded in the snow, the coffin was lowered into its resting place." When the chaplain finished reciting the time-caressed service, the honor guard crashed out

Merritt's gravesite is marked by an unpretentious black marble memorial, with his last name etched on the sides. *A. E. Bennett*

three volleys. As the gunfire echoed across the river, a lone trumpeter hauntingly blew "Taps." As the last plaintive note rose into the night sky, "the minute guns took up their iterated count."[12]

Several attending officers noted that this was the first time in more than 30 years that a service had been conducted by lamplight. It is hard to imagine a more appropriate farewell for a man who had conducted his business quietly in the background, eschewing the limelight for the good of the service. Merritt is buried next to his first wife, Caroline, in Lot IX, just behind the quaint Victorian buildings that house the cemetery's administrative offices. As if to underscore the symbolic power of his funeral, Merritt's grave is marked by a black marble memorial with his name etched simply on the side, rock solid and understated in its simplicity and elegance.

Everyone Here Wants to be a Warrior

Although their journeys ended at West Point in drastically different ways, Custer and Merritt began their military careers in exactly the same manner—on the road that winds its way up to the drill fields and barracks of the United States Military Academy. Morris Schaff vividly recalled the strenuous, 160-foot climb four decades later. "Soon we were at the dock, and soon we were ascending the slope that Grant, Lee, McPherson, Stonewall Jackson, Longstreet, and Warren, and many a high-hearted one—boys like ourselves—had ascended." The cramped roadway swept to the left and to the right, shrouded with trees and retained by lichen-covered rocks. In places, the gloom of the road gave way to swathes of dappled, golden light. "The hills rise immediately, stern and shaggy, forming a mighty and lofty background for West Point," reminisced Schaff with emotion. "Whoever has climbed up . . . has a memory which time cannot efface."[13]

To a certain extent, obtaining an appointment to West Point was an exercise in political patronage. Every member of Congress could nominate one cadet each year, and the president held the power to appoint a few at large. Schaff explained how the system worked at the time of his own admittance in 1858. "It was in the days before competitive examinations," he wrote, "when appointments to West Point and Annapolis were coveted, and usually secured, by sons of the leaders in

12 Ibid.

13 Schaff, *The Spirit of Old West Point*, 15-16.

business, political influence, and social standing." Luckily, political activism ran deep through the lives of both the Merritts and the Custers.[14]

Merritt's family was staunchly Democrat. His father, John Willis Merritt, had started out as a lawyer in New York City. The financial crisis of 1836 drove him from his practice to seek a new life for the Merritt clan on the western frontier of Ohio. In 1848, he abandoned his attempt at farming to become editor of *The Belleville Advocate*. Three years later, sensing greater opportunity, he moved the family to Salem, Illinois, a small, bustling town astride the St. Louis and Vincennes stage routes. There, he founded the town's first newspaper, *The Salem Advocate*. The senior Merritt served as editor and his sons, E. L. Merritt and J. D. Merritt, joined him as business partners. *The Advocate* met instant success and John Merritt established himself as a pillar of the community. His moderate political tendencies, neither abolitionist nor disunionist, shaped the editorial current of the family newspaper. Articles castigating Lincoln and the Republicans appeared daily. Congressman William H. Bissell of the 8th District of Illinois certainly could not ignore the clout of John Willis Merritt.[15]

A brief biography of Wesley Merritt, published in the *New York Times* on May 29, 1898, portrayed a reluctant soldier. Born in New York City on December 1, 1836, young Merritt had long cherished thoughts of practicing law and had managed to obtain a low-level sinecure in the office of Judge Haynie in Salem. "He was congratulating himself upon his advantageous start in his chosen profession," noted the *Times*, "when his father broached the subject of his going to West Point." Despite his own legal ambitions, Merritt formally applied for admission to the Academy in 1855. That April, Congressman Bissell forwarded his recommendation of Merritt's application to Secretary of War Jefferson Davis, who signed off on it a month later. The timing was highly fortuitous for Merritt. Not long after, Bissell

---

14   Ibid., 2.

15   Robert P. Howard, *Mostly Good and Competent Men: Illinois Governors, 1818-1988* (Springfield, IL, 1988), 109-113. Bissell's political career began in 1840, when he won nomination and election as a Democrat to the Illinois House of Representatives, serving until 1842. That whetted his appetite for public service, which took him all the way to the Illinois governor's mansion. Bissell left his law practice in 1845 to enlist in the 2nd Illinois Volunteer Regiment just prior to the Mexican War. His comrades soon elected him captain, and then colonel, of the regiment. In 1848, he was asked to stand as the Democratic candidate for Congress. Running unopposed, he went to Washington, winning re-election handily in 1850 and 1852. In the middle of his third term, he became paralyzed and walked on crutches for the rest of his life. Many attributed the paralysis to his wartime service in Mexico. In March 1860, at the age of 49, he caught a common cold that turned into a fatal bout of pneumonia.

split from the Democratic Party and threw his lot in with the Republicans, the emerging new political force in the country. In 1856, the Democratic convention endorsed the Kansas-Nebraska Act, and that reopening of the slavery question in the territories dramatically changed the face of politics as America headed inexorably toward war. It is doubtful that Merritt's Democratic credentials would have impressed the newly converted Republican had his application to West Point been made later.[16]

The Custers, too, were proudly Democratic. "Of course he was a Democrat," bragged Emmanuel Custer of his son George, known by the nickname of "Autie." "My boys were all Democrats. I would not raise any other kind." Unfortunately, his father's deeply held Democratic beliefs proved to be an obstacle for George Custer. Emmanuel had always been an opinionated individual, ready to join in a political debate at the drop of a hat. His arguments, although articulate, were always delivered in a loud, brassy voice that was easily heard by anyone whose business took them by his blacksmith shop. Highly respected by the citizens of New Rumley, Ohio, he would serve four successive terms as a justice of the peace.[17]

Unlike Merritt, Custer longed to begin his military career at West Point, and he needed the endorsement of John Bingham, congressman for the 21st District of Ohio, an anti-slavery and almost abolitionist Republican. Emmanuel Custer made it clear that his antipathy toward Bingham, and all that he stood for, would prevent him from becoming involved in Autie's campaign for Bingham's support. To compound the problem, in October 1856, young Autie joined a march of youthful Democrats against a campaign rally for John C. Fremont, the first Republican presidential candidate, which was taking place in Congressman Bingham's hometown of Cadiz. The protesters turned themselves out dressed as Kansas "border ruffians." The boisterous demonstration angered the Republicans and Bingham in particular.[18]

---

16 "Gen. Wesley Merritt," *The New York Times*, May 29, 1898.

17 Jeffry D. Wert, *Custer: The Controversial Life of George Armstrong Custer* (New York, 1996), 24.

18 Tom O'Neill, "Two Men of Ohio: Custer & Bingham," *Little Big Horn Association's Research Review* (January 1994), Vol. 8, No. 1, 10-11. John A. Bingham's political career began in 1841, after his graduation from the study of law at Franklin College. His loquacious manner in the many debates of the times, including slavery and the Mexican War, gave an early indication of the reputation he would develop as the "Cicero of the House of Representatives." With the dissolution of the Whig Party in the 1850s, he joined the Republicans, and was elected to Congress in 1854. He would become a powerful political figure and counted Abraham Lincoln as a friend and confidant.

George Armstrong Custer's official
Class of 1861 portrait

United States Military Academy Library

Brazenly, young Custer wrote to Bingham, "I am told that you can send a boy to West Point. I want to go there and I hear that you don't care whether a boy is a Democrat or Republican. I am a Democrat and I hope that you can send me to West Point for I want to be a soldier." Bingham informed Custer that he had already made one appointment and had promised a second to a young man from a neighboring county. Undaunted, Custer persisted in his efforts. "If that young man from Jeff. County of whom you spoke," he wrote Bingham, "does not push the matter, or if you hear of any other vacancy, I should be glad to hear from you." Custer's direct approach struck a nerve with the new congressman. Forty years later, the aging Bingham still remembered the letter. "It was a boy's letter, in a boyish hand, but the writing despite the painstaking effort showed a firmness of purpose, a determination to succeed seldom apparent in one so young," wrote the octogenarian. "I was struck with the originality and blunt honesty of his expressions." Finally, Bingham met with Custer in Cadiz. In November 1856, he wrote to Secretary of War Davis, endorsing Custer's candidacy to the Military Academy.[19]

Bingham would always treasure their first meeting after the start of the war. One day, Custer appeared at Bingham's office unannounced. "He was out of breath, or had lost it from embarrassment." Almost in a stutter, Custer addressed his benefactor: "Mr. Bingham, I have been in my first battle. I tried hard to do my best. I felt I ought to report to you, for it's through you I got to West Point. I'm . . . I took his hand. 'I know, you're my boy Custer!'" Bingham would never regret his choice. "Up, up he went, never a cowardly action, never a deed marring his war

19 Reynolds, *The Civil War Memories of Elizabeth Bacon Custer*, 11-12.

record," he wrote, "[c]ourteous to his friends, magnanimous to his foes, just and true and noble in every relation of his life. He was a most manly man, the most soldierly soldier, the most heroic hero I've ever met."[20]

Merritt reported for classes at West Point on July 1, 1855, followed by Custer in 1857. The two young men joined an institution that was in the midst of great changes, and that was about to face an even greater challenge.

A Sorry Substitute for Battle

In the 1850s, West Point was steeped in tradition and slow to change. In its own cumbersome fashion, the Academy trained the future leaders of the army with a curriculum heavy in mathematics and engineering but light on the military sciences. One historian points out that "the men who controlled the institution viewed its mission as being the production of engineers who could also function as soldiers rather than the reverse."[21]

Engineering and mathematics represented nearly 50% of a cadet's class ranking, and 70% of his total class time. The rigorous schedule required a great deal of study time. One mathematics professor warned his fourth-year students, "From three and a half to four hours should be given daily by the cadet to render him thoroughly proficient in the prescribed lessons of the mathematical course."[22]

A circular published by the war department for new cadets admonished "that only about a third of all who entered were graduated, and counseled the appointee that unless he had an aptitude for mathematics, etc., it might be better for him not to accept the appointment, thus he would escape the mortification of failure for himself and his family."[23]

In the early years of the decade, the army was still digesting the results of its heady victory in the Mexican War of 1846-48. Recent breathtaking advances in the technology of war sparked an intense debate at all levels of the officer corps, particularly a growing concern over the long-range effects of the rifled musket then

20 Merington, *The Custer Story*, 13; Reynolds, *The Civil War Memories of Elizabeth Bacon Custer*, 12-13.

21 Jacob Kobrick, "No Army Inspired: The Failure of Nationalism at Antebellum West Point," *Concept: An Interdisciplinary Journal of Graduate Studies* (April 2004), Vol. 27, 8.

22 "West Point, Training and the Development of Tactics," web.archive.org/web/20050207210403/ http://www.usregulars.com/USMAhome.html.

23 Schaff, *The Spirit of Old West Point*, 2.

coming into vogue in the European armies. This concern, in conjunction with George McClellan's report of his observations of the Crimean War in 1856, led to the creation of the Department of Tactics in 1858, headed by reform-minded Lt. Col. William J. Hardee, who used the well-drilled long gray line to practice and perfect his theories. Hardee's *Rifle and Light Infantry Tactics* would become the standard infantry drill manual used by both sides in the Civil War. Hardee's tenure at West Point was marked by innovation in both academic training and military thought, and officers and cadets were encouraged to test new tactics and formations. Rightfully, the Academy's new mission was to prepare the future leaders of the army to fight a modern war.

West Point's academic board, however, remained mired in the past and shackled to the teachings of Professor Dennis Hart Mahan, who taught the notorious course on engineering and the "science of war." It was Mahan's contention, wrote one historian, that "the great goal of the military academy . . . was to furnish a solid foundation of scientific and military education. . . . Anything that distracted from this governing objective must be pruned away ruthlessly." Mahan's intractability placed him in conflict with the board of visitors, an influential group of outside observers that bemoaned the narrow focus of the curriculum. "The subject of history is not taught, very much to our regret," they complained in their annual report for 1854, "as it is certainly a branch of great importance, especially the history of our country and military history—this should not be neglected."[24]

In addition to its continued application of Mahan's dogmatic tomes on fortifications and military engineering, the academic board enforced strict discipline and endless hours of precision drill. It was a sacrosanct technique for preparing junior officers for training raw recruits in the rudiments of the intricate close-order drill of 19th century armies, but it did nothing to advance the military education of a force that needed to be girding for a new style of warfare. "West Point is after all," sneered one cynic, "only a training school to fit men to discipline the militia."[25]

When the board balked at implementing any reforms that would change the basic thrust of the curriculum, Secretary of War Davis saw no recourse but to add a year to the term of the course, beginning with Merritt's class in 1855. As designed,

24 Kobrick, "No Army Inspired," 9.

25 Edward C. Boynton, "History of West Point; its Military Importance during the American Revolution, and the Origin and Progress of the United States Military Academy," *The North American Review* (April 1864), Vol. 98, Issue 203, 7.

the extended curriculum mercilessly pared down the initial class of 121 cadets; in the end, only 41 of them received their commissions. "During the five years which followed," recalled Maj. Gen. James H. Wilson, one of Merritt's classmates, "the exactions were severe and the standard high. . . . It is not to be denied that the extra year was well and profitably employed, and in the end gave us an unusually good preparation for the great war which broke out within a year after we graduated."Meanwhile, Hardee espoused these dictums in a class entitled "Tactics of Artillery, Cavalry and Infantry and Equitation." The students gained practical experience in the field and developed proficiency in the use of a variety of small arms. Davis's experiment to increase the term of the course would end with Merritt's class, as the need for new officers at the outset of war forced the war department to shorten it. In 1861, this desperate shortage of officers would also result in the hasty graduation of two classes, one of them being Custer's.[26]

Captain Edward C. Boynton, adjutant at West Point during the Civil War years, described the change taking place at the core of the Academy's curriculum. "Long a warlike people, we are becoming, we must be, a military nation," he expounded. "The best assurance of success will be, to teach all our sons that noble art which can defend our freedom, and hurl back the invader, with readiness, address, and the least bloodshed. West Point must ever be the great mother of our future educational development in arms." On the other hand, Captain Boynton acknowledged the validity of charges that the Academy and its young cadets were kept too isolated from the rest of the world. "It is shut off topographically on a narrow point, guarded on all sides from ingress and egress," he agreed. The first two years of the curriculum were meant to be relentless, with no vacations or letup in the "vigorous exercise of mind and body." It was as monastic an existence as could be created. A perturbed Boynton stated, "[t]he Academy is their microcosm."[27]

Isolated high up on the banks of the Hudson—the real world held deliberately at arm's length—the Academy went about its perceived task. "The doctrine of our perpetual nationality was ever placed in the fore-front of instruction and practice there," asserted Boynton. The symbol of that doctrine, the national flag, stood at the center of the cadets' "daily lesson of reverence and love." The boom of the morning gun signaled the flag's majestic ascent up the flagstaff. Likewise, a solitary

---

26 James H. Wilson, *Under the Old Flag: Recollections of Military Operations in the War for the Union, the Spanish War, the Rebellion, Etc.* (Westport, CT, 1971), 1:7.

27 Boynton, "History of West Point," 12.

gun echoed from the hills each evening to mark its descent. These ceremonies served to teach the "truest lessons, that the Union meant our country, and that disunion was the rankest treason."[28]

Despite the harsh lessons of four years of civil war, the Academy's curriculum would remain stagnant, mired in obsolescence and disconnected from developments in the military field. Only after the war did innovation in the military sciences begin to take place at West Point. "From the date of its establishment up to a period after the civil war the Military Academy at West Point continued by law [to be] a part of the Engineer Corps of the army," explained Merritt. The transformation truly began with a simple bureaucratic sleight-of-hand. In 1866, Congress transferred the institution from the Corps of Engineers to the war department. From that point on, the new leaders of the army would be taught by officers drawn from all branches of the service. "The Academy . . . produced results of which its friends are justly proud," wrote Merritt approvingly. The influx of new professional instructors infused West Point with "vigor and vitality in the performance of its important work."[29]

Born and Raised in Black and White

A rigid code of conduct regulated the tight confines of the cadets' world, administered through the issuance of demerits, which at least one West Point superintendent described as a "system of terror." Demerits were dispensed liberally for just about any imaginable breach of military decorum. Each cadet was permitted 100 demerits over a six-month period, and all knew that number 101 meant automatic expulsion. Throughout the four years of the course, Custer flirted continuously with expulsion, acquiring very close to the limit of demerits allowed by Academy regulations. Cadet Joseph Farley paid tribute to his happy-go-lucky classmate. "Glorious old boy!" he exclaimed, "Daredevil of the class! How well did you hang on to the tail end—always ahead of the deficients."[30]

Of her husband's career at West Point, Libbie would recall, "I never heard anything about his successes at West Point. It was a tale of demerits, of lessons unlearned, of narrow escapes from dismissal, of severe punishments." These

---

28 Ibid., 9.

29 Wesley Merritt, "The Army of the United States," *Harper's New Monthly Magazine* (March 1890), Vol. 80, No. 476, 500; Alberts, *General Wesley Merritt*, 284.

30 Joseph P. Farley, *West Point in the Early Sixties* (Troy, NY, 1902), 21-22.

punishments included performing many extra tours of guard duty on Saturdays. The irrepressible and unrepentant Custer would later write, "If memory serves me right, I devoted sixty-six Saturdays to this method of vindicating outraged military law during my cadetship of four years." Custer used to tell Libbie that "[i]t required far more skill to graduate at the foot of the class than at the head, and there was no effort to conceal the fact that his fun-loving, daring spirit nearly cost him his appointment in the Army. He was 'found' so often til at last one demerit more would have been the end."[31]

Cadet Schaff, who marched off his own share of punishment tours of guard duty, described moments of self-satisfaction on those long and lonely nights. Guard duty was meant to be punishment, but for those walking the rigid path of the sentry, the moments before dawn were transformative. Every hour on the hour, the big tower clock chimed away the moments until dawn. The moonlight that bathed the campus waned, the mists that covered the Hudson began to disperse, and the sun finally cracked the horizon. The staccato notes of "Reveille" brought forth "the appearance of the soldier at the morning gun, the corporal standing with the colors in his hands till the sun clears the east, when the gun fires, and the colors ascend lovingly to the head of the mast."[32]

In contrast to the wealth of anecdotes about Cadet Custer, very few exist regarding Cadet Merritt, which is rather telling in its own way. Merritt's classmates seemed to have fond memories of their time together. Merritt, recalled Schaff, "was a sergeant in my first camp, and had, I think, more of the sunshine of youth in his fair, open face and clear blue eyes than any other cadet in the corps. I can hear his fine tenor voice now, rising high and sweet over the group that used to meet at the head of the company street and sing, in the evening."[33]

Merritt graduated 22nd, right in the middle of his class. His tenure was neither distinguished by brilliance nor marred by mediocrity. He was a square peg in a square hole who always saluted his officers and reported for parade and guard duty in the proper uniform. He arrived promptly to class, fully prepared for his lessons. It is doubtful that he even worried about his demerit count. In 1857, Merritt's second year, the offenses for which demerits could be awarded became more lenient, and finally, the awful attrition of cadets slowed down.

---

31 Reynolds, *The Civil War Memories of Elizabeth Bacon Custer*, 19-20, 35, 40.

32 Schaff, *The Spirit of Old West Point*, 64-65.

33 Ibid., 57.

The practice of hazing, according to James Wilson, "was practiced in full force." Anson Mills, a classmate of Merritt and Wilson, recalled, "I knew nothing of military discipline or ways and was received, as were others at the time, in a most cruel manner by the older cadets." Wilson took a more philosophical view of the whole matter. "It was good-natured, but at times rather rough play between old and new cadets," he wrote, "which so far as I could see, did no harm but much good to all. . . . It certainly did no injury whatever to such as met it with good-natured resistance and were fit for the life they had chosen." Mills seems to have taken the hazing in stride, but warned of the "extreme case of hazing of the kind that eventually brought it into disrepute." He believed hazing, "held within bounds," produced some benefit by teaching "the bumptious and presumptuous how little they are prepared to enter a life of absolute discipline, and how little imaginary personal, social or political superiority has to do with their future training."[34]

Merritt opposed hazing from the start of his five-year tenure as West Point superintendent in the 1880s, viewing it as sprit-damaging and prejudicial to good military order and discipline. Accordingly, he spent an inordinate amount of time trying to combat it. Sternly, Merritt admonished his staff and professors that "[t]he authorities here will indulge in no half-hearted measures to detect the offenders." To any caught in the act, justice would be meted out swiftly and remorselessly. "The best means of maintaining discipline in any organization," wrote the superintendent, "is the certainty of summary punishment, just but severe, in all cases of intentional offense." The practice, however, proved to be too deeply entrenched. Many of the young officers, having just gone through the fires themselves, "were diametrically opposed to my views on hazing—so much so, in fact, that I could not obtain their cheerful acquiescence in what I was trying to do to 'stop the practice.'"[35]

Southron by the Grace of Gawd

While the cloistered isolation of West Point kept the world at bay, it also locked together men of opposing beliefs into a confined proximity. "The Kansas troubles were then at their height," recalled Mills, "and there were many encounters between the extremists of the North and the extremists of the South, but, after a

---

34 Wilson, *Under the Old Flag*, 1:7-8; Mills, *My Story*, 43.

35 Alberts, *General Wesley Merritt*, 285; "A Gentleman to Witness," *The Washington Post*, January 30, 1901.

year or two at the academy, each became reconciled to the other's ways so that the corps, as a body, was more homogenous than the people at large." The Corps of Cadets, like the rest of the nation, broke into factions. By the late 1850s, room assignments and, more importantly, company assignments were made on a regional basis. "They questioned me on my political and moral principles," Mills remembered, "adding that they must observe great caution in assigning room-mates, lest injury might happen." Another cadet, Peter S. Michie of the class of 1863, recalled that, "At this time the cadets had by some gradual process become separated into two parties, hostile in sentiment, and even divided into barracks."[36]

These passions intensified during Custer's term. On February 22, 1861, the commemoration of Washington's Birthday began at "Reveille" with the playing of the national airs by the assembled band of the Corps of Cadets. The Southern side of the barracks erupted with hisses and catcalls, and the Northerners counterpunched with loud cheers. At 11:30 a.m., the entire complement of officers and cadets assembled in the Old Cadet Chapel for a reading of Washington's Farewell Address, which was, ironically enough, a plea for national unity. "The very air" recalled Schaff, of that vast, cold stone room, "was filled with foreboding."[37]

As the cadets prepared for the staccato beat of "Tattoo" to end the day, the gathering storm finally broke. Once more, the band assembled on the great drill plains in front of the barracks; Northerners occupied the east wing, while Southern sympathizers congregated in the west and south wings. The sally port in the center served as the demarcation line. After a lifeless rendition of "Washington's March," the band launched into the "Star-Spangled Banner," and the spirited tune was easily heard throughout the barracks. "Every room fronting the area was aglow, every window up and filled with men," according to Schaaf. Ignoring the likelihood of earning another demerit, George Custer burst into a cheer. As one cadet remarked, "it took a man of his courage and heedlessness [to openly] violate the regulations." Within moments, the entire east wing resounded with the hearty cheers of the Northerners. Recognizing the voice of his close friend, Thomas L. Rosser responded with his own cry for the band to play the de facto Southern anthem. "Dixie, Dixie, Dixie!" Rosser and his cohorts shouted.[38]

---

36 Mills, *My Story*, 41, 44; Stephen W. Sears, "West Point in the Civil War," in Robert Cowley and Thomas Guinzburg, eds., *West Point: Two Centuries of Honor and Tradition* (New York, 2002), 78.

37 Schaff, *The Spirit of Old West Point*, 204.

38 Ibid., 208.

In this atmosphere, rife with bitter divisions, open conflict frequently erupted. After evening formations, the civility that characterized the official day gave way to a free, sometimes violent, expression of an individual's political beliefs. The Southern boys—"hot-headed, masterful, intolerant fellows who classed Black Republicans with the abolitionists, and believed in slavery as a divine institution"—openly espoused states' rights and hinted darkly at resignation. Disunion was the watchword of the day. In heated arguments, a few misspoken words could quickly lead to fisticuffs. On one occasion, recalled James Wilson, "[Cadet McCreery], a brilliant and ambitious Virginian . . . had provoked me, unfortunately for himself, into the only fight I had during my cadet days, ostensibly because of impatient words I had used towards him at artillery drill, but really because I was a Northerner, and he and his friends thought a good licking would do me good."[39]

At least the Southerners stood united. The same could not be said of their Northern brethren, who splintered into precise cliques: the radical Republicans, the abolitionists, and the remnants of the old Whig and Democratic parties. A fist fight was just as likely to break out between Northerners, and there were even established protocols in which seconds were selected. These fights, recounted one participant, were "with bare fists, 'rough and tumble,' to a finish without a break, according to the local rules."[40]

As much as he tried, Merritt could not avoid trouble. "During my whole time at West Point," he recalled, "I had but one fight, and that was with a fellow classman over a personal issue." Anson Mills, the classmate in question, remembered the fight as one of the high points of his career at West Point—a career curtailed when he failed to qualify in mathematics. A small party gathered in a lantern-lit circle, down by the Francis Dade monument, within which the two combatants squared off. Mills described it as "one of the hardest fights that took place while I was at the academy." Neither man had an advantage, being of the same size and stature. With no apparent victor, and with both combatants covered in blood, the seconds stepped in and stopped the fight. As the aggrieved parties staggered back to camp, they were astounded when "nearly a hundred cadets, secretly assembled as spectators, arose from the surrounding foliage." Mills would

---

39 Wilson, *Under the Old Flag*, 1:19-20.

40 Ibid., 1:20.

Some of Custer's best friends at the academy and in later life were Southerners, particularly his West Point roommate James Parker of Missouri, John "Gimlet" Lea of Mississippi, James Washington of Virginia (shown here with Custer as a prisoner on the Virginia Peninsula), and Pierce M. B. Young of Georgia. *LOC*

come to regret his hot-headed words. He and Merritt, he insisted, "were always the best of friends afterward."[41]

Cadet Custer seems to have remained above the fray. Some of his best friends at the Academy and in later life were Southerners, particularly his West Point roommate, James Parker of Missouri, as well as John "Gimlet" Lea of Mississippi, James Washington of Virginia, and Pierce M. B. Young of Georgia. Acquaintances from other classes included John Pelham of Alabama, Stephen Dodson Ramseur of North Carolina, and Tom Rosser from Texas. "My husband told me," Libbie recounted, "his only sad [days] were when his Southern classmates were watching for their states to secede during the winter of 1861. But my husband told me that

41 "A Gentleman to Witness," *The Washington Post*; Mills, *My Story*, 46.

they fell so on each other's necks and cried like children at parting during that tempestuous winter of our history."[42]

When Union troops captured Confederate Captain Washington on the Peninsula in 1862, Custer's efforts on behalf of his former classmate were not forgotten by Washington's mother. Years later, while serving with Sheridan in the Shenandoah Valley, Custer's march took him past the Washington mansion. "Mrs. Washington had sworn never to speak to a Yankee," wrote Libbie in her diary, "but her son had told her that she must make an exception of Custer should he ever come her way, and now she wanted to thank him for his kindness to her son. She did more; she forced him to accept a gift, a precious heirloom in the family, one of a set of buttons from a coat made for and worn by George Washington."[43]

During the Peninsula campaign, Custer served as best man at Capt. "Gimlet" Lea's wedding, which was held deep in enemy territory. Clad in his regulation dress uniform of blue, Custer stood out in a room full of Confederate dress gray. The saucy Rebel women swooned in Custer's presence, and one whispered, "You should be in our army." The Union cavalryman would also stand at the foot of Maj. Gen. Stephen Ramseur's deathbed in the small hours of the morning after the battle of Cedar Creek in 1864, and cut off a lock of Ramseur's hair for his widow and the newborn child his friend would never see. Following the Confederate surrender at Appomattox, witnesses never forgot the sight of Custer and some of his Rebel friends romping on the ground like children.[44]

Many others would soon find themselves on opposite sides of the killing fields. "Each graduate made his choice in honest and conscientious belief that he was in the right," declared Edgar Dudley. "They were called upon to decide between their legal and moral duty, to support and maintain the Union, and what they believed to be their moral and personal duty to their kindred, their homes, their locality and their states." The division ran so deep that upon graduation, Custer simultaneously received both an official and unofficial class ranking as the "foot of the class of thirty-four and head of the class of seventy-four." Custer explained that his lowly ranking was the result of a roster that had been cut almost in half by the resignations of the Southern cadets, "[which] took away from the Academy a few

42 Reynolds, *The Civil War Memories of Elizabeth Bacon Custer*, 26.

43 Merington, *The Custer Story*, 129-130.

44 Frederick Whittaker, *A Popular Life of Gen. George A. Custer. Major-General of Volunteers, Brevet Major-General U.S. Army, and Lieutenant-Colonel of the Seventh U.S. Cavalry* (New York, 1876), 128; Schaff, *The Spirit of Old West Point*, 182.

individuals who, had they remained, would probably have contested with me the debatable honor of bringing up the rear of the class."[45]

Before long, the Academy came to be viewed as a hotbed of sedition, with some flippantly calling it "a nursery of treason." The few young men inside its confines never understood the vituperative nature of those outside its walls. "I cannot help thinking that there is something wrong with this institution," charged the Radical Republican Senator Benjamin Wade. "I do not believe that in the history of the world you can find as many men who proved themselves utterly faithless to their oaths, ungrateful to the Government that supported them, guilty of treason and a deliberate attempt to overthrow that Government which has educated them."[46]

Into the Hands of the Masters

In this atmosphere of escalating trouble, Wesley Merritt graduated as a second lieutenant of cavalry in the United States Army. On November 11, 1860, commission in hand, he reported to the 2nd Regiment of Dragoons, stationed at Camp Floyd in the Department of Utah—the heart of Indian country. He began his apprenticeship with a temporary posting as second lieutenant of Company E, commanding the unit in the absence of officers away on detached service. He received a short-lived posting to Company A in April 1861. A month later, he was promoted to first lieutenant of Company B, which was commanded by Capt. John Buford.

Many of the officers in the 2nd Dragoons, both Northern and Southern, would rise to high command in their respective armies. Several of those officers would have a tremendous impact on shaping Merritt's subsequent career as a cavalryman, particularly the regiment's commander, Col. Philip St. George Cooke, and Capts. John Buford and Alfred Pleasonton. In 1858, after his promotion to colonel, Cooke took a leave of absence and traveled extensively throughout Europe. His observations of European mounted forces resulted in his preparation of a manual

---

45 Farley, *West Point in the Early Sixties*, 21-22; John M. Carroll, ed., *Custer in the Civil War: His Unfinished Memoirs* (San Rafael, CA, 1977), 86; Reynolds, *The Civil War Memories of Elizabeth Bacon Custer*, 23, 27.

46 Sears, "West Point in the Civil War," 102.

Philip St. George Cooke, seen here as a brigadier general, commanded the 2nd Dragoons and enjoyed a storied prewar career fighting Indians on the western frontier. His noteworthy role in the Civil War would be overshadowed by his more flamboyant and famous son-in-law, Confederate cavalryman Jeb Stuart. *LOC*

entitled *Cavalry Tactics*, which he hoped would be adopted as the standard for the U.S. Cavalry.[47]

Cooke had been busy prior to Merritt's arrival. In late March 1854, he hastily marshaled a strike force to go to the aid of the 1st Dragoons at Fort Burgwin after that regiment had been defeated with heavy losses. His pursuit of the hostile Jicarilla Apache covered more than 150 miles, much of it conducted over the Rocky Mountains, which were still blanketed with deep winter snows. "He overtook them at *Aguas Calientes* April 8th, and defeated them, killing about twenty," wrote Merritt. "The tribe was so humbled by their pursuit and defeat they begged for peace." During the Kansas disturbances of 1856, he so impressed Gen. Persifor Frazer Smith that in his report, that Smith lauded Cooke for his "sound judgment." Cooke's "promptness, energy and good management" had been instrumental in preventing "the most fatal and extended disasters" in Kansas.[48]

Merritt's other mentors in the 2nd Dragoons were equally experienced soldiers. His company commander, Capt. John Buford, would achieve everlasting fame for his truculent stand in the opening hours of the battle of Gettysburg. Considered by many to be the finest cavalry officer in the army, Buford took a personal interest in Merritt's career and served as the young officer's mentor until his untimely death from typhoid fever in late 1863. Captain Alfred Pleasonton, who later wormed his way into command of the Cavalry Corps of the Army of the Potomac, would promote Merritt to brigadier general just days before the opening salvoes at Gettysburg.

Abraham Lincoln's election as president of the United States coincided with Merritt's arrival at Camp Floyd, and the irrevocable split in the Union gathered momentum and rolled like an avalanche toward war. As at West Point, sectarian strife splintered the 2nd Dragoons, and its officer corps broke into factions.

---

47 Cooke entered West Point in 1823 and joined the ranks of the 6th Infantry after graduating. In 1829, he transferred to the western frontier, where he began piling up a record of action and success against marauding Indians, starting with skirmishes against the Comanches. He participated in the Black Hawk War of 1832 and fought in the battle of Bad Axe River that same year. In 1833, he was promoted to first lieutenant and was assigned to the 1st Dragoons. In 1847, he attained the rank of major and commanded the 2nd Dragoons in the war with Mexico. By 1853, he was back on the frontier and in quick succession battled the Apaches at Agua Caliente, led mounted troops against the Sioux at Blue Water, and commanded the cavalry during the Utah expedition.

48 Wesley Merritt, "Life and Services of General Philip St. George Cooke," *Journal of the United States Cavalry Association* (June 1895), Vol. 8, No. 29, 82-83.

A cavalryman's cavalryman. Shown here in his prime as a brigadier general, John Buford graduated from West Point in 1848 and saw extensive service against the Sioux in Texas and during the Utah War. Buford served as Lt. Wesley Merritt's company commander in the 2nd Dragoons, and mentored the younger officer in the nuances of small unit command. *LOC*

The swelling volume of resignations of Southern officers soon took its toll on the unit, and it resulted in Merritt's temporary posting as regimental adjutant to Cooke. "My relations with General Cooke . . . were as intimate as was possible between a mature man and a youngster just from West Point," Merritt would write of his association with Cooke. Merritt attributed much of his early success to "this prince of cavalry soldiers."[49]

The troubles endemic to West Point followed Merritt westward. Life on the frontier was bleak and dark, with a dearth of entertainment. Most evenings, the post's officers and the wives of the married men would gather at a designated parlor—most often the commanding officer's, as his was the roomiest. At some point, the women would retreat to another room, leaving the men to enjoy their pipes, cigars, and libations. Inevitably, discussions turned to the gathering clouds of secession and war, often becoming heated as the evening progressed. Eben Swift, a future aide to Merritt, wrote of those contentious times, "Political discussions may have led these men of conservative opinions to express themselves too freely and perhaps caused them to be misunderstood."[50]

Insidiously, reports denouncing officers with Southern ties began to wend their way to Washington, drawing Merritt onto treacherous ground. "Their career as soldiers was in danger, as suspicion poisoned many a cup in those days." Allegations of backstabbing came to the attention of Col. Cooke, who promptly ordered the arrest of the miscreants. He sent Merritt, decked out in full uniform, to read the arrest warrant in "formal style." Merritt's youthful, cool countenance belied a hot temper, and he felt deeply affronted by the perfidy of those who doubted the loyalty of the accused officers. Throughout his life, Merritt struggled mightily to control his "impetuous temper, a quality which he often considered a fault, but which he soon schooled himself to hold in complete subjugation." On this occasion, he failed miserably, and "proceeded to take personal satisfaction at once."[51]

"General Cooke labored under the suspicion which attached to officers of Southern birth, of a want of loyalty to the government," asserted Merritt. "Of one thing I am certain, and that is, that this great, noble, chivalrous man never for one moment wavered or faltered in his allegiance to the government." Cooke proved

---

49 Ibid., 84.

50 Eben Swift, "General Wesley Merritt," *Journal of the United States Cavalry Association* (March 1911), Vol. 21, No. 83, 829.

51 Ibid., 829-830.

guilty of nothing more than guilt by association, based on the fact that his son-in-law was the future Confederate cavalry chieftain, James Ewell Brown ("Jeb") Stuart. Other loyal officers under suspicion included Capt. Buford, a native of Kentucky; Buford's close friend Capt. John Gibbon, who received his appointment to the Academy from North Carolina; and Capt. William Price Sanders, a Mississippian who would die at Knoxville in November 1863 dressed in Union blue. Merritt's superiors, Swift wrote, were "all of them officers who were entirely loyal to the cause of the government but were not in sympathy with the ultra-abolitionists of the day." Fortunately for the Union's prospects in the impending struggle, these scandalous allegations were handled before any real damage was done.[52]

The beginning of the war found much of the Regular cavalry stranded on the far-flung frontier. Many members of the 2nd Dragoons feared the war would be over before the regiment could reach the theater of action. "In those days," Merritt later wrote, "the means of communication were slow compared to the present. The pony express connecting with the telegraph in the States brought us the news of the disaster at Bull Run. I recall how the impatient spirits in the far-off cantonment in Utah chafed at the delay in expected orders." In early July, Cooke finally received marching orders from the war department, and he instructed the regiment to pack its gear and begin the long trek to the war in the east. In anticipation of the arduous march, Cooke made Merritt's staff posting permanent. In this capacity, Merritt became intimately involved in a complex military movement that was to span two months.[53]

The march east did much to prepare Merritt as an officer of cavalry. The characteristics that would stamp his style of leadership were nurtured by Cooke and further polished by his company commander, John Buford. "This period of my acquaintance with General Cooke," recalled Merritt, "is especially interesting to me, for it was on this march from Utah to Fort Leavenworth that I learned much of marching troops, which has served me since in the cavalry service." Over those two months, Cooke gave Merritt a masterful demonstration of how to move a mounted column between two points. Merritt attributed his later success to two precepts on which Cooke had hammered away: the need for constant attention to detail on the

---

52 Merritt, "Life and Services of General Philip St. George Cooke," 84-85; Swift, "General Wesley Merritt," 829.

53 Merritt, "Life and Services of General Philip St. George Cooke," 85.

part of cavalry officers, and the value of instant and impetuous mounted charges against the enemy.[54]

Despite the short duration of his frontier service, Merritt had cemented the official relationships that would influence his career. More importantly, he also had established a firm foundation in small unit leadership. "As for Merritt's service in Utah, he had a lot of mundane duties," notes historian Eric Wittenberg, "but they taught him a lot. He often served on boards of survey with his company commander, Buford, where they had the job of assessing and evaluating horse flesh. What better way is there to learn about horses?" Merritt came to appreciate the contributions of the various staff roles, particularly the logistical nightmare that was the quartermaster's department. He became a firm believer in the adage that an army moved on its belly. "It is not difficult, then, to conclude how easily a poorly conducted Quartermaster-General's Department embarrasses and paralyzes an army," he would later write with the blunt sagacity of a life spent in pursuit of his country's enemies. Drawing on that experience, Merritt declared, "Any neglect in the Subsistence Department is quick to be felt and resented, and soon ends in demoralization."[55]

A young professional soldier's career benefits greatly from both experience and patronage. Staff positions place young officers in intimate proximity to their commanders and help them to create close, lifelong associations. Merritt's counterpart in the 1st Dragoons, Lt. George B. Sanford, provided his opinions on the subject. "I liked the work, [and] more especially the inside view it gave me of affairs pertaining to the army," he explained. "A certain amount of staff service tends to broaden [an officer's] views, enlarge his knowledge of his profession and enables him to come in contact with the older and more distinguished officers of the service."[56]

Sanford himself found an excellent mentor in Capt. Benjamin F. "Grimes" Davis, West Point class of 1854. The 28-year-old officer from Alabama would remain loyal to his oath of service despite his thoroughly Southern breeding. By June 1863, he was colonel of the 8th New York Cavalry, serving under Buford in the 1st Cavalry Division of the Army of the Potomac. During the battle of Brandy

---

54 Ibid.

55 Eric J. Wittenberg, correspondence with the author, August 7, 2017; Merritt, "The Army of the United States," *Harper's New Monthly Magazine* (March 1890), Vol. 80, No. 476, 496.

56 E. R. Hagemann, ed., *Fighting Rebels and Redskins: Experiences in the Army Life of Colonel George B. Sanford* (Norman, OK, 1969), 217-218.

Station on June 9, he was killed while leading his regiment into action at Beverly Ford. "He kept me 'on the jump.' He was a thorough officer, and as far as I can remember, never missed an opportunity to impart the instruction I required," recalled Sanford fondly. "On the march he taught me to notice the character of the country, the advantages of positions for attack and defense, sites for camp etc. At a halt he would practice with me in the sabre exercise and give me instruction in posting pickets and sending out scouts."[57]

At night, mentor and student huddled around a fire. Cooke opened up to Merritt, and the young subaltern was eager to learn. "More than once at this time I talked with General Cooke on the subject of his loyalty to his government, the conversation being introduced by himself," wrote Merritt with some astonishment, "and on one occasion he expressed the hope that if he ever faltered in devotion to the cause of the Union, his best friend should stab him to the heart. His patriotism was inborn, and part of his chivalrous nature."[58]

But Cooke presented a dichotomy. He believed that the ultimate tactical expression of cavalry was the mounted charge, and that dismounted cavalry was a misuse of the service. It was therefore paramount to husband the strength of the command's horses, so that when the moment to strike came, they would be able to help deliver the killing stroke. "His motto," recalled Merritt, was "[s]harp sabers and sharp spurs,' and his orders and example forcing a free, fast and furious charge on the enemy wherever found." This philosophy was somewhat at odds with the stated purpose of the dragoons, and Merritt never made much of an effort to reconcile the discrepancy.[59]

The cross-country march to the contested fields of Virginia served as Merritt's classroom. He witnessed the methods of the old warhorse Cooke in close and personal detail. "His interest in the command while marching never relaxed for a moment. He observed every trooper, man and animal in the command. His care, with reference to grazing and watering, was constant," observed Merritt. By journey's end, Merritt felt assured "that the officer who keeps his command in good condition by careful attention to what may be called trifles, is of more service to his country in time of war than are some men in battle." This would prove to be

---

57 Ibid., 147-148.

58 Merritt, "Life and Services of General Philip St. George Cooke," 85.

59 Ibid., 84.

another of the many vexing issues over which Merritt and Custer fought tooth-and-nail.[60]

Merritt would become known for the tight march discipline of his various field commands and for the constant attention paid to the welfare of their horses. In later life he would lay down his principles for conducting an efficient cavalry march, and even offered detailed instructions on the correct mental attitude and physical posture of officers beginning a march. "In the preparation and start, as well as in the smallest details of the march, the closest supervision of the Commanding Officer must be exercised," he began. "The active interest in every incident of the march," he continued,

> must begin with all the officers of a column the moment the "Forward" is sounded. That officer who throws himself into the saddle and listlessly settles into his haunches for the—to him—dull routine of a march, is bad as an example and useless in control. Better for the command that he should make the march rolled in a blanket in an ambulance.

> My advice to an officer commanding a march is to arrest an officer . . . who willfully neglects attention to the smallest details of the march, so necessary to the preservation of the endurance of men and horses.[61]

In a stark conclusion, Merritt made his point in language that all could understand: "In reviewing the foregoing one is impressed with the simplicity of the problem to be solved in order to march successfully, cavalry or mixed commands for long distances." His old mentor, Philip St. George Cooke, once sent him a personal note, praising his efforts. "Any unusual success I may have had in cavalry marches," Cooke wrote, somewhat tongue-in-cheek, "I suspect may be attributed to my constant thoughtfulness and attention—my great interest felt in the welfare and comfort of horses and men—I fear in that order."[62]

---

60 Ibid., 85-86.

61 Wesley Merritt, "Marching Cavalry," *Journal of the United States Cavalry Association* (December 1890), Vol. 3, No. 11, 72-74.

62 Ibid., 78.

Not the Recommended Way to Go to War

While Merritt was establishing a firm career foundation, Custer was scrambling to salvage his own prospects. "West Point," recalled upperclassman Morris Schaff, "has had many a character to deal with; but it may be a question whether it had a cadet so exuberant, one who cared so little for its serious attempt to elevate and burnish, or one on whom the tactical officers kept their eyes so constantly and unsympathetically searching as upon Custer. And yet how we all loved him."[63]

Of his notoriety at West Point, Custer would later write unabashedly:

> My career as a Cadet had little to commend it to the study of those who came after me, unless as an example to be carefully avoided. The requirements of the academic regulations, a copy of which was placed in my hand the morning of my arrival at West Point, were not observed by me in such manner at all times to commend me to the approval and good opinions of my instructors and superior officers. My offences against law and order were not great in enormity, but what they lacked in magnitude they made up for in number.[64]

With war fever gripping the campus in the waning weeks of his last term in 1861, Custer punctuated the end of his West Point tenure in a resounding manner. While standing duty as officer of the guard, he not only failed to stop a fight, but actively encouraged it. "Stand back, boys; let's have a fair fight!" he shouted. The officer of the day, Lt. William B. Hazen, heard the commotion and investigated. Shocked by Custer's gross neglect of duty, Hazen placed him under arrest. Hauled before a court-martial board, Custer could only claim, "My duty as Officer of the Guard was plain and simple. I should have arrested the two combatants and sent them to the guard tents for violating the peace and regulations of the Academy. But the instincts of the boy prevailed over the obligations of the officer of the guard."[65]

Custer didn't wait for his sentencing. Not wishing to trust such an important issue as his commission to luck, he fell on the mercies of his classmates who had preceded him to Washington. Luckily, several of them had powerful friends and Custer was able to defuse the situation. It was but "a few days after my trial that the

---

63 Schaff, *The Spirit of Old West Point*, 194.

64 Carroll, *Custer in the Civil War*, 86; Reynolds, *The Civil War Memories of Elizabeth Bacon Custer*, 23.

65 Carroll, *Custer in the Civil War*, 87.

superintendent of the Academy received a telegraphic order from Washington, directing him to release me at once," chuckled Custer. He reported as ordered to the adjutant general's office for assignment to duty. Custer never found out the results of the court-martial, for his new orders made the decision effectively "nugatory."[66]

Hastily departing West Point, Custer rushed to New York City to purchase his "lieutenant's outfit of sabre, revolver, sash, spurs, etc." He arrived in Washington on the eve of the battle of First Bull Run. There he fortuitously met the legendary General of the Armies, Winfield Scott. Custer, carrying war department dispatches, managed to make it to the front and join his Regular Army regiment, the 5th U.S. Cavalry, in time "to run with the rest at the battle of Bull Run." Of his part in the battle, Custer wrote, "We were formed in column of companies, and were given to understand that upon reaching the crest of the hill we would probably be ordered to charge the enemy." With the Confederates in full view, Custer pondered his choice of weapons: pistols or sabers? "From my earliest notions of the true cavalryman," he ruminated, "I had always pictured him in the charge bearing aloft his curved saber, and cleaving the skulls of all with whom he came in contact." Holstering his revolver, he yanked out his shiny new saber from its scabbard, "and rode forward as if totally unconcerned."[67]

Three companies of the regiment were ordered to support the artillery. They watched as Federal troops pushed back the Rebels to the crest of Henry House Hill. They had been stunned when Brig. Gen. Edmund Kirby Smith's Confederate brigade, screened by a line of timber, crashed into Brig. Gen. Irvin McDowell's right and rear. "The soldierly discipline of the regulars was of inestimable value during the retreat," wrote Lt. George F. Price. "When the panic began the cavalry and a section of artillery formed a line of battle and held the enemy until the infantry had retired from the field. They then retired in good order."[68]

The Confederate rout of the Federal army, coupled with the unexpected bloodshed of the war's first major battle—all told, over 5,000 casualties—quickly dispelled the notion held by both sides that the war was going to be over quickly. Concepts such as chivalry and the romance of war, the last vestiges of the conflict with Mexico, died a quick and merciless death in the first blast of rifle fire. The

---

66 Ibid., 88-89.

67 Ibid., 89; Reynolds, *The Civil War Memories of Elizabeth Bacon Custer*, 5; Carroll, *Custer in the Civil War*, 103.

68 George F. Price, *Across the Continent with the Fifth Cavalry* (New York, 1883), 103.

long-range accuracy of modern weaponry had already changed the face of battle forever, but both sides were slow to notice, much less adapt to, this fact. The Yankees and Rebels would continue to struggle tactically as they tried to cope with this new way of war.

Like Training for a Prize Fight

The 2nd Dragoons arrived in Washington in the aftermath of the battle and collectively breathed a sigh of relief that the war was not over yet, and that they would still get a chance to do what they had trained for over the years: fight. Once in the capital, they found that the four regiments of Regulars had been amalgamated into one brigade. The Regulars were augmented by the 6th Pennsylvania Cavalry, known as "Rush's Lancers." This organization was maintained, for the most part, throughout the next four bloody years of war. "Those who formed a part of this magnificent body of men, will never forget the hours spent day after day east of the Capitol at Washington in brigade drills," wrote Merritt. With their hard-won experience, they could focus on higher level tactics without having to worry about company or regimental drills.[69]

During this time "the seeds of the future efficiency" were sown. More important to the future growth of the service, the Regular Cavalry provided the "leaven," which, spread throughout the rest of the Cavalry Corps, "perfected the entire cavalry organizations of the superb army which for four years bore the brunt of the great Civil War." Merritt showered all the credit on Cooke. Acting with the vitality of ten men, Cooke set "the pace and establish[ed] the standard of the cavalry that later became the admiration of the country, if not the whole world."[70]

Counterbalancing these positives, the veteran troopers brought with them the baggage of preconceived military practices that had been espoused by the cavalry officers of the remote western frontier. They had no clue as to the enormity of the role the cavalry would play in the full-scale war to come. Even such great soldiers as Cooke and Maj. George Stoneman were mired in traditions that were the result of years of fighting Indians. Their vision of cavalry in action consisted of lightning raids into enemy territory, or grand mounted charges whose sweep changed the course of battles. Some were unable to rise to the challenges presented by the tactics of the hard-riding Confederate cavalry and were soon cast aside. The

---

69 Merritt, "Life and Services of General Philip St. George Cooke," 86-87.

70 Ibid., 89.

headquarters of the Army of the Potomac contributed to their demise by maintaining an operational stranglehold that nearly throttled the Union cavalry to death.

Custer saw combat before Merritt. An inexperienced junior officer straight from West Point, unencumbered by assimilation into an existing Regular Army unit and its constricting traditions, he viewed the panorama of war with all the wonder of an inquisitive child. With wry humor, he would describe himself as a "schoolboy . . . but three days before I had quitted West Point . . . and as yet had never ridden at anything more dangerous or terrible than a three-foot hurdle, or tried my saber on anything more animated or combative than a leather-head stuffed with tan bark." James Wilson remembered well the sight of Custer on horseback, "six feet tall, with broad shoulders, deep chest, thin waist and splendid legs, he had a perfect figure and was one of the best horsemen of his day."[71]

At this stage of the war Custer was still just a horseman—a damn fine one according to some—but a horseman just the same. Even his enemies admired his horsemanship. "Custer was the beau ideal of a perfect horseman. He sat in the saddle as if born in it, for his seat was so very easy and graceful that he and his steed seemed one," attested an article published in the *Southern Historical Society Papers*. "At West Point he was at the head of all the classes in horsemanship."[72]

There was more to becoming a cavalryman, however, than lopping off the heads of practice dummies while at a full gallop. Custer had not yet grasped the full meaning of being a cavalryman. Unwittingly, as early as First Bull Run, Custer was already asking himself the key question faced by cavalrymen in the Civil War: sabers or firearms? "As we rode at a deliberate walk up the hill," Custer wrote of those indecisive moments, "I began arguing in my own mind as to the comparative merits of the sabre and revolver as a weapon of attack."[73]

For Custer, the thought was starting to crystallize that tradition did not hold much water in the face of superior firepower. Just as he bucked the system at West Point, so too would he flout tradition on the battlefield. And in so doing, he would end up going toe-to-toe with Wesley Merritt.

---

71 Wilson, *Under the Old Flag*, 1:101.

72 "Generals in the Saddle," *Southern Historical Society Papers* (January 1891), Vol. 19, 172.

73 Carroll, *Custer in the Civil War*, 103.

CHAPTER TWO

Days of High Adventure with the Army

O N AUGUST 3, 1861, CONGRESS passed legislation authorizing the sweeping reorganization of the cavalry into six regiments. One week later, General Order No. 55 officially consolidated the existing cavalry regiments into one corps, and the storied names of the Dragoons and Mounted Rifles ceased to exist.

"Each regiment . . . had its proud record of service and individual prowess," wrote Bvt. Brig. Gen. Theophilus F. Rodenbough after the war. Rodenbough volunteered for the Union army and joined the 2nd Dragoons in early 1861, later becoming a trusted subordinate of Wesley Merritt. "For long years they had been distinguished by various marks, and none more conspicuous, perhaps, than by the facings of their uniforms." Each regiment wore a different color: orange for dragoons, green for mounted riflemen, and cavalry yellow for the rest. The troopers treasured this "apparently trivial" system and resisted the unwelcome changes to their uniforms and traditions. Well stocked with orange-faced uniforms, the 2nd U.S. Cavalry managed "to postpone for more than two years the thorough execution of the order." Given the uncertainty of what dangers lay in wait on the battlefield, holding onto a tangible object from the past gave soldiers a much-needed measure of comfort.[1]

---

1 Theophilus F. Rodenbough, ed., *From Everglade to Cañon with the Second United States Cavalry* (New York, 1875), 237-238. The regiments were renumbered as follows:1st Dragoons to 1st Cavalry; 2nd Dragoons to 2nd Cavalry; The Mounted Riflemen to 3rd Cavalry; 1st Cavalry to 4th Cavalry; 2nd Cavalry to 5th Cavalry; 3rd Cavalry to 6th Cavalry.

The first brush with war can be intoxicating to a young man traveling far from home for the first time. For many of the volunteer cavalrymen just beginning to congregate around Washington in October 1861, it was all one grand adventure. "At last I am off for the National Capitol [sic]," wrote an excited Pvt. Henry Elijah Alvord. "We have a full company of seventy-nine men, students, cadets and a few friends of each. It is a fine set of fellows. I never expect to regret going." Any open field in the vicinity large enough to accommodate a body of cavalry was packed with men, horses, and war materiel of every description.[2]

Artillery and muskets banged away at target practice, the heavy weather holding the thick clouds of gun smoke tight to the ground. The air rang with the steady tramp of marching feet and the shouted curses of impatient drill instructors. Dozens of regimental bands blasted amateurish renditions of patriotic music. At night, a fellowship of ardent young men gathered around campfires. "Though we know nothing about it, we suppose we shall see no active service in the field, don't anticipate being under fire," Alvord wrote. "Think of me during the next three months not as at war, but as on a pleasant journey on horseback, a vacation of three months spent at Washington."[3]

He had no clue as to what lay in store for him.

Everybody Gets a New Flag

It seemed like it had been raining forever and if it was not raining, it was either snowing or the wind was howling like a hungry coyote on the prowl for dinner. One gale ripped through the stables of the 6th U.S. Cavalry "and blew down several of [them]. . . . Portions of the roof in several cases were carried many yards." The troopers struggled desperately to save the horses trapped in the wreckage. According to Lieutenant Sanford, the 1st U.S. Cavalry encamped nearby in Alexandria lived under the most squalid of conditions. "The weather, he complained, "was perfectly dreadful, and the mud seemingly bottomless. . . .We lay for some days in a perfect swamp," he continued,

the men shivering in their tents and the horses at the picket line. Drill was out of the question, and it was almost out of the question to keep the animals supplied with forage

---

2   Caroline B. Sherman, ed., "A New England Boy in the Civil War," *The New England Quarterly* (April 1932), Vol. 5, No. 2, 314-315.

3   Ibid.

and the men with rations. . . . It was a bitter foretaste of the sufferings and privation that we were to go through for three long years, but which was to make of our raw volunteers a compact body of veteran soldiers, such as has been rarely equaled, and never excelled.[4]

On October 8, General Cooke ordered his command to hold a full-fledged brigade drill. On the muddiest of fields, 6,000 mounted men in columns of companies paraded past President Lincoln, Gen. Winfield Scott, various cabinet members, and a host of other dignitaries. "The regiment returned to the camp at Bladensburg in the late afternoon, tired, hungry, and muddy after an entire day in the saddle," wrote one disgruntled participant. "The newspapers spoke very highly of the apparent state of discipline among the regiment, furnishing a theme of conversation for some time among the men." Cooke also instituted a strict training regimen to prepare the troops for the spring campaign, including drilling the men in the evolutions of a brigade-sized unit.[5]

As miserable as October had been, it had felt absolutely balmy when compared to November, a harbinger of the hard winter to come. A correspondent from the *New York Times* hopped into his carriage for an observatory drive around the camps. It had been some time since his last excursion through the army and he was astounded by the improvement that had taken place. At Long Bridge, he pulled to the side of the road, shivering in his open conveyance as regiment after regiment of cavalry trooped across it. They just "kept pouring over," he reported. "The encampments that crowned the summits and dotted the slopes, did not look so cheerful in the cold light of the Wintry sun."[6]

Congress appointed Brig. Gen. George Stoneman to command the cavalry. Stoneman "applied himself during the winter of 1861-62 to the task of creating a valuable cavalry organization," recalled George F. Price. "His energy, sound judgment,"

and ripe experience overcame, so far as it was possible, many obstacles arising from the deficiency of small arms and equipments, and when the army was ready to move in the spring of 1862 he had succeeded in organizing a force which was capable of achieving excellent results. . . . The volunteer cavalry was in an excellent condition, and the regular

---

4   Donald C. Caughey and Jimmy J. Jones, *The 6th United States Cavalry in the Civil War: A History and Roster* (Jefferson, NC, 2013), 39; Hagemann, *Fighting Rebels and Redskins*, 151.

5   Caughey and Jones, *The 6th United States Cavalry*, 31, 37-38.

6   "Our Washington Correspondence," *The New York Times*, November 24, 1861.

cavalry had been drilled to their habitual state of efficiency. But, unfortunately, there was a well-developed fondness displayed at corps, division, and brigade headquarters for the presence of numerous and well-mounted orderlies. The details for ornamental service, combined with those for picket or escort duties, about absorbed the cavalry regiments.[7]

The results of this training showed at the review of the brigade held in the middle of January. There would be no repeat of October's sedentary parade, which had taken three and a half grueling hours to completely pass the presidential reviewing stand. "Wheeling now in column and then in line, it closed with a magnificent charge in column of squadrons of the whole brigade," was how one officer in the 2nd U.S. Cavalry, sparing his readers the technicalities of the evolutions, described th event. "We returned home at four o'clock P.M., tired and muddy, having been six hours in the saddle." Captain August Kautz's view was less sanguine. "Notwithstanding the condition of the drill ground, General Cooke had a brigade drill and even had our regiment to charge in echelon," he wrote with some indignance. "We were covered in mud by the time the drill was over. Many of the horses fell, and though there were some narrow escapes, no one was seriously injured."[8]

In February, just as preparations for the upcoming spring campaign were getting into full swing, the cavalry held one last grand drill that was later described by a participant as a "very exciting one." The 2nd U.S. furnished the spectacular finale with a charge by three full squadrons advancing through the mud in a line stretching some 300 yards. Like the knights of old on their sturdy and dependable war horses, the movement began at the walk, and then increased to a trot, and finally burst into a full gallop. When the command "Charge!" rang out, recalled Rodenbough, "[a]way we went, every man at a full run, cutting at an imaginary foe with his sabre. At eighty yards the men were brought to a trot, and then a halt, every man in his place." The horsemen yanked their reins and pulled to a stop, with their newly issued company guidons snapping snappily in the brisk bitter wind. All the regiment's distinctive pennants had been painted to resemble the national colors;

---

7 Price, *Across the Continent with the 5th Cavalry*, 105. A veteran cavalryman, Stoneman accompanied the Mormon Battalion as assistant quartermaster during its epic march from the Iowa territory to San Diego during the Mexican War. After further service on the frontier, he quickly rose through the ranks like many other Regular officers at the beginning of the war, receiving a promotion to brigadier general in August 1861, just three months after his promotion to major in the 1st U.S. Cavalry.

8 Rodenbough, *From Everglade to Cañon*, 255; Caughey and Jones, *The 6th United States Cavalry*, 38.

Brigadier General George Stoneman graduated from West Point in 1846 (where he shared a room with Thomas J. "Stonewall" Jackson), fought in the Mexican War and then against Indians on the frontier, and commanded the cavalry division in Maj. Gen. George B. McClellan's Army of the Potomac. *LOC*

the red and white guidons of frontier service had been consigned to the dustbin of history.[9]

9 Rodenbough, *From Everglade to Cañon*, 256.

Cooke's command consisted of two wafer-thin brigades. Colonel William H. Emory commanded the 5th and 6th U.S. Cavalry Regiments and the 6th Pennsylvania Cavalry, while Col. George Blake led the 1st U.S. Cavalry, the 8th Pennsylvania Cavalry, and a squadron of Illinois volunteer cavalry. Artillerist Samuel Marks of Horse Battery D, 2nd U.S. Artillery, wrote home about his new assignment. "We are now with some regular Cavalry called the reserve, but a curious reserve it is, and contrary to what the word implies, as we are on the move, the same as last summer."[10]

Merritt continued in his role as adjutant general and then aide-de-camp for General Cooke. He held these positions, reported the *New York Times*, "with that gallant officer for two or three years." The *Times* lavishly praised Merritt, who was already making a reputation for himself. "His intelligence, quickness and military sagacity made a most favorable impression on the commanding officers with whom he was brought in contact," extolled the paper's editorialist. "Persons high in authority recognized in the active young officer the ready qualities of a first-class soldier."[11]

After months of preparation, the cavalry finally went into action on February 10, 1862, when General Stoneman led a large force toward the Rappahannock River. The 5th U.S. Cavalry was attached to Brig. Gen. Phillip Kearny's New Jersey brigade. As the most junior lieutenant in the regiment, Custer reported to Kearny's staff, serving first as aide-de-camp and then as assistant adjutant general. Kearny turned out to be a tough taskmaster and a hard man to please, but somehow Custer managed.

His time on Kearny's staff proved to be "both agreeable and beneficial." Custer opined, "Of the many officers of high rank with whom I served, Kearney was the strictest disciplinarian. So strict was he in this respect that were it not for the grander qualities he subsequently displayed he might have been considered as simply a military martinet." Custer noted that Kearny reserved his wrath for high-ranking officers, rather than subalterns and enlisted men. Some officers submitted their resignations rather than subject themselves to the "torrent of violent invectives, such varied and expressive epithets, that the limit of language seemed for once to have been reached." Custer most likely learned to curse like a

---

10 Samuel J. Marks to Carrie Marks, April 26, 1864, Personal Letters of S. J. Marks, United States Army Heritage and Education Center (USAHEC).

11 "Gen. Wesley Merritt," *The New York Times*, May 29, 1898.

salty trooper from Kearny, and he would later struggle mightily to control and finally overcome the habit.[12]

Custer's tenure on Kearny's staff would be short-lived. Army headquarters issued a directive prohibiting officers of the Regular army from serving on the staff of officers holding their commissions in the volunteers. The 5th U.S. Cavalry rode back to the camps of the Cavalry Reserve. Despite the brevity of their association, Kearny served as more than just a role model to Custer; he inspired the first seeds of Custer's tactical philosophy, which would evolve over the course of the war. This philosophy of cavalry operations required both an understanding of the inner workings of a death-dealing mobile force, coupled with the technical ability to apply that force on any opponent. As Gen. George S. Patton later declared, "There is only one tactical principle which is not subject to change. It is: 'To use the means at hand to inflict the maximum amount of wounds, death and destruction on the enemy in the minimum time.'"[13]

Kearny was "a man of violent passions, quick and determined impulses, [and] haughty demeanor, largely the result of his military training." Custer considered him as "brave as the bravest of men can be." Rubbing elbows with Kearny, Custer noted his many idiosyncrasies. Kearny could be "imperious in command, and at times domineering," traits Custer chose not to emulate. "He constantly chafed under the restraint and inactivity of camp life and was never so contented and happy as when moving to the attack. . . . And whether it was the attack of a picket post or the storming of the enemy's breastworks, Kearny was always to be found where the danger was the greatest." Custer never forgot this profound lesson on the basics of combat leadership.[14]

In October 1861, Custer suddenly left the army on a mysterious medical leave, returning the following February. The reasons for his leave remain speculation, some of it bordering on the contemptible. The papers of the adjutant general's office for this period are terse and uninformative. Some of his detractors insinuated that Custer had contracted syphilis from one of the notorious camp followers that attached themselves to the army. They would buttress their argument by pointing

---

12 Carroll, *Custer in the Civil War*, 114, 115.

13 George S. Patton, *War as I Knew It* (Boston, 1947), 405.

14 Carroll, *Custer in the Civil War*, 115. Kearny's combative nature would lead to his untimely death at Chantilly on September 1, 1862. During that rainy battle, Kearny rode into the enemy lines by mistake and, when called on to surrender, tried to fight his way out, dying ingloriously in a hail of musket fire.

out the Custers' childless marriage. "Although the nature or seriousness of his affliction is unknown," explained historian Jeffry Wert, "the leave was extended until February 1862. When he returned to the army, he wrote to Tully McCrea, stating that he had been so sick at one time that he was not expected to live."[15]

It was not until March 10, 1862, that George Custer found himself cantering along the first of the countless roads headed south in front of the newly re-designated Army of the Potomac. He took a special pride in commanding a company of Regular cavalry. Five months after his fond adieu to General Kearny, he was finally about to obtain his "first experience with cavalry advance guards." The Rebels had begun to pull back to the Rappahannock and Rapidan rivers the previous day, and the Union horsemen followed hard on the road to Centreville, with the 5th U.S. Cavalry in the vanguard. Custer recorded that the enemy's pickets "were discerned in considerable force on a hill about one mile in our front." The information was quickly conveyed to General Stoneman. The crusty cavalryman's orders came back immediately: Drive the damn pickets in! "When this order reached us the officers of the regiment were generally assembled in a group at the head of the column," recalled Custer. Years after the fact he still thrilled at the memory. "I at once asked permission to take my company," he wrote, and with "permission being accorded" he advanced his men. In the face of light opposition, Custer's troopers reached the base of the hill where the Rebel picket line was posted. "I gave the command 'Charge' for the first time," he recalled. "My company responded gallantly, and away we went. Our adversaries," he continued,

> did not wait to receive us, but retreated hurriedly and crossed the bridge over Cedar Run, setting fire to it immediately after. We pursued them to the bank of the run and then exchanged several shots with the enemy, now safely posted on the opposite side. Being unable to advance across the stream, and exposed to a serious fire from small arms, I ordered my command to retire, which it did in excellent order.[16]

Kearny would have been proud of Custer's first participation in the nitty-gritty of cavalry operations. Like Kearny, Custer always wanted to be at the point of attack and in the thickest of the fighting. Although it was an insignificant action, Custer managed to stretch the story into two lengthy paragraphs. "Battles and skirmishes at that time were unfamiliar events to the men composing the Army of

---

15 Wert, *Custer*, 45.

16 Carroll, *Custer in the Civil War*, 129-130.

the Potomac," he explained, doing his best to stake out his place in the history of the army, "and the little episode furnished a topic for general discussion and comment. . . . [It was] the shedding of the first blood by the Army of the Potomac."[17]

Sea Voyages and Balloon Rides

For some observers in Washington, it had taken too long for that first drop of blood to be shed. The dilatory pace of Maj. Gen. George B. McClellan's methodical approach to waging war thoroughly exasperated President Abraham Lincoln. "I shall take my own time to make an army that will be sure of success," McClellan wrote to his wife in October 1861 in a letter heavy with messianic fervor. "So soon as I feel that the army is well-organized, and well-disciplined, and strong enough, I will advance, and force the rebels to a battle on a field of my selection. A long time must yet elapse before we can do this."[18]

To Lincoln's dismay, the last four months of 1861 dragged by at the glacial pace dictated by McClellan. According to James B. Fry, who had served on Irvin McDowell's staff, "[t]he offensive was demanded from all quarters, and in all ways; but McClellan would not move. He was fully aware of the deep and widespread feeling, and no doubt knew that his own prestige was endangered by ignoring it." Despite weather conditions that were "remarkably favorable for military operations in Virginia," McClellan refused to budge. Eventually, with the worst of the gray, chilling winter behind, the advent of campaign season rolled around in March 1862.[19]

McClellan could no longer escape the demands of his president. Just to make sure "Little Mac" knew who was in charge, Lincoln issued War Order No. 2 on March 8, 1862. The order divided the Army of the Potomac into several corps with commanders appointed by the president. That same day Lincoln followed up with Order No. 3, which laid out a plan of campaign that upset the schemes McClellan had been formulating. The tersely written order dictated immediate action. "Any movement," Lincoln ordered, "shall begin to move upon the [Chesapeake] bay as

---

17 Ibid., 130

18 James B. Fry, "McClellan and His 'Mission,'" *The Century Magazine* (October 1894), Vol. 48, No. 6, 935.

19 Ibid., 934.

George Custer idolized Maj. Gen. George B. McClellan, the young commander of the
Army of the Potomac who assured his wife, "I shall take my own time to
make an army that will be sure of success. *LOC*

early as the 18th of March, instant, and the General-in-Chief shall be responsible
that it so moves as early as that day."[20]

20 Carroll, *Custer in the Civil War*, 128.

On March 13, McClellan called a war council of his corps commanders. After a long, contentious meeting they hammered out a plan. McClellan's intention had been to move along the line of the James River and, supported by the navy, attack Richmond from the south. In his memoirs, Custer stated that after the council of war, the operations would "best be undertaken from Old Point Comfort, between the York and James rivers." By taking a more northerly route, McClellan ended up besieging Yorktown, and having to fight at Williamsburg before moving south to attack Richmond from the north. "I have . . . supported General McClellan and obeyed all his orders with as hearty a good will as though he had been my brother or the friend I owed most," wrote IV Corps commander Erasmus D. Keyes in a letter to Senator Ira Harris, sent with the expectation that it would be shown to Lincoln. "I shall continue to do so to the last, and so long as he is my commander." The statement demonstrated the faith that all levels of the Army of the Potomac had in George McClellan.[21]

Whatever McClellan's faults, an inability to inspire the loyalty of his men was not one of them. "No commander which this army had from the beginning to the end of the war ever exercised one-tenth of the personal influence on the feelings or affections of his men that McClellan did," attested Sanford. "I feel sure that no one deserved that affection more. That he made mistakes is granted; but so did his successors. Certainly the morale of the army at the end of the Peninsula and Antietam campaigns was infinitely better than at any other time during the war up to its close." Custer's admiration for McClellan predated his assignment to his staff. "I have more confidence in General McClellan than in any man living," he wrote to his parents in March. "I would forsake everything and follow him to the ends of the earth. I would lay down my life for him. . . . Every officer and private worships him."[22]

Embarkation of the army began on March 17, one day prior to President Lincoln's mandate. A steady, seemingly unending stream of ships headed down the Potomac River and out into Chesapeake Bay, destined for Fort Monroe. "This transfer involved the shipment of 121,500 men, 14,592 animals, 1,150 wagons, 44 batteries, 74 ambulances, besides pontoon bridges, materials for telegraph lines, and other miscellaneous matter," recounted Custer. The "stupendous undertaking" required the acquisition of 113 steamers, 118 schooners, and 88 barges. Custer marveled at the accomplishment. "In thirty-seven days from the

---

21 Ibid., 129, 142.

22 Hagemann, *Fighting Rebels and Redskins*, 160; Merington, *The Custer Story*, 27-28.

time the order was given to secure the transportation necessary for so extensive a movement, the transfer of the Army of the Potomac was effected from Washington to Fort Monroe."[23]

The troopers of the Cavalry Reserve rode with high spirits on their way down to the embarkation point at Alexandria, Virginia. As transports became available at the wharves, the horse soldiers and their mounts boarded them. "My company was soon embarked, including sixty horses, which were shipped in the same manner and in about as short a time as the human portion of our cargo, by a gang-plank," recalled one officer in the 2nd U.S. Cavalry. "On Monday, at six A.M., a large North River steamer came alongside, filled with troops, and took our schooner, with two others, in tow."[24]

The perfect weather helped to raise the spirits of the men. "The change of camp and scene was to all of us a pleasant experience," declared the 3rd Pennsylvania Cavalry's regimental history. "The trip down the Potomac and across Chesapeake Bay was very enjoyable." By March 26, however, a note of caution was apparent. "Weather lovely; a clear sun and smooth sea. The fleet continues on, vessels scattered and become separated." As each ship made its best speed to the south, the organizational integrity of the regiments fell apart, with companies jumbled in the mass of shipping. The price for this disorganization was exacted at Fort Monroe.[25]

The cavalry units began to arrive at the fortress on April 1. Hampton Roads teemed with ships of every description. "Here we are, snugly anchored under the guns of this stronghold of the Union in Virginia," wrote a 2nd U.S. Cavalry diarist. "At six this morning we cast anchor in the midst of two hundred and fifty sail . . . all loaded with troops, stores, etc., for Uncle Sam." Hovering over the fleet like a hen protecting her chicks steamed the USS *Monitor*, determined to prevent any disruption of the landing by her rival, the Confederate ironclad CSS *Virginia*. Warships, steamers, schooners, and barges jockeyed their way through the vast armada to the very tip of the peninsula formed by the confluence of the York and James rivers.[26]

23 Carroll, *Custer in the Civil War*, 134.

24 Rodenbough, *From Everglade to Cañon*, 257.

25 William Brooke Rawle, ed., *History of the Third Pennsylvania Cavalry, Sixtieth Regiment Pennsylvania Volunteers, in the American Civil War, 1861-1865* (Philadelphia, 1905), 42, 44.

26 Rodenbough, *From Everglade to Cañon*, 256, 257. The author of these reminiscences is only referred to as "An Officer of the Regiment."

As soon as one transport finished unloading, tugboats rushed in to remove it and shove another into its place. Artillery, baggage wagons, pontoon trains, and other wheeled vehicles piled up along the shore. "The little village surrounding the fortress [was] being crammed to overflowing with 'horse and foot,'" recalled one agitated cavalry officer, "while the wharves were thronged with anxious [officers] . . . waiting their turn to unload, unloading, or, upon being dumped on the pier, watching their men, who, after several days' confinement between decks, were kicking up their heels in honor of their emancipation." The officer, however, had noticed problems already surfacing along the waterfront. "I found that many vessels, loaded with horses and men had been lying in the stream for four or five days, the facilities for unloading not being in proportion to the demand."[27]

From Confederate batteries along the south side of the James River opposite Fort Monroe, bored gunners lobbed "occasional compliments in the shape of ten inch shells . . . and added liveliness to the scene." Twice the *Virginia* sortied down the river shadowed by the *Monitor*, looking very much like "a medieval knight in armor riding down the lists." George Sanford was on board his transport long enough to see the entire Union fleet attack one of the Rebel batteries. "It was a magnificent sight to me," he wrote, "for I had never seen men of war in action."[28]

"Little Mac," surrounded by his large staff, came ashore in the middle of this mess. In those early, heady days of April 1862, he was buoyed by the knowledge that the public still believed in him. More importantly, his soldiers still worshipped him. Their hoarse cheers followed him as he rode through his army. At this point, McClellan should have been all confidence; instead, with the campaign barely underway, he already found himself wringing his hands at the disorganization at the disembarkation point. He wrote disconsolately to Lincoln. "I found five divisions of infantry, Sykes's brigade of regulars, two regiments of cavalry, and a portion of the reserve artillery disembarked. Another cavalry regiment and a part of a fourth had arrived, but were still on shipboard. . . . Of the troops disembarked, only four divisions, the regulars, the majority of the reserve artillery, and a part of the cavalry, could be moved, in consequence of the lack of transportation."[29]

Stepping into the middle of the chaos, the self-styled master organizer "began giving his personal attention to the disposition of his troops as they arrived and

27   Ibid, 257.

28   Hagemann, *Fighting Rebels and Redskins*, 153.

29   George Brinton McClellan, "The Peninsular Campaign," in Robert U. Johnson and Clarence C. Buel, eds., *Battles and Leaders of the Civil War*, 4 vols. (New York, 1887-88), 2:169.

disembarked." It was imperative that McClellan get cavalry to his front, so their disembarkation became a priority. "We were suddenly taken in tow by a tug," wrote an astonished officer of the 2nd U.S. Cavalry, "and run over to a wharf in advance of troops who had been waiting for a week, and unloaded." As the squadrons landed, they pushed out through the network of roads and by-ways that crisscrossed the lower Peninsula. By the evening of April 3, the cavalry had established a line four miles from Fort Monroe in anticipation of a general advance on the morrow. Despite McClellan's foot-dragging, the Army of the Potomac was beginning to move.[30]

As dawn broke the next day, April 4, the troops stepped off to the advance in two columns. McClellan rode among them, enjoying a fine start along what he thought was his personal road to glory. "A cloud of dust heralded his approach, with his numerous staff clattering after him," wrote one trooper. Jauntily waving his cap toward the cheering soldiers, he cut through the morass of his stalled infantry and artillery. The road opened "as by magic." The cavalry followed through at "a slashing pace." "Onward to Richmond," wrote a correspondent from the *Philadelphia Inquirer*, somewhat cheekily. Just before dawn the army had struck its camps and taken to the victory roads. "The advance struck . . . along a most beautiful and romantic road, the birds singing sweetly through the woods. It seemed as if the grand army was a grand pageant, celebrating some gala day."[31]

Merritt and Custer served in different capacities during this part of the campaign. Merritt continued his close association with Cooke, as reported later by the *New York Times*. "When Col. Cooke was made a brigadier general and placed in command of the cavalry of the Army of the Potomac, young Merritt became his aide de camp, and on April 5, 1862, was promoted to be Captain." For his part, Cooke would lavish praise on Merritt's performance throughout the early phases of the campaign and the cavalry's advance to the Chickahominy. Custer summarized his role at the time in his memoirs. "I had left Alexandria, Virginia with my company of the Fifth U. S. Cavalry as second lieutenant of the company, and was among the first to arrive at Fortress Monroe. I served with my company during the march from Fortress Monroe to the Warwick."[32]

---

30 Whittaker, *A Popular Life of Gen. George A. Custer*, 98; Rodenbough, *From Everglade to Cañon*, 257.

31 Rodenbough, *From Everglade to Cañon*, 257-258; Brooke Rawle, *History of the Third Pennsylvania Cavalry*, 45.

32 "Gen. Wesley Merritt," *The New York Times*; Carroll, *Custer in the Civil War*, 143.

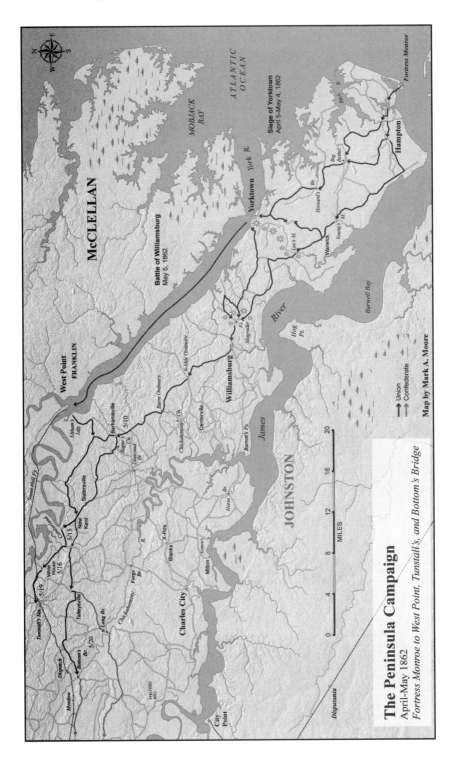

The Peninsula Campaign
April–May 1862
Fortress Monroe to West Point, Tunstall's, and Bottom's Bridge

Map by Mark A. Moore

For Custer, the Peninsula campaign began with the attachment of his regiment to Gen. William F. "Baldy" Smith's division of the IV Corps. Smith was one of those irascible characters who seemed to populate the "Old Army." Theodore Lyman, a staff officer with army headquarters, described him as "a short, portly man, with a light-brown imperial and shaggy moustache, round, military head, and the look of a German officer, altogether." Another officer wrote that Smith was "a contentious controversialist who spent most of his time criticizing the plans of other generals, particularly those of his superiors."[33]

On April 5, Smith's division spearheaded the advance of the IV Corps as it tramped slowly along the James River Road to Warwick Court House. Heintzelman's III Corps was tasked with advancing past Big Bethel, a vital crossroads in the center of the Peninsula deep within a vast and marshy area. Its capture would trap the Confederate defenders of Yorktown while preventing reinforcements from reaching the city.

The cavalry, noted one officer, "has been employed night and day making reconnaissances, etc." These forays into enemy territory exposed the character of the terrain. "[The] topography and soil of the peninsula presented a most difficult field for cavalry operations," reported Col. William Woods Averell of the 3rd Pennsylvania Cavalry, one of the few volunteer cavalry outfits in the field. Chopped up by forests thick with brambled underbrush, the open fields could not accommodate more than a squadron or two at a time. "After a rain, the deep alluvium became, under the tread of horses," groused the old-fashioned colonel, "a bed of mortar knee deep."[34]

As the 3rd Pennsylvania approached Big Bethel, "the enemy disputed our approach, and we exchanged shots in a lively manner for a short time, fortunately without any casualties, our opponents falling back as we advanced." On the far left Smith's division unexpectedly encountered a heavy force of Rebel infantry strongly entrenched at the Warwick River crossing at Lee's Mill. "The enemy opened upon Smith's troops with artillery and musketry," reported Lt. Custer. The enterprising Confederates had constructed a series of dams that had the effect of widening the Warwick, usually more of a stream than a river, making it "an almost impassable

---

33 Mark Mayo Boatner, III, *The Civil War Dictionary* (New York, 1959), 776.

34 Rodenbough, *From Everglade to Cañon*, 258; William W. Averell, "With the Cavalry on the Peninsula," in Johnson and Buel, eds., *Battles and Leaders*, 2:429.

barrier to the advance of troops." General Keyes found it impossible "to carry the enemy's position by assault."[35]

In the face of Yorktown's "strong earthworks," McClellan's battle plan came to a complete standstill. General Keyes's description, written on April 7, gives more detail. "We are stopped by a line of defence nine or ten miles long, strongly fortified by breastworks, erected nearly the whole distance, behind a stream or succession of ponds nowhere fordable." Bastioned works stretched as far as the eye could see, and the only approaches were "through low, swampy, or thickly wooded ground, over roads which we are obliged to repair or make before we can forward our carriages." Confederates streamed down the York and James rivers to the fighting line. Keyes grimly wrote that these reinforcements were "one of the strongest ever opposed to an invading force in any country." In addition, Rebel gunboats commanded both the York and the James from fortifications so strong "that the navy are afraid to attack."[36]

A very skittish McClellan began to vacillate as his road to glory began to narrow. He tended to exaggerate the obstacles in his path, but in this case the Confederate works had been masterfully constructed. As reports filtered back to his headquarters, McClellan came to "perceive that what he had supposed would be an undertaking of perhaps a day was likely to detain him indefinitely." The circumstances warranted his first-hand inspection. "At all events, my personal experience in this kind of work was greater than that of any officer under my command," he wrote pompously, "and after personal reconnoissances more appropriate to a lieutenant of engineers than to the commanding general, I could neither discover nor hear any point where an assault promised any chance of success. We were thus obliged to resort to siege operations." This ended McClellan's vision of a rapid advance up the Peninsula to the gates of Richmond.[37]

Lieutenant Sanford, for one, was thunderstruck. "Everyone supposed that we would attack at once," he wrote, much chagrined at the lost opportunity. "There is little doubt that if we had done so, we should have broken their lines," he snorted, though he readily admitted that "[i]n this business the mounted force of course had

---

35 Brooke Rawle, *History of the Third Pennsylvania Cavalry*, 44; Carroll, *Custer in the Civil War*, 136-137.

36 McClellan, "The Peninsular Campaign," 2:169; Carroll, *Custer in the Civil War*, 140-141.

37 Carroll, *Custer in the Civil War*, 137; McClellan, "The Peninsular Campaign," 2:171.

little part." To underscore the grim realization that the war wouldn't be over in the next few weeks, a nor'easter blew in with leaden skies and blustery winds.[38]

One veteran recorded that the men "lived in mud literally fifteen inches deep, and drowned out every other day." Without tents the troopers had nothing with which to protect themselves from the inclemency "except india-rubber ponchos spread on sticks." Abandoned on the picket line and standing braced against the frigid storms without benefit of blankets or protection, the horses suffered even more. For sustenance they received little more than half-rations, which had to be carted from the York River. "At this time the heavy rains had put the ground in very bad condition," recalled Lt. William H. Carter of the 6th U.S. Cavalry, "and, transportation being limited, the regiment was compelled to pack its forage on the horses." In the muddy conditions the wagons were more hindrance than help. "We were kept fully occupied just the same in escorting supply trains up to the army," complained another officer. "I suppose there are no worse roads on the planet than those dreadful quagmires through which we forced those wagons."[39]

When not engaged in scouting, escort, or picket duty, the cavalrymen spent their time "perfecting the instruction of the regiment in the details of field service." Training at all levels intensified, filling entire days with mind-numbing drills— mounted and dismounted, by company and by regiment, with both saber and pistol. The 6th U.S. Cavalry constructed obstacle courses in the open fields. Each trooper was forced to showcase his skills in front of his peers "through such a course of exercises as they had never before experienced."[40]

Like true veterans, after realizing that they might be in camp for a while, the men immediately set about making themselves "as comfortable as possible." They constructed snug shelters from their canvas tents, buttressed by brush piles to cut the wind. Many of their efforts centered around food. Lucky was the collective mess that featured a real cook. One officers' mess in the 6th U.S. Cavalry boasted just such a gem, "an ancient dragoon," according to one member. The staff mess affectionately addressed him as "Old Carr":

> Our cook . . . who, having been a soldier for thirty-five years, during which time he gained
> much culinary wisdom, now concocts savory messes out of onion, a little salt pork, two or

---

38 Hagemann, *Fighting Rebels and Redskins*, 154.

39 Rodenbough, *From Everglade to Cañon*, 258-259; William H. Carter, *From Yorktown to Santiago With the Sixth U.S. Cavalry* (Austin, TX, 1989), 25; Hagemann, *Fighting Rebels and Redskins*, 154.

40 Carter, *From Yorktown to Santiago*, 25; Caughey and Jones, *The 6th United States Cavalry*, 44-45.

three potatoes, salt, pepper, etc. After living for two weeks on pilot bread and salt pork, we have fresh beef four times a week, potatoes, hot rolls twice a day, delicious pea and bean soup, oysters once a week, and such little matters as rice, molasses, pickles, etc.[41]

This proved too sedentary a life for George Custer, who "received an order which greatly changed the character of my duties" and jumped at the chance. "When it was decided to commence a siege there was a demand for young officers competent to serve as subordinates to the engineer officers," he recalled. His new duties included supervising the erection of field works, including fascines and gabions. Custer blossomed under Smith's chief of topographical engineers, Lt. Nicholas Bowen, with whom he cemented a lasting friendship.[42]

During the campaign McClellan embraced many new-fangled gadgets and innovations, including lighter-than-air balloons, which allowed for unprecedented views of the extensive Rebel works. The famed "aeronaut," Professor Thaddeus Lowe, directed the operations of the balloons. In the initial stages of the program the aeronauts also served as observers. Untrained in the ways of war, their reports consisted of generalities that offered no substance as to the enemy's dispositions or movements. It was decided that the observers had to be trained military men.

That very thought crossed Brig. Gen. Fitz John Porter's mind and prompted him to ascend in the balloon to see everything for himself. As the basket rose higher and higher, the crew paid out the restraining rope. Suddenly, when the balloon reached its operating height of 1,000 feet, the rope snapped, and balloon, basket, and general drifted at the mercy of prevailing winds. Thousands of Union soldiers watched the drama "with breathless interest" as the winds blew the balloon toward the Confederate lines. Reacting quickly, Porter opened the valve and released some of the gas, then a little more, and then maybe a little too much. The basket and its hapless occupant plunged down at a dangerous speed. Fortunately, "the branches of a tree were encountered, and the balloon caught and secured, the General narrowly escaping what seemed likely to prove a serious disaster."[43]

Smith refused to repeat Porter's mistake. Why send a brigadier general up into the clouds when a mere lieutenant would do fine? "I was directed by the General to make a reconnaissance in a balloon, an order which was received with no little trepidation," trembled Custer. "It was a kind of danger that few persons have

41 Rodenbough, *From Everglade to Cañon*, 258, 259.

42 Carroll, *Custer in the Civil War*, 143.

43 Ibid., 146.

Professor Thaddeus Lowe operated several lighter-than-air balloons, which were used to observe the extensive Rebel works in front of Yorktown. *LOC*

schooled themselves against, and still fewer possess a liking for." He armed himself with field glasses, compass, notebook, and pencil, with which he "was supposed to be able, after attaining the proper elevation, to discover, locate, and record the works and encampments of the enemy." Custer steeled himself and proceeded to Smith's headquarters, where the balloon was tethered. "Thither I proceeded, my mind not entirely free from anxious doubts as to how the expedition would terminate."[44]

44 Ibid., 146, 147.

Custer and other staff officers of the Army of the Potomac, in an Alexander Gardner photo taken on May 20, 1862. At the time, Custer was serving as a topographical engineer on Brig. Gen. W. F. "Baldy" Smith's staff. A little more than a week later he made his celebrated foray across the Chickahominy River and as a result was posted to Maj. Gen. George B. McClellan's staff. *LOC*

Held to the earth by a series of guy ropes, the balloon looked to Custer like "a wild and untamable animal." Despite the efforts of the accompanying aeronaut to assuage his fears, Custer's apprehensions "were redoubled, and I expected to see the bottom of the basket giving way, and one or both of us dashed to the earth." As the balloon rose "noiselessly, almost imperceptibly," Custer cowered in the bottom of the basket, holding onto the iron safety bar with white–knuckle intensity. "Gradually I became more familiar with the car," said Custer, gaining confidence. Peering over the rim of the basket, he beheld "a most beautiful landscape." With the eye of a soldier, he marveled at a "theatre of operations of armies larger and more formidable than had ever confronted each other on this continent before."[45]

45 Ibid., 147.

From on high Custer observed that the Confederates had pitched their camps deep in the shielding woods and had cunningly camouflaged their earthworks along the Warwick with trees and underbrush. He recounted that "[g]uns could be seen mounted and peering sullenly through the embrasures, while men in considerable numbers were standing in and around the entrenchments, often collected in groups, intently observing the balloon." This dry narrative concealed Custer's fear that the Rebels would take the balloon under fire. In order to reduce that risk, he came up with a plan to ascend in the darkness just before reveille, as the Confederates' breakfast fires were first stoked. "The result fulfilled my expectations," declared Custer. The enemy's campfires painted a perfect picture of their lines, from which he could deduce their strength. "So satisfied was General Smith with the information derived in this manner that ascensions were frequently ordered to be made thereafter in the morning before daylight."[46]

On the evening of May 3, Smith directed Custer to make two nocturnal ascents, one immediately after dark, the other just before sunrise. "Nothing unusual was observed during the first ascent," reported Custer. The second ascent, at 2:00 a.m. on May 4, revealed the reality of the situation, although Custer initially missed all the clues. Later he admitted that "[a]s yet no idea of evacuation had occurred to me." Off toward Yorktown, he witnessed heavy fires and the unmistakable booming of exploding ordnance. As the hour for "Reveille" approached, he noticed the sparking campfires as the Union troops prepared to cook their breakfasts. Looking toward the Confederate lines, he saw no such activity. As his suspicions began to grow the light of dawn enabled him "to inspect the works of the enemy. . . . The entire absence of their usual occupants surprised me. A second and more careful examination convinced me that the works of the enemy were deserted. Descending as rapidly as possible, I hastened to General Smith's headquarters to report my information." The Rebels had slipped away in the night like gray ghosts in the mist.[47]

Contrary to popular belief, it was not Custer's observations that alerted the Union command to the Confederate withdrawal. A steady stream of reports had flowed into headquarters from all along the line, with many others coming from the multitude of contrabands that populated the vicinity. For once McClellan moved with alacrity, immediately issuing an "order . . . for the advance of all the disposable cavalry and horse batteries, supported by infantry divisions." Of course, not much

---

46 Ibid., 148-149.

47 Ibid., 149.

"disposable" cavalry was available, as most of it had been parceled out for picket or escort duty. "The force [on] which General Cooke and his officers had spent so much time, and the government so much treasure in perfecting for the legitimate duties of cavalry," castigated Wesley Merritt, was "scattered to the four winds." Cooke, likely with Captain Merritt's assistance, scrounged up a very "attenuated cavalry command" and immediately made an aggressive move against the Confederate rearguard.[48]

The Cavalry Does its Best, but Not Good Enough

The Confederate lines, built in the fall of 1861, were by no means a masterpiece of military engineering. Even the engineer who supervised their construction, Lt. Alfred M. Rives, seriously doubted their ability to prevent a large Federal force from rolling them up like a piece of worn carpet. The Rebel defense was centered on Fort Magruder, two miles southeast of Williamsburg, which guarded the convergence of the roads from Yorktown and Hampton. Pentagonal in shape, its 70-foot-long front featured 15-foot-high walls, formed with earth that had been excavated to create a moat along its length. The fort could mount eight artillery pieces. The rains of the previous few days had filled the moat with nine feet of water. Union Pvt. Warren Lee Goss called it "a muddy-looking heap of dirt."[49]

Fourteen smaller earthworks extended to the right and left flanks and guarded all the key roads and bridges leading up the Peninsula toward Williamsburg. Redoubt Number One anchored the right flank at the dam that created Tutters Neck Pond. Redoubt Number Fourteen, on the far left flank and hidden from Fort Magruder's view by a tree line, covered the left flank at the strategically important crossing of the Cub Creek Dam at Jones Pond. Confederate rifle pits studded the entire line.

---

48 McClellan, "The Peninsular Campaign," 2:172; Merritt, "Life and Services of General Philip St. George Cooke," 87. In August 1861, three escaped slaves sought shelter at Fort Monroe, then commanded by Maj. Gen. Benjamin Butler. In order to avoid sending them back to their Confederate owners, he declared that they were being used to wage war against the Union and therefore were subject to confiscation. Congress confirmed his decision shortly thereafter with the first Confiscation Act. As a result, escaped or liberated slaves in Union-occupied regions of the South, particularly those in close proximity to the Union army, became known as "contrabands," from the phrase "contraband of war."

49 Warren Lee Goss, "Why Don't You Hide Behind a Tree?", in Ned Bradford, ed., *Battles and Leaders of the Civil War* (New York, 1956), 147.

Even without the recent heavy rains, the treacherous ground in front of the redoubts itself proved to be a defensive impediment. Ravines, ditches, and gullies crisscrossed the land directly to the front of the Rebel line, and the marshlands created by Tutters Neck Pond and Jones Pond made any flank approaches difficult. In addition, Custer noted in his memoirs, "[t]he heavy timber in front had been slashed so effectually so as to bar the progress of any organized body of troops, infantry skirmishers alone being able to overcome the obstacles." To the south a piece of wooded high ground dominated the approaches to the Rebel positions, descending toward them in undulating folds.[50]

Stoneman's orders were clear enough. "My instructions were to pursue and harass the rear of the retreating enemy, and if possible to cut off his rear guard." Assigned to the task were the 1st and 6th U.S. Cavalry, along with the 3rd Pennsylvania Cavalry, the 8th Illinois Cavalry, and four batteries of horse artillery. Stoneman advanced the men along two roads. Recently promoted to brigadier general, William H. Emory struck up the Hampton Road directly to Fort Magruder with the 3rd Pennsylvania and the 8th Illinois, while Cooke's Regulars maneuvered along the Yorktown Road toward the Rebel left flank.[51]

A little before noon and six miles from Yorktown, according to Stoneman, "we came upon the enemy's pickets. Two miles farther we came up with the rear of his rear guard, consisting of a regiment of cavalry, with a deep ravine and bad crossing between us and him." Aided by the deep ravine that yawed across its front, the battle-hardened Confederate rearguard did its job well. Because of this staunch resistance, the Union troopers did not come into view of the Confederate line of redoubts until 3:00 that afternoon; by then, Fort Magruder was teeming with Confederate troops and guns, but some of the outer redoubts remained unoccupied.[52]

The two columns of Union cavalry debouched from the wooded hilltop, much to the consternation of the startled Confederates. Firmly accustomed to McClellan's stodgy approach, the enemy had left the redoubts almost completely unoccupied. Stoneman's sudden appearance in strength changed the situation dramatically. The Confederates raced to man their defenses while their

---

50 Carroll, *Custer in the Civil War*, 150.

51 *The War of the Rebellion: A Compilation of the Official Records of the Union and Confederate Armies*, 128 vols. (Washington, DC, 1880-1901), Series 1, vol. 11, part 1, page 424. Hereafter cited as *OR*. All references are to Series 1 unless otherwise noted.

52 Ibid.

commander, Gen. Joseph E. Johnston, steadily worked to augment his force with infantry, cavalry, and artillery.

Cooke directed his efforts to the Confederate left. As his cavalry prowled up the roads toward Williamsburg, they struck the Rebel rearguard, which consisted of two companies protected by strong breastworks. Cooke deployed a section of his artillery, causing the Confederates to retreat further. The Federal troopers followed, encountering the enemy ensconced behind a defile created by a nearby mill and its dam. Cooke ordered Capt. John Savage's squadron of the 6th U.S. Cavalry to advance to the charge, forcing the enemy to give way. Meanwhile, another squadron of the 6th found a forest road that skirted the earthworks on the enemy's left flank.

Determined to press on, Cooke ordered Maj. Lawrence Williams and four large squadrons of the 6th U.S. Cavalry "to take that road and attack the enemy's left flank." Facing the Confederate center, Cooke placed the three small squadrons of Lt. Col. William Grier of the 1st U.S. Cavalry in a shallow swale, ready to charge in support of its sister regiment. But the Confederates continued to augment their forces, and from a mere 400 yards away their "cross-fire of shell and shrapnel became destructive, killing and wounding many horses and a number of officers and men, he having the advantage of a well-ascertained range."[53]

Cooke moved his meager forces to the attack, but due to the unforgiving nature of the saturated terrain, he could only bring one battery into play, supported by a little more than 300 cavalry. As the Rebels strengthened their position, Cooke's artillerymen struggled to get their guns unlimbered in the unforgiving mixture of heavy forest and marshy ground. For the next 45 minutes the Union and Confederate batteries dueled. As more and more Rebel infantrymen joined the fray, they began to move out of their lines in an effort to turn Cooke's right flank and cut off his command. Cooke sent Wesley Merritt to check in with Stoneman and "report the state of affairs, and to ask if you had orders to give."[54]

Stoneman arrived on the scene soon thereafter, and quickly decided that the overwhelming superiority of the enemy's artillery and increasing infantry support, coupled with his own lack of infantry, made any attack by cavalry an exercise in futility. "I deemed it worse than useless to try to hold our position at the junction of the roads in front of a strong earthwork and overwhelming force," Stoneman wrote in his official report, "and therefore gave directions to withdraw and take up

---

53 Ibid., 428.

54 Ibid.

a defensive position, which we had determined to try and hold at all hazards." Cooke confirmed the results of Merritt's mission, stating in response to Stoneman, "He returned with an order to retire. You undertook, at his request, to send an order to Williams to withdraw." Cooke complied with Stoneman's order and withdrew his command. As soon as the Rebels saw the Federal cavalry falling back, the 4th Virginia Cavalry, Lt. Col. Williams C. Wickham commanding, sallied out of the lines and charged the 1st U.S. Cavalry's rearguard. Captain Benjamin "Grimes" Davis wheeled a squadron about and countercharged, driving the Rebels back, and the rest of the regiment soon followed. Colonel Wickham was slashed in the side by a saber during this action.[55]

"In this charge," wrote Colonel Grier in his official report, dated May 7, "a regimental standard, with the coat of arms of Virginia, was captured and a captain taken prisoner." If his claim is true, the flag of the 4th Virginia would qualify as the first one taken by the Army of the Potomac. So the possibility exists that the intrepid Custer was as close to the scene of the action as he wrote in a letter to his sister. "The 4th Virginia's colors were seized in the melee around the guns," cavalry historian Donald C. Caughey states unequivocally in his painstakingly researched history of the 6th U.S. Cavalry. Many historians, however, doubt that claim. Among them is Jeffry Wert, who argues that "none of the Confederate regiments reported the loss."[56]

Major Williams's column on the Confederate left flank also was forced to retreat with the Southern cavalry snapping at its heels. While traversing the narrow ravine that approached the enemy's works, the rearguard of the 6th U.S., commanded by Capt. William Sanders, suffered greatly when the enemy cavalry "appeared on the edge and opened a destructive fire from carbines and pistols. . . . The enemy followed across the ravine and up the hill." As the chase continued, Sanders's men turned on their pursuers, who were "handsomely charged and

---

55 Ibid., 425, 428.

56 Ibid., 430; Caughey and Jones, *The 6th United States Cavalry*, 47; Wert, *Custer*, 52. John C. Rigdon challenges this claim, stating that the "4th served from First Manassas to Appomattox Court House [never surrendering its colors], participating in every major battle and campaign which involved the Army of Northern Virginia." This cryptic statement may be technically misleading. At the time of the battle of Williamsburg, General Johnston still called his command the "Army of the Potomac." Not until the end of May, when Robert E. Lee replaced the wounded Johnston, were the Southern forces near Richmond renamed the Army of Northern Virginia. Rigdon's response is emphatic but possibly a little disingenuous. John C. Rigdon, *Historical Sketch and Roster of the Virginia 4th Cavalry Regiment* (Centersville, GA, 2015), Kindle edition.

driven back by this squadron . . . and suffered severely in [their] turn in passing the ravine." At the top of the hill, Captain Sanders turned his command to face the enemy and ordered a second charge. His men swept down the hill and were "upon them, with glittering sabers, like an irresistible avalanche, and crushed them back into the marsh with considerable loss." After driving the Rebels, Stoneman regrouped his command half a mile back from the front line; his losses were one man dead and 22 wounded.[57]

Contentious Cavalry and Custer's Flag

Several points of contention dogged the aftermath of the Union attack of May 4. In large part, its defeat was due to the failure of the infantry to lend its support. Additionally, the cavalry's attack on Fort Magruder and its supporting redoubts was a confused affair from the start due to the presence of both Stoneman and Cooke, who maintained separate headquarters on the battlefield at the same time. It is easy to see how the multiple overlapping levels of command overly complicated the issuance of orders. To make matters worse, the Federal mounted arm lacked experience in coordinated operations at that early stage of the war.

As would become standard procedure in the Army of the Potomac, whenever there was failure, recriminations and finger-pointing were sure to follow. Major Williams averred that he had received conflicting orders from the two respective headquarters. Clearly upset, Cooke chastised Williams, claiming that Williams had not received orders to "'take a battery on the enemy's right flank, or left flank either. He was ordered to attack the enemy's left flank." Williams claimed to have done nothing wrong since the order had been obeyed "as it was communicated by his aide-de-camp," thereby blaming Merritt for bungling his transmission of General Stoneman's orders.[58]

Moreover, Williams had compounded the misunderstanding, written off as a clerical error, by prematurely withdrawing from the field. "General S[toneman] undertook, at the request of Captain Merritt, to send you an order to retire, but your report shows you did not wait for it," Cooke wrote in an addendum to Williams's official report. "The expression that your report, 'regarding the order to take the battery on the enemy's extreme left may or may not be correct in the opinion of the commanding general,' cannot be understood. Do you mean the

---

57 OR 11, pt. 1, 439; Caughey and Jones, *The 6th United States Cavalry*, 48.

58 OR 11, pt. 1, 437, 439.

alternative, that in his opinion it may be correct?" Aside from stating Cooke's actions "were admirably managed," Merritt himself left no account of that day. [59]

The greatest challenge in tracing the career of George Armstrong Custer is separating fact from mythology, particularly those myths claiming to exemplify "Custer's Luck." Some historians grant Custer the distinction of capturing the first Confederate colors taken by the Army of the Potomac. An in-depth study of the official records of the Peninsula campaign fails to provide any tangible proof that Custer ever captured a Confederate battle flag, not on May 5, 1862, as claimed by Marguerite Merington, nor on May 24, as asserted by Frederick Whittaker.

The origin of both versions lies in a letter Custer wrote to his sister, Mrs. Lydia Reed, on May 15. His bold-faced claims are contained in Marguerite Merington's *The Custer Story*. In the last paragraph of that transcribed letter, Custer bragged to Mrs. Reed that he had been "in the thick of the fight from morning till night." Grandly he boasted that he had, "without any assistance," taken a captain and five men prisoner. He also mentioned the capture of a large Confederate flag, "afterwards sent up by McClellan to the President at Washington." Due to this statement, Merington accords Custer the credit for "the first Confederate flag captured by the Army of the Potomac."[60]

If Colonel Grier's report of capturing the flag of the 4th Virginia Cavalry is taken at face value and accepted as true, it still leaves the question of whether Custer was even on the field that day. The answer to that question is definitely "yes." Custer's corps commander, Gen. W. F. Smith, establishes his presence on the left flank of the Union army as it advanced on Williamsburg, paralleling the James River. On the morning of May 4, Brig. Gen. Winfield Scott Hancock informed Smith that the Confederate works to his front at the Lee's Mill Dam had been abandoned. "Before, however, the troops arrived at the points designated," Smith reported, "at about 5:30 a.m., Lieutenant Custer, Fifth Cavalry . . . had crossed the dam and taken possession of the works." The dam was made passable for the movement of artillery and cavalry by 7:00 a.m., and Custer had continued down the Lee's Mill Road toward Williamsburg. By about 11:30 a.m., Smith's command had advanced as far as Skiff Creek, where the men discovered that the

59 Ibid., 438.

60 Merington, *The Custer Story*, i, 29-30. Due to the sorry state of the Custers' correspondence, Merington's work is riddled with errors. To further confuse the matter, much of the correspondence was later burned at the behest of family members.

bridge had been set afire. "In the endeavor to put out the fire," lauded Smith, "Lieutenant Custer had burned his hands."[61]

This puts Custer within a mile of the Yorktown-Williamsburg Road.

Williamsburg, Round Two

After the cavalry failed to take the Rebel earthworks on May 4, Union commanders decided to send in the infantry the next day. Officers from the Engineer Corps studied the Confederate works in detail, and the head of the Army of the Potomac's Left Wing, Maj. Gen. Edwin V. Sumner, made a personal reconnaissance on the morning of May 5. Sumner also was acting as overall army commander in McClellan's absence. During their scouting mission, the engineers discovered that Redoubt Number Thirteen, on the Confederate left flank, was unoccupied, and Hancock's brigade was ordered to capture it. Custer asked General Smith if he could tag along with Hancock, and Smith gladly gave his permission. "The writer of this tendered his services to General Hancock for that day, which tender was accepted," wrote Custer. "In this way personal association with the battle of Williamsburg was enjoyed which otherwise would not have been probable."[62]

Shortly after 7:00 a.m., a sporadic exchange of fire between the lines quickly escalated into a continuous roll of musketry as Brig. Gen. Joseph Hooker began pressing his attack against Fort Magruder opposite the Union left. Uncharacteristically, Hancock's forward movement had gotten off to a late start, which rendered any plans for coordinated Union action moot. "In obedience to his orders, Hancock conducted his brigade to the unoccupied redoubt on the enemy's left," explained Custer in his memoirs. "Before reaching it, it was necessary to cross a narrow dam over which it was barely possible to march infantry in column of fours. Half a regiment stationed in the redoubt could have held the crossing against an entire division." First Lieutenant Arthur Holbrook of the 5th Wisconsin verified the perilous passage, describing his regiment's approach to what he labeled the "dirty, sluggish creek." The only crossing point they could discover was what he described as "a mud dam, about seventy-five yards in length, on which we could cross, but only in single column. . . . A few good sharpshooters could have easily

---

61 OR 11, pt. 1, 526.

62 Carroll, *Custer in the Civil War*, 151.

held back an entire army at that place," he concluded. By this time it was almost noon.[63]

Modestly, Custer made no mention of his part in the affair, but his leadership was noted by others. One member of the 5th Wisconsin remembered his presence clearly. The regiment had begun to deploy its skirmishers when "a young lieutenant came dashing up on horseback. We learned that he was of the 5th Cavalry and had been sent to lead us. His sudden appearance at once interested the men and they welcomed him with a shout. The Fifth Regiment will never forget that figure or face." Hancock himself took time to acknowledge Custer's contribution. "I . . . deployed skirmishers on the right and left of the road," he wrote in his official report, "then sent the Fifth Wisconsin . . . followed by the Sixth Maine in column of assault across the dam and into the work, Lieutenant Custer, Fifth Regular Cavalry, volunteering and leading the way on horseback."[64]

Occupation of the redoubt placed Hancock in position to roll up the Confederate left flank. His men stormed and captured the next two redoubts in line, but Fort Magruder still lay tantalizingly out of reach. Hancock advanced his artillery even further to the front, and "a well-directed fire was poured into Fort Magruder, giving great annoyance to the occupants of the fort." Commanding from the center of his line, Hancock could hear opportunity knocking at the door, but he was running out of time. Unfortunately, he had orders to hold his position, not take the offensive. Stalling for time, Hancock sent a series of requests for reinforcements, becoming more insistent as the rejections from Sumner mounted. Sumner had long had the reputation of being a damn good soldier, but he was not a damn good general.[65]

Inevitably, Hancock received an order to withdraw. "Those who have seen Hancock when affairs with which he was connected were not conducted in conformity with his views," wrote Custer sardonically, "can imagine the manner in which he received the order to retire." One succinct account recalled that Hancock "turned the air blue with curses." He was left to hope that some untoward event would change Sumner's mind. "Taking out his watch, Hancock, in conversation

63 Carroll, *Custer in the Civil War*, 152; Arthur Holbrook, "With the Fifth Wisconsin at Williamsburg," in *War Papers Read Before the Commandery of the State of Wisconsin, Military Order of the Loyal Legion of the United States*, 4 vols. (Milwaukee, WI, 1891-1914), 3:530.

64 Holbrook, "With the Fifth Wisconsin at Williamsburg," 3:534; Merington, *The Custer Story*, 30.

65 Carroll, *Custer in the Civil War*, 153.

with the writer, remarked, 'It is now two o'clock. I shall wait till four: if no reply reaches me from headquarters, I will then withdraw.'"[66]

Only Custer was around to hear this statement; the rest of Hancock's staff officers had been sent back to Sumner for orders or reinforcements. Just as Hancock uttered the words, the woods to his front and right suddenly erupted with musketry. Hancock directed Custer to inform the battery commander "to retire to the crest on which the redoubt was located and take position on the left of and near the redoubt." The enemy's fire was intensifying, and Custer later expressed relief that "[t]he order for the battery to retire had been given none too soon."[67]

Arthur Holbrook of the 5th Wisconsin was struck by the dashing appearance of Hancock's messenger. "We can never forget the coming of the aide who delivered that order, for he was the only mounted officer in that part of the field, and as the enemy was close at hand and approaching us, he was a fine target for the whole rebel line," he recalled about the rider, who was likely George Custer. "The bullets flew about him like hailstones, and he stretched his whole length along the neck and back of his big bay horse. As soon as he was sufficiently near to be heard, he shouted his message to Colonel Cobb, and then retired at breakneck speed."[68]

Southern officers marshalled their infantry in columns of regiments as the Rebel cavalry made a show of force at the edge of the woods. The Confederates struck Hancock's command just as it transitioned from the offense to a withdrawal to the main Union position. Hancock cantered up and down his line, with Custer riding behind much like a nervous bird dog prancing around its master's heels. "Aim low, men—aim low. Don't be in a hurry to fire until they come nearer," Hancock commanded in his magnificent voice. Undaunted, the Confederates continued to advance. "The intention of the enemy was now plainly evident," recalled Custer. From the attacking Confederates an ungodly screech emanated, its volume increasing. For the first time, according to Custer, the Federals heard the "Rebel yell," "which ever afterward was made an important auxiliary in every charge or assault made by the Confederates." Hancock's men scrambled back to the nearest high ground and straggled into line.[69]

---

66 Ibid., 152-154.

67 Ibid., 154.

68 Arthur Holbrook, "With the Fifth Wisconsin at Williamsburg," in *War Papers* Read Before *the Commandery of the State of Wisconsin, Military Order of the Loyal Legion of the United States*, 4 vols. (Milwaukee, WI, 1891-1914), 3:534.

69 Carroll, *Custer in the Civil War*, 155, 156.

Brigadier General Jubal A. Early began an ill-advised assault against Hancock's reformed line across the open fields at about 3:00 p.m. Using a thick sheaf of woodland as cover, Early deployed his brigade; the 24th Virginia formed on the far left with the 38th Virginia and the 23rd North Carolina in the middle of the line. The 5th North Carolina anchored the right. In order to reach their starting points, however, the Confederates would have to leave the sanctuary of the woods and cross an open field. In retrospect, the brigade had a very low chance of exiting the thick forest in any semblance of a cohesive unit. The uncoordinated attack would go far toward damaging Early's reputation. Adding injury to insult, Early was wounded twice and was forced to leave the field.

The 24th Virginia was the first to emerge from the woods, followed a few minutes later by the 5th North Carolina. To the dismay of the Rebels crossing the field, the 38th Virginia and the 23rd North Carolina got tangled in the dense underbrush and failed to fill the 300-yard gap between the 24th Virginia and the 5th North Carolina. Despite the lack of support, both regiments slogged forward.

Hancock withdrew even further and consolidated his position. The 5th North Carolina was forced to make an oblique march across the field until it reached the Queen's Creek Road. Once there it turned onto the road and headed straight into the teeth of Hancock's assembled artillery, suffering casualties that few other units would incur during the war. "Theirs was a high type of Southern soldiery which fought to the death," wrote Holbrook, overcome with admiration. "Their charge upon our position the fifth of May 1862, was one of the great and remarkable deeds of the war. These fellows came rushing down upon our line unswervingly, undaunted, and unhesitatingly to meet their doom."[70]

By that time, about 5:00 p.m., darkness settled over the field. A hard rain falling for some time only added to the gloom. Major General Daniel Harvey Hill, Early's commanding officer, later confessed to Maj. Gen. James Longstreet with stark horror that the "slaughter of the Fifth North Carolina Regiment was one of the most awful things I ever saw." Sadly, it was caused by a blunder. The Rebel high command had completely underestimated the Federal troops. In his after-action report, Brig. Gen. James Ewell Brown (Jeb) Stuart ruefully admitted his conviction that his opponent was "either weak, timid, or feigning, and in neither contingency to be feared." The long tramp across the sodden fields had sapped the

---

70 Thomas L. McMahon, "The Flag of the Fifth North Carolina, the First Southern Banner Captured in the East, Has Been Rediscovered," *America's Civil War* (May 2002), Vol. 15, No. 2, 69; Holbrook, "With the Fifth Wisconsin at Williamsburg," in *War Papers*, 3:530.

Confederates of their strength, and they began to falter. Hancock galloped up and down his line, hat in hand, yelling, "Men, you must hold this ground, or I am ruined!"[71]

Though only recently mustered into the service, the 5th Wisconsin proved to be ruthless on that battlefield, standing firm in line and pouring an incredible volume of fire into the Rebel ranks, which were about 100 yards away. Under the hail of shot, shell, and canister, the 5th North Carolina wilted. Watching as the Rebels slogged their way through the morass, Col. Amasa Cobb ordered his Wisconsin riflemen to focus their fire on the 5th's color guard. Up and down the line the lieutenants barked the orders; Cobb easily heard Lt. Enock Tolten urging his men to knock down that "bastard flag." Cobb recalled that he watched as the man holding the flag dropped to the ground in short order.[72]

The 5th North Carolina's after-action report was filed by its commanding officer, Col. Duncan McRae, who had left the regiment to take over the brigade when Early was wounded. McRae's account shows how much eternal glory can be attributed to a tattered, blood-stained, and bullet-riddled piece of silk. The original flag bearer went down at the opening fusillade of the 5th Wisconsin. Another man grabbed for the flag and he too fell, as did the third man. The fourth to try was an officer, Capt. Benjamin Robinson of Company A. He took hold of the staff and carried it until it was "shivered to pieces in his hands." The proud banner of the 5th North Carolina then fell into the mud and was trampled underfoot.[73]

After the attack, the dead and wounded littered the wet, grassy plain. "The smoke of battle hung dense, heavy and low," wrote Holbrook with bated breath, "and when it lifted and was wafted aside, the scene upon that field was one never to be forgotten." Of the 460 men present with the 5th North Carolina, 252 were killed, wounded, or captured, one of the highest casualty rates of any unit during the war.[74]

J. R. Ensign, a member of the 5th Wisconsin, recovered the Rebel flag from the mud. He dutifully made his way back to headquarters to turn in his prize when he

---

71 McMahon, "The Flag of the Fifth North Carolina," 70; OR 11, pt. 1, 571; Carroll, *Custer in the Civil War*, 157.

72 McMahon, "The Flag of the Fifth North Carolina," 69.

73 OR 11, pt. 1, 610; McMahon, "The Flag of the Fifth North Carolina," 69-72. Over the next 140 years, the flag followed a circuitous route back to the "Tarheel State." When the federal government returned captured Confederate banners to their home states in 1905, it mistakenly ended up in Arkansas, and was finally sent back to North Carolina in 2002.

74 Holbrook, "With the Fifth Wisconsin at Williamsburg," 3:535.

ran into "a staff officer," to whom he relinquished this first captured flag. Some have stated that the unnamed officer appropriated the flag. Regardless of the circumstances of the transfer, there is no doubt that the staff officer in question was George Custer. As flag historian Thomas McMahon opined, "In typical style, Custer over-glorified his role in the flag's capture . . . boasting in a letter that he had 'captured . . . a large Rebel flag.'"[75]

"One of the French princes serving on General McClellan's staff, the Duc d' Orleans, arriving on the battlefield at this moment," attested Custer, "was made the bearer of the captured colors." Such an event should have figured prominently in Hancock's official report, but no such mention of it was made. Even Whittaker failed to do so. To his credit, Custer stated in his memoirs, "They also captured one battle flag." As McMahon would conclude, it counted as but "one of the many embellished stories used in the lionization of General George A. Custer."[76]

Ultimately, at least in General Hancock's view, Custer had acquitted himself in a highly laudatory manner. "For the success of the day," recorded Hancock, "I am much indebted to the valuable staff officers of my own and other commands whom circumstances placed with me on this occasion. Their intelligence and promptness in carrying orders prevented any errors." Among the officers listed was "Second Lieutenant G. A. Custer, Fifth Regular Cavalry, acting topographical engineer."[77]

Custer described the battle in a letter home to his sister. "Gen'l Hancock's brigade was charged by two rebel brigades with bayonets. Our troops stood firm, then when the rebels were twenty paces [away], Gen'l Hancock gave orders to advance at a charge of bayonets. They did so, putting the enemy to a complete rout, killing and capturing a large number." The account of the battle of Williamsburg in Custer's memoirs illustrates his tendency to exaggerate the events transpiring on the battlefield. Unfortunately, his official reports also display his "talent" for embellishment, which can prove dangerous for an incautious historian.[78]

Although bayonets were certainly affixed to rifles, there had been no bayonet charge. Eyewitness accounts describe it more as a fierce gunfight rather than close-up, hand-to-hand combat. "The whole line moved forward," recorded

---

75 McMahon, "The Flag of the Fifth North Carolina," 70.

76 Carroll, *Custer in the Civil War*, 158; McMahon, "The Flag of the Fifth North Carolina," 72.

77 *OR* 11, pt. 1, 543.

78 Merington, *The Custer Story*, 30.

Colonel Cobb of the 5th Wisconsin, "with a short and well directed fire. Driving the enemy before them like chaff." This fire was directed with the "rapidity and coolness worthy of veterans."[79]

After the battle, attending surgeons also contradicted Custer's claim as to the efficacy of the bayonet charge, recording that few of the wounded sported the distinctive stab of a bayonet. Throughout the course of the war most successful bayonet charges succeeded through intimidation, with defenders turning to flee before the moment of impact. Few men could stomach the thought of death by cold steel.

---

79 OR 11, pt. 1, 555.

Chapter Three

We Thought We Were Soldiers

A MUCH MORE SUBDUED army—a bloodied army—filled the roads heading up the Peninsula toward Richmond. It grew as it marched, in both logistics and manpower. A depot was established at White House on the Pamunkey River, which was deep enough at that point to accommodate gunboats and schooners. The West Point Railroad crossed the Pamunkey at White House then curved toward its terminus at West Point, a spit of land that separates the Mattaponi and Pamunkey rivers at their confluence with the York River.[1]

On May 18, General McClellan ordered the formation of the new V and VI Corps. McClellan's close friend, Brig. Gen. Fitz John Porter, received a promotion to major general and was given command of the V Corps. Porter, West Point class of 1845, began his career in the artillery and was wounded in the Mexican War, receiving two brevets. After serving a stint as an artillery and cavalry instructor at West Point he went west to serve on the frontier. On May 14, 1861, he was appointed colonel of the 1st U.S. Cavalry, and three days later was promoted to brigadier general of volunteers.

Once reorganized, the army set off ponderously up the roads toward Richmond—or at least what passed for roads in rain-soaked Virginia. McClellan deeply resented the line of march he was forced to follow. He petulantly obeyed the

---

1 White House had belonged to Martha Dandridge Custis before her marriage to George Washington. In another of the Civil War's infinite store of ironies, the plantation's current owner was Confederate Col. W. H. F. "Rooney" Lee, commander of the 9th Virginia Cavalry and the son of Gen. Robert E. Lee.

letter of the orders he had received, but not the spirit in which they were written. His visionary mind had crafted a different plan, and he needed more men with which to implement it. Specifically, he wanted those men moved up the James River so he could operate against Richmond from the south. McClellan demanded that the politicians in Washington quit dictating the course of his campaign to him.

The irascible secretary of war, Edwin Stanton, rejected outright this notion of reinforcements via the James River. On May 18 he informed McClellan that any further augmentation of his force would only come from the north, where Maj. Gen. Irvin McDowell was marching from Fredericksburg to a rendezvous point somewhere northeast of Richmond. "[Stanton] directed me to extend the right of the Army of the Potomac . . . in order to establish communications," wrote McClellan. To his disbelief, McClellan was also required to supply McDowell from his own resources by establishing a connection on the far bank of the Chickahominy River. This, reported McClellan to the war department, "caused great delay in constructing practicable bridges across that stream." He pointedly reminded Washington that he had desired his resupply from the James River, which would have allowed reinforcements to "have reached me . . . rapidly and safely."[2]

"How slow and cautious was his advance," sneered one skeptic, "may be judged from the fact that it was not till the 22nd of May, seventeen days after the battle of Williamsburg, that his advance reached the Chickahominy." Once there his momentum stalled again. "Those who think McClellan is slow must remember that his army has never been defeated," wrote an officer in his overworked escort detail, "and that it is better to move two or three miles a day and hold the ground than advance ten and retire twenty." President Lincoln dismissed this defense. Since early April, his frustration barely constrained, the president had continually goaded McClellan into action. "I think it is the precise time to strike a blow," he urged McClellan with a phrase that he repeated several times. "By delay the enemy will relatively gain upon you—that is, he will gain faster by fortifications and reinforcements than you can by reinforcements alone," he warned. "Once more, let me tell you, it is indispensable to you that you strike a blow. I am powerless to help this."[3]

---

2 McClellan, "The Peninsular Campaign," 2:173-174.

3 Whittaker, *A Popular Life of Gen. George A. Custer*, 107; Rodenbough, *From Everglade to Cañon*, 261; Carroll, *Custer in the Civil War*, 139.

One Slippery Rock and There Goes Glory

McClellan established his headquarters at Cold Harbor, about a mile back from the Chickahominy River. From there he slowly prepared for battle, first carefully reconnoitering the terrain and becoming intimately acquainted with the capricious nature of the Chickahominy. "It was subject to frequent, sudden, and great variations in the volume of water," he wrote, presenting yet one more reason to dally. "A single storm of short duration sufficed to cause an overflow of the bottom-lands for many days, rendering the river absolutely impassable without long and strong bridges." Two roads crossed the Chickahominy: one at Bottom Bridge, located one mile below the West Point Railroad, and the other eight miles above the railroad at New Bridge. Both had been destroyed by the retreating Rebels, leaving only the bridge pilings standing above the water.[4]

The Chickahominy would play a defining role in the career of young Lieutenant Custer, who was still attached to the army's topographical engineers, "obtaining a most invaluable experience—until the army found its advance to Richmond obstructed by the treacherous and tortuous windings of the Chickahominy River." In fact Custer would later describe the river as "a stream which, however chargeable with some of the misfortunes of the Army of the Potomac, was almost literally a stepping-stone for my personal advancement."[5]

Another way had to be found, and on May 20, Brig. Gen. John G. Barnard, chief engineer of the Army of the Potomac, set off for New Bridge after visiting Bottom Bridge the previous day. His personal inspection confirmed that the enemy was not present at that point and that the stream was fordable on horseback. As Barnard mounted his horse he spied Custer, who was still attached to the topographical engineers, idling nearby, and he beckoned for Custer to accompany him. Soon they crossed the Union picket line and sat their horses side by side on the river's bank. In his usual brusque manner Barnard told Custer to "jump in."

There are multiple accounts concerning Custer's next action. Frederick Whittaker heard a stylized version from Libbie, who had probably heard an embellished version from her husband. Barnard's order was "instantly obeyed" by Custer, who "forded the stream . . . and ascended the opposite bank." Holding his revolver above the water, the young officer waded into the river, perfectly exposed and expecting at any moment to become the target of a hidden Rebel sharpshooter.

4 McClellan, "The Peninsular Campaign," 2:175.

5 Carroll, *Custer in the Civil War*, 143.

Custer is ordered by the army's chief engineer, Brig. Gen. John G. Barnard, to reconnoiter across the Chickahominy River. Frederick Whittaker, *A Popular Life of George Armstrong Custer*

Once over, Custer crawled up the embankment and peered through the bushes at the Confederate dispositions, enjoying "a distinct view of the enemy's picket fires some distance off and by the sight of their nearest sentry lazily pacing his post, quite unconscious of the proximity of any foe."[6]

Custer overstayed his visit and Barnard, visibly perturbed, gestured furiously for the young lieutenant to return. "But the young fellow never heeded them till he had carefully examined the whole of the enemy's position," recounted Whittaker, "and had found that their main picket post was so situated in the midst of a bend of the river that it might be easily cut off by a bold dash from a point either higher up or lower down.... Then he waded his way back to Barnard, and briefly reported the stream as being 'fordable.'"[7]

On reporting back to headquarters, General Barnard, much to his credit, brought Custer's actions to the direct attention of General McClellan. Barnard's report inspired McClellan to yank the scruffy, mud-caked lieutenant up by the bootstraps and remove him from the anonymity of the staff herd, which gave Custer the chance to shine on his own. "McClellan was the first man whom he found to lend him a helping hand in the course of his life," wrote Whittaker, "and

6   Whittaker, *A Popular Life of Gen. George A. Custer*, 111-112.

7   Ibid.

he never forgot that fact. . . . The feeling with which Custer, then and after, regarded McClellan, was such as he never gave to any subsequent general. . . . It was a compound of respect, gratitude, and love amounting to adoration, which remained with him to the last."[8]

Shortly after Custer's death, McClellan sent Libbie a thoughtful letter of condolence, reminiscing about that moment of opportunity. "He was reported to me as having accomplished an act of desperate gallantry on the banks of the Chickahominy," recalled McClellan. "I sent for him at once,"

> and, after thanking him, asked what I could do for him. He seemed to attach no importance to what he had done, and desired nothing. Whereupon I asked him if he would like to come upon my staff as Captain. He gladly accepted, and remained with me until I was relieved of my command.[9]

On May 24, the 4th Michigan Infantry, commanded by Col. Dwight A. Woodbury and considered "one of the finest bodies of men in the Army of the Potomac," was ordered to take the picket outpost that Custer had discovered. Woodbury's cavalry support consisted of Capt. George A. Gordon's squadron of the 2nd U.S. Cavalry and a company of the 5th U.S. Cavalry commanded by Custer. The plan of attack had the infantry deploying a line of skirmishers to cross the stream and strike the flank of the Rebel picket force posted in the bend of the river. "As a subaltern I knew we were to make a reconnaissance of the position named and surmised it was directed from Headquarters of the Army for there were many staff officers with us," wrote Lt. William H. Harrison of the 2nd U.S. Cavalry, and "[a]mong them I noticed Col. Alexander and Captains Custer and Forster." Custer had a personal stake in the attack and asked McClellan for the honor of leading it. Whittaker asserts that McClellan assented and gave young Captain Custer command of a detachment consisting of two companies of cavalry and one company of infantry. Given the presence of Colonel Woodbury, a senior officer, this is a ludicrous statement.[10]

---

8   Ibid., 114-115.

9   Merington, *The Custer Story*, 31.

10   William H. Harrison, "Personal Experiences of a Cavalry Officer," in Michael A. Cavanaugh, ed., *Military Essays and Recollections of the Pennsylvania Commandery of the Military Order of the Loyal Legion of the United States, 1866-1903*, 2 vols. (Wilmington, NC, 1995), 1:235-236.

The commander of the Army of the Potomac, Maj. Gen. George B. McClellan, with members of his staff. *LOC*

Whittaker's account, as mistake-ridden as it is, provides more insight into Custer's character during this relatively insignificant action. Although much of what Whittaker wrote in *A Popular Life* needs to be taken with a large dollop of salt—and in truth, some of it is simply pure invention—his insider's knowledge, some of it based on his communications with Elizabeth Custer, works in his favor. "Whittaker had come under Libbie's spell," explained Shirley A. Leckie, one of Libbie's biographers. "Elizabeth provided him with Armstrong's personal correspondence with family and friends." This bit of luck would prove invaluable to Whittaker because Custer was a prolific letter writer with a gift for extended, detailed storytelling. After Little Bighorn, he visited with the grief-stricken family members on a trip to Monroe, Michigan. "The surviving members of the Custer family," recalled Whittaker, did not think that "they had no right to withhold information as to Custer's career from the nation whose trusted and honored servant he was."[11]

As Custer waited on his horse next to the side of the road, the advance guard of the 4th Michigan approached the bank. The young officer knew that state well. His sister Lydia Ann had married David Reed, a farmer in Monroe, Michigan. Since Monroe had better schools than Custer's hometown of New Rumley, Ohio, Custer spent each school year living with his sister and her husband and attending school there. These particular soldiers recognized Custer immediately. "As the light was growing stronger, he heard a voice say 'I want to know! If that ain't Armstrong!'" Whittaker recounted years later. Company A had been recruited in Monroe, "composed almost entirely of his old school friends and playmates. With the peculiarly refreshing republicanism of the western and all-American country volunteers, the boys recognized no barrier of rank between them and their old playmate . . . he hastily grasped the proffered hands nearest." Custer quickly cut the frivolity short and addressed the company, giving the order for all to hear: "All Monroe boys, follow me; stick to me, and I'll stick to you! Come!' . . . And they did."[12]

The infantry managed to overcome the challenge of the rain-swollen stream. "In the men plunged," read one account, "all accoutered as they were, but contrived to keep their muskets in use. In some places the stream . . . was so deep that the men were obliged to swim, and none got over without wading waist-deep." They came under an immediate and incessant fire from the Rebel pickets stationed on the far bank. Custer went in with them. "There was one officer, who was not to be brooked in this fashion," Lieutenant Harrison maintained, "but putting spurs to his horse, jumped into the stream, swam to the opposite bank, dismounted, picked up a Rebel musket and bowie knife, remounted and swam back." When Custer returned he was dumbfounded to find that the cavalry had yet to ford the Chickahominy.[13]

As planned, the cavalry's part in the action was simple enough, recalled Harrison. Accordingly his squadron waited in a column of fours on the road that ran parallel to the river, perfectly hidden by the heavily wooded banks. They were to move forward at the sound of the infantry's gunfire. "It was not long before a

11 Leckie, *Elizabeth Bacon Custer*, 212.

12 Whittaker, *A Popular Life of Gen. George A. Custer*, 116-117.

13 John Robertson, ed., *Michigan in the War. Report of the Adjutant General* (Lansing, MI, 1882), 225; Harrison, "Personal Experiences of a Cavalry Officer," 1:236.

sharp musketry fire told us our infantry had crossed and were in action," Harrison wrote. With drawn sabers the regiment charged to the bridge, but the head of the column suddenly skidded to a halt. It remains a bit of a mystery as to why the 2nd U.S. Cavalry thought it could cross on the bridge, as General Barnard, among others, had already confirmed that all the bridges in the vicinity had been destroyed by the Rebels. Temporarily stymied, the head of the column made a tempting target for two pieces of artillery the Confederates had placed overlooking the remnants of the bridge.[14]

Custer's eager rush into the fray prevented him from seeing that the cavalry's attempt to cross the river had failed. The event reveals one of Custer's defining traits: he never looked over his shoulder to see if his men were following, and he never even imagined that they would fail to do so. His total focus was on the enemy to his front. He never noticed that Lieutenant Bowen, his close friend and immediate superior, had jumped into the swirling waters behind him, only to have his horse shot out from under him, causing great consternation to the supporting cavalry.

In the latter stages of the war the Union cavalry often would attack first with the infantry in support. Still lacking that confidence, the cavalry did not go over the river even though the infantry's crossing had shown the water to be only chest-high in most places. For men on horseback the lack of a bridge should not have presented an obstacle. "This prevented Field-officers and the cavalry from attempting to cross the stream." One officer in the 2nd U.S. expressed his displeasure at the cavalry's lack of initiative, writing, "The nature of the ground and the impassability of the Chickahominy at that point—New Bridge—prevented the cavalry from taking a very active part."[15]

Whittaker's account makes for a rollicking tale, but it is contradictory at best, at one point placing Custer in the middle of the infantry attack. "Just before sunrise they opened fire on the surprised post of the enemy, part of the Louisiana tigers, shot several and stampeded the rest, driving them down toward the river, and taking arms, prisoners," writes Whittaker, who then makes his own dubious claim about Custer's legendary capture of the Confederate flag, "the first ever taken by the Army of the Potomac, captured by Custer himself." Around this time, Custer realized that the cavalry had not crossed the river. "Custer came raging back to the riverbank," Whittaker recounted, "urging, entreating, storming at the cavalry

---

14 Harrison, "Personal Experiences of a Cavalry Officer," 1:235-236.

15 Robertson, *Michigan in the War*, 225; Rodenbough, *From Everglade to Cañon*, 261-262.

commander to come over, that a grand chance awaited them. The officer refused to be persuaded."[16]

Absent the cavalry, all credit for the victory went to the infantrymen of the 4th Michigan. "The Michigan boys behaved very gallantly, took thirty-five prisoners, and completely routed the Fifth Louisiana, which was in the woods at the bridge." Going down to the river, McClellan personally demonstrated his appreciation and "grasped Colonel Woodbury warmly by the hand and said, 'General, I am happy to congratulate you again on your success, I have had the occasion to do so before, and do so again with pleasure.'" In the two-hour skirmish, the 4th Michigan lost one man killed, two mortally wounded, and four more seriously injured. Enemy casualties included 100 killed and wounded and 37 taken prisoner. A correspondent with the *New York Herald* joined the 4th Michigan on the raid. "Our men partook of the dinner the Louisiana Tigers had prepared for themselves," he marveled. "They captured their company books, and brought away rifles, muskets, swords, sashes, etc." The correspondent made no mention of a captured flag.[17]

The Rivers of Virginia are Treacherous with Undercurrents

May 31, 1862, would prove to be one of the most important days of the entire Civil War, though no one, including the major participants involved, would immediately realize it. With McClellan's army divided by the flooding Chickahominy, Confederate Gen. Joseph E. Johnston saw his chance and attacked at Seven Pines/Fair Oaks. The offensive was overly complex, especially for a green army, and little went off as planned. Late in the day, a lead slug tore into Johnston's right shoulder, followed by a chunk of shrapnel to the chest. The wounds were severe and he was carried off the field. Major General Gustavus Smith assumed temporary command and continued the muddled affair through June 1. An unimpressed President Davis appointed his military advisor, Gen. Robert E. Lee, to command of the primary Southern army.

For George B. McClellan and the Army of the Potomac, the war had just taken a convulsive turn down a road that would be long and bloody, but bathed in the burnished sunlight of eternal fame and glory that shines down on heroes. First,

16 Whittaker, *A Popular Life of Gen. George A. Custer*, 117. The name "Louisiana Tigers" originated specifically with the 1st Louisiana Special Battalion, but as the war continued the term came to be used loosely to describe all units from Louisiana in the Army of Northern Virginia.

17 Rodenbough, *From Everglade to Cañon*, 261-262; Robertson, *Michigan in the War*, 225.

Maj. Gen. James Ewell Brown (Jeb) Stuart, the darling of the Southern horsemen.

Library of Congress

however, Merritt, Custer, and the veteran horsemen of the plains would bear the brunt of many humiliations at the hands of the Confederate mounted arm led by the Union cavalry's arch nemesis, Brig. Gen. "Jeb" Stuart.

James Ewell Brown Stuart graduated from West Point in 1854. Clean shaven during his tenure at the Academy, his receding chin earned him the unflattering sobriquet of "Beauty" from his classmates. Even then, his effervescent, fun-loving personality was in full bloom. Surprisingly, his carefree nature was coupled with a devout Christian faith. Upon graduation he served on the frontier with the 1st Cavalry and was active against the border ruffians in "Bleeding Kansas" in the late 1850s. He served as aide-de-camp to then-Col. Robert E. Lee in the capture of John Brown during the latter's abortive raid against the United States Armory at Harpers Ferry in October 1859.

When Stuart met with his new commander, Lee ordered him to "make a secret movement to the rear of the enemy, now posted on [the] Chickahominy, with a view of gaining intelligence of his operations, communications, etc., of driving in his foraging parties, and securing such grain, cattle, etc., for ourselves as you can make arrangements to have driven in. Another object is to destroy his wagon trains." Without divulging his plans but offering just enough information to give purpose to Stuart's movements, Lee had just handed Stuart a ticket to ride.

Stuart brashly announced that he "could do more than ascertain the position of the Federal right; if the commanding General permitted, he would ride entirely around McClellan's army." Lee, a man of great equanimity, must have shuddered at the thought of his cavalry loose in the rear of the Union army and surrounded by peril on all sides. In his final orders to Stuart he cautioned his young subordinate to remain vigilant. "You will return as soon as the object of your expedition is accomplished," Lee admonished, sternly warning the young cavalier "not to hazard unnecessarily your command or to attempt what your judgment may not approve; but be content to accomplish all the good you can without feeling it necessary to obtain all that might be desired."[18]

Stuart's force of 1,200 veteran troopers began preparing for action on the afternoon of June 11, congregating around Ashland to draw three days' rations and 60 rounds of ammunition. "The officers and men were in high spirits in anticipation of a fight," remembered Lt. W. T. Robins, the adjutant of the 9th Virginia Cavalry. "Orders were issued enforcing strict silence and forbidding the use of fires, as the success of the expedition would depend upon secrecy and celerity." The column consisted of Col. W. H. F. "Rooney" Lee's 9th Virginia

18 OR 11, pt. 3, 590; Edwin Cole Bearss, *Encircling the Union Army: Jeb Stuart's Controversial Ride Around McClellan During the Peninsula Campaign, June 1862* (El Dorado Hills, CA, 2013), Part 1 (Kindle Edition); Douglas Southall Freeman, *Lee's Lieutenants: A Study in Command*, 3 vols. (New York, 1942), 1: 277.

Cavalry, Col. Fitzhugh Lee's 1st Virginia Cavalry, and the Jeff Davis Legion under Col. William T. Martin. Artillery support was provided by a section of horse artillery commanded by Lt. James Breathed. The Stuart Horse Artillery under Capt. John Pelham was beginning to earn its fearsome reputation; the young Alabaman helped redefine the role of horse artillery with his innovative tactics, eventually earning the sobriquet of "The Gallant Pelham."[19]

In accordance with Lee's strictures on the need for the utmost secrecy, Stuart played his cards close to the vest. Quite unexpectedly at 2 o'clock on the morning of June 12, Stuart went around and shook the members of his staff from their slumber. "Gentlemen," he informed them crisply and cheerily, "in ten minutes every man must be in his saddle." The word worked its way down the chain of command until it reached the sergeants and corporals who, in their typical brusque manner, rudely kicked the men out of their bedrolls. The troops were mounted and ready for action by the time Stuart's 10-minute deadline passed; not a single bugle had blown. As the day's march, a diversionary feint to the north, began, Stuart cut a swashbuckling figure as he sat mounted by the side of the road in the moonlight. "He was a gallant figure to look at," admired Lt. John Esten Cooke of Stuart's staff. "The gray coat buttoned to the chin; the light French saber balanced by the pistol in its black holster; the cavalry boots above the knee, and the brown hat with its black

---

19   W. T. Robins, "Stuart's Ride Around McClellan," in Johnson and Buel, eds., *Battles and Leaders*, 2:271; William Henry Fitzhugh Lee, better known as "Rooney," was the second-eldest son of Robert E. Lee. Three years into his academic career at Harvard, he left to accept a commission in the Regular Army, serving as a lieutenant in the 6th Infantry. He participated in the lackluster campaign against the Mormons during the Utah expedition but abruptly resigned his commission in 1859, taking up the life of a gentleman farmer and managing the affairs of the White House plantation that had been bequeathed to him by his grandfather. At the outbreak of the war, he accepted a commission in the Confederate cavalry and in April 1862 he was elected to the colonelcy of the 9th Virginia Cavalry; Eric J. Wittenberg, *The Battle of Brandy Station: North America's Largest Cavalry Battle* (Charleston, SC, 2010), 52. Like George Custer, Fitzhugh Lee had barely avoided expulsion from West Point to graduate in the class of 1856. Like many officers of his time he served on the western frontier, where he took an arrow to the chest in 1859. He tendered his resignation soon after the war began and joined the Confederate army, serving in a series of staff positions before being promoted to the colonelcy of the 1st Virginia Cavalry in April 1862. Cut from the same ebullient cloth as Stuart, he never attained his close friend's stature. His war career was marked by inconsistency, with moments of brilliancy negated by incidents of the "slows." Lieutenant General James Longstreet would later comment that "he was anything but an efficient cavalryman." Marylander Jim Breathed was practicing medicine in Saint Joseph, Missouri, when the war broke out and enlisted as a private in the 1st Virginia Cavalry. He lucked into command after a chance meeting with Stuart on a rail car. Stuart took a chance on the young man and was amply rewarded with Breathed's skill and imaginative employment of shot and shell. At the end of the war, then-Major Breathed calculated that he had engaged in at least 86 battles, battery exchanges, and minor skirmishes.

plume floating above the bearded features, the brilliant eyes and the huge moustache, which curled with laughter at the slightest provocation."[20]

The next day, Stuart's command streamed without pause through the porous Union cavalry cordon on its way to Hanover Court House and the crossing of Totopotomoy Creek. "Soon the Confederate cavalry fell on the emasculated ranks of the thin right wing of what was left of Cooke's cavalry, and made a raid to the rear of our army," reported Merritt. On the other side of Hanover the Rebels finally spotted their first Yankees, who wisely took to their heels.[21]

Just past Haw's Shop, the vanguard of the 9th Virginia Cavalry encountered the first line of enemy skirmishers, part of Capt. William B. Royall's command of three companies of the 5th U.S. Cavalry. Three times the Regulars tried to stand their ground, and three times the Confederates forced them back. During the desperate charges and countercharges, Royall personally confronted Capt. William Latané of the 9th Virginia, the commander of the Rebel advance. Before he finally shot Latané off his horse, Royall suffered multiple saber wounds. Weak from loss of blood, he relinquished his command. Stuart's men eventually forced their foes across the Totopotomoy and down to the vital crossroads of Linney.[22]

Farther down the road lay the crossroads at Old Church, and, beyond that, Tunstall's Station, which was just nine miles southeast of Stuart's position. A stop on the Richmond & York River Railroad, Tunstall's Station linked the Army of the Potomac's far-flung corps with the supply depot at White House. As the key to the heart of the Union logistical effort, its loss would be catastrophic, which was just what Jeb Stuart intended. Taking the station would be a gamble, but by then Stuart had a glint in his brilliant, expressive eyes, and despite Lee's imprecations, he had made up his mind to roll the dice.

Before setting out, Stuart gathered his staff and regimental commanders and told them that rather than head back the way they had come, they were going to ride around the backside of McClellan's army and strike "a serious blow at a boastful and insolent foe, which would make him tremble in his shoes." They would then head south toward Charles City on the James River and thence on to Richmond.[23]

---

20 John E. Coke, *The Wearing of the Gray: Being Personal portraits, Scenes and Adventures of the War* (New York, 1867), 166.

21 Merritt, "Life and Services of General Philip St. George Cooke," 88-89.

22 Royall's wounds would keep him out of the field for the rest of the war. Latané would be the only Confederate fatality during Stuart's raid.

23 OR 11, pt. 1, 1058.

Stuart's actions exposed the fractured nature of the Union command structure, and placed George Custer and Wesley Merritt in opposing camps of sometimes misguided loyalty. The trail we need to follow is that of the Union commanders—Maj. Gen. Fitz John Porter, Col. Gouverneur K. Warren, and Brig. Gen. Philip St. George Cooke—and how they responded to the dangers of Stuart's raid. Theirs was a lackluster effort at best, characterized by sloppiness and disorganization. Worst of all, in light of the rapidly developing situation, the quickly deteriorating lines of command and the rancor that existed at the top only increased the confusion caused by Stuart and his cavalry.

At 2:50 p.m. on June 13, a breathless courier from Captain Royall arrived at Cooke's headquarters with news of the Rebel incursion. His report estimated that more than 3,000 Confederates and four pieces of artillery were poised to strike at any moment. Eventually that figure would be pared to a lower number of 600 men and two guns. Adding to the pressure on Cooke, Lt. Richard Byrnes of the 5th U.S. Cavalry claimed to have seen a column of five regiments of Confederate infantry on the march. "When about 1 mile from Old Church," he reported, "I saw the head of a column of infantry advancing on the road leading into the Hanovertown Ferry road. The pickets which were driven in saw the same body of infantry." Throughout the next few days Cooke would be unable to put that column of Rebel infantry out of his mind.[24]

Soon the urgent, raucous blare of bugles blowing "To Horse" resounded throughout the camps of the "emasculated" Union cavalry. Cooke had six squadrons present in camp and ordered Brig. Gen. William H. Emory to take six companies to buttress Royall's force. As soon as Cooke had his men in motion, he contacted the commander of the nearest infantry division, Brig. Gen. George Sykes, who saw the urgency of the situation. The brigade of Col. Gouverneur Warren was soon under arms and ready to march up the Old Church Road in support of the cavalry.

Riding hard, Emory's command reached Linney sometime after 10:00 p.m. and discovered that the Rebels had already passed through on their way to Tunstall's. This placed the Union cavalry firmly astride what should have been Stuart's line of retreat. Shortly after 3:00 the next morning, Cooke himself joined his 380 troopers, ready to pursue his son-in-law down the Old Church Road to Tunstall's Station.

24 Ibid., 1024.

And then the meddling began. Cooke's report of the enemy's activity and of his intention to attack at daylight reached Fitz John Porter about dusk on June 13. Unaware that Warren's brigade had nearly caught up with Cooke, Porter cautioned against attacking a possibly superior force without infantry support. Cooke was to await the arrival of Sykes's infantry in the morning, at which point Sykes would take over as the officer in charge of the pursuit. In the interim, Cooke was to hold his position.

Porter's communiqué caused a storm of debate within Cooke's inner circle of staff officers, including Merritt. Cooke felt duty-bound to ignore Porter's injunctions and continue his pursuit of the enemy. "[He] was only deterred from doing so by the earnest advice of those around him, who thought they knew how suicidal such a course would be under the conditions which then obtained in the army," Merritt wrote years later. With the wisdom of old age, Merritt debunked the military consequences of Stuart's raid. "I have since regretted that I opposed the infraction of orders," he conceded, "and the entire blame was unworthily thrown on the cavalry and on General Cooke."[25]

Cooke went ahead with his plans anyway, later informing Sykes in a dispatch that "the orders to maintain my position, could not be considered as binding. . . . At the moment I felt confident of a fine opportunity at daylight." Still convinced that the future held a fight with Rebel infantry, Cooke determined to drag the infantry along with him, although Warren protested mightily. He urged Cooke to allow the infantry to stay behind and discredited Lieutenant Byrnes's report of having observed multiple regiments of enemy infantry on the march. "Knowing the country well, and convinced that it would not have allowed seven infantry regiments to display themselves at Hawes Shop," asserted Warren, "together with the little time for observation left to Lieutenant Byrnes, I never for a moment believed we had any evidence of an infantry force."[26]

Warren strongly resented the fact that Cooke had marched his brigade into the ground, forcing them to cover 41½ miles in 38 hours, all the while staying within supporting distance of the cavalry. "We were too much exhausted to have any hope of keeping up with an efficient cavalry pursuit, even if it were a possibility ever to do it," he complained. "He told me to keep on till further orders, and we did so . . . but the roads were heavy, the men tired, and the sun intensely hot. It was

25 Merritt, "Life and Services of General Philip St. George Cooke," 88-89.

26 OR 11, pt. 1, 1011, 1030.

impossible for all to keep up. They fell down exhausted and faint and some were sun-struck." Warren would be one of the first officers to stand up against Cooke.[27]

As Cooke saw it, the Rebels had only two options. If Stuart retraced his line of advance back to its point of origin, he would need the rumored infantry column to ensure success against the superior force of the enemy. If Stuart chose to escape to the south, pursuit would be irrelevant, in Cooke's opinion. "If the enemy did not return I know he had been 8 miles or more ahead ten hours before at least, so that cavalry alone could not overtake him," rationalized Cooke, "even if it should pursue to attack three times its strength in numbers, supported by artillery."[28]

Stuart chose the latter, more daring course. On June 15 a courier galloped up to Cooke with a dispatch from Emory. It caught Cooke at a most awkward moment; it was already three in the afternoon and his command, after a lengthy respite, was preparing to move out in support of Emory, who had advanced four or five miles ahead. Once hearing this news Cooke held "the least hope in the world of overtaking retreating cavalry with the start I knew he had." Emory's dispatch affirmed "that the enemy had escaped over the Chickahominy," thus making his decision to retire a foregone conclusion. The various commands bivouacked around Tunstall's Station that night and were back at Gaines' Mill the next day.[29]

In his official report, Emory attempted to quantify the damage inflicted by the raiders at Tunstall's Station, and was less than impressed. "The damage done by the enemy is not commensurate with the bold spirit with which the raid was dictated," he reported. "He left faster than he came, and the attempt to break up the railroad communication was an entire failure." Of course, mere numbers could never truly express the residual effects of the raid. The Rebels were expected to crow—and they did. Lieutenant Robins of the 9th Virginia described the euphoria that swept through the country, which "rang out with praises of the men who had raided entirely around General McClellan's powerful army, bringing prisoners and plunder from under his very nose. The Southern papers were filled with accounts of the expedition, none accurate, and most of them marvelous."[30]

The Federals of course were expected to make excuses—and they did. "Stuart's raid did more damage through its effect on the public mind than it really

---

27 OR 11, pt. 1, 1030.

28 Ibid., 1012.

29 Ibid.

30 Ibid., 1014; Robins, "Stuart's Ride Around McClellan," 2:275.

accomplished against the army," insisted one officer in the 6th U.S. Cavalry. The raid was to have severe repercussions for Cooke, whose neck was now placed firmly on the chopping block, awaiting the stroke of the executioner's axe. Wesley Merritt, if he was not careful, would have a spot reserved on the next available chopping block.[31]

Gouverneur Warren quickly voiced his concerns. "I deem it my duty to say that I do not believe from the way in which General Cooke conducted the operations," he wrote in his report of the raid, "that the enemy would have been prevented from returning to Hanover Court House by taking the road along the Pamunkey River. It was impossible for the infantry to overtake him, and as the cavalry did not move without us it was impossible for them to overtake him."[32]

Warren's negative comments were a perfect setup for Fitz John Porter's own assessment, which he forwarded to McClellan on June 19. "General Cooke seems to have regarded his force as a reserve for the day of battle, and not therefore expected to perform any picket duty; at least no picket duty had been performed by it until ordered by me, except by Captain Royall's command," he wrote in the overly-verbose manner of all his correspondence. He lambasted Cooke for allowing himself to be tied to the slow-moving infantry. "I have seen no energy or spirit in the pursuit by General Cooke of the enemy [nor did he exhibit] the characteristics of a skillful and active guardian of our flanks."[33]

Naturally, Merritt staunchly defended his mentor, and placed the blame for the debacle on Porter. "General Cooke immediately made arrangements to pursue and punish the intrepid foe," wrote Merritt brazenly, in a biography of Cooke he penned for the *Journal of the Unites States Cavalry Association,* "but was thwarted in his design by positive orders from the Commanding General of the left wing of the army . . . to regulate his pursuit by the march of an infantry column detached to intercept Stuart, and on no account to precede this infantry march."[34]

Instead of attempting to improve the chain of command and better define the role of the Union cavalry, the commanding officers of the Army of the Potomac intensified the problems revealed by the raid. "From this time on affairs with the cavalry went from bad to worse," Merritt observed. "Detachments from its

---

31 Carter, *From Yorktown to Santiago,* 49-50.

32 OR 11, pt. 1, 1031.

33 Ibid., 1006.

34 Merritt, "Life and Services of General Philip St. George Cooke," 88.

strength were constantly increased, and it was hampered by instructions which crippled it for all useful action. . . . It had no freedom of action, and was not allowed to select its position for the better attention to its work." Lieutenant Eben Swift recalled those inglorious days—a poisoned atmosphere in which the "most dangerous enemy was at Army Headquarters, and not at the front. Cavalry generals often had to fight their own high commanders in rear, and the result was sometimes as disastrous as defeat by the enemy."[35]

Headquarters of the Army: A Swamp Unlike Any Other

Merritt's true introduction to the internal politics of the Army of the Potomac occurred on June 27, 1862, at the battle of Gaines' Mill. Occurring close on the heels of Stuart's ride around McClellan's army, this disastrous Union defeat would lead to the downfall of Merritt's mentor, Philip St. George Cooke. Like a falling line of dominoes, Cooke almost took Merritt with him. As one of the principal culprits, Maj. Gen. Fitz John Porter, was to write, "the events immediately preceding the 'Seven Days' Battle on the Peninsula,' in June of 1862, have been subjects of historical interest, and the causes which precipitated certain movements connected with that campaign have given rise to much dispute and controversy." In his own bull-headed way, Merritt contributed amply to the debate.[36]

For weeks Porter's V Corps had been stranded on the north side of the Chickahominy River as the Army of the Potomac advanced on the Confederate capital. A staunch McClellan man, Porter had been made privy to the commanding general's strategy. "His plans embraced defensive arrangements against an attack from Richmond upon our weak right flank. We did not fear the results of such an attack if made by the forces from Richmond alone; but, if, in addition, we were to be attacked by Jackson's forces, suspicions of whose approach were already aroused, we felt that we would be in peril."[37]

Now it seemed these fears were coming true. Already cavalry scouts were reporting large concentrations of enemy infantry in front of Porter's lines, as well as alarming rumors of the advance of the enemy from the north. Learning that Maj. Gen. Thomas J. "Stonewall" Jackson had evaded the forces of Irvin McDowell and

---

35 Ibid.; Swift, "General Wesley Merritt," 831.

36 Fitz John Porter, "The Battle of Gaines's Mill and Its Preliminaries," *The Century Magazine* (June 1885), Vol. 30, No. 2, 309.

37 Ibid., 311.

was making a beeline toward McClellan's army, Porter chose to fall back. In the space of 24 hours, the positions of the contending armies were reversed. One moment McClellan was "rejoicing over the success of his advance toward Richmond," and the next, wrote Porter, "all the united available forces in Virginia were to be thrown against his right flank, which was not in a convenient position to be supported."[38]

By June 27, the V Corps held a somewhat defensible position on the forward slope of a plateau. Facing to the west and north, the infantry divisions of Brig. Gens. George Sykes and George Morell lined up in a gentle arc behind a small, heavily wooded stream named Boatswain's Creek. The south side of the line plunged in a steep descent into the open marshland along the Chickahominy. The waters of the river had finally receded and engineers, working feverishly, managed to throw several spans across it. If the Union line collapsed, the army possessed a way to safety. The V Corps artillery had been placed to cover all the approaches, with the rest of the guns held in reserve along the brow of the plateau. Three of these batteries would play a major role in the confusing action to come. The cannons of Capts. Hezekiah Easton and Mark Kerns, recalled Col. Abraham K. Arnold of the 1st U.S. Cavalry, stood "on the extreme left and rear, a few yards in front of the eastern brow, facing the unoccupied woods about 500 yards in front. [Capt. James M.] Robertson was furthest to the left, covering the approaches via the bottom land."[39]

An hour before the Confederate attack began, Cooke's troopers arrived on the field and took up a position "on the extreme left and rear of our line, 200 yards from the foot of the south and east slopes of the plateau, facing the west and covering the bottom land in that direction." Cooke placed the 5th U.S. Cavalry on the right, the 1st U.S. Cavalry in the center, and the 6th Pennsylvania Cavalry on the left. "By 11:30 A. M.," reported Colonel Arnold, "the dispositions of the forces heretofore mentioned were about finished, and we awaited the first onslaught of the approaching enemy." Unfortunately, Cooke's understrength command only numbered about 665 men.[40]

According to Cooke, his command had been severely diminished by "its extraordinary duties and exposure for the day or two previous in covering the right

38 Ibid.

39 Abraham K. Arnold, "The Cavalry at Gaines' Mill," *Journal of the United States Cavalry Association* (December 1889), Vol. 2, No. 7, 356.

40 Ibid., 357.

and rear of the army [which] had caused the detachment of about half of my forces." At the time of the battle the Cavalry Reserve was comprised of two meager brigades. The first brigade, under Cooke's direct command, consisted of five troops of the 5th U.S. Cavalry, commanded by Capt. Charles Whiting, and six troops of Col. R. H. Rush's 6th Pennsylvania. All told, Cooke's command numbered fewer than 500 saber arms. The second brigade, under Col. G. A. H. Blake, approximately 165 sabers, consisted of four troops of the 1st U.S. Cavalry under Lt. Col. William Grier and a small detachment of the division's provost guard. Although no such documents appear in the *Official Records*, Porter claimed that he issued very specific orders to Cooke. "General Cooke was instructed to take position, with cavalry, under the hills in the valley of the Chickahominy—there with the aid of artillery to guard our left flank. He was especially enjoined to intercept, gather and hold all stragglers and, under no circumstances to leave the valley for the purpose of coming upon the hill held by our infantry, or pass in front of our line on the left." Cooke's account does not contradict Porter, but maintains that he voiced serious objections to the deployment of his cavalry, to which "General Porter evidently yielded, instead of 'enjoining' me; for the cavalry remained quite near his first station, Adam's house; and I was there repeatedly."[41]

On the left of Porter's line, Morell's men belatedly attempted to chop down enough trees to erect a defensive position on the clear, undulating plain to the east of Boatswain's Creek. Off in the distance immense clouds of dust marked the advancing columns of the enemy. Soon the distinctive bark of the Colt rifles employed by Berdan's Sharpshooters, stationed to Morell's front as skirmishers, echoed through the woods. Shortly after noon the first Rebel skirmishers appeared from the wood line along the creek and began probing for a weak point in Porter's line. The advancing infantry, supported by artillery, made a series of attacks along Porter's entire front. "Dashing across the intervening plains, floundering in the swamps and struggling against the tangled underbrush," reported Porter, "brigade

---

41 OR 11, pt. 2, 41. After graduating from West Point in 1835, Whiting only spent a year in the army, serving as an engineer in the Second Seminole War. He then worked as a surveyor, and founded a school in Ellsworth, Maine, where he taught a young Joshua Lawrence Chamberlain. In 1855 he rejoined the army as a captain in the 2nd Cavalry Regiment, which would later become the 5th U.S. Cavalry after the reorganization of the mounted arm in 1861. He served with the regiment in combat against the Comanches, then fled Texas when that state left the Union. Although Buford held him in high regard, Whiting's opinionated personality would work against him; Porter, "The Battle of Gaines's Mill," 316; *OR* 11, pt. 2, 224; Philip St. George Cooke, "The Charge of Cooke's Cavalry at Gaines's Mill, *The Century Magazine* (September 1885), Vol. 30, No. 5, 778.

after brigade seemed almost to melt away before the concentrated fire of our artillery and infantry."[42]

As the afternoon wore on and the dreadful carnage continued, Union regiments began to cycle in and out of the firing line, stocking up on ammunition, then heading back to take up their positions again. Three times the Confederates advanced and three times they were repulsed. The Federal artillery fired shrapnel with lethal accuracy as the enemy crested the plateau, beautifully outlined against the now darkening sky. False hope began to permeate the Union lines. "The sun had sunk below the horizon," wrote Porter, "and the result seemed so favorable that I began to cherish the hope that the worst that could happen to us would be a withdrawal after dark, without further injury—a withdrawal which would be forced upon us by the exhausted condition of our troops, greatly reduced by casualties, without food, and with little ammunition." As sundown approached, the Rebels, finally augmented by Jackson's fresh regiments, gathered to force the issue with irresistible power. Cooke, closely shadowed by Merritt, could clearly discern the preparations for the coming assault.[43]

Cooke anticipated that the Confederates would strike hard on the left to capture the bridges over the Chickahominy and cut off Porter's corps, ensuring its complete and utter destruction, and he sent his trusted aide to warn Porter of the impending disaster. But even as Merritt galloped off to Porter's headquarters the Rebel onslaught burst out of the dense battle smoke that choked the woods along the creek. Merritt found the headquarters in pandemonium, with everything "in the most wretched confusion." He found one of Porter's aides ludicrously reading McClellan's premature congratulations to Porter on his defensive stand even as that defense disintegrated. While the center of his line collapsed Porter began to lay the groundwork for his historical exoneration. "The enemy again massed his fresher and re-formed regiments and threw them in rapid succession against our thinned and wearied battalions, now almost out of ammunition, and with guns so foul that they could not be loaded rapidly," he recounted. Nevertheless, Porter wrote, the enemy was driven back, though the Union lines had been seriously compromised in the center of Morrell's position. All was not yet lost, at least according to Porter.[44]

---

42 Porter, "The Battle of Gaines's Mill," 319.

43 Ibid., 322.

44 Merritt, "Life and Services of General Philip St. George Cooke," 89; Porter, "The Battle of Gaines's Mill," 322.

Cooke and his officers in the cavalry, however, saw things differently. In their view only the cavalry could save Porter's corps from annihilation. "This attack was stubbornly resisted," reported Colonel Arnold, who witnessed the disintegration of the left and center. This was no soldierly retreat but more of a pell-mell rout, "the men scattering and pushing to the rear as fast as possible. The reserved artillery was thus left without any support, and some of the batteries limbered up and moved to the rear."[45]

At 6:00 p.m., with the daylight waning fast, Pickett's brigade suddenly materialized out of the smoke-shrouded woods and made a beeline for the V Corps's artillery. Cooke rode up to the guns and ordered their commander to "go into battery and he would support him." Cooke reported, "I observed all the infantry of the left wing, in rear of which was my position, giving way, and three batteries, which in reserve positions had been silent the whole day, opened a violent fire upon the advancing lines of the enemy." Cooke marshalled his meager force just to the rear of the batteries. The cavalry had work to do.[46]

A storm of case shot wreaked havoc on the advancing infantry, but did not stop their advance. With the steadiness of veterans, Pickett's men advanced inexorably up the slope, wasting no time to load and fire. It was going to be cold steel. Once the range dropped to 100 yards the Union guns switched to canister, tearing huge gaps in the center of the Rebel ranks. Men dropped by the dozens as the gunners served their pieces like men possessed. The Confederate lines staggered, then wavered. Just as it seemed that they would be forced back, the batteries began going silent; they were running out of ammunition. Frantic gunners tried to limber up their pieces, but with the onrushing enemy so close, this proved impossible. The decimated crews fled for their lives. Catching their breath, the Rebels leapt forward and climbed up and over the crest of the plateau. On the backside of the hill, the cavalry's position came into full view, and the troopers were quickly exposed to a withering fire.

The Rev. W. H. Hitchcock's memories of the Battle of Gaines' Mill remained vivid two decades later. He claimed to be so close to General Cooke and Captain Whiting that he heard everything that transpired between them. "Captain," ordered Cooke, "as soon as you see the advancing line of the enemy, rising the crest of the hill, charge at once, without any further orders, to enable the artillery to bring off the guns." As the command "Draw Sabers" was relayed up and down the thin line

---

45 Arnold, "The Cavalry at Gaines' Mill," 357.

46 Ibid., 358; *OR* 11, pt. 2, 41.

of mounted men, the shimmering bayonets of the enemy topped the hill about 50 yards away. "Captain Whiting at once gave the order, 'Trot! March! and as soon as we were fully under way he shouted 'Charge!'" recalled Hitchcock. "We dashed forward with a wild cheer." Starting from behind the batteries, the orderly lines of horsemen had to veer to the right and left of the guns. When they emerged in front of the artillery, they had lost most of their unit cohesion. "Arriving near the line," reported Arnold, "we were received by a heavy fire from the right and front, the effect of which placed all the officers except one, *hors de combat* and quite a few of the men. . . . A part of the command passed forward and through the ranks of the enemy, while fragments turned to the right and moved to the rear."[47]

It looked as though the line of mounted men had simply disappeared into a cloud of smoke. In the face of such impetuosity, the Rebel attack wavered and in some places stalled, never to regain its momentum. "The charge of the Fifth Cavalry," bemoaned Cooke in his after action report, "failed to be carried home." When fate plucked Capt. William P. Chambliss from his saddle, "[it] threw the rest of the line into disorder. Its success, beyond enabling the batteries to get off was impossible. It lost most severely and did not rally." To make matters worse, a battery of Federal guns 400 yards behind the firing line, "in the obscurity of evening and smoke and dust, opened a fire of shrapnel, which fell among us instead of the enemy." It was too much to bear, and Cooke, having heard several times that Porter had ordered a retreat, ordered the men to retire. Cooke reported losses of nine officers and 92 men killed, wounded, or missing, and 128 horses destroyed.[48]

The post-battle recriminations began almost immediately. Unsurprisingly, the attacks came from the biggest loser of them all, Fitz John Porter. In his official report the V Corps commander placed the blame for the disaster squarely on the cavalry in general, and on Cooke in particular. The devastating charges sealed the fate of Cooke's long, storied career. Porter's official report was as lengthy as it was self-serving. "All appeared to be doing well, our troops withdrawing in order to the cover of the guns, the enemy retiring, and victory, so far as possession of the field was concerned, had already settled upon our banners, when, to my great surprise, the artillery on the left were thrown into confusion by a charge of cavalry coming from the front," he wrote in astonishment. Agitated by the heavy enemy fire, "the bewildered horses, regardless of the efforts of the riders, wheeled about, and

---

47 W. H. Hitchcock, "Recollections of a Participant in the Charge," *The Century Magazine* (September 1885), Vol. 30, No. 5, 779; Arnold, "The Cavalry at Gaines' Mill," 359.

48 OR 11, pt. 2, 442.

dash[ed] through the batteries. . . . To this alone is to be attributed our failure to hold the battle-field and to bring off all our guns and wounded."[49]

Shocked by the effrontery of Porter's accusations, cavalry officers responded with indignation. "Instead of censure, the highest praise should have been awarded to it [the cavalry], for thus sacrificing itself to support the batteries which otherwise would have retired without checking the victorious enemy, who were about to envelop our left and center," complained Colonel Arnold. "This combined effort, of the batteries and cavalry, giving time and opportunity to our infantry to retreat to a safe position, where, with fresh troops the enemy was held at bay until too late in the day for him to make another attack."[50]

Merritt would eventually come to the aid of his beleaguered mentor. In early 1864, with two stars on his shoulder straps to add more credence to his claims as well as increased protection from Cooke's detractors, he wrote to the army's adjutant general. "Sir," he began,

> There are a thousand and one misrepresentations in regard to the operations of the cavalry at Gaines' Mill, arising from statements of persons who were ignorant of the facts or circulated falsehood maliciously. The cavalry did much on that field to restore the fortunes of the day in charging and supporting under the most merciless fire batteries which otherwise, on account of having no supports, would have been obliged to retire much earlier than they did, thus suspending a fire that kept the enemy in check.[51]

In a more subtle defense, Arnold suggested that "[n]ot one of the officers connected with the batteries, we were supporting—in submitting their reports—made any allusion to having lost their guns through the conduct of the cavalry."[52]

Unfortunately, the fog of war clouded many vantage points on that hard-fought field, and some eyewitness accounts place part of the blame on the cavalry. The division commander on that part of the line, Brig. Gen. George Morell, described the effects of the cavalry's withdrawal. "General Cooke's cavalry, having been repulsed in a charge upon the enemy's right, rode at full speed obliquely through a large portion of the artillery, carrying men and horses along with them." The Prince de Joinville, a member of McClellan's staff who witnessed

---

49 OR 11, pt. 2, 225-226; Porter, "The Battle of Gaines's Mill," 322-323.

50 Arnold, "The Cavalry at Gaines' Mill," 362.

51 OR 11, pt. 2, 43.

52 Arnold, "The Cavalry at Gaines' Mill," 362.

the retreat, was extremely laudatory in a subsequent chance meeting with General Cooke; but he also noted that "[t]he fusillade and cannonade are so violent that the projectiles striking the ground raise a permanent cloud of dust. At that moment General Cooke charged at the head of the cavalry; but that movement does not succeed, and his horsemen on their return only increase the disorder. He makes every effort, aided by all who felt a little courage, to stop the panic, but in vain."[53]

Morell conceded that the "cavalry reformed under the hill beyond the reach of musketry, and advancing . . . imparted some steadiness to the infantry near them." Continuing his report, Morell inadvertently opened a new line of accusations by stating that he had "urged their immediate commanding officer, Colonel Blake . . . to make a demonstration on our left, which he seemed disposed to do, when he received a peremptory order from General Cooke to retire from the field, and they rode at a brisk pace to the rear." Porter himself would later claim that "[m]ost unaccountably this cavalry was not used to cover our retreat or gather the stragglers, but was peremptorily ordered to cross to the south bank of the river. I never again saw their commander."[54]

According to Merritt, nothing could have been further from the truth. In 1885, as superintendent of West Point, he wrote to Cooke (who was still seeking vindication) and described his recollections of the final stages of the battle. "The cavalry remained, with you in immediate command, on that portion of the field, until after midnight . . . the last force to leave the field and cross the Chickahominy, and the bridge on which it crossed . . . rendered impassable by your order."[55]

The morass of accusations and finger-pointing gained impetus in 1862 when Fitz John Porter was relieved of his command by Maj. Gen. John Pope for disobedience, disloyalty, and misconduct in the face of the enemy. The charges led to Porter's dismissal from the service in early 1863, and spawned a controversy that would rage for almost 24 years until his reinstatement to the army rolls in August 1886. Cooke wasted little time in pouncing on the discredited Porter. In January 1864, while perusing a copy of McClellan's final report of the operations of the Army of the Potomac, Cooke read McClellan's derogatory extract of his actions at Gaines' Mill. McClellan's version was in large measure based on his friend Porter's report of the battle. "They write in the same spirit, they use the same materials, and they work to a common end," complained Cooke, "thus showing a mutual

---

53 OR 11, pt. 2, 273; Cooke, "The Charge of Cooke's Cavalry," 778.

54 OR 11, pt. 2, 273; Porter, "The Battle of Gaines's Mill," 323.

55 Cooke, "The Charge of Cooke's Cavalry," 777.

understanding, as was to have been expected from their intimacy during the war." Livid with rage, Cooke ripped into McClellan. "The whole paragraph . . . is essentially false." It was the cavalry, declared Cooke, that managed "to save some of the artillery and some of the honor of an army after it had suddenly retreated in disorder." Cooke dared the war department to publish further information.[56]

Ever loyal, Merritt once again rose to the defense of his mentor. "I thought at the time, and subsequent experience has convinced me," he argued, "that your cavalry and the audacity of its conduct at the time, together with the firing of canister at short range by the battery mentioned, did much, if not everything, toward preventing the entire destruction of the Union army at Gaines's Mill."[57]

Merritt's view of McClellan and of the army's politics would be forever tainted by the tawdry affair. "The fact that I know General Cooke felt keenly this aspersion on his character as a soldier has induced me to give more extended notice to this episode in his military career," he wrote. Merritt's pent-up bitterness was evident: "The events of that day at Gaines' Mill are pictured on the mind of the writer of this imperfect sketch as on a never fading photograph." Merritt was particularly offended by McClellan's statement that Cooke "was relieved from command for his part in the battle of Gaines' Mill." Merritt knew better; Cooke had resigned in protest at his own request. The exhausted old cavalier was done dealing "with the incompetence of his superiors in the handling and treatment of the cavalry."[58]

"He was the incarnation of a cavalry soldier," wrote Merritt in 1873 in a heartfelt tribute to his mentor on his retirement after 46 years of service. "His greatest ambition was to excel in this, his favorite arm. On the frontier he gloried in making long and rapid marches without injury to his horses. During the war he was among those who thought that the legitimate sphere of cavalry action was mounted and in the crisis of battle." The first real test of the "hussar school" of tactics had been found wanting.[59]

---

56 Boatner, *The Civil War Dictionary*, 661-662; "General McClellan's Change of Base," *North American Review* (October 1885), Vol. 141, No. 347, 335; OR 11, pt. 2, 43.

57 Cooke, "The Charge of Cooke's Cavalry," 778.

58 Merritt, "Life and Services of General Philip St. George Cooke," 90-91.

59 Ibid., 92.

CHAPTER FOUR

An Army Cannot Dawdle

ROBERT E. LEE'S AGGRESSIVE maneuvering knocked the methodical McClellan—who was already convinced he was outnumbered two to one—completely off stride and dealt "Little Mac's" grandiose plans several embarrassments. First was Stuart's earlier foray, conducted with such impunity and élan, around the Army of the Potomac. Then "Stonewall" Jackson, recalled from the Shenandoah Valley, arrived off his right flank on June 26, which was assailed in front at Beaver Dam Creek by A. P. Hill. On June 27, Lee coalesced an array of forces against Fitz John Porter's V Corps, isolated on the north side of the Chickahominy River at Gaines' Mill, and attacked. The hammering Southern assaults eventually broke through Porter's front late in the day and nearly destroyed the right wing of the Federal command. Fortunately for McClellan, Jackson had failed to reach his assigned position and attack as planned. Lee's carefully crafted trap was simply too complex for a large green command to execute as designed, though it did succeed in turning the Union threat away from Richmond.

Taking heed of his fears, McClellan gave up any hope that Irvin McDowell would reach the area of operations in time to be of any help and decided to withdraw from the approaches to Richmond and regroup the army at Harrison's Landing on the James River. Despite his outward optimism, a deep anxiety gnawed at McClellan. "After deducting the garrisons in rear, the railroad guards, non-combatants, and extra-duty men, there were not more than 75,000 men for battle. I now bent all my energies to the transfer of the army to the James," he later rationalized, "fully realizing the very delicate nature of a flank march, with heavy

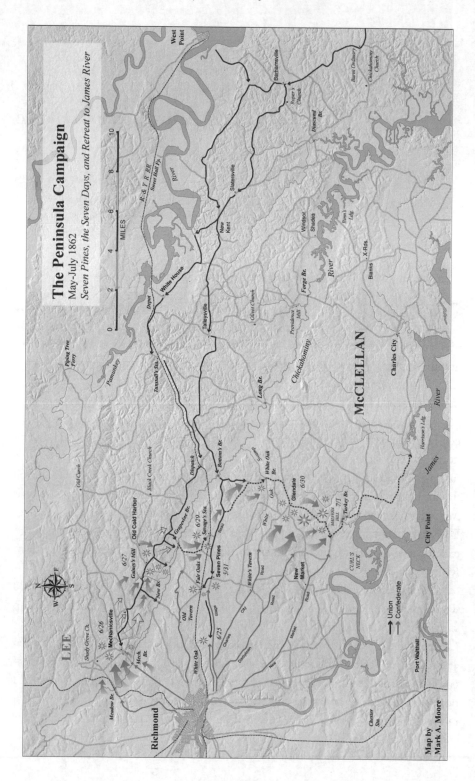

The Peninsula Campaign
May–July 1862
Seven Pines, the Seven Days, and Retreat to James River

Map by
Mark A. Moore

trains, by a single road, in the face of an active enemy, but confident that I had the army well in hand."[1]

The day after the fighting at Gaines' Mill, McClellan put the army in motion. He directed the transfer of the carefully accumulated horde of supplies at White House and ordered the destruction of the storage facilities there. The Army of the Potomac gratefully said goodbye to the pestilential swamp lands of the Chickahominy and headed south, making its way across the Peninsula while fighting off constant Rebel attacks. On the morning of July 1, the Federals began to concentrate on Malvern Hill.

Posted in an "admirable position," McClellan felt able to face the impending battle "with perfect confidence." By then, his chief worry had been removed, as his ponderous wagon trains were parked at Haxall's plantation, safe under the covering fire of the navy's gunboats. When that movement was successfully accomplished, a satisfied McClellan wrote, "The Army of the Potomac was at last in a position on its true line of operations, with its trains intact." Once again, the mantle of protector of the nation lay heavy on McClellan's shoulders. Once again, he alone could save the Union. And once again, his self-doubt would rule his judgment, failing both the country and the men of the Army of the Potomac.[2]

On July 1, the bloody repulse of the Confederate piecemeal assaults at Malvern Hill brought The Seven Days' Battles to an end. Every member of McClellan's staff, including aide-de-camp Custer, labored through four grueling days of unrelenting activity to ensure that the army remained in sync with the commanding general's orders. "Dear Brother and Sister—The rebels came nearer being successful in this engagement than any other," he wrote on July 13. "I was in the saddle four consecutive nights and as many days. I generally had but one meal—coffee and hard bread—breakfast." Yet somehow Custer managed to live up to his well- known reputation for stamina. At one point Colonel Grier, commander of the 5th U.S. Cavalry, told General Stoneman that Custer could "eat and sleep as much as anyone when he has the chance. But he can do without either when necessary!"[3]

On August 8, a 300-man detachment of cavalry under the command of Col. William Woods Averell moved out on a 40-mile reconnaissance of Confederate lines near White Oak Swamp, hoping to "surprise a regiment of cavalry stationed

1 McClellan, "The Peninsular Campaign," 2:180-181.

2 Ibid., 2:186.

3 Merington, *The Custer Story*, 27, 32.

there." In the greater scope of things, the smallish action (officially listed as the "Skirmish at White Oak Swamp Bridge") was just another in a string of inconsequential events in which men would die, suffer horrendous injury, or perhaps find themselves within the hands of the enemy as prisoners of war hoping for an expeditious parole or exchange. Custer's narrative of the affair, which is contained in a letter to his sister, reveals two interesting points. First, Custer's frame of mind in regard to his ever-more complicated and evolving view of war, and second, it affords an unvarnished, raw, and inglorious view of life and death at the small unit level.[4]

Averell's detachment arrived at the Rebel encampment around 11:00 a.m. and instantly moved to the attack. "Away we went, whooping and yelling lustily," recorded Custer. "The rebels broke and scattered, we following as fast as our horses could go." The officer now focused his attention on a Confederate officer. "I took deliberate aim at his body and fired. He sat for a moment in his saddle, reeled and fell to the ground, his horse ran on and mine also. Lieutenant Byrnes," continued Custer, "told me that he saw him after he fell, and that he rose to his feet, turned around, threw up his hands and fell to the ground with a stream of blood gushing from his mouth."[5]

Custer's account of that skirmish is, like many of his missives home, lengthy, detailed, and set forth with the relish of a big game hunter on safari. Exhilarated by the chase, Custer declared it "the most exciting sport I ever engaged in." Throughout the narrative he invokes the spirit of a hunt in the far reaches of America's "Wild West," using terms such as "I selected him as my game," "exciting in the extreme," "seemed to enjoy the sport," and "a splendid trophy." It was a terrible dichotomy: death, pain, and suffering on the one hand, and the adrenalin-pumping exhilaration of a sport where the game shoots back "and every leap of the charging steed is a peril escaped or dashed aside" on the other. In October, still grappling with the issue, he wrote to his cousin Augusta Ward, seeking solace and understanding. "You ask me if I will not be glad when the last

---

4 Cautious by nature, Averell would thrive when acting independently. He joined the Mounted Rifles in 1855 after graduating from West Point. Seriously wounded in combat in New Mexico in 1858, he was on the disabled list until the outbreak of the war. Considered old fashioned by the new breed of young cavalry officers coming up through the ranks, Averell would prove to be obdurate and dilatory under the direction of superior officers, eventually finding himself relieved from command on two occasions.

5 Whittaker, *A Popular Life of Gen. George A. Custer*, 123-124.

battle is fought," he started by way of reply to her previous letter. "I must say," he continued,

> that I shall regret to see the war end. I would be willing, yes glad, to see a battle every day during my life . . . when I think of the pain and misery produced to individuals as well as the miserable sorrow caused throughout the land I cannot but earnestly hope for peace, and at an early date. Do you understand me?[6]

One Last Hurrah for the General, Lads!

Averell cited Captain Custer in his after-action report for "gallant and spirited conduct." The exhilaration of the August 5 skirmish quickly dissipated in light of the news that met the returning troopers: The Army of the Potomac would withdraw from the Peninsula and join the command of Maj. Gen. John Pope, forming the new Army of Virginia. Thus began the final, convoluted phase of McClellan's lackluster career.[7]

As soon as his field desk was set up at Harrison's Landing, McClellan began to badger Lincoln and Stanton for more men to continue the offensive against Richmond. But the two savvy veterans of the political power wars, having learned their lesson on previous occasions, inserted a layer of command between themselves and McClellan's constant carping. They chose Maj. Gen. Henry Wager Halleck for that arduous task. His appointment as commander of "the land-forces of the United States as general-in-chief" was signed by the president on July 11, 1862. Halleck reported to Washington forthwith and on his arrival in the capital on July 23, he immediately went to Harrison's Landing to confer with McClellan as to the course of future operations.[8]

Halleck spent July 25 closeted with McClellan, and for hours forced himself to listen as the aggrieved commander of the Army of the Potomac alternated between pontificating about lofty military principles and pleading his case for another chance at immortal glory. Two days later, Halleck filed a report on this meeting with Secretary Stanton. "He expressed the opinion that with 30,000 reinforcements he could attack Richmond with a 'good chance of success,'" noted Halleck dutifully. "I replied that I was authorized by the President to promise only 20,000,

---

6 Ibid., 123-124, 157-158; Wert, *Custer*, 59.

7 *OR* 11, pt. 2, 955.

8 Fry, "McClellan and His 'Mission,'" 941.

and that if he could not take Richmond with that number, we must devise some plan for withdrawing his troops." McClellan's initial impression of Halleck plummeted, and in later life he was wont to declare that "of all the men I have encountered in high position, Halleck was the most hopelessly stupid. . . . I do not think he ever had a correct military idea from beginning to end." There was just cause for the strained relationship, wrote one veteran staffer. "His peninsula campaign had failed, his army had been brought back to Washington against his will, and Halleck had superseded him as Commander-in-Chief." Halleck's sharply administered slap in the face certainly stung McClellan's pride.[9]

On August 23 McClellan took one last nostalgic tour of the deserted campsites along the James River and then boarded a steamer for Washington with his staff. It must have been a dreary passage, for McClellan's return as a has-been general without a command meant that his staff had lost their jobs as well. Custer found himself once again waiting for a new assignment.

Less than a week later, Lee struck Pope near the old Bull Run battlefield, deftly coordinating Jackson's and Longstreet's commands to crush the Union's left flank and force Pope's army back toward Washington. The Federal army suffered losses of 16,054 killed, wounded, and missing, and the Confederates counted 9,197 casualties. President Lincoln reluctantly fired Pope and reinstated the last man on earth he wanted to see commanding a Union army, a general who had lost 15,849 soldiers on the Peninsula without a single tangible result other than inflicting higher casualties on the Rebels, which were reported as 19,749 men.

Lincoln, however, possessed no other recourse than to reappoint McClellan on September 2 to command "the fortifications of Washington, and all the troops for the defense of the capital." He had little choice: Lee was at the Potomac River and there was no army in the field to oppose him. It was a controversial move and much of Lincoln's cabinet objected. "We must use what tools we have," he explained to his secretary John Hay. "There is no man in the Army who can man these fortifications and lick these troops of ours into shape half as well as he. If he can't fight himself, he excels in making others ready to fight." McClellan's dealings with the president and his subordinates had turned into one of those embarrassing on-again, off-again relationships that satisfied no one, left the participants spent, and gave an impression of desperation.

On September 4 Lee began crossing the Potomac into Maryland, boldly pushing the war onto Northern soil. This time, nothing unfolded as Lee had

9 Ibid., 942, 943.

planned. When the garrison at Harpers Ferry failed to withdraw, Lee divided his army in a dangerous attempt to besiege and capture it. Jackson, with a majority of the Army of Northern Virginia, moved to encircle the garrison while Longstreet and Lee remained behind the South Mountain range near Hagerstown with what remained of the army. McClellan, meanwhile, reorganized the Union forces around Washington in record time and began pushing westward much faster than Lee believed possible. Skirmishes broke out on September 13 at Catoctin Mountain, Middletown, and Jefferson as the head of the Army of the Potomac pressed west to find the enemy. The next day McClellan surprised his opponent by driving aggressively into the South Mountain passes at Crampton's, Fox's, and Turner's gaps. The under-strength defenders there under Maj. Gen. D. H. Hill were unable to hold their positions and were mostly in retreat by nightfall. Federal troops had wrested control of the high ground away from the Confederates and camped that night on a victorious field of battle for the first time in the war. The victory opened a clear path into the rear of Lee's widely separated army.[10]

Unwilling to retreat to Virginia, Lee regrouped around Sharpsburg after Harpers Ferry fell. He spent the entire day of September 17 fighting off McClellan's assaults in the bloodiest single day in American history at Antietam. Although a tactical draw, the battered Virginia army had suffered a major strategic defeat and was unable to continue its campaign north of the Potomac. Lee withdrew on the evening of September 18. "You are perhaps, in doubt whether I am still among the living or numbered with the dead. These few lines will show you that I belong with the former," wrote George Custer as he shared the news with his sister that he had survived the carnage. "We have fought three battles, one the greatest ever fought on this continent." Custer mistakenly overestimated the impact of the battle on McClellan's fortunes. "General McClellan . . . by his last campaign in Maryland has put it beyond the power of the most lying to injure him."[11]

Lincoln realized that the political and military climate was as good as it was going to get, and on September 22 issued his preliminary Emancipation

---

10 For an outstanding treatment of the South Mountain events, see Brian Matthew Jordan, *Unholy Sabbath: The Battle of South Mountain in History and Memory, September 14, 1862* (El Dorado Hills, CA, 2012).

11 Recent scholarship of the Maryland Campaign has reexamined McClellan's decision-making in a fresh light, although it remains controversial. See, for example, Steven R. Stotelmyer, *Too Useful to Sacrifice: Reconsidering George B. McClellan's Generalship in the Maryland Campaign from South Mountain to Antietam* (El Dorado Hills, CA, 2019); Whittaker, *A Popular Life of Gen. George A. Custer*, 125-126, 129; also in Merington, *The Custer Story*, 34.

A frustrated President Lincoln (center) confronts General McClellan at his headquarters near Sharpsburg, Maryland. Captain George Armstrong Custer is visible on the far right wearing a broad-brimmed slouch hat. *LOC*

Proclamation, which was to take effect on the first day of 1863. In McClellan's eyes this news superseded the glorious achievements of his victorious army, and instead focused the war on the issue of slavery. As Custer would later explain to his father-in-law, Judge Daniel Bacon, "Throughout the war I never heard slavery mentioned as an issue. The Union—it was the Union we were fighting for!" And Lieutenant Sanford adamantly declared that although slaves of Southern plantation owners were "not actually forbidden to enter our lines," the majority opinion within the Army of the Potomac held "that they were not wanted."[12]

In early October Lincoln visited with McClellan at his headquarters near Sharpsburg. Try as he might, Lincoln was never able to make a dent in McClellan's firmly held belief that the future of the nation was in his hands, and in those of the men of his army. For hours Lincoln listened to McClellan's time-worn complaints and requests—more men, more horses, more supplies, more time. Only this time Lincoln made up his mind that enough was enough; on November 5, he fired McClellan once again and selected Maj. Gen. Ambrose E. Burnside as his replacement.

---

12 Merington, *The Custer Story*, 56; Hagemann, *Fighting Rebels and Redskins*, 161.

Burnside, most famous for his mutton chop whiskers, had enjoyed early success in command of Union forces in North Carolina, where he established a base that was valuable in maintaining the naval blockade of the South. His later record fell short, particularly as leader of the IX Corps at Antietam. Burnside freely admitted his own shortcomings as a potential army commander, and in fact had refused the post on two prior occasions. The story spread throughout the army that Burnside had tearfully begged McClellan to stay a few more days in order to help him over the hump.[13]

Shortly after the announcement, Maj. James H. Wilson, McClellan's aide-de-camp and topographical engineer, visited headquarters and found the staff on the edge of rebellion. "I found a bad state of feeling among the officers of his staff, three of whom were drinking heavily, while others were talking both loudly and disloyally," recounted a perturbed and disapproving Wilson. In abrasively loud voices they called on McClellan to disobey his orders, retain his command, and march on Washington. "One of the number in a loud and resonant voice declared that he wouldn't serve Lincoln's abolition government any longer," Wilson recalled in disgust, "but intended to send in his resignation and go home at once."[14]

Was Custer one of the instigators? Was his one of the voices that was raised in such anguish? Witnesses placed him at the heart of the disturbance, but no names were ever mentioned. Whether Custer took the lead in advocating for the near insurrection will always inspire speculation, but McClellan knew. He had heard the commotion and his sense of duty was deeply offended; his arrival in their midst immediately produced an embarrassed silence. He addressed his unruly staff in a low, sad voice and they were chastened. "He told them how surprised and grieved he was to hear such sentiments from men who had served with the Army of the Potomac," wrote Frederick Whittaker. "He reminded them that he and they were soldiers . . . and bound to obey the nation they served, whatever its orders might be."[15]

On the morning of November 10, 1862, McClellan took his time riding out of the army's camps. Snow had blanketed the landscape just a few days earlier, providing a stark contrast with the rich blues of the uniforms and overcoats worn

---

13 Before the war, Burnside had invented a .54-caliber breech-loading carbine. Although unsuccessful commercially, the Burnside carbine was adopted by the Union army and was produced in significant numbers.

14 Wilson, *Under the Old Flag*, 1:126.

15 Whittaker, *A Popular Life of Gen. George A. Custer*, 132-133.

by McClellan's brokenhearted troops. Brigade after brigade lined the Centreville Pike and wept shameless tears for their loss. They roared out their love for the man who had made them into soldiers, and who had instilled in them a pride in arms that would last to the end of their time on earth. They would forever be McClellan's Army—"Little Mac's" men. The general rode his horse effortlessly, a dapper little man astride one of the black, full-blooded chargers he favored, made taller in the saddle by the occasion. He took solace in the knowledge that he had cared as best he could for the lives and welfare of the men entrusted to his care.

Eventually he came to the last two corps of the army: Sumner's II on one side of the pike, and Porter's V on the other. They could hear him coming. The shouts and yells and cheers preceded him like the roar of a massive wave crashing with all of nature's fury against a craggy cliff side—10,000 men cheering for all they were worth. In an instant their caps came off, waving high in the sullen light of the wintry day. Then McClellan was parading through the throng, "one of the handsomest men on horseback in the Federal service," sitting his horse with a "grace and ease peculiarly his own, [and] all his appointments were in the most correct taste." The moment passed too soon, and the men's last view of their beloved commander was blocked by the staff that herded behind him, George Custer among them. When he disappeared over the horizon, the pageantry of war left with him, leaving behind only a grim determination to see the deed done, and to go home.[16]

The newly unemployed George Custer returned home to await orders. The most momentous event that occurred during this interlude was his meeting with Libbie Bacon at a Thanksgiving party in Monroe. He stayed in Michigan until the middle of December; as a result, he missed the battle of Fredericksburg, although the cavalry played only a minor role in that disastrous defeat. He returned for a brief stay with the army, possibly putting out feelers for a future posting. He visited with Brig. Gen. Andrew A. Humphreys, ostensibly on behalf of Lt. Jim Christiancy, the son of one of Custer's future benefactors. More than likely, he sought an appointment for himself on the staff of the 3rd Division of the V Corps. Custer returned to Monroe in time for the holiday season and remained on furlough until April 1863.

Custer itched to get back to the army, and when his leave expired he departed Monroe and reported for duty at the war department. Mentally prepared to return to battle, a surprised Custer was informed that his services had been requested by the former commander of the Army of the Potomac. In the aftermath of his

16 "Generals in the Saddle," *Southern Historical Society Papers*, 19:169.

removal from command, McClellan found himself promptly banished to his home in Trenton, New Jersey; Lincoln, however, had allowed him to retain his rank and perquisites. Unwilling to abide exile in the backwaters of the war, McClellan soon managed to get his posting changed to New York City, the business and financial heart of the country. He took up temporary residence at the Fifth Avenue Hotel before moving into an ostentatious mansion provided by some of his many admirers. The day after his arrival, Custer met with the McClellans, spending a grand evening in talk and reminiscences. Spellbound by Mrs. McClellan, Custer "could find no words for his admiration."[17]

The next day, the serious work of securing George Brinton McClellan's place in history began. *The Official Report of the Army of the Potomac* was a study in self-aggrandizement, with Custer its most willing contributor. After its publication, the *New York Times* deemed it to be nothing more than "a McClellan memoir printed at government expense." Dismissing the *Times* as "among the most prominent of the vile sheets that have assailed General McClellan," Custer wrote to Judge Bacon in spirited defense of his mentor. "Although by politicians abused, dishonored, disgraced, he will yet come forth. If in command without interference from persons intending to do right, but whose plans are the ruin of the Army, every soldier will follow, for he is no blind guide." In Custer's eyes, McClellan would always be a martyr to the political agenda of the government. Years later he would write, "The defeat of McClellan was not the result of . . . the open opposition of enemies in his front, but the half-hidden interference of foes in his rear.[18]

Despite the continuous attacks on McClellan, his celebrity could not be denied. The social pages of the New York dailies were replete with accounts of his attendance at the many gala events of the well-to-do—lavish parties, the theater, the opera, and hobnobbing with the rich and famous, including August Belmont, chairman of the Democratic National Committee. A firm believer in the need for a military presence in Lincoln's cabinet, Belmont also worked assiduously to convince McClellan to seek the party's nomination for president in the 1864 election. For the fun-loving Custer these were heady times, and in a country bumpkin kind of way he fondly remembered his "first introduction to the financial,

17 Reynolds, *The Civil War Memories of Elizabeth Bacon Custer*, 77.

18 Stephen W. Sears, *George B. McClellan: The Young Napoleon* (New York, 1988), 352; Whittaker, *A Popular Life of Gen. George A. Custer*, 129; Merington, *The Custer Story*, 52; Carroll, *Custer in the Civil War*, 112-113.

political and journalistic elite of the metropolis." Accompanying the McClellans, he was often spotted dining at some of the city's best restaurants.[19]

But all the gaiety of New York's nightlife couldn't conceal the rancor that simmered just below the surface, a bitterness as palpable as a suppurating wound. Even a decade after the end of the war, the controversy endured. While travelling in Europe after Custer's death, Libbie was asked about her husband's relationship with McClellan. "I found the hottest discussions were going on regarding General McClellan," she recalled, "and sometimes the vehemence of his admirers got them in trouble, for feeling ran so high it broke friendships and made an officer a target for persecution. It did no good to try and defend General McClellan with the fanatics who persecuted him."[20]

Custer uncharacteristically stayed silent. As one of McClellan's most ardent supporters, he had no immunity from this discord. In the latter stages of the war, he would recall a note he received from a prominent U.S. senator while his confirmation to brigadier general languished before that august body. "Sir: Your appointment as brigadier-general U.S. Volunteers has been sent to the Senate. Before I can vote for your confirmation, I desire to be informed whether you are what is termed 'A McClellan man.'" Flabbergasted, Custer pointed out to a ranking officer that in the space of a few short weeks he had three horses shot from under him and had personally led two successful charges at enemy batteries, which resulted in their capture. "All this was known to the Senator," wrote Custer with a pen dipped in acid. "Yet these facts were to go for naught if, forsooth, it should be ascertained that I was what is termed a McClellan man. . . . This incident shows the extent and bitterness of the opposition which McClellan encountered."[21]

Trained by the Best

As the Army of the Potomac headed into yet another round of misery, discomfort, and hardship in the brutal winter of 1862-63, its morale, already teetering on the edge, threatened to plunge into discontent. McClellan's dismissal still rankled. "On the 7th (of November) a light snow fell so that on the morning of the next day the ground was covered," wrote newly promoted Captain Sanford, an

---

19 John C. Calder, "President George Armstrong Custer," *Research Review: The Journal of the Little Big Horn Associates* (Winter 2005), Vol. 19, No. 1, 15.

20 Reynolds, *The Civil War Memories of Elizabeth Bacon Custer*, 78.

21 Carroll, *Custer in the Civil War*, 113.

unapologetic McClellan supporter. "Soon after reveille that morning and while expecting the order to move, an aide de camp brought the news that General McClellan had been relieved . . . and that Burnside was to command the army. It was a wretched morning greeting, and a very miserable body of men who received it."[22]

To make matters worse, the two heterogeneous elements composing the army never melded into one. Sanford would describe their relationship—perhaps with some understatement—as "by no means cordial." The authorities and the press showed McClellan's former divisions the cold shoulder, disheartening the veterans of the Peninsula. Pope's former command, meanwhile, threatened to slip into an irreversible bout of demoralization. "The condition of this force . . . was exceedingly bad," assessed Sanford. The men reeled from "the rough handling they had received and the ease with which their leaders had been out-manoeuvred by Lee and Jackson."[23]

Seemingly unending bouts of rain and mud became the foundation of the squalor of camp life. The entire army seemed to write about it in letters home or in memoirs. Typical of the experiences of other troopers, Capt. James H. Kidd described his regiment's first foray from its camps near Washington in early February. "The night was dark and dismal," he starkly remembered. "The rain began to fall. It was cold and raw, the air surcharged with moisture, chilling one to the marrow. . . . It was a sorry scene; and a sullen welcome to the soil of Virginia, that was then as often before and afterwards, a slippery, sticky mud." A few months later the situation was unchanged. "The rain fell constantly during the whole time and the country was like a sea," attested Captain Sanford. "We marched all day in the rain and lay down at night in the mud in our wet clothes, often unable to get a cup of coffee owing to the impossibility of making fires with wet wood."[24]

---

22 Hagemann, *Fighting Rebels and Redskins*, 188.

23 Ibid., 171.

24 James H. Kidd, *Personal Recollections of a Cavalryman with Custer's Michigan Cavalry Brigade in the Civil War* (Ionia, MI, 1908), 88-89. When the war began, Kidd did not believe it would last very long and decided to continue his studies at the University of Michigan. Pursuing a career in journalism, he spent much of his time interning at the *Detroit Free Press*. By 1862 he had changed his mind about the direction of the war and sought a post in one of the new cavalry regiments being organized by Congressman Francis W. Kellogg. With his easy, outgoing personality, he quickly recruited enough men to earn the rank of captain and the command of Company E, 6th Michigan Cavalry. After the war he returned to journalism, writing and lecturing about his former brigade commander, George Custer; Hagemann, *Fighting Rebels and Redskins*, 197.

Given Burnside's well-known lack of confidence in his own ability to command an army, his decision to advance in the dead of winter against a resilient and experienced foe was either a stroke of genius or evidence of epic stupidity. In Burnside's case, a strong argument can be made for the latter option. His plan led directly to two successive, resounding defeats that proved to be the severest tests of the mettle of the Army of the Potomac to that point in the war.

On December 11, 1862, the army's engineers flung a pontoon bridge across the Rappahannock River directly at the city of Fredericksburg. The infantry regiments supporting them during the construction suffered heavy casualties. The particularly vicious battle culminated in the Federal assault on Marye's Heights on December 13. "It was a horrible business, relieved only by the wonderful gallantry of the men and officers," marveled one member of Burnside's escort who watched from the vantage of his headquarters on the opposite bank. "I think perhaps it was the most desperate piece of fighting in the war, as from the first men realized the utter futility of the attempt. It was simply to go up and be killed without even the hope that finally the position would be taken." To add to the horrors of the battle, entire regiments spent the freezing night amongst the dead, entirely without shelter.[25]

On January 20, 1863, Burnside followed up that disaster with the embarrassment that came to be known as the "Mud March." An unseasonably warm front moved in just before the start of the advance, bringing rain that liquefied the roads. What should have been a bold, surprise move against Lee's left foundered in the treacherous Virginia mud in plain sight of an alert, taunting crowd of Rebels. As wagons and artillery sank axle-deep into the muck, Confederate pickets on the opposite bank called out derisively, volunteering to cross the river and give the struggling Yankees a helping hand. Burnside's mud-caked army retraced its steps to its winter camps, beaten without a shot fired.[26]

On January 26, Burnside's brief tenure as head of the Army of the Potomac came to a merciful close when he handed over command to Maj. Gen. Joseph "Fighting Joe" Hooker. Hooker's long career included service in the Seminole Wars and the war with Mexico. He actively campaigned to obtain a high commission at the start of the war, but was twice rebuffed by the war department. In May 1861, he was finally commissioned a brigadier general in the volunteer service. In the long run fate—and Lee, Longstreet, and Jackson—would not be

---

25 Hagemann, *Fighting Rebels and Redskins*, 192.

26 Ibid., 193-194.

kind to Hooker. Lee demolished Hooker's reputation with Stonewall Jackson's last great assault, on the Union's unguarded right flank at Chancellorsville in May.

In spite of his failures, Hooker left one enduring legacy that undoubtedly contributed to the ultimate victory of the Army of the Potomac. Understanding the need for a cavalry force capable of meeting Stuart and his saddle-bred men on equal terms, Hooker set about organizing the mounted arm "into compact brigades and divisions, remounted and carefully drilled and equipped. That corps certainly owes to General Hooker a debt of gratitude, which it would be difficult to repay. From the date of its reorganization by him until the close of the war, its career was constantly growing more and more glorious, until at the end of the rebellion nothing could stand before the rush of its squadrons."[27]

On February 5, Brig. Gen. George Stoneman left his post as III Corps commander to return to the saddle as head of the Cavalry Corps. The scattered cavalry regiments were aggregated into three divisions, commanded by Brig. Gens. Alfred Pleasonton, William Woods Averell, and David McMurtrie Gregg. The Regular cavalry—the 1st U.S. Cavalry, 2nd U.S. Cavalry, 5th U.S. Cavalry, and 6th U.S. Cavalry, along with the 6th Pennsylvania Cavalry—were organized into the Regular Reserve Cavalry Brigade under the command of the redoubtable John Buford.[28]

"Buford was known throughout the army as 'Old Reliable,'" lauded Captain Kidd, "not because of his age, but for the reason that he rarely if ever failed to be in the right place at the right moment—solid rather than showy, not spectacular but sure." Another contemporary described Buford as follows: "His was a unique character. He was full of dash. . . . He despised ostentation and display of any kind,

---

27 Ibid., 194.

28 Pleasonton, West Point class of 1844, participated in a wide variety of actions before the Civil War, including combat in Texas during the Mexican War, fighting the Apaches in 1848 and the Sioux in 1856, and serving with the 2nd Dragoons in Florida against the Seminoles. As a staff officer to Brig. Gen. William S. Harney, he saw the troubles in "Bleeding Kansas" at close range. Although he attempted to present the suave, debonair facade of a true cavalier, he never managed to attain the panache of his nemesis, Jeb Stuart. After the spectacular failure of the Kilpatrick-Dahlgren raid on Richmond in 1864, Pleasonton was relieved of command of the Cavalry Corps and sent to the Department of Missouri. Modest and self-effacing, Gregg was one of the most experienced and effective cavalry officers in the Army of the Potomac. After graduating from West Point in 1855, he commanded a company of the 1st Dragoons. During the Peninsula campaign, he led the 8th Pennsylvania Cavalry with distinction. Like many of his Old Army contemporaries, Gregg held strong beliefs against the presence of the new breed of news correspondents that permeated the army. As a result, the exploits of his veteran 2nd Cavalry Division rarely made the pages of the nation's most widely read tabloids.

[and was] genial and natural in social intercourse, but a very tiger when aroused." Custer left no known opinion with respect to Buford, having never served under his command.[29]

On the other hand, Custer clearly expressed his low opinion of Stoneman. "With Stoneman, however, it was different," he wrote. In his view, Stoneman, then in the prime of his military life, received the plummest job in the cavalry service. "He failed, however," opined Custer, "in every respect to realize the expectations of those to whom he owed his selection as chief of cavalry. . . . The record of cavalry while operating under Stoneman contains nothing to its credit as a separate organization."[30]

No McClellan Man Here

Wesley Merritt was happy. The young cavalryman greeted McClellan's removal with unconcealed glee, blaming him for the onerous dispersal of the Army of the Potomac's cavalry in trivial duties that "consisted in supplying details as orderlies for mounted staff officers, following them mounted on their rapid rides for pleasure or for duty, or in camp acting as grooms and bootblacks." McClellan had failed Merritt's beloved army, leaving its "cavalry regiments . . . emasculated and disorganized." In his anger and frustration, Merritt lashed out at what he perceived as gross mismanagement. "Nor did he know how to use the cavalry he had in hand. His treatment of cavalry and cavalry commanders was proverbially harsh and unjust." In fact, continued Merritt with some relish, "[i]t was not until McClellan was removed that the cavalry of the Army of the Potomac was fairly organized under Stoneman, with Buford and David Gregg as his lieutenants. . . . From the day of its reorganization under Hooker, the cavalry . . . commenced a new life."[31]

General Cooke had tendered his resignation as soon as the cavalry arrived at Harrison's Landing in the wake of Gaines' Mill. As an immediate consequence, Merritt's career entered a long and arid spell. Cooke returned to Washington to sit on some courts-martial, leaving Merritt to take an extended leave until September

---

29 Kidd, *Personal Recollections of a Cavalryman*, 94; James H. Wilson, "General John Buford," *Journal of the United States Cavalry Association* (July 1888), Vol. 1, No. 2, 143-144.

30 Carroll, *Custer in the Civil War*, 118.

31 Wesley Merritt, "Reminiscences—Beverly Ford to Mitchell's Station (1863)," in Rodenbough, ed., *From Everglade to Cañon*, 284-285.

1862, thus missing the battle of Antietam. Because of his close association with the discredited Cooke, Merritt's career lost some of its luster.

Cooke finally talked Merritt into taking a position on the staff of Maj. Gen. Samuel P. Heintzelman, commander of the Military District of Washington, who was responsible for the capital's defenses. Merritt wrote that he had been lucky "changing horses in the middle of the stream." His duties during the winter of 1862-63 consisted of requisitioning supplies and inspecting cavalry camps. Despite his staff experience, the crash of musketry and the roar of artillery beckoned to Merritt from the distant front. He pictured himself riding into the line of fire at the head of his men, "with his red cheeks and boyish face and airs of Knighthood's days and joust and tourney."[32]

The course of his duties put Merritt in close touch with the cavalry screen that stretched for miles around the city. He disliked the conditions that he saw and attributed all these shortcomings to the aftereffects of McClellan's stewardship. Late in October 1862, a report circulated that pinpointed the problem. "Our cavalry has been constantly occupied in scouting and reconnoissances, and this severe labor has worked down the horses and rendered many of them unserviceable," wrote the observer. "The enemy is well provided with cavalry, while our cavalry force . . . even with every man well mounted, would be inadequate to the requirements of the service." The writer was none other than George McClellan.[33]

McClellan noted that in the opening weeks of the war, Winfield Scott had put the development of the cavalry on a very restricted path to nowhere. "Gen. Scott had little confidence in its ability, or experience in handling it, and from the first had deprecated its use," wrote another observer. "Recognizing the great length of time required to train men and animals for this service and apparently believing that the war would be of but-short duration, he considered it as on the whole advisable to confine its use within the smallest limits possible."[34]

Sadly, McClellan—who always believed that the Union was just one grand campaign away from total victory over the Confederacy—did nothing to change the trajectory of cavalry development brought on by Scott's antiquarian thinking. For his part, Merritt could not resist taking one last shot at "Little Mac." "If General McClellan had organized his cavalry properly in first place," he jabbed,

---

32 Alberts, *General Wesley Merritt*, 42; Swift, "General Wesley Merritt," 832.

33 Merritt, "Reminiscences," 284.

34 Hagemann, *Fighting Rebels and Redskins*, 184.

"treated it in a becoming manner, and used it only for its legitimate objects, he would never have had to make the report recorded in the foregoing paragraph."[35]

Joe Hooker immediately implemented a multi-faceted program for raising the Union cavalry up to the level of combativeness exemplified by the Southern horsemen. His time was limited, for the spring campaign season was fast approaching. This lofty if not daunting goal entailed recruiting, arming, equipping, and training over two dozen regiments of citizen-soldiers, many with their ranks filled with raw recruits who required additional acclimation to a life of service in the field. Each step of this process was fraught with problems.

The shortage of carbines was a perfect example. During the Peninsula campaign, only two squadrons carried the Sharps carbine, and thus they were forced to assume the brunt of the toughest duties as flankers, skirmishers, and rear guard, tasks normally parceled throughout the regiment in an equitable manner. One trooper groused about the added burden. "We have had the advance of the army, marching in front all day, deploying as skirmishers, running through brush, driving in the enemy's pickets, and then standing picket guard all night," grumbled Pvt. Beriah N. Owen in a letter to his hometown newspaper. "At one time I only had two hours sleep in four nights. . . . While on the march some of our men would drop asleep and fall off their horses. To add to this, we only had hard crackers to eat."[36]

The troopers of the 6th U.S. Cavalry rejoiced on that most memorable day in early June 1862, when ordnance officers finally issued brand new Sharps carbines to those who didn't already have them. "The boys are overjoyed with their new arm," grinned one sergeant. "Indeed it is a splendid weapon, bright and new and warranted to carry 1000 yards." Only a week before, "Rush's Lancers" (the 6th Pennsylvania Cavalry) had turned in their useless lances, "found to be illy adapted to cavalry service," and received enough carbines to arm the entire command. Hooker's next priority was to ensure that every trooper in the Cavalry Corps was similarly equipped. Thanks to the munificence of their state government, the 5th and 6th Michigan regiments were armed with the Spencer rifle, a breech-loading, seven-shot repeater of revolutionary design. After firing the Spencer in a private session with its inventor, gunsmith Christopher Miner Spencer, President Lincoln used every bit of his considerable power to force the army to give the weapon a test. "The Michigan men were fortunate in being among the very first to receive these

---

35 Merritt, "Reminiscences," 284.

36 Caughey and Jones, *The 6th United States Cavalry*, 50.

repeating rifles which, after the first year in the field, were exchanged for the carbine of the same make, a lighter arm and better adapted for the use of cavalry," wrote James Kidd. "A better gun had never been issued."[37]

The task of training all these volunteers in the finer points of horse soldiery fell to the officers of the Regular cavalry. The war had worn away at the Regulars; the enlistments of many had expired, and others had attained better positions in the many new volunteer regiments. With five to 10 years of cavalry experience under their belts, even the noncommissioned officers were in great demand and "were almost certain to get commissions as Lieutenants, almost for the asking. . . . Of course in the end this worked well for the Government, as it distributed the traditions and discipline so well imbued in the regulars throughout the mass."[38]

Even attaining a level of comfort in camp life required training and experience for new troops. The lifestyle found in the camps of the Regulars contrasted starkly with that attained by inexperienced volunteers; the camps of the former "were well policed, the rations ample and well cooked, the clothing on hand where wanted and always properly fitted by the regimental tailors," recorded one career soldier. "These and many other matters, trifling in themselves, but which taken together make up the life of the soldier, and include the difference between what he regards as comfort and misery, were very apparent to the volunteers when camped in the vicinity of regular troops of any arm of the service."[39]

By contrast, one volunteer officer recalled with a shudder his regiment's first night of "roughing" it after marching through the rain for three days. "Late that Saturday night we bivouacked with the campfires of Hooker's army all around," he described. His exhausted soldiers required succor, but received none. "No forethought had been taken; no rations were drawn or issued; no wood was supplied . . . the entire command was forced to lie on the ground, in pools of water, in the midst of a drenching rain without food, or fire, or shelter of any kind whatever. It was dreadful."[40]

The pace of training increased dramatically. In every camp those not assigned to outpost duty drilled and drilled again until every movement and evolution became instinctual. The untrained horsemen drawn from urban areas established a

37 Ibid., 56; Samuel L. Gracey, *Annals of the Sixth Pennsylvania Cavalry* (Philadelphia, 1868), 148-149; Kidd, *Personal Recollections of a Cavalryman*, 78.

38 Hagemann, *Fighting Rebels and Redskins*, 185.

39 Ibid., 186.

40 Kidd, *Personal Recollections of a Cavalryman*, 94.

rapport with their steeds, which learned to respond to the touch of spur and knee. The accouterments of war were buffed and oiled with care and strapped down tight to the saddle, ready for any eventualities of the march. To Captain Kidd it seemed like "the work of drilling and disciplining went on without relaxation throughout the winter." One of the Regulars noted the increased pace as April 1863 approached. "We are drilling twice a day now and have been doing so for the last two weeks," he announced in a letter home. "All of this is intended to perfect our recruits as much as possible during the leisure that we have and as the calm sometimes proceeds a storm, it is well that we should be prepared."[41]

During the early days of April, Merritt accepted a position on General Stoneman's staff, a move that required little pushing from General Cooke. With the ascendancy of Stoneman and Buford, Merritt's career looked like it might get back on track. The very week of his arrival on Stoneman's staff, the entire corps paraded before President Lincoln, Hooker, and Stoneman in one long, resplendent column of Union blue, cavalry yellow, burnished steel, and proudly waving flags.

At their head rode Brig. Gen. John Buford. "We appeared in our best uniforms and with flying colors," wrote one trooper as he recalled the emotional moment. "It was an occasion not to be forgotten, the sight being one of the most magnificent many of us ever saw. The column was between three and four hours passing in review."[42]

---

41 Ibid., 94; Caughey and Jones, *The 6th United States Cavalry*, 74.

42 Willard Glazier, *Three Years in the Federal Cavalry* (New York, 1872), 162-163.

CHAPTER FIVE

To Joke, or Not to Joke—That is the Question

I**N** EARLY NOVEMBER 1862, shortly after McClellan's ouster as head of the Army of the Potomac, George Custer made his first concerted effort to seek a line command. Custer felt he had boomeranged between assignments long enough, and despite all of his best efforts, he was still only a lieutenant in the 5th U.S. Cavalry. He had held the rank of captain while serving on General McClellan's staff, but had reverted to his Regular Army rank of lieutenant when "Little Mac" was dismissed.

Although he sensed greater opportunity for promotion on staff duty rather than in a fighting unit, he launched his campaign for the colonelcy of the soon-to-be-organized 7th Michigan Cavalry. Home on leave in Monroe while awaiting reassignment, Custer focused his considerable energies on the task. He went straight to Governor Austin Blair, who stoutly refused to give him the time of day. Regimental commands, he informed Custer bluntly, were only for those who recruited regiments. Moreover, Custer was not a born-and-bred Michigan man, coming as he did from Ohio.

Custer next visited Congressman John Bingham, who quickly set him on the right course. Bingham suggested that Custer see Judge Isaac P. Christiancy, a man with a formidable reputation in Michigan politics as a justice on the Michigan Supreme Court and founder of the state's Republican Party. Unfortunately, not even Christiancy's considerable clout could overcome Governor Blair's ingrained antipathy toward Custer. "[He] is using you to his advantage," Blair railed at the judge. "His people are Rebel Democrats. He himself is a McClellan man; indeed McClellan's fair-haired boy, I should say. Sorry, your Honor." The plum patronage

Maj. Gen. Alfred Pleasonton, the Army of the Potomac's Cavalry Corps commander.
Once again a lieutenant, Custer was posted to his staff. *LOC*

position would be awarded to Col. William D. Mann, who had somehow survived the behind-the-scenes wheeling and dealing of the politicians.[1]

Despite the setback, Judge Christiancy wrote Custer a letter brimming with confidence that Custer eventually would prevail. In reply, Custer wrote, "You had been speaking of the Governor's refusal to appoint me and encouraged me by saying I would yet acquire a position." In a letter written some years after the Civil War, Christiancy congratulated Custer on avoiding the political obligations that would have accompanied his appointment. "How fortunate that Governor Blair had nothing for you," noted the judge with perfect hindsight. "Every step of your remarkable advancement has been due to your own merit, without favor . . . often in the face of opposing influences, often of political origin."[2]

Custer's efforts to obtain command of a regiment continued unabated in the ensuing months. He rejoined the Army of the Potomac in early May 1863 and was posted to Brig. Gen. Alfred Pleasonton's Cavalry Corps staff in the capacity of aide-de-camp, remaining a lieutenant. Michigan newspapers, however, extolled his virtues in print. "General Hooker asserts that we have not a more gallant man on the field," wrote one tabloid, "and that wherever there is a daring expedition or hard fighting to be done he is always among the foremost." Never trusting to luck alone, Custer made it a habit "while on Staff duty [to accompany] the reconnaissances and expeditions conducted by the cavalry, and to this in a great measure was due my subsequent promotion to the grade of general officer."[3]

On February 27, 1863, the commander of the 5th Michigan Cavalry, Col. Freeman Norvell, well-known throughout the regiment as a drunkard, resigned his commission. The vacancy still had not been filled in May, and Custer compiled his resumé and called on half a dozen high-ranking officers to endorse him for the colonelcy of the regiment. "Captain Custer has been strongly recommended to Governor Blair," proclaimed one Michigan newspaper, "by Generals Burnside, Stoneman, Humphrey, Copeland, Stahl and Pleasonton." The 5th's officers expressed their sentiments in a petition delivered to Blair, beseeching him to "appoint an outsider to the vacancy." When Custer visited the regiment, however, they quickly changed their minds. According to Lt. Samuel Harris, "About the 1st of June a slim young man with almost flaxen hair, looking more like a big boy, came

---

1 Wert, *Custer*, 66-67.

2 Robert A. Servacek, *Custer: His Promotion in Frederick, Maryland,* Privately Published, (Frederick, MD, 2002), 30; Merington, *The Custer Story*, 55.

3 Merington, *The Custer Story*, 55; Carroll, *Custer in the Civil War*, 75.

to us and, as the line offcers expressed it, with the cheek of a government mule, actually asked us to sign a petition to Gov. Austin Blair to appoint him as Colonel of the Fifth. He said his name was George A. Custer, and that he was a West Pointer. No petition was sent."[4]

On June 11, Blair, after hearing of their doubts regarding Custer's age and qualifications, chose Lt. Col. Russell A. Alger of the 6th Michigan Cavalry for the job. Judge Christiancy sent Custer another optimistic missive, and Custer again thanked him for his support.[5]

No Accolades for a Duty Done

If the daring actions of Jeb Stuart's horsemen—such as the raid on Chambersburg, Pennsylvania, in October 1862—were the benchmark for cavalry operations, then the argument can be made that there was nothing spectacular about the Stoneman Raid. Raiding after all is one of the things that cavalry is supposed to do, and the Rebels had done it more often, and better. That the Federal troopers were able to do it at all speaks volumes about the growth of the cavalry of the Army of the Potomac. Was it a spectacular operation in the mold of Stuart? No. Instead, much like George Stoneman himself, the command performed in a competent, workman-like manner. Unfortunately, the raid accomplished only part of its mission.

Unlike previous commanders of the Army of the Potomac, Hooker planned for the cavalry to take a prominent role in his next campaign, as shown in the orders Stoneman received on April 12. "You will march at 7:00 a.m., on the 13th instant, with all your available force except one brigade, for the purpose of turning the enemy's position on his left," read the order. "The general desires you to understand," it added, "that he considers the primary object of your movement the cutting of the enemy's connections with Richmond by the Fredericksburg route, checking his retreat over those lines, and he wishes to make everything subservient to that object."[6]

Hookerpompously exhorted Stoneman to let his "watchword be fight, and let all your orders be fight, fight, fight." The weather, which had a different idea, took a

4 Merington, *The Custer Story*, 55; Kidd, *Personal Recollections of a Cavalryman*, 107; Samuel Harris, *Personal Reminiscences of Samuel Harris* (Chicago, 1897), 23-24.

5 Servacek, *Custer: His Promotion*, 30.

6 OR 25, pt. 1, 1066-1067.

turn for the worse. The river crossings were soon impassable, and Hooker reluctantly delayed the start of his offensive. The original orders of April 12 were pushed back to a start date of April 29. Army headquarters again instructed Stoneman to be ready to move according to the original plan—the infantry would maneuver Lee into battle east of Chancellorsville while the cavalry swept around the enemy's left to interdict Lee's lines of communication and retreat. At the last moment Hooker advanced the date of the river crossing by two days, catching Stoneman flat-footed. "I had previously been directed to hold my command in readiness to move on the following morning, April 29," he complained, "and consequently no preparations had been made to move on the 27th, such as drawing in the pickets, calling in scouting parties, & etc."[7]

The sudden change of schedule turned the usually simple approach to the Rapidan River into a major exercise. "It was quite late at night before the command was all assembled and ready to start," recounted Stoneman, "owing to the state of the roads, the result of the recent heavy rains, and the darkness of the night, rendered doubly obscure by a dense fog, the corps did not reach the river until near 8:00 a.m." Restricted in his forward movement by the wording of his instructions, Stoneman found himself limited to using just one ford, which was passable to all but the pack mule train and the artillery. By 5:00 p.m., "by dint of great exertion," he had his entire command across the river; he then "assembled the division and brigade commanders, spread our maps, and had a thorough understanding of what we were to do, and where we were each to go."[8]

New to the raiding game, the Yankee cavalry continued to make mistakes. With the rivers still running too high for wheeled transport and pack trains, Stoneman ordered these sent to Germanna Mills, where they were to follow in the rear of the army. "Each officer and man [was] to take with him no more than he could carry on his horse," read the orders, and Stoneman and his staff led by example as the columns headed south. Stoneman's trust that he would re-establish communication relied on the optimistic supposition that the rest of the Army of the Potomac "would be within communicating distance of us before the end of six days, during which time our supplies were supposed to last." The plan did not take into account the vulnerability of the army's right flank, and certainly underestimated the risk-taking temperaments of Robert E. Lee and Stonewall

---

7 Ibid., 1066, 1058.

8 Ibid., 1058.

Jackson. This decision to accept Hooker on faith would come back to haunt the command.[9]

"Four a.m. came, and with it a cold, drenching rain . . . and we started on our way, a command numbering about 3,500, as unencumbered and determined a set of men as ever started upon any expedition in this or any other army." By 10:00 p.m. on May 1, the entire command had crossed the Rapidan at Raccoon Ford and pitched another cheerless camp. Fearing the loss of the element of surprise, Stoneman forbade fires for the duration of the raid "lest the enemy should become aware of our whereabouts and strength," a practice which added to the discomfort of the men.[10]

As the cavalry advanced, Stoneman lost a division commander and 4,000 desperately needed saber arms without a shot being fired. Averell's division had no sooner started on its march than it halted and went into camp. Hooker intervened directly, relieving the erratic Averell and recalling his division from the raid. "General Averell's command . . . [was] a larger cavalry force than can be found in the rebel army between Fredericksburg and Richmond," charged an enraged Hooker. "I could excuse General Averell in his disobedience if I could anywhere discover in his operations a desire to engage the enemy." Averell would be made into an example for the rest of the army.[11]

With great bitterness, Stoneman denounced Hooker's decision to recall Averell. Whatever punitive action needed to be taken could have easily waited until the conclusion of the operation. "Had not General Averell been recalled, and had he formed a junction with me, as was to be expected, I could have detached a force to Charlottesville, which is almost unguarded, and destroyed the depot of supplies said to be there." Stoneman was unaware of those opportunities at the time, but he had fully expected Averell to perform his part of the plan to occupy Brandy Station.[12]

Other seemingly insignificant decisions turned out to be far-reaching in their ramifications; such was the case with Stoneman's decision to keep his men on constant alert. "Gen. Stoneman evidently considered that as we were far within the enemy's lines and entirely cut off from all assistance from our own army," recalled a

9 Ibid., 1058, 1064.

10 Ibid., 1059.

11 Ibid., 1072-1073.

12 Ibid., 1064.

member of his staff, "that it was necessary to remain in constant readiness to meet attack, and therefore kept the horses saddled night and day, and the men under arms during the whole expedition almost. In fact we may be said never to have 'camped' during the whole time we were south of the Rappahannock river." As Stoneman prepared for his move on Louisa Court House, his already exhausted command "lay down on the wet ground to get a couple of hours sleep."[13]

The men were to be in motion at 2:00 a.m. on May 1, reported Stoneman, "but the fog was so thick that it was impossible to move, more particularly as we had no guide to show us the road. Daylight came, and we pushed on." Twelve hours later, in the early morning hours of May 2, Gregg's lead regiment finally reached Louisa Court House, and immediately entered into a frenzy of destruction. "After having destroyed the Virginia Central Railroad and telegraph, burned the depots, water-tanks, &c. for 18 miles," reported Stoneman, "and accomplished all that time would permit, we pushed on to Yanceyville, on the South Anna, and from there to Thompson's Cross Roads, 10 miles lower down the river."[14]

Deep in enemy territory, Stoneman called a halt and decided to use Louisa Court House as a central hub from which his striking forces would radiate. "Here I determined to make the most of my 3,500 men in carrying out my previously conceived plan of operations," he reported. He dramatically informed his assembled regimental commanders that they "had dropped in that region of country like a shell, and that I intended to burst it in every direction, expecting each piece or fragment would do as much harm and create nearly as much terror as would . . . magnify our small force into overwhelming numbers."[15]

General Gregg took the 1st Maine Cavalry, the 1st Maryland Cavalry, and a section of artillery to operate in the northeast quadrant, driving along the South Anna in order to destroy as many bridges as possible, particularly the railroad bridges. The 12th Illinois under Col. "Grimes" Davis was to move southeast toward Ashland Station and wreck the two railroads in the vicinity. Colonel Hugh Judson Kilpatrick and the 2nd New York Cavalry were to make a dash for the bridges over the Chickahominy, destroying them and threatening Richmond, while inflicting the greatest possible damage on the enemy as they moved. Stoneman admonished Kilpatrick to make sure the "destruction was complete." The 5th U.S. Cavalry moved directly south, creating mayhem and eventually destroying the canal

13 Hagemann, *Fighting Rebels and Redskins*, 205; OR 25, pt. 1, 1060.

14 *OR* 25, pt. 1, 1060.

15 Ibid.

facilities at Goochland on the James River. Colonel Percy Wyndham and the 1st New Jersey Cavalry struck to the southwest toward Columbia and the James River. The large aqueducts at the confluence of the James and Rivanna rivers that supplied fresh water to Richmond were prime targets. Stoneman, meanwhile, would hold Louisa Court House with 500 men from Buford's brigade providing a "nucleus, and upon which the different parties could rally in case of necessity after they had performed the work assigned them to do."[16]

Thus far Wesley Merritt had been limited to relaying orders aimed at nudging the recalcitrant Averell to move against the enemy. Itching to get into the fray, he asked Stoneman for a combat command. In a fatherly gesture, the general gave Merritt a squadron and a free hand, and, by extension, a chance at glory. "Captain Merritt, with a flying party of the First Maryland," Stoneman reported, "was sent out to do what he thought he could accomplish in the way of destroying bridges, &c."[17]

Over the course of 48 hectic hours, Merritt and his 50 men, including pioneers, set out to destroy as many bridges, ancillary buildings, and supplies as they could. Inserting his command between Gregg on the north and the 5th U.S. Cavalry to the south, Merritt clung to the South Anna River. He reported a litany of destruction, including the burning of five bridges, all "strongly built, and [averaging] 50 feet in length." Bringing these structures down proved to be an arduous and time-consuming task, but Merritt noted that "[t]hey were all effectually destroyed by fire

16 Boatner, *The Civil War Dictionary*, 459. To observers, H. Judson Kilpatrick aroused either deep admiration or abject hatred, with his detractors nicknaming him "Kill-Cavalry." Immediately after graduating from West Point, he took command of the 5th New York Volunteer Infantry, and at the June 1861 battle of Big Bethel earned the dubious honor of becoming the first Union officer wounded in battle during the war. Later that year he transitioned to the mounted arm as lieutenant colonel of the 2nd New York Cavalry. The failure of the Kilpatrick-Dahlgren raid in March 1864 ended his career in the Army of the Potomac and led to his transfer to William T. Sherman's command. Sherman welcomed him, stating, "I know Kilpatrick is a damned fool, but I want just that sort of man to command my cavalry." *OR* 25, pt. 1, 1061; Born at sea to English parents, Sir Percy Wyndham described himself as a soldier of fortune, and claimed to have served in the French navy, the Austrian cavalry, and Giuseppe Garibaldi's Italian army of liberation. King Victor Emmanuel knighted Wyndham for his actions during the conquest of Sicily. Noted for a set of whiskers that spanned two feet, he next turned his adventurous spirit to the Civil War. In and out of trouble while with the Union army, he was finally cashiered by Secretary of War Stanton in July 1864. Fascinated by aerial balloons, Wyndham began giving demonstrations. On one such flight in January 1879, he perished when the balloon exploded 300 feet above a lake near Rangoon, Burma. His body was never recovered. *OR* 25, pt. 1, 1061.

17 *OR* 25, pt. 1, 1061.

and the axes of the pioneers, so that they cannot be rebuilt save by preparing new material for their construction."[18]

Just before sundown on May 3, Gregg mounted one more effort, ordering Lieutenant Colonel Smith to take his 1st Maine Cavalry along with Merritt's men to destroy the railroad bridge across the South Anna at Ashland. The regiment, reported Merritt, "pushed toward the bridge, driving in the enemy's pickets, and discovered artillery in position. In the meantime my command fired the depot buildings, burning a quantity of ammunition, stores, and tools of workmen engaged on public works . . . [and] also a culvert on the railroad, and the track, as far as practicable, for some distance." The Federal raiders began to reach the limits of what they could accomplish and started filtering back to Stoneman's position that night. By May 5, the scattered units had reunited with the main body, and Stoneman pondered his next move. Merritt would write glowingly of his time in command of an independent body of soldiers: "These men worked and endured beyond my preconceived notions of human capacity without a murmur. . . . All the work done by the detachment I commanded during my absence was well done."[19]

As the dispersed detachments withdrew to the main column they foraged and scoured the land, adding to the misery of a population that had been the doormat of the opposing armies for almost two years. The desolation of the area deeply moved correspondent William Croffutt of the *New York Tribune*. "Farms had been plundered of their stock; bridges, depots, and settlements had been burned," wrote the veteran reporter. The air was rife with the smell of putrefying animals, and only the blackened chimney shafts remained as witness to what had been "the centre of a homestead."[20]

Deep in enemy territory and clearly out-manned, Stoneman worried that it would only be a matter of time before the Rebels responded to the destruction. His nights passed "in no little anxiety. . . . To take the enemy by surprise and penetrate his country was easy enough; to withdraw from it was a more difficult matter." As the command reunited, Stoneman began to cover his line of retreat; at this point he had a clear picture of the enemy's dispositions and capabilities. Rooney Lee and Col. Wade Hampton hovered to the west of Stoneman's position with one strong force in and around Gordonsville, another waiting at Louisa Court House, and a

---

18 Ibid., 1071.

19 Ibid., 1072.

20 J. Cutler Andrews, *The North Reports the Civil War* (Pittsburg, PA, 1955), 367-368.

small detachment of infantry occupying Tolersville. The situation was fast becoming precarious.[21]

Besides the eminent danger of overwhelming Confederate attacks, the Union troopers had used up all their supplies. "We were entirely out of rations and had been living off the country for some days," reported Captain Sanford. "Of course, this means of supply was too uncertain to depend on much longer, and in addition both men and horses were nearly exhausted by the incessant work." Gregg commented on the hit-or-miss nature of this form of supply in his after-action report. "When provisions could properly be taken, the men were supplied; if none could be procured, there was no complaint."[22]

The rest of the Army of the Potomac was nowhere to be seen; in fact, rumors from the area's slave population indicated that Hooker had been turned back. Over the first few days of May, the army had suffered another humiliating defeat at Chancellorsville, culminating in Stonewall Jackson's devastating flank attack on the unprepared XI Corps of Maj. Gen. Oliver O. Howard. Although Jackson was mortally wounded by his own men during the battle, his troops rolled up the Union right and threw the entire army into confusion. "In every direction that we turned," wrote a worried Sanford, "we came across parties of the enemy." It seemed to him "as if there should have been no escape for our little force, which by casualties and detachments was now reduced to about two thousand men."[23]

The resourceful Stoneman soon cobbled together a plan to extricate his command from behind Rebel lines. Captain Theophilus Rodenbough of the 2nd U.S. Cavalry was sent to the left "with the view of threatening the enemy's communication in that direction." Buford, meanwhile, took a picked force of 650 of "the best men and horses from his brigade" to the right toward Gordonsville and the Virginia Central Railroad. Buford's diversion would allow Stoneman to move with his main force to the Rapidan River; pushing past that point would open the Rappahannock crossings. Buford would be left to his own devices to find a way

---

21 *OR* 25, pt. 1, 1061-1062; One of the wealthiest plantation owners in South Carolina, Hampton recruited a combined legion of infantry, artillery, and cavalry at his own expense at the beginning of the war. Despite a complete lack of military experience, he proved to be a brave and competent leader, repeatedly suffering wounds during the war. In July 1862, during the reorganization of the Army of Northern Virginia, Hampton transferred to the cavalry after a year of infantry service. Much older than Stuart's other officers, he brought a balancing maturity to the mounted arm of the Army of Northern Virginia. After Stuart's death he would assume command of Lee's cavalry.

22 Hagemann, *Fighting Rebels and Redskins*, 201; *OR* 25, pt. 1, 1083.

23 Hagemann, *Fighting Rebels and Redskins*, 201.

of returning safely to the Union lines. "It was a forlorn hope, but it was the only thing left us, and Buford was the man of all the others to be entrusted with such an undertaking."[24]

The return march began on the afternoon of May 5, and by early evening, rain began to flail the hooded heads and bent shoulders of the marching column. "We were in a strange country, and the roads bad beyond description," recorded the historian of the 6th Pennsylvania. Horses floundered in the viscous mud and were abandoned. The luckless troopers gamely carried their mounts' heavy "traps" over their shoulders, tramping on the more solid embankments beside the road. Past exhaustion, many a soldier fell by the wayside wrapped "in his horse-blanket. . . . Many of our men thus dropping out by the way, were captured by the enemy."[25]

In the end, Stoneman's "calculations worked admirably," and by daylight on May 7 the command had crossed the Rapidan at Raccoon Ford. There, for the first time, "the horses were unsaddled and fed what little forage we had on hand; the men permitted to build fires and cook whatever meat and meal they might still possess, and to rest until 10:00 a.m." That night the head of the column reached Kelly's Ford on the Rappahannock. Nothing was sweeter to the exhausted and hungry troopers than the welcome sight of the ghostly white tents of the encamped army on the other side of the river and upon the distant hills. "I say nothing was more exciting," wrote Lieutenant Harrison of the 2nd U.S. Cavalry, "than the swimming of the Rappahannock at Kelley's Ford on our return."[26]

By May 8, "Stoneman's Raid" had officially ended. In the final accounting, the raid did no major damage to the enemy, as much of the destruction was repaired by the Confederates within a week. More important were the lessons that the Union cavalry took away from the raid. "The fact is that from the commanding general down," recalled Sanford, "we were all new at the business of 'raiding' and in consequence made many errors, which were subsequently corrected."[27]

The first lesson concerned how to fill the stomachs of men and horses, which had not been empty because of a simple lack of food or forage. The cavalry's quartermaster, Lt. Col. C. G. Sawtelle, reported finding "bacon, corn meal, flour, corn, and frequently hay or fodder, in sufficient quantities to supply the whole

24 OR 25, pt. 1, 1062; Hagemann, *Fighting Rebels and Redskins*, 201-202.

25 Gracey, *Annals of the Sixth Pennsylvania Cavalry*, 149.

26 OR 25, pt. 1, 1062-1063; Harrison, "Personal Experiences of a Cavalry Officer," 244.

27 Hagemann, *Fighting Rebels and Redskins*, 204-205.

command. Foraging parties were sent out from time to time from the different regiments, and generally came back with forage and provisions." At one farm the quartermaster confiscated $25,000 worth of corn. The problem lay in the proper management of so much abundance. "Large amounts of provisions and forage were destroyed and wasted by the troops," complained Sawtelle.[28]

Sawtelle's report buttressed Merritt's belief that cavalry could operate far from any logistical support and subsist solely off the land. "There was no lesson so readily and regularly learned by our cavalry in the late war as that of taking care of and subsisting itself in the enemy's territory," claimed Merritt. To be effective, however, foraging had to be managed in a systematic manner. "I have known an entire force of ten thousand cavalry to be fed by these parties," attested the cavalry officer, who continued,

> They would run grist mills and grind large quantities of meal and flour. They would secure salt or fresh meat in abundance, often-times driving live-stock into camp, and turning that, as well as all else obtained, into an issuing department. Everything was regularly served out to the command, the issues being as regularly made as if the entire subsistence and stores had been drawn from the Government by a responsible staff officer.[29]

The management of foraged provisions was easily rectified, however, when compared to the serious issue of the sorry condition of the horses. "Our loss in horses on the Stoneman raid was terrible," recalled Sanford. "In no other expedition during the war was it as great, and this owing primarily to bad management on the part of the men and officers." The horses started the expedition in relatively good shape but deteriorated rapidly, "exhausted and weakened by the march," as reported by Quartermaster Sawtelle. "I have not yet received full reports of the number of horses abandoned on this march. The number will not, however, vary much from 1,000. . . . Most of those abandoned were killed." Captain Sanford pondered long and hard on this problem and his conclusions validated much of Merritt's thinking. "When not marching the whole command was practically on picket, expecting an attack at every moment. The result of course was broken down horses and exhausted men," he criticized, "and by that means still more contributing to the injury of their [the horses'] backs,

---

28 *OR* 25, pt. 1, 1069.

29 Merritt, "Reminiscences," 300-301.

already in a dreadful condition from being kept under saddle for such a length of time."[30]

Other logistical lapses hampered the expedition. The experiment with the pack-mule train garnered much criticism. "Two sturdy army wagons could do the work of 25 mules, with a lot less trouble," observed Sawtelle. In his professional opinion, pack-mules "as a means of transportation instead of the army wagons . . . are not advantageous to the service." Sawtelle also heaped scorn on the absurdity of trying to destroy bridges with just matches and kindling. "I would suggest that, in view of similar expeditions being made in future," he pointed out with a touch of sarcasm, "a number of copper cans be provided . . . to be filled with turpentine, and carried by the pioneer parties of each regiment, to facilitate the burning of bridges, store-houses, &c." He pointed out the obvious fact that "if you're going to go out and destroy bridges and burn buildings . . . go prepared with the necessary accelerants to light and feed a fire."[31]

In Stoneman's final assessment, the most important outcome of the expedition was its positive effect on the Federal troopers. The composure of the command showed them "what we are able to accomplish if we but have the opportunity and in convincing the country that it has not spent its men and money in vain in our organization." Later in the war, as the cavalry flexed its hard-earned muscles, it would point to the Stoneman Raid as the moment when professionalism took hold and the command became imbued with the spirit that would carry it through the trying times ahead. At least that is what John Buford believed. "All, without exception, were full of enthusiasm, ready for any emergency, and did their duty with hearty good-will. I have not heard of a complaint or murmur.[32]

Friends They Were Not

Despite the boost to the cavalry's morale from the recent expedition, it had proved too costly and ineffective, and someone had to go. Shortly after the raid, Stoneman returned to Washington on medical leave for the treatment of a saddle-inflamed case of hemorrhoids. For his part, Hooker, who never really cared for Stoneman, needed a scapegoat for the Chancellorsville debacle. Even as Stoneman recuperated, Hooker relieved him, effective May 22, 1863. Stoneman

---

30 Hagemann, *Fighting Rebels and Redskins*, 204-205; *OR* 25, pt. 1, 1069.

31 *OR* 25, pt. 1, 1069-1070.

32 Ibid., 1064, 1090.

found himself unceremoniously transferred to the cavalry bureau, where he would spend most of his time dealing with complaints about the quality and quantity of field-worthy remounts.[33]

Stoneman's departure played right into the hands of Brig. Gen. Alfred Pleasonton, an officer long covetous of Stoneman's position, and Hooker fulfilled these desires by appointing Pleasonton to the temporary command of the Cavalry Corps. Pleasonton wasted little time moving into the commanding officer's tents. His tenure would prove to be both uplifting and somehow depressing at the same time. "Alfred Pleasonton is something of an enigma to most modern Civil War historians and students," claims cavalry historian J. D. Petruzzi. "[He] was more directly responsible for its reorganization into an effective, cohesive fighting force than any chieftain before him." Unfortunately, Pleasonton possessed a mottled soul. "Yet, because of his shabby treatment of foreign-born commanders, a lead-from-behind style, his tendency toward political conniving, and his proclivity for weaving official reports into fanciful, self-serving yarns, he is rarely taken seriously by most."[34]

Pleasonton moved expeditiously to fill the vacancies in the larger staff he was now entitled to. Within hours of his appointment, both George Custer and Wesley Merritt were offered sinecures in his inner circle. Pleasonton knew Merritt well from their days together in the old 2nd Dragoons, and Custer had frequent interactions with Pleasonton during the Peninsula campaign as aide-de-camp to McClellan. Custer often attached himself to Pleasonton's command, nominally as an observer to report back to headquarters, but really with the intention of getting into a good fight.

Both men probably settled comfortably into their new positions. Pleasonton could be charming, witty, and engaging. With his white kid gloves, knee high boots, rakishly angled wide straw hat, and cigar clamped firmly in his mouth, he was elegant in attire and manners, almost bordering on the foppish. Merritt likely figured he would have no trouble working under Pleasonton's low-key but eccentric auspices.

Few officers trusted Pleasonton, however, and his reputation would suffer as he rose in rank during the war. "I don't call any cavalry officer good who can't see

---

33 Stoneman would later serve with Sherman in the Western Theater and be captured during the Atlanta Campaign. After his release, he led a series of ambitious raids into Virginia and North Carolina. In 1866, Stoneman was forced to deploy Federal troops to suppress rioting in Memphis. He served one term as governor of California (1882 to 1887) as a Democrat.

34 J. David Petruzzi, *Alfred Pleasonton's Civil Wars* (Unpublished Manuscript, 2004).

the truth and tell the truth," remarked Col. Charles Russell Lowell of the 2nd Massachusetts Cavalry. "Cavalry are the eyes and ears of the army and ought to see and tell the [truth]—and yet it is the universal opinion that Pleasonton's own reputation, and Pleasonton's late promotions are bolstered up by systematic lying." Around Alfred Pleasonton, it was best to be wary, for his opinions could turn on a dime. One officer described him as "not so cordial . . . indeed [he] was a trifle frigid." Merritt would have several encounters with this iciness in the years to come.[35]

Custer's relationship with Pleasonton differed greatly from Merritt's experience. The outgoing and amiable Custer established an instant rapport with his new chief. "I do not believe a father could love his son more than Genl. Pleasonton loves me," Custer wrote to Annette Humphrey, the facilitator of his romance with Libbie Bacon. "He is solicitous about me and my safety as a mother about her child. You should see how gladly he welcomes me on my return from each battle. His usual greeting is, 'Well, boy, I am glad to see you back. I was anxious about you.'"[36]

In the headquarters of the Army of the Potomac, Custer found a culture in which his hedonistic qualities could flourish. He fell into the wanton ways of the staff like he did everything else: at full tilt. If anything, Custer's bad habits grew worse. Headquarters had earned a horrid reputation among the moral and religious men in the army. "I can say from personal knowledge and experience, that the headquarters of the Army of the Potomac was a place which no self-respecting man liked to go to, and no decent woman would go," opined prolific writer Charles Francis Adams. "It was a combination barroom and brothel." Others confirmed this dim view. "It must be remembered that at that time the Army of the Potomac had gathered to itself, along with many good men, many worthless, dissapeted [sic] scamps, even among the highest officers," wrote another. "The amount of hard drinking that was done by all, from general to lieutenant, was frightful, and the language in common use was of the vilest description."[37]

With the contending armies entrenched on opposite sides of the Chickahominy, life for young staff officers consisted of boredom, socializing,

---

35 Edward Waldo Emerson, *Life and Letters of Charles Russell Lowell* (Boston, 1907), 279; Harrison, "Personal Experiences of a Cavalry Officer," 229.

36 Merington, *The Custer Story*, 69.

37 Charles Francis Adams, *Charles Francis Adams, An Autobiography, 1835-1915* (Boston, 1916), 161; Reynolds, *The Civil War Memories*, 67.

gambling, drinking, and toasting to "promotion or death," as young subalterns in most armies of the time were wont to do. They sang, "Here's a health to the living and hurrah for the next one who dies," and as they did so they looked into each other's eyes and wondered who would be next. Custer easily "fell in with the prevailing habits, [and] drank as deep and swore as hard as any man in the army."[38]

During his 1862 furlough in Monroe, Custer became quite inebriated with a group of soldiers at a local bar, and traded war stories that probably grew more exaggerated with each retelling. He was in that sorry condition when he had turned down the street where his future *amour* lived and staggered past the reproachful gaze of the old magistrate, Judge Daniel S. Bacon. Soon afterward he met Judge Bacon's daughter, Elizabeth Clift Bacon, quite by accident at a Thanksgiving party, and life as Custer had known it ended. Libbie, as she preferred to be called, later remembered their brief introduction only as a blur. She subsequently confessed to Custer that "what we said I am dying to know for I remember nary a word." A flustered Custer wrote of the spell she had cast over him. "My heart could have told her of a promotion far more rapid in her power only to bestow. How I watched her every motion, and when she left . . . in that throng of youth and beauty she had reigned supreme . . . when she left Armstrong Custer went home to dream."[39]

Libbie's father would never countenance a military romance, and certainly not one with a lowly staff officer, much less a man of Custer's low moral standards. Libbie would always remember "that terrible day." Afterward, she wrote, "We had forbidden ourselves to speak on account of Father." From that point on, their romance continued undercover, with all their correspondence going through an intermediary so the judge would not realize what was taking place. Libbie later recorded that young Captain Custer had eventually "taken a pledge . . . realizing, himself, that there was no future for him if he continued to drink, as like everything else he did at that time there was no likelihood of its being done with moderation." As Whittaker relates the story, "Custer . . . in the presence of God, gave his sister a solemn pledge that never henceforth to the day of his death should a drop of intoxicating liquor pass his lips." Nonetheless, the damage had been done and it would be months before Judge Bacon even deigned to talk with Custer.[40]

---

38 Reynolds, *The Civil War Memories*, 67; Whittaker, *A Popular Life of Gen. George A. Custer*, 88, 89.

39 Merington, *The Custer Story*, 47.

40 Ibid.; Reynolds, *The Civil War Memories*, 24; Whittaker, *A Popular Life of Gen. George A. Custer*, 91.

Merritt, apparently, did not fit in well at headquarters. He longed to be out on the picket line, reveling in the traditions that common soldiers and officers shared. Just like his mentors, everything Merritt did was understated, removed from the prying eyes of the press and completely out of public view, performed solely out of love for the army. To Merritt there was nothing more relaxing than a convivial gathering around a campfire with serious men telling serious stories with that glint in the eye that only a good pull from a whiskey flask could instill. And after a few nips in the cooling evening, around cheerful campfires, the staff would gossip unabashedly.

It was Custer's favorite time of the day, as Libbie learned one startlingly clear fall night shortly after their wedding. "My husband's avocation of his profession came home to me so impressively one night when we were camped where we could see the lights of the tents rising far up around surrounding a hill," she remembered. "I was called out and in such tones asked if there could be any sight finer on earth. I began to take in the absorption of my husband in his life."[41]

We Are All Friends Here, Are We Not??

The social life of a general's staff created a forced intimacy. Under normal circumstances, the staff officers' mess was a convivial affair. After the officers finished up their duties for the day, they would gather leisurely under the tent fly that had been set up for dinner. Some would light up pipes filled with their favorite aromatic tobacco, while others would take sips from flasks made precious by memories and filled with their favorite libations. Still others engaged in a less discreet pastime: gossiping about the goings-on in the Cavalry Corps. All eagerly anticipated the night's meal. Some generals were known to enjoy the perquisites of their positions, maintaining opulent dinner tables that were, if not ostentatious, at least a few cuts above the rations the enlisted men were issued.

Pleasonton had a well-established reputation as a gourmand, albeit a rather private one. "General Pleasonton was always a gentleman whenever you found him, always and at all times," recounted Lt. James Franklin Wade, one of Pleasonton's staff officers and the son of the feared Radical Republican Senator Benjamin Wade. "He was not assertive [austere], but he always seemed to keep to himself. He was like a captain of a ship. He always messed alone. He would invite

---

41 Reynolds, *The Civil War Memories*, 118-119.

members of his staff to dine with him, but only one at a time. He seemed always old; he must have been born old."[42]

Custer's letters home left no doubt that he was one of the favored few in Pleasonton's inner circle. He described the nightly spread laid out for Pleasonton and his chosen aide in a letter to his anxious sister, who worried continuously about his eating habits. "Everyone should live in a tent, during the summer months at least. There would be less sickness, more enjoyment of health," Custer wrote reassuringly. "You need have no anxiety about my food, sister. I live with the General. He sends daily to Baltimore for fresh fruit and vegetables—radishes, onions and—fine Tomatoes. The General has a negro cook; her husband waits on table. . . . You see we don't go hungry when not moving or fighting."[43]

In the two short weeks in which they served together on Pleasonton's staff, Custer and Merritt probably sat at the same dinner table—maybe next to each other, or perhaps separated by the width of a rough camp table. Merritt's only biographer, Don E. Alberts, notes that, at this moment in time, "[t]he two young officers were not yet rivals . . . and Merritt left no impressions of his feelings towards Custer." This is not surprising, considering Merritt's aversion to committing derogatory statements about fellow officers—except in the case of General McClellan—to paper.[44]

Some of the seeds of the future contention between Custer and Merritt can be seen even at this early juncture, especially regarding their respective mentors. Merritt, as a first-hand witness, could not overlook the fact that McClellan had been instrumental in the ruination of Gen. Philip St. George Cooke. Merritt was unpretentious, unflappable, and affable, but he could also be obdurate, autocratic, and prickly when the occasion demanded it. He was not, however, the forgiving type, and Custer's loyalty to McClellan certainly did not escape his notice.

The greatest fundamental difference between the two men could have been something as simple as a sense of humor. Whether the serious, contemplative Merritt even possessed one at all is open to debate. Merritt likely considered Custer a little too gregarious in his off-duty hours—perhaps even obnoxious, and occasionally quite inebriated. Regardless, by the time Merritt left Pleasonton's staff, the feelings they had toward each other had already begun to crystallize.

---

42 William B. Styple, ed., *Generals in Bronze: Interviewing the Commanders of the Civil War* (Kearney, NJ, 2005), 131.

43 Merington, *The Custer Story*, 53.

44 Alberts, *General Wesley Merritt*, 51.

Custer—naively perhaps—believed they would be life-long friends, drawn together by the fraternal bonds of their West Point experience and the shared hazards of the battlefield. Reports Custer filed in connection with his participation in the upcoming cavalry battles indicated the personal warmth he felt for Merritt at that time.

There are also indications that the reserved Merritt did not fit into the social atmosphere that pervaded the Cavalry Corps headquarters, and fell a little out of favor as a result. In some ways, the Alfred Pleasonton of the pre-war 2nd Dragoons no longer existed. Overweening ambition and a growing reputation for obfuscation had made him unrecognizable to those who had known him in the antebellum years. The short duration of Merritt's tenure with Pleasonton begs the question: Did Pleasonton send Merritt packing? Or did Merritt so miss working with the professionals with whom he had started his career so much that he was willing to give up the laurels that went with staff positions at the corps level? He had never been the voluble type, and already was beginning to distance himself from the boisterousness of Custer and others of his ilk. His discomfort with the goings-on at headquarters probably led to his request to move back to a field position. As soon as it was approved, Merritt packed his saddle bags with pleasure and went back to the company of serious men practicing that most serious of all professions—that of the combat soldier.

He Who Laughs Last, Laughs Best

Six years later, a practical joke would throw the differences between Merritt and Custer into sharp relief. The summer of 1869 had been a good one for the Custers. Armstrong was well on his way to cementing a solid reputation as one of America's premier big game hunters. Writing under the pseudonym of "Nomad," Custer placed extensive accounts of his hunting exploits before an avid public in the pages of *Turf, Field and Farm*. "[He] was placed on waiting orders and recommended to the lieutenant-colonelcy of one of the new regiments of cavalry," Libbie recalled with a hint of trepidation. "In the autumn, the appointment to the Seventh Cavalry came, with orders to go to Fort Garland." Prior to reporting, Custer lovingly packed his hunting rifles and fishing rods, as he also was an avid fisherman.[45]

---

45 Elizabeth Bacon Custer, *Tenting on the Plains or General Custer in Texas and Kansas* (Norman, OK, 1994), 207-208.

Custer used his palatial campsites to mount buffalo hunts on the plains that often ranged as far as 20 miles. By this time he had become a full-fledged celebrity. *LOC*

In 1868, Custer moved the regimental headquarters of the 7th Cavalry to Fort Hays, Kansas. As they had during the war years, the Custers enthusiastically answered the call to outdoor camp life. A palatial campsite was set up in a secluded habitat, far from the prying eyes of the rest of the command. A monstrous 14' x 16' hospital tent served as the entertainment parlor and centerpiece, while a tent fly stretched along its front, providing "a shady overhang under which the Custers sat with their guests afternoons and evenings." The couple enjoyed their own sleeping quarters, and, for more private moments, the camp carpenter built a restraining balustrade at the rear of the tent; from there the Custers watched the evening sun descend over the soothing flow of a nearby stream. Thoughtfully, the Custers provided a dormitory-style tent for the bevy of young girls "who would add sparkle to camp life as well as attract and amuse the many bachelor officers." Other tents contained the dining room, kitchen, storerooms, and quarters for the cook and coachman. Eliza Brown, "the Custers' black cook, who had been with the General since 1863," ruled the roost. The stories of her impact on the Autie-Libbie relationship are legendary.[46]

From these safari-like quarters, Custer mounted frequent hunting expeditions, often ranging 15 to 20 miles in search of buffalo. Soon a steady stream of the rich

---

46 Minnie Dubbs Millbrook, "Big Game Hunting with the Custers, 1869-1870," *The Kansas Historical Quarterly* (Winter 1975), Vol. 41, No. 4, 430-431.

and famous lined up to hunt with him. Five grand hunts were planned throughout the summer of 1869, each one more elaborate than the last. Of the September hunt, Custer reported to his publishers, "Letters from Lieutenant General Sheridan and Major General Schofield . . . informed us that two youthful scions of English nobility—two real lords—proposed visiting us, who, to use the words of the distinguished Lieutenant General were 'chock full of buffalo-hunting.' . . . When this intelligence reached us, we began perfecting our arrangements for a hunt, which would be the grandest of the season."[47]

"What a party it was!" recalled one of the participants. "General Custer was the hero of all who knew him, and Mrs. Custer, who attended in a carriage, was like a queen, surrounded by her court." The long hunting season, however, began to wear on the normally resilient Libbie. "We had so many buffalo hunts this summer for strangers who came with letters to Autie, that it is such a bore to us," she complained as the last hunt neared its end. "We tremble at every dispatch for fear it announces buffalo hunters."[48]

The weather soon began to turn, and the Custers made plans for a quiet winter. Alas, it was not to be. From General Schofield came orders for one more hunt. Ostensibly, wrote Libbie, Schofield "had in mind the diversion, exercise to the soldiers as well as giving the companies a supply of buffalo meat." But as the veteran military wife she was, Libbie noted that there was an ulterior motive behind everything the army did. This last hunt was planned with Lt. Col. Wesley Merritt as one of the principal guests.[49]

After You Have Hunted Men, What Then?

Merritt's place in this hunt had followed a circuitous and oft-times dismaying route. His post-war years were marred by a series of debilitating health issues. A serious bout of dysentery throughout the summer of 1867 required an extended sick leave, which began in November of that year and lasted until June 1868. In January 1869, Merritt slipped and fell while trying to hoist himself up into a moving wagon. His left arm snapped like a dry twig when it fell into the path of a moving wheel. The serious compound fracture was beyond the scope of the post surgeon, who could do nothing more than place it in a cast. The arm obstinately refused to

47 Ibid., 434.

48 Ibid., 441, 447.

49 Ibid., 450.

heal, and Merritt's discomfiture increased over the next seven months. He conveyed his worries to the staff at district headquarters. "My hand and arm are stiff and lame," he wrote, "and I despair of recovering the full use of them unless some means and appliances are used which cannot be obtained here." Relinquishing command of the 9th Cavalry in August 1869, Merritt sought the best doctors he could find, little dreaming that it would be two years before he would command troops in the field again.[50]

As befitting a frugal postwar army, the high command tried to kill two birds with one penny-pinching stone. While Merritt obtained the necessary medical care at Fort Leavenworth in St. Louis, he was assigned to the so-called "Schofield Board," presided over by its namesake Major General Schofield. Its distinguished array of officers from the respective branches were tasked with performing a top-to-bottom review of the various systems employed by the U.S. Army.

Merritt, with his experience in the Civil War and on the frontier, represented the cavalry. It was a god-sent opportunity for him to firmly stamp his vision on the future operations of front-line cavalry regiments. Merritt believed that in years to come, the Army would no longer find itself campaigning on the thankless frontier against a militarily primitive but battle-hardened warrior society. The next war, he predicted, would pit America's military forces "against the best that the Europeans could throw at them." He outlined the parameters of future wars in an article written for *Harper's New Monthly Magazine*. The role of the Regulars would require a vast departure from long-established dogma, he warned; they would have to train all the raw recruits. "The militia of the United States will answer well the purpose of a 'second line' in case of war with a foreign power," he argued, noting that "if we are involved in war with a foreign power a year's time will not be given us to prepare."[51]

Merritt became heavily involved in choosing the cavalry's weapon of choice for the future. Almost shockingly, the board rejected the adoption of the reliable Spencer or any other war-proven, breech-loading carbine. A consensus of the board briefly chose the Remington rolling block carbine for universal use by the mounted arm; the ordnance board, however, overruled even this inexplicable decision and awarded a contract to the Springfield Arms Company. Thousands of single-shot, muzzle-loading firearms left over from the war had been stashed in government warehouses. These Springfields would be machined into

50 Alberts, *General Wesley Merritt*, 212.

51 Wesley Merritt, "The Army of the United States," 508.

cartridge-firing, breech-loading carbines. Frugality at the highest levels once again dictated policy, and the "Trapdoor Springfield" would serve as the standard weapon of the army until well into the 1890s.

The "Trapdoor" carbine lay at the heart of the cavalry's future tactics and necessitated a new system of drill, which meant that the cavalry could finally break away from the two-rank system prevalent in the Civil War. The evolutions for the new formations were sent to Custer at Fort Hays for a practical evaluation, and the 7th Cavalry worked its way meticulously and professionally through the manual. In the end, Custer reported that the cavalry should adopt the drill as written. At some point, Merritt traveled to Kansas to meet with Custer and discuss the switch to single-rank tactics, hence the addition of one last hunt to end the season. Custer could not resist a chance to have some fun with Merritt.

Libbie's writings never mention Merritt by name, alluding only to "the guest officer whom we were entertaining with the hunt, for it was not wholly for the girls." But in the midst of her campaign to have the Custer statue at West Point removed, she wrote to General Sherman and verified that "[o]n the plains we entertained him [Merritt] and he seemed to have conquered his enmity and jealousy that was so bitter in the Army of the Potomac." Unlike prior expeditions, the last one started off on the wrong track and stayed there. "This hunt however differed from all the rest," observed historian Minnie Dobbs Millbrook, "which seemed to have been expertly organized and carried out with the famed army efficiency." In Custer's eyes, such meticulous preparations were wasted on Wesley Merritt.[52]

To begin with, noted tracker and nationally renowned frontiersman George Armstrong Custer succeeded in getting the party lost. The group wandered aimlessly miles from the intended campsite where they were to meet up with the buffalo hunters hired for the expedition. "It got dark sooner than expected as a storm came up," recounted Libbie. The small creeks and draws began churning with torrents of rainwater. After attempting a few treacherous crossings, they decided to camp for the night. "A bend in the creek was selected as a sort of a screen, hiding [us] from the Indians as the underbrush on the creek banks [formed] a sort of protection from our being seen." Streaks of lightning illuminated the small party and thunder—"the artillery of heaven"—rolled over the wagons, which shook like the proverbial leaves in a storm. The rain found every hole, opening, and loose stitch in the canvas of each wagon. The servants rode in the first vehicle,

---

52 Millbrook, "A Monument to Custer," 278-279; Millbrook, "Big Game Hunting with the Custers," 451; Leckie, *Elizabeth Bacon Custer*, 233.

followed by the Custers in their personal wagon. Strategically placed next to that of their hosts was the third wagon, with its coterie of "tittering, jabbering" young lady friends of the Custers. The last one carried "the chilled, drenched officers."[53]

"At dawn," recalled Libbie, "the officers climbed out . . . water-soaked, mud-stained, crumpled, creased men." Among them strode Merritt, rapidly working his way into a foul mood. Aggravated by the cramped accommodations and the inclement weather, his unhealed arm gave him a great deal of pain. Sometime in the course of the restless, sleepless night, several of the young officers had slipped into the wagonload of single women; there "followed frolic and merrymaking not dampened by climatic influences," wrote Libbie, who could hear everything from her position next to the wagon in question. And what Libbie could hear, Merritt could also; to say he was displeased probably would be an understatement.[54]

As the rain-soaked night turned into a gray sultry morning, the bad situation worsened when dark figures appeared in the distance. Custer grabbed his field glasses, took a long searching look, and called all the officers to his side: they were beset by Indians, he declared. "This consultation was the most ominous of all," recalled an alarmed Libbie. "They returned and said they had resolved on the only plan of action left open to them, and must ride at once to the foe." Custer pointedly left Merritt in charge of the women. "Leaving the now thoroughly alarmed guest as our champion in the oncoming massacre they put spurs to their horses and disappeared down the gully."

Before long, an exchange of gunfire could be heard, dull and menacing in the humidity of the morning. "While we looked and gasped . . . we saw a horseman approach us," wrote Libbie. "As he reached us on a dead run . . . he called out waving, gesticulating wildly—'corral the ambulances, the Indians, the Indians!'" The women quailed in terror. "The guest officer was walking up and down clinching his fists, muttering in tones of fury, 'It's a pretty fix Custer's got us into.'" When one of the girls spotted a give-away twinkle in the rider's eyes, word quickly spread. "It was all a hoax, one of those practical jokes that General Custer loved to play. The invading horsemen were from the hunting camp, coming to find the hunters who had not arrived the night before as planned."[55]

It is safe to assume that the "guest officer" was not in the least bit amused.

---

53 Leckie, *Elizabeth Bacon Custer*, 233; Millbrook, "Big Game Hunting with the Custers," 450-451.

54 Ibid., 451.

55 Ibid., 451-452.

CHAPTER SIX

Finally, Cavalry the Way It Was Meant to Be

FROM ITS SOURCE HIGH up in Chester Gap in the Blue Ridge Mountains, the Rappahannock River meanders southeasterly for 184 miles through the northern part of Virginia's Piedmont region, eventually emptying into Chesapeake Bay a mere 15 miles south of the Potomac River. Just to the southeast of Fredericksburg, it widens into a brackish tidal estuary, renowned then as now for its oyster beds and scrumptious crab. The Rapidan River joins the Rappahannock upriver of Fredericksburg to form a triangular spit of land known locally as the "Great Fork." During the Civil War, the strategically important Orange and Alexandria Railroad cut across both rivers on well-engineered bridges. Farther upstream the Rappahannock is neither wide nor deep, a fact recorded by Maj. W. W. Blackford of Jeb Stuart's staff. "I was ordered to make a topographical map showing the strategical strength of positions along the banks to force a crossing," recalled the budding cartographer, and "[a]s we ascended the stream it became smaller and smaller and the fords more and more frequent."[1]

The Rappahannock nonetheless presented a formidable barrier to the passage of Union troops; its high banks were heavily fringed with trees and dense undergrowth, and its marshy bottom made passage difficult. Further impeding the soldiers' movement on the north-south axis were the remnants of a barge canal system that had been built in 1840. The advent of the railroads had made the canal obsolete, and it had fallen into ruin and decay. The crib dams remained in place and still worked efficiently, creating reservoirs and pools which would require bridging

---

1 W. W. Blackford, *War Years with Jeb Stuart* (Baton Rouge, 1992), 210.

with pontoons. Just such a dam obstructed the flow of the river above Beverly's Ford, but the waters below the dam were easily fordable. "The rivers, the roads and the fords seemed to have been placed as if to lure an invader into a maze," wrote historian Douglas Southall Freeman.[2]

For its Confederate defenders, the area offered a veritable warren of thickly wooded forests and narrow country lanes. Vast rolling fields under cultivation with young shoots of corn, wheat, and oats provided perfect ground for the movement of large masses of cavalry. The many knolls, bluffs, and ridges seemed tailor-made for the deployment of artillery and offered clear lines of sight for observing the enemy. The land was cut up by numerous ditches, fences, and the ubiquitous stone walls of an agrarian society practicing the latest in farming techniques.

As May gave way to June, a trickle of information began to find its way to cavalry headquarters. To date the only tools available for penetrating the Confederate screen south of the river had been rumor and speculation, and Pleasonton's staff was clueless as to the Rebels' intentions. On June 1, Pleasonton received a message written by a Mr. G. S. Smith, who asked the courier to "[p]lease show the inclosed note to Major-General Hooker. He knows who Mr. Smith is." According to the seemingly well-placed Mr. Smith,

> There is one thing that looks very apparent to me, and that is, that this movement of General Lee's is not intended to menace Washington, but to try his hand again toward Maryland, or to call off your attention while General Stuart goes there. I have every reason for believing that Stuart is on his way toward Maryland. I do not positively know it, but have the very best of reasons for believing it.

Pleasonton added his own endorsement saying that, in his opinion, "the rebel army has been weakened by troops sent west and south, and that any performance of Stuart's will be a flutter to keep us from seeing their weakness." Typical of Pleasonton, he had misunderstood the report entirely.[3]

Not satisfied with Pleasonton's analysis, Hooker authorized an aerial reconnaissance. At first light on June 4, two balloons made their majestic ascent above the south basin of the Rappahannock. The balloon overlooking the Salem Church area reported seeing a line of dust and twenty wagons moving north. The

---

2 Joseph W. McKinney, *Brandy Station, Virginia, June 9, 1863: The Largest Cavalry Battle of the Civil War* (Jefferson, NC, 2006), 39; Douglas Southall Freeman, *Lee's Lieutenants*, 1:694.

3 OR 27, pt. 3, 3.

other, floating over Banks Ford, noted the disappearance of two camps "and several batteries in motion." That same day, a patrol of troopers from the 2nd New York Cavalry intercepted a missive from Jeb Stuart to a local secessionist, "assuring him that he would have a sufficient force of cavalry in that neighborhood by Sunday evening to relieve the anxiety of the county and stop the raids of the Yankees."[4]

In Washington, Henry Halleck's informants believed that Jeb Stuart was preparing to launch a large-scale mounted raid with a force numbering between 15,000 and 20,000 men, including the cream of the Confederate horse artillery. Union patrol activity increased as a result of this news, and the next day a solid report arrived from the always-vigilant Buford. "I have just received information," he wrote, "which I consider reliable, that all the available cavalry force of the Confederacy is in Culpeper County. Stuart, the two Lees, Robertson, Jenkins, and Jones are all there. . . . Since the Chancellorsville fight, their cavalry has been very much increased. . . . My informant—a refugee from Madison County–says Stuart has 20,000."[5]

John Buford had known Alfred Pleasonton for a long time, ever since the days when the cavalry learned its trade fighting the marauding bands of Indians who inflamed the frontier from Texas to the northern plains. They developed a workable relationship that took into account the obvious strengths of Buford and the weaknesses and foibles of Pleasonton. Of course, Pleasonton always believed it was the other way around. "Now Buford was a very laconic man," he once told sculptor James Edward Kelly. "He would never tell enough in his reports, but I could always read between the lines and fill them up. . . . I would take the Reports to Headquarters and tell what happened. [The commanding] General would say, 'That's not in the report.' 'No, but I know what they mean.'"[6]

This was precisely what Buford feared. As his biographer, Edward G. Longacre, notes, Buford recognized Pleasonton's "sometimes lax leadership and especially his frequent failure to separate wild rumor, baseless speculation, and hard intelligence." Buford knew Pleasonton to be "an opportunist, an inveterate politician and intriguer, a seeker of promotion and preference." On the other hand, Pleasonton possessed undisputed administrative abilities, and as long as he stayed off the battlefield—which rumor said he was prone to do anyway—then Buford

---

4   Ibid., 5; Glazier, *Three Years in the Federal Cavalry*, 212.

5   *OR* 27, pt. 3, 8.

6   Styple, *Generals in Bronze*, 116.

could work with him to achieve the cavalry's goals. Later in life Pleasonton would lament what he perceived as his detrimental effect on Buford's promotion. "You know I recommended Gregg and Buford very highly for promotion; but do you think they would promote them?" he asked an acquaintance. "No. It seemed that everything I touched I contaminated." Only Custer and Merritt seemed to escape the Pleasonton curse.[7]

Hooker presented his analysis along with the information at hand directly to President Lincoln. "It was impossible for me to determine satisfactorily whether this movement had merely been a change of camps," he vacillated, "but, taken in connection with the fact that some deserters came in from the divisions of Hood and Pickett, I concluded that those divisions had been brought to the front . . . and that this could be for no other purpose but to enable the enemy to move up the river, with a view to the execution of a movement similar to that of Lee's last year."[8]

But Hooker, still living down the fiasco of Chancellorsville, was beginning to feel handcuffed by the orders that had been issued to him back in January. "I am instructed to keep 'in view always the importance of covering Washington and Harper's Ferry, either directly or by so operating as to be able to punish any force of the enemy sent against them.'" He reminded Lincoln of these restrictions in an extended communiqué. "After giving the subject my best reflection, I am of opinion that it is my duty to pitch into his rear, although in so doing the head of his column may reach Warrenton before I can return. Will it be within the spirit of my instructions to do so?" President Lincoln clearly disagreed and in his usual folksy way informed Hooker of his concerns: "In one word, I would not take any risk of being entangled upon the river, like an ox jumped half over a fence and liable to be torn by dogs front and rear, without a fair chance to gore one way or kick the other."[9]

Taking heed of the president's words, Hooker decided to defang the dogs that threatened to attack front and rear. On June 6, he ordered Pleasonton to prepare to deal with the concentration of Stuart's cavalry. "As the accumulation of the heavy rebel force of cavalry about Culpeper may mean mischief," he informed General Halleck, "I am determined, if practicable, to break it up in its incipiency. I shall send all my cavalry against them, stiffened by about 3,000 infantry. . . . It is my intention

---

7 Edward G. Longacre, *General John Buford: A Military Biography* (Cambridge, MA, 1995), 140-141; Styple, *Generals in Bronze*, 127.

8 *OR* 27, pt.1, 30.

9 Ibid., 30, 31.

to attack them in their camps." This decision would lead to one of the most indecisive and yet far-reaching clashes of cavalry thus far in the war. The opposing forces had worked their way toward the Rappahannock, concealed from one another by the dense timber lining the banks of the river.[10]

Keep Your Powder Dry, Boys!

General Hooker's instructions left little doubt as to the ultimate aim of the cavalry's mission. His chief of staff, Maj. Gen. Daniel A. Butterfield, passed on the commanding general's orders to General Pleasonton:

> From the most reliable information at these headquarters, it is recommended that you cross the Rappahannock at Beverly and Kelly's Fords, and march directly on Culpeper. For this you will divide your cavalry force as you think proper, to carry into execution the object in view, which is to disperse and destroy the rebel force assembled in the vicinity of Culpeper, and to destroy his trains and supplies of all description to the utmost of your ability.[11]

Buford led the right wing, which was slated to cross the Rappahannock at Beverly's Ford. Buford's 1st Cavalry Division consisted of the brigades of Cols. Benjamin F. "Grimes" Davis and Thomas C. Devin, as well as the Regular Brigade, commanded by Maj. Charles J. Whiting. They were accompanied by three batteries of artillery and one of the two infantry brigades assigned to the operation, led by Brig. Gen. Adelbert Ames. Merritt arrived in the camp of the 2nd U.S. Cavalry in early June expecting to take command of a squadron of two companies due to his seniority. He soon discovered that he was had become the ranking officer, as other,

---

10 Ibid., 33.

11 Before the war, Butterfield worked for American Express, a company founded by his father. He rose rapidly through various volunteer regiments to command a corps at Fredericksburg. Although there is some debate on the details, Butterfield either composed or adapted "Taps" for use by the army. Hooker selected him for the chief of staff post in January 1863. Butterfield was blamed for much of the poor moral reputation of Hooker's headquarters, but also contributed greatly to the recovery of the Army of the Potomac after the battle of Fredericksburg; OR 27, pt.3, 27. See also, generally, Al Conner and Chris Mackowski, *Seizing Destiny: The Army of the Potomac's "Valley Forge"* (El Dorado Hills, CA, 2016), for a deep treatment of this period of the war, including Butterfield's role therein.

A rare image of a young Capt. Wesley Merritt.

Courtesy of Cowan's Auctions

more senior men had left the regiment to accept higher positions in volunteer units. He was now Capt. Wesley Merritt, commander of the 2nd U.S. Cavalry.[12]

The left wing, which was to cross at Kelly's Ford several miles downstream, was commanded by Brigadier General Gregg, and consisted of his own 3rd Cavalry Division of two brigades under the command of Cols. Kilpatrick and Wyndham, along with Col. Alfred N. Duffié's 2nd Cavalry Division. Colonels Luigi P. di Cesnola and J. Irvin Gregg led the two brigades of Duffié's division. Augmenting Gregg's command were two batteries of artillery and a brigade of infantry under Brig. Gen. David Russell. Horsemen could cross easily at Kelly's Ford, but the deeper water presented problems for Russell's infantry. The army provided a couple of boats to ferry them across, but it was destined to be a slow process, and the resulting delay in crossing Kelly's Ford would gravely jeopardize Pleasonton's coordinated plan of attack.[13]

12 Eric Wittenberg, *The Devil's to Pay: John Buford at Gettysburg* (El Dorado Hills, CA, 2014), 22. The start of the war found Devin running a house-painting business with his brother. Devin also had a martial side, however; he served in the militia in New York, and eventually was promoted to captain of the 1st New York State Militia Cavalry. Later, as commander of the 6th New York Cavalry, he won the respect of Buford, who stated, "I can't teach Col. Devin anything of cavalry tactics, he knows more than I do." Captured at Gaines' Mill when his horse was shot out from under him, Whiting spent a month at Richmond's notorious Libby Prison before being paroled and exchanged for a Southern officer.

13 Luigi P. di Cesnola to Erasmus Corning, March 10, 1863, Gettysburg National Military Park. Son of an Italian count, di Cesnola graduated from the Royal Military Academy at Turin, Italy. After serving with distinction in the Crimean War, he emigrated to America in 1860. At the war's outbreak, di Cesnola received a commission as lieutenant colonel of the 11th New York Cavalry, but resigned in June 1862 to become colonel of the 4th New York Cavalry. From then on, a string of minor incidents tarnished his reputation. In February 1863, he was accused of the theft of six Remington revolvers and was summarily dismissed from the service. After an investigation exonerated him, di Cesnola returned to his regiment, but his resentment lingered. On March 13, he wrote his close friend, Congressman Erasmus Corning. "It is impossible for me to continue in the service, [and] tho I have been restored I have not received from the administration that full justice I was entitled to. . . . I am therefore going to the regiment with a broken heart—to stay there some weeks and then I shall resign as it is incompatible with my character to continue." His fortunes improved after the war. Appointed American consul to Cyprus, he became fascinated with antiquities and eventually was named the first director of the Metropolitan Museum of Art in 1879. Gregg followed a very different path. He enlisted as a private in the Mexican War and mustered out as a captain. When the Civil War broke out, he accepted a commission as captain, and soon thereafter a post as colonel of the 5th Pennsylvania Reserve. He transferred to the newly formed 6th U.S. Cavalry under his cousin David McMurtrie Gregg and served conspicuously through the Peninsula, Second Bull Run, and Maryland campaigns. In November 1862, he took command of the 16th Pennsylvania Cavalry, and later led a brigade under General Averell. After Gettysburg, he served with distinction under Sheridan through the Overland, Shenandoah Valley, and Appomattox campaigns. After the war Gregg stayed in the army, taking command of the 8th Cavalry in 1866.

At 2:00 p.m. on June 8, Pleasonton began moving his troopers and supporting infantry to the river fords, 12 miles away from their various campsites. "Saddles are hastily packed, horses mounted, and many speculations indulged as to destination," wrote Samuel Gracey, the chaplain of the 6th Pennsylvania Cavalry. "All indications point to a severe fight." Darkness soon descended upon the men and no fires or lights were allowed. The hungry troopers slapped a slice of salt pork between two bone-dry pieces of hardtack, munched down the unappealing fare, and "spread our saddle-blankets on the ground, and with saddles for pillows, prepare[d] for a night's rest."[14]

Despite these privations, the commands were in fine fettle, according to Capt. Edwin Eustace Bryant, adjutant of the 3rd Wisconsin Infantry of Ames's brigade. "At about eight o'clock in the evening, [the cavalry was] drawn up by the roadside to give us the front. A merry bandying of jokes, as we passed this seemingly vast array of horsemen, showed the light-hearted humor of brave soldiers," Bryant wrote approvingly. "The boys chaffed the cavalry because they could not keep up with us and had to turn out and let us pass." Officers took the utmost precautions to ensure that the enemy remained unaware of the movement. "Buford's whole column was now concealed in the woods," recalled Capt. Daniel Oakey of the 2nd Massachusetts Infantry. "The cheerful clank and jingle of the cavalry was, by some means, suppressed; there was no merry bugle breaking upon the still hours of the night; and, as the moon threw deep shadows across the quiet country road, there seemed no trace of 'grim-visaged war.'"[15]

A feeling of confidence also permeated the ranks of the Confederate horsemen stationed on the southern side of the Rappahannock. The Rebel cavalry now stood at the height of its strength, and soon would wield its power. "A grand review was ordered for the 5th of June and all at headquarters were exerting themselves to the utmost to make it a success," recalled Blackford. Officers and men wore their best uniforms, and the horses, fit and fat after a winter of grazing, were brushed to a shine. From a slight knoll which served as the reviewing stand, the vast, open field "could be seen to great advantage." The columns of squadrons, 12,000 men in all, took one stately walk around the field, then broke into a trot. One hundred yards from the knoll, they took the gallop, "then at the 'charge' [moved] at full speed past

---

14 Gracey, *Annals of the 6th Pennsylvania Cavalry*, 156.

15 Edwin Eustace Bryant, *History of the Third Regiment of Wisconsin Veteran Volunteer Infantry, 1861-1865* (Madison, WI, 1891), 166; Daniel Oakey, *History of the Second Massachusetts Regiment of Infantry: Beverly Ford, A Paper Read at the Officer's Reunion in Boston, May 12, 1884* (Boston, 1884), 5.

the reviewing stand, yelling just as they do in a real charge, and brandishing their sabers over their heads. The effect was thrilling."[16]

As the troopers passed the reviewing stand, Maj. Robert F. Beckham's battery of horse artillery began firing its guns as fast as they could be loaded, belching out great gouts of flame and swirling gun smoke. The scene, recalled one witness, "would make your hair stand on end to see [it]." The festive event could be heard quite clearly on the northern side of the Rappahannock. "Yesterday cannon fire was heard toward Culpeper," reported Buford. "I suppose it was a salute, as I was told Stuart was to have had that day an inspection of his whole force."[17]

Three days later, a more business-like review was held solely for the benefit of Gen. Robert E. Lee, who had not been able to attend the more ostentatious affair of June 5. The stately and dignified Lee, noted Maj. Henry B. McClellan, Stuart's adjutant general, was "always careful not to tax his men unnecessarily, [and] would not allow the cavalry to take the gallop, nor would he permit the artillerymen to work their guns. He would reserve all their strength for the serious work which must surely ensue."[18]

And that momentous task, Lee had determined, was nothing less than another incursion into northern territory. On June 8, adhering to the chain of command, Lee shared his thinking with Confederate Secretary of War James Seddon. "As far as I can judge there is nothing to be gained by this army remaining quietly on the defensive," he explained. "All our military preparations and organizations should now be pressed forward with the greatest vigor, and every exertion made to obtain some material advantage in this campaign." That same day, part of Lee's infantry under Richard Ewell began moving out of Fredericksburg toward Culpeper Court House, and from there enter the Shenandoah Valley on their way north to the Potomac River.[19]

Lee ordered Stuart to cross the Rappahannock the next day and protect the flank of the army as it advanced. "In preparation for this movement," recorded Major McClellan, "the [cavalry] brigades were, on the evening of the same day, moved down toward the river." Stuart had established his headquarters on the eastern slope of Fleetwood Hill, a long, elevated spit of land overlooking the rolling

---

16 Blackford, *War Years with Jeb Stuart*, 211-212.

17 Ibid., 212; OR 27, pt. 3, 14.

18 Henry B. McClellan, *The Life and Campaigns of Major-General J. E. B. Stuart* (Bloomington, IN, 1958), 262.

19 *OR* 27, pt. 3, 868-869.

farmland south of the Rappahannock. Brandy Station, on the Orange and Alexandria Railroad, lay a few hundred yards to the south. It was a commanding position from which he could survey all the open ground around him. In anticipation of the next day's advance, Stuart had already packed all his camp equipage into the headquarters' wagons, and was "roughing it" like the rest of his boys.[20]

Fitzhugh Lee's brigade, temporarily commanded by Col. Thomas T. Munford, camped north of Hazel Run, a tributary of the Rappahannock, perfectly placed to guard the northernmost fords. Munford's defenses centered on the Oak Shade Church, and Fleetwood Hill lay seven and one-half miles to the northwest. Rooney Lee's brigade, headquartered at the Welford plantation, picketed the fords from the south side of Hazel Run, keeping a particularly close watch over the Beverly's Ford crossing. This crossing was further guarded by the famed "Laurel Brigade," led by the colorful and cantankerous Col. W. E. "Grumble" Jones. The bulk of Jones's command was bivouacked several hundred yards back from the ford. Unaware of their extreme exposure, four batteries of horse artillery parked between Jones's position and the Rappahannock, hoping to steal an early march and avoid potential traffic. Brigadier General Beverly H. Robertson's brigade covered the crossing at Kelly's Ford, and its camping grounds extended back to Stevensburg. Wade Hampton's brigade stood by within supporting distance, its camps also stretching toward Stevensburg.[21]

---

20 McClellan, *The Life and Campaigns of Major-General J. E. B. Stuart*, 262.

21 Munford graduated from the Virginia Military Institute in 1852. Before the war he spent time as a cotton planter in Mississippi, and farmed in Bedford County, Virginia. He led a brigade of cavalry under Stonewall Jackson in the 1862 Valley campaign and assumed command of all of Jackson's cavalry after the death of Brig. Gen. Turner Ashby. Munford led troops with distinction at Cross Keys, White Oak Swamp, Second Bull Run, and South Mountain. Although Munford commanded brigades on multiple occasions and eventually led a division, he was never formally promoted to brigadier general; John D. Imboden, "Fire, Sword, and the Halter," in Alexander Kelly McClure, ed., *The Annals of the Civil War. Written by Leading Participants North and South* (Philadelphia, 1879), 173; McKinney, *Brandy Station*, 39. Jones, West Point class of 1848, served in the Mounted Rifles before the war. His irritable disposition earned him the nickname "Grumble." Fellow general John Imboden considered him "brave as a lion," but also a "man of temper, morose and fretful." Jones recruited and commanded a company of the 1st Virginia Cavalry at the start of the war. In March 1862, he took command of all Confederate cavalry in the Valley District. He served with Stuart in the Peninsula campaign, at Second Bull Run, and in the opening stages of the Gettysburg campaign. Jones disdained pageantry and ceremonial claptrap. During the review for Lee, he angered Stuart by allowing his brigade to relax "at ease" until the last moment; Jones himself was found lounging on the ground next to his horse. This event, along with Jones's generally disagreeable disposition, led Stuart to leave Jones and his brigade behind when he launched his ill-starred ride around the

The Union troopers were shaken awake at 2:00 a.m. "Quietly we saddle up, mount, and move stealthily to the ford," recalled Chaplain Gracey. "Just as the gray dawn of approaching day begins to brighten up the deep darkness of the hour, we arrive at the riverbank." A detachment of the 2nd Massachusetts Infantry snuck down to the ford and reported the presence of Jones's unsuspecting cavalrymen. "The Confederates," recalled Adjutant Bryant, "were not expecting visitors at this time. . . . They had withdrawn their pickets from the lower fords of the river . . . the horses were picketed, the men at fatigue duty or lying about camp, no one suspecting the presence of an enemy."[22]

As the infantry fortified itself with a cold breakfast, the road to the crossing began to teem with cavalry. "As the hazy June morning dawned upon us, troopers appeared to rise out of the ground and swarm out of the woods, till the whole country seemed alive with cavalry," recounted Captain Oakey. "The early morning mist, hanging upon the riverbanks, concealed our approach." Pleasonton and Buford, followed by their staff officers, headed down to the riverbank, quietly urging the troops along. "General Buford was there, with his usual smile," Capt. Frederick C. Newhall recalled. "It was always reassuring to see him in the saddle when there was any chance of a fight." His confident manner, though understated, proved infectious. The general, said Oakey, "whom we had never seen before, impressed us with his commanding presence and his manly and picturesque simplicity of dress. He looked as if his division might idolize him, as it was said they did."[23]

As Ames's men plunged into the stream, Captain Bryant noticed the assemblage "of the distinguished group of horsemen." With the respect of one soldier to another, he wrote that Pleasonton's "staff on that morning formed a

Union army. Beginning in 1849, Robertson served with the 2nd Dragoons at outposts in the territories of New Mexico, Kansas, and Nebraska. After fighting the Apache and Sioux with the regiment, he transferred to the 5th Cavalry as a 1st lieutenant, eventually becoming the acting assistant adjutant general for the Department of Utah. Despite being promoted to captain in March 1861, he resigned his commission to join the Confederate adjutant general's department. After his election to the colonelcy of the 4th Virginia Cavalry, he took part in Stonewall Jackson's Valley campaign and served at Second Bull Run. Sent to North Carolina to recruit and train new cavalry regiments, he later returned to Virginia at the head of a brigade of two regiments from that state; McClellan, *The Life and Campaigns of Major-General J. E. B. Stuart*, 263; *Atlas to Accompany the Official Records of the Union and Confederate Armies* (Washington, DC, 1891-95), Plate 44, Map 3.

22 Gracey, *Annals of the 6th Pennsylvania Cavalry*, 157; Bryant, *History of the Third Regiment*, 167.

23 Oakey, *History of the Second Massachusetts*, 6-8, 10.

party who came out of the war with high distinction." Among them he identified A. J. Alexander, Elon Farnsworth, Ranald McKenzie, Ulric Dahlgren, and "the model chevalier," George Custer. "These young and gallant hard-riders," he noted, "were full of the enthusiasm of the true bred soldiers they were." In this group, noted Captain Newhall, "General Pleasonton had certainly no lack of intelligence, dash, and hard-riding to rely on in those about him." Custer, accompanied by his bugler and staunch admirer Joseph Fought, soon peeled away from the group and hastened up the narrow road to the front. "Lt. Custer and I crossed the Ford and took the inside of the field," wrote Fought. "There were two or three Rebels near the woods, but we clipped along towards them, and they fired at us and we fired back. . . . We rode on through the woods, and met our advance guard, Col. Davis and his command, and reported to him."[24]

"Grimes" Davis, commanding the 1st Division in Buford's absence, personally led the advance element of the 8th New York Cavalry across the ford; a cooler mind might have chosen a brigade headquarters a little farther back and left his regimental commanders to deal with the Rebel pickets. A thick fog lay close to the water's surface, muffling the splashing of the horses' hooves. "By 4 o'clock our advance guard is across," reads Chaplain Gracey's account, "and surprise the picket of the enemy; and before they have time to fall back upon their reserve, or rub the sleep from their eyes, we are upon them and capture them. Now our men dash upon the reserve, and away they run without exchanging a shot."[25]

The Rebels wasted little time in mounting an effective rearguard action. "Part of Jones' troopers were soon in the saddle, charging furiously down upon the Eighth New York, who broke," wrote Oakey. Davis was losing control of the fight.

---

24 Bryant, *History of the Third Regiment*, 168; Oakey, *History of the Second Massachusetts*, 8; Merington, *The Custer Story*, 58; Edward G. Longacre, *Custer: The Making of a Young General* (New York, 2018), 74-77. Fought looms as one of the biggest enigmas in the Custer mythology. He supposedly joined the Union army as a drummer boy, and then became a bugler. His commanding officer in Company D, 2nd Cavalry—soon to become the 5th U.S. Cavalry—described him as a "small boy." Early in the war he met and attached himself to George A. Custer, who was then a lieutenant, and would remain with the budding young officer until the war's end. Fought's accounts of his adventures with Custer are archived in the Marguerite Merington collection at the New York Public Library. Modern historians suspect that Fought's anecdotal stories were heavily redacted, but Merington states that his accounts were already in very brittle condition when the historian took possession of Libbie Custer's papers after her death. Custer, as he rose in rank, continued to promote Fought, who eventually achieved the rank of lieutenant. The Grand Army of the Republic (GAR), which listed him as an active member, recorded his death on September 9, 1913, and his subsequent burial at Rockwell Cemetery in Washington, D.C.

25 Gracey, *Annals of the 6th Pennsylvania Cavalry*, 157.

His line of advance, up a narrow road bordered on both sides by woodlands, prevented him from bringing the bulk of his forces into action. Trotting up the road ahead of his men, Davis roared his troopers back to the line. Caught up in the thrill of battle and brandishing his sword, he advanced toward the enemy, venturing dangerously far from support. Some reports indicate that he was 75 yards in front of the line. Suddenly, "before Colonel Davis could turn to rally his leading regiment, a Rebel soldier sprang from behind a tree and shot him dead." Few events disrupt an attacking force more than the loss of a key commander in the opening phase of a complicated battle plan, and Davis's death would be no different.[26]

Custer, with Fought in tow, had reported to Davis just minutes earlier. A staff officer with no specific orders, Custer lingered on the fringes of the divisional command group, observing the action on behalf of his commander. "Genl. Pleasonton, a very active officer, was always anxious to be posted about what was doing in front," wrote Fought. "If Lt. Custer observed that it was important to make a movement or charge he would tell the commander to do it, and the commander would have to do it, would not dare question, because he knew Lt. Custer was working under Genl. Pleasonton who would confirm every one of his instructions and movements."[27]

One hundred men of the 6th Virginia Cavalry charged the Union troopers and stalled their attack, allowing the Confederate artillery to limber up and escape. "Grumble" Jones arrived along with the 7th Virginia Cavalry, and Davis's brigade made a fighting retreat. In the distance, the hillside camps of the Confederates erupted in a bedlam of noise and movement. "Our firing has alarmed the main force of the enemy," recalled Gracey. "Do you hear the sharp bing! bing! bing of the carbines? Let us on their support! They have cleared the woods, and roused the whole force of Stuart's rebel cavalry, and now there is earnest work before us."[28]

The Rebels had hit the Federal chain of command hard. Colonel Davis lay dead in the road; command of his brigade passed to Maj. William S. McClure. Major Alpheus Clark, leading the 8th Illinois Cavalry, took a bullet in his hand—a

---

26 Oakey, *History of the Second Massachusetts*, 7.

27 Merington, *The Custer Story*, 58. Unfortunately, several of Fought's stories conflict with known facts, making his testimony highly questionable. Yet the nature of his relationship to Custer gives his tales some weight, and several have become important in the Custer mythology over time. Custer uncharacteristically left no accounting of his actions during Brandy Station, forcing historians to rely mainly on Fought's account.

28 Gracey, *Annals of the 6th Pennsylvania Cavalry*, 157.

wound that would prove mortal. Moments later his second in command, Capt. George Forsyth, was shot in the thigh. Company E of the 8th New York Cavalry lost its leader, Capt. Benjamin F. Foote. It is likely that Custer personally delivered the discouraging news to Pleasonton and Buford, both of whom were at the Rappahannock crossing. Fought suggested that he and Custer returned to the ford. "We saw a Battery on the hill and found that it was Robinson's," he wrote somewhat sketchily. "We rode up to it, and Lt. Custer told of Col. Davis's death. It was a great shock."[29]

Buford quickly spurred his way to the front to restore order and regain the initiative. He directed Major McClure, with Davis's brigade, to move to the left of the Beverly's Ford Road with orders to clear out the woods to his front. The Regulars deployed to the right, with the 6th Pennsylvania Cavalry in front guiding on the road. Ames's infantry passed through the massed ranks of the Reserve Brigade to clear the woods on that flank. The infantry scrambled up the banks and broke through to the edge of the timber. "There before us was a large open country, excellent ground for a cavalry battle," explained Adjutant Bryant. "Thousands of Confederate horsemen were hurrying to and fro on the farther side of the opening. Our cavalry were coming up, squadron after squadron, forming on the edge of the woods, and a galling fire from dismounted skirmishers was making considerable havoc with the animals."[30]

Buford then ordered Colonel Devin to the front to take command of Davis's brigade. The riverbank and woods were now swarming with advancing troops. Among those in the process of crossing was Capt. Wesley Merritt with the 2nd U.S. Cavalry, who recalled the scene:

> It was only the work of a few moments, (though minutes seem long under such circumstances), to cross from the peaceful hither side of the Rappahannock to where the over-confident and lately-augmented horse of the Southern army was making hasty

---

29 Merington, *The Custer Story*, 59. This is one of those Fought statements that requires additional examination. A close look at the Union order of battle does not list any battery commanded by an officer named Robinson. There is, however, a Captain James M. Robertson listed in *Putnam's Rebellion Record*, volume 7, page 18, not only as commanding a horse battery with the cavalry, but also serving as "chief of artillery on General Pleasonton's staff." When Custer and Fought found him, they found Pleasonton and Buford. Custer informed them of Davis's death.

30 Bryant, *History of the Third Regiment*, 168.

preparations to meet us. And while we crossed and ascended the opposite bank, the first news of battle, borne on the wings of the morning, reached us.[31]

Merritt had known Davis in the pre-war army, and considered him to be "a gallant man, an ambitious soldier, [and] a courtly gentleman." Merritt respected the decision made by Davis, although Southern born and bred, to honor his oath to the Constitution and the army. "He stood firm by the flag under which he had received his qualifications and commission as an officer. . . . He died for that flag—under that flag fell too soon, but oh! so bravely. . . . He was dearly beloved throughout the brigade, and many a veteran . . . awaited the shock of battle, anxious to avenge the death of this hero."[32]

Whether Merritt had let go of the "martinetism" practiced as a style of leadership by many in the prewar Army, but eschewed by his former commander, Buford, is unknown. Cooke, Buford, and Stoneman had certainly been major influences on Merritt's development as an office. But there were also others, including but not limited to Davis, Whiting, and Pleasonton, who had put in their time but had not grasped the future role of the cavalry, stubbornly refusing to update their command styles to match. These men also had some influence over the young subaltern. Davis obviously clung to the ways of the martinet. There can be no sorrier epitaph for an officer than a complete lack of heartfelt loss from his own regiment—no lamentations, no expressions of sorrow, no prayers for a happy afterlife. "Our Brigade Commander Col. Davis was killed," Dr. Elias Beck, surgeon for the 3rd Indiana, wrote bluntly to his wife. "Davis was a Regular, a Mississipian by Birth—a proud tyrannical devil—& had the ill will of his whole Command. & I'll bet was Killed by our own Men. . . . General rejoicing among our Brigade that Davis was Killed he was such a Tyrant."[33]

Once the 2nd U.S. Cavalry was fully deployed beyond the woods, it was ordered to move in concert with and in support of a charge by the 6th Pennsylvania Cavalry. Devin's command peeled off to the left along the heavily wooded Beverly's Ford Road. Buford moved into the open fields on the right, a move Rooney Lee easily parried by moving from the north and taking up a strong position behind a stone wall. Hampton arrived from the south and took up

---

31 Merritt, "Reminiscences," 287-286.

32 Ibid.

33 E. W. H. Beck, "Letters of a Civil War Surgeon," *Indiana Magazine of History* (June 1931), Vol. 27, Issue 2, 132-163.

position on Jones's right. In response to these movements, Buford ordered the infantry into the middle of the line between the two cavalry commands. While debouching from the woods, Ames's and Devin's brigades came under heavy fire from the Rebel horse artillery massed at St. James Church. Dismounted sharpshooters hidden behind a stone wall began wreaking havoc amongst Devin's horses. "The woods were full of wounded horses," recalled Captain Bryant, "limping along on three legs, with that look of pleading in their great, expressive eyes that appealed as strongly to sympathy as did the sufferings of the wounded men."[34]

Like Custer, many officers loved being in battle. Lieutenant Christian Balder of the 6th U.S. Cavalry was one of them. "The fight grew beautifully larger & larger. The rebs contested every inch of the ground manfully," he wrote in stirring fashion. Balder openly criticized the delays that occurred after Davis's demise. "That hill should have been occupied by us, and we could have gotten it very early in the day but 'somebody' thought it was of no consequence." The artillery roared continuously, and every inch of Buford's line—anchored on his right by the Hazel River, a tributary of the Rappahannock, and stretching in a wide arc down to the Rappahannock on his left—seemed ablaze with fire and shrouded in battle smoke.[35]

Buford moved to attack the Rebel guns stationed at St. James Church. "The old, time-honored Second Dragoons, the Fifth Regulars, and that crack young regiment, the Sixth Pennsylvania Cavalry . . . were massing on the southern bank of the river," recalled Captain Oakey. "The sharp report of infantry rifles, the rising smoke, and the thousand indescribable sounds, with the tramp of fresh cavalry pressing forward to take their part in the fray, showed that the battle was now waging in good earnest." The trickle of wounded wending their way back to the ford grew to a flowing river of misery, with the "stretcher-bearers plying their trade in the hot sun."[36]

As the Reserve Brigade deployed into attack formation, two regiments from Rooney Lee's brigade began to pressure Buford's right flank, threatening to uncover Beverly's Ford, where much of the command was still wading across the

---

34 Bryant, *History of the Third Regiment*, 169.

35 James W. Milgram, "The Libby Prison Correspondence of Tattnall Paulding," *The American Philatelist* (December 1975), Vol. 89, No. 12, 1116. Sadly, Lieutenant Balder would die less than a month later at Gettysburg.

36 Oakey, *History of the Second Massachusetts*, 8.

river. "The Rebels made desperate efforts to capture the ford," recounted Captain Oakey, "and pressed us hard on the right. This part of our line made little progress and was forced at times to assume simply the defensive." Major Whiting, Merritt's immediate superior, overrode Merritt's orders to support the 6th Pennsylvania Cavalry's charge and "while executing this order the regiment was recalled for an emergency, while two squadrons . . . were detached to the front [the right flank]," reported Merritt. "From this hour (it was about five in the morning) the fighting for the regiment commenced and was kept up continuously for more than twelve hours."[37]

Buford, already committed to the offensive and unaware that Whiting had detached two squadrons of the 2nd U.S. Cavalry, ordered the now much-diminished Reserve Brigade to attack the Confederates clustered around the guns at St. James Church. The two remaining squadrons under Merritt fell in to support the 6th Pennsylvania Cavalry and the 6th U.S. Cavalry. "The consequences of this miscommunication would have devastating effects upon the attempts to seize the guns," explained Donald Caughey in his regimental history of the 6th U.S. "Instead of three regiments attacking in unison, only thirteen under-strength companies made the attempt."[38]

The troops on the ground saw the action in a totally different light. "It is one of the most exciting scenes in war to see, as we saw on that soft, June morning," recalled Captain Bryant, attesting to the ferocity of the fight. "The loud shouts, the sabers flashing and swinging in the air," he wrote, "then the clash, the hewing strokes, the indescribable jumble and melee, the rearing of horses, the snapping pistol shots, the huddling together, horses overthrown, riders unhorsed and trodden under foot of the wrestling squadrons."[39]

Bursting through the Confederate lines, Buford's attacking squadrons turned their attention to the cannons. Their charge "was made over a plateau fully eight hundred yards wide, and the objective point was the artillery at the church," recalled Maj. J. F. Hart of Stuart's Horse Artillery. "Never rode troopers more gallantly than did those steady Regulars, as under a fire of shot and shrapnel, and finally of canister, they dashed up to the very muzzles." The mounted charge sliced through the junction of "Grumble" Jones's and Wade Hampton's commands.

37 Ibid., 9; Merritt, "Reminiscences," 287-286.

38 Caughey and Jones, *The 6th United States Cavalry*, 86.

39 Bryant, *History of the Third Regiment*, 169-170.

Buford's Union regiments charge the Confederate position at Old St. James Church on the Brandy Station field. *Harper's Weekly*

"Here they were simultaneously attacked from both flanks and the survivors driven back."[40]

From the Federal lines, the infantry could see that the Rebels were lining up for one more desperate charge. "It seemed, this time, as if they would carry all before them. But we stood our ground and opened on them at close quarters with our guns," reported Oakey. With their long-range rifles, Ames's infantrymen made "every bullet tell," and the Rebel attack began to show unmistakable signs of faltering. "The Dragoons dropped their carbines, and, drawing sabres, rushed upon them, driving them in confusion," Oakey wrote. "It was hot work all along the line; and although our cavalry suffered severely at times, nothing could surpass their gallant conduct."[41]

Pleasonton moved forward, taking position at the edge of the tree line where the charge had started. "Here we met General Pleasonton, who commands his bugler to sound the 'rally,'" wrote Chaplain Gracey of the 6th Pennsylvania, hardly believing that he had just ridden through a hail of lead unscathed. "Companies and regiments are all mingled in perfect confusion, all flying for life. But the well-known sound recalls them to thoughtfulness; and in a few minutes the men left of the two

---

40 McClellan, *The Life and Campaigns of Major-General J. E. B. Stuart*, 268.

41 Oakey, *History of the Second Massachusetts*, 9.

Sixes crowd again into column and await orders." Pleasonton's staff clustered around him, including Lieutenant Custer, who was itching to have another go at the Southerners.[42]

Custer got his chance, for Fought recalled that "[t]he next move was of the cavalry, Col. Merritt's regiment. . . . Custer and I had the lead." "We all got across the road and charged a force of rebels five times our number. . . . At one point we thought we should have to run, but we captured a good many and pushed the others back, driving them towards Brandy Station." Were Custer and Fought leading Merritt's regiment? It seems highly unlikely. This appears to be another typical Fought statement, fanciful and exuberant, yet offering just enough veracity to titillate.[43]

The Confederate cavalry enjoyed superiority in numbers, and although the gallant band of Yankees rode in like heroes, the withering enemy fire drove them away. As usual, finger pointing and bitter recriminations followed soon after the battle. "Owing to the overpowering numbers opposed to it," wrote William H. Carter, "and being exposed to a heavy artillery fire at close range on its left, the regiment was compelled to retire through the woods, instantly reforming on its edge to re-advance." Others took a different view. "You have undoubtedly read in the *Chronicle* of yesterday the account of our fight with the rebs. Don't believe the half of it," warned Lieutenant Balder. "I looked in vain for the 2d, 6th Pa. and ours, but they had commenced a hurried advance towards Washington." He was astonished that the Regulars had turned and slunk back to their lines. "I think it is a great shame. . . . I never gave the rebs so much credit before, but I must now say, they go in with such a will."[44]

By 10:00 a.m., Buford's advance had stalled. With the situation on his right stabilizing, Stuart turned his attention to his left, since Buford seemed to be marshaling his forces for a push in that direction. Worried about being flanked, Buford withdrew the Reserve Brigade from the action in front of St. James Church and moved it to the open fields of the Cunningham and Wiltshire farms on his

42 Gracey, *Annals of the 6th Pennsylvania Cavalry*, 161.

43 Merington, *The Custer Story*, 58-59.

44 Carter, *From Yorktown to Santiago*, 85. At the time of the battle, Carter was only 12 years old, and was serving as a mounted messenger. After the war, Carter graduated from West Point, and he retired as a major general in 1915 after extensive service both on the frontier and in shaping the technological development of the modern United States Army. Briefly recalled to duty in World War I, he also wrote extensively on military history and biography. Milgram, "The Libby Correspondence of Tattnall Paulding," 1115-1117.

right. The fight slackened as Ames's infantry shifted to cover the resulting gap in the line. "Much to our relief," wrote Captain Oakey, "the enemy now appeared to be attacked in the rear, as they made no further attempt to capture the ford, and the force in our front was evidently reduced."[45]

If You Can't Punch His Nose, Kick His Butt

General Gregg, meanwhile, was finally making his presence felt. Though busy with Buford's force, Stuart knew of the precarious position of his brigades. He recognized the possibility that the Yankees might cross the Rappahannock at one of the lower fords and had already sent his trains to Culpeper Court House. Robertson's brigade of two regiments of North Carolina boys, armed with the long-range Enfield rifle, picketed the area to the south. Colonel M. C. Butler's 2nd South Carolina Cavalry had been moved to the rear of Hampton's and Jones's brigades at Brandy Station. Just to be on the safe side, Stuart ordered the 4th Virginia Cavalry to join Butler. "Having made these dispositions," attested Major McClellan, "Stuart proceeded to the front, at Saint James' Church, to urge on the battle. . . . These dispositions seemed to be all that circumstances required. Robertson's brigade, with the Second South Carolina and the 4th Virginia, constituted a force of at least fifteen hundred men, and Stuart was justified in expecting them to protect his rear from attack by way of the lower fords." To give ample warning of a Federal incursion, Stuart ordered McClellan to establish an observation post on the southernmost extremity of Fleetwood Hill.[46]

Gregg intended for Alfred Duffié's division to lead the way across the Rappahannock at the early hour of 3:00 a.m., but the luckless Frenchman had managed to get his command lost and did not begin his crossing until 8:00 a.m. By that time, the guns in Buford's front could be heard clearly, and any chance of launching a coordinated effort was long gone. The colossal waste of time would have a tremendous impact on Duffié's career. In a few weeks, the xenophobic Pleasonton would begin his long-awaited reorganization of the cavalry, which included the removal of all foreign-born officers from command. Once across the Rappahannock, Duffié continued his westward advance to Stevensburg with Gregg following.

45 Oakey, *History of the Second Massachusetts*, 9.

46 McClellan, *The Life and Campaigns of Major-General J. E. B. Stuart*, 268-269.

About this time, one of Robertson's couriers approached Major McClellan and reported the advance of the enemy's columns. An incredulous McClellan reported that, "[n]ot having personal acquaintance with the [courier], and deeming it impossible that such a movement could be made without opposition from Robertson's brigade," he refused to believe the information and sent the messenger back to confirm it. Robertson defended his report simply, claiming that he had "acted according to orders and the dictates of judgment," and had followed Stuart's orders to the letter. It apparently worked, for Stuart later responded, "General Robertson's report appears satisfactory."[47]

Sometime between 11:00 a.m. and noon, Gregg's two brigades turned onto the cut-off road to Brandy Station, the old Fredericksburg Plank Road, leaving Duffié to continue on to Stevensburg. Fleetwood Hill was now a little more than four and one- half miles away. Why Gregg followed Duffié as far as the cut-off to the secondary road rather than cutting cross country toward the sound of the guns is not known; Gregg's official reports certainly do nothing to resolve the mystery. Thus were another two hours wasted.

Now McClellan could see the advance of the Federal troopers for himself. The thoroughly alarmed sentinel shot off a message to Stuart and began to take stock of the situation. "Matters looked serious!" recalled McClellan; "Lieutenant [John] Carter's howitzer was brought up, and boldly pushed beyond the crest of the hill; a few imperfect shells and some round shot were found in the limber chest; a slow fire was at once opened upon the marching column. . . . It was all important to gain time." Stuart viewed McClellan's report with the same skepticism that McClellan had for Robertson's. The flamboyant cavalier had in fact ordered McClellan's courier to "ride back there and see what all that foolishness is about," when the first of Lt. Moses Clark's guns cut loose and Stuart's disbelief quite literally disappeared in a puff of battle smoke.[48]

Neither Custer nor Merritt participated in the clash of cavalry on Fleetwood Hill. Since this part of the battle has been covered by a number of great historians, the focus here will remain with Buford, on the far right.

47 Ibid., 269; OR 27, pt. 2, 735.

48 McClellan, *The Life and Campaigns of Major-General J. E. B. Stuart*, 270-271. Lieutenant Clark's guns belonged Capt. John Martin's 6th Battery, New York Light Artillery.

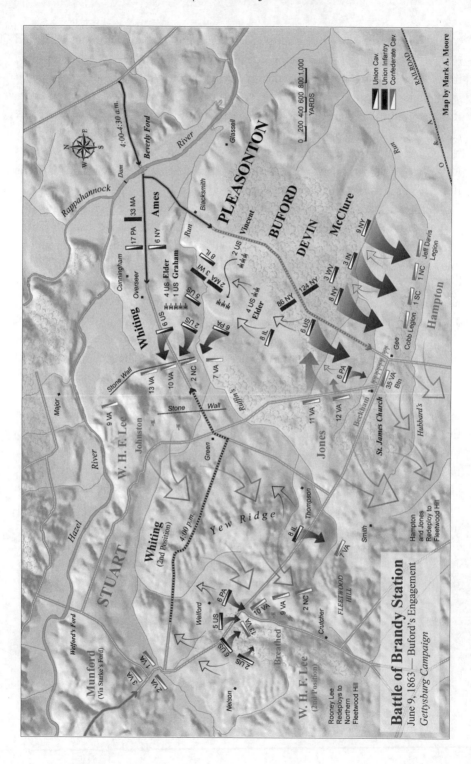

Map by Mark A. Moore

Battle of Brandy Station

June 9, 1863 — Buford's Engagement

Gettysburg Campaign

Chafing for Some Hot Action

Buford had been in the middle of re-aligning his forces when Gregg began his attack. By the time Buford was ready, Gregg had decided enough was enough and was headed northeast to link up with Buford's command. With the threat to his rear eliminated, Stuart established a new battle line facing Buford along the full length of Fleetwood Hill. Assigning responsibility for the left of the line to Colonel Devin, Buford moved to the far right, taking up a position behind a section of guns which had unlimbered "upon a knoll in the open fields in front and to the right of the ford. . . . General Buford and some of his staff officers were standing near the guns, their horses awaiting them in rear, where the artillery horses had taken refuge." As the Union troops began to file into position, a battery of Rebel guns stationed in a patch of woods 600 yards to their front opened fire. "Our guns," wrote Captain Oakey, "belched forth their fire and smoke, and the enemy's shells came howling overhead and bursting behind us with that spiteful, sharp, clean-cut bang which we used to know so well."[49]

Seemingly oblivious to the thunder about them and with nothing to do but smoke their pipes, Oakey and his companions lolled nonchalantly in the grass about 30 yards behind the guns and "studied our cavalry friends." The group around Buford buzzed with activity. "Staff officers arrived from time to time, and, plunging into the group, on their reeking horses, spoke to General Buford, and then dashed away again." Even then, observed Oakey, "Custer was the most striking figure in the group, with his fanciful uniform, his long hair, and spirited manner. He seemed to enjoy the shelling, and appeared to beam all over, almost dancing with excitement." This scene was also witnessed by Adjutant Bryant of the 3rd Wisconsin, who recalled that "Custer was there, his long hair waving in the breeze and his manner full of animation."[50]

Despite the incessant roar of the guns, a feeling of ennui began to pervade the field. "During this time, and for an hour longer," reported Merritt, "the regiment, subjected to a well-directed artillery fire, remained in support of a battery of artillery." The 10th Virginia Cavalry added to the discomfort of Merritt's regiment. According to Captain Oakey, the Rebel troopers "were on foot behind a stone wall down in the open fields in front. . . . They had already annoyed our artillery very much, popping at them with their carbines," and now "endeavored to interfere

49 Oakey, *History of the Second Massachusetts*, 9-10.

50 Ibid., 10; Bryant, *History of the Third Regiment*, 170-171.

with us as much as possible." Finally, their fire became too much for Buford. "He seemed much annoyed at the Tenth Virginia Cavalry behind the wall, and at last summoned the commander of the infantry supports," recalled Oakey:

> "Do you see those men down there?" Says Buford: "They've got to be driven out. Do you think you can do it?" . . . We thought we could. . . . The General, with this group around him, was drawing the fire of the stone wall people, and was urged to keep out of range, while the rest of us scattered to less dangerous positions. Some of the staff came back and watched the men "fall in," as if to see us off.[51]

This was a perfect opportunity for another dashing Custer exploit, but this time he did not join in the fun. Perhaps a clue can be found in that one little remark from Fought—"Custer and I had the lead." Did Custer, in that mad, crazy dash to strike the Rebel horsemen in front of the old church, somehow manage to get his horse in front of the commanding officer of the 2nd U.S. Cavalry? Captain Wesley Merritt would never have tolerated such a slight. Was there an awkward moment between the two at some point in time during the march to the right flank? Was Custer so emboldened by the powers he believed he derived from his position as Pleasonton's aide-de-camp that he did not even see the faux pas he had committed? If the two hot-tempered youths exchanged words, what was said? The answers to those questions are securely hidden in the mists of time. Although one officer stated that "Custer showed much interest, and evidently would have enjoyed going with us," it is clear that when Merritt and the 2nd U.S. moved against the Virginians behind the stone wall, George Custer did not ride out at the side of his old comrade from Pleasonton's staff.[52]

Crawling through the corn fields, the rifle-toting infantrymen took a circuitous route until they finally found themselves skirting the flanks of the enemy's position. On command they delivered a devastating enfilading volley into the ranks of the startled Rebels. "Having killed, wounded and captured the entire party," recounted Captain Oakey, "we retired to a rising ground to the left of our guns, and covered the approaches to the stone wall. . . . General Buford now advanced the right of the line." The men of the Reserve Brigade eagerly anticipated the attack. "At last an order—which we all had hoped and all but asked for," was received, wrote Merritt.

---

51 Merritt, "Reminiscences," 287; Oakey, *History of the Second Massachusetts*, 10-11.

52 Swift, "General Wesley Merritt," 837; Cyrus Townsend Brady, *Indian Fights and Fighters* (New York, 1904), 392; Oakey, *History of the Second Massachusetts*, 10-11.

"We were ordered to advance and deal on their ground with the batteries and sharpshooters which had wrought such havoc among our men and horses. Right gallantly did the Second advance to this work."[53]

The advance of the Reserve Brigade—Merritt's 2nd U.S. Cavalry, along with the 6th U.S. Cavalry and the 6th Pennsylvania Cavalry—found the Confederate horsemen of Rooney Lee's brigade alone and in peril. The sounds of combat to Lee's rear underscored the Union threat to the Rebel right flank at Fleetwood Hill. Hampton's and Jones's brigades had swung around to deal with Gregg's assault, uncovering Lee's right flank and leaving him to face Buford's division with only one brigade of cavalry. Lee fell back approximately two miles to the southwest, with the bulk of his men taking up position on Yew Ridge, a commanding spur on the northern slope of Fleetwood Hill. As Lee began to pull back he ordered Col. Richard Beale's 9th Virginia Cavalry and a section of Capt. James Breathed's battery to cover his rear. This brought Merritt's command to a halt, and a battery of Union guns rushed to the front. For a while the opposing batteries exchanged fire. Merritt's men took shelter in a shallow depression, oblivious to the rounds that passed harmlessly over their heads. Buford despised the idea of not attacking, and shortly Merritt "received orders from General Buford to advance in conjunction with the Sixth Cavalry."[54]

As the Rebels fell back to Yew Ridge, the terrain over which they withdrew became more difficult for the advancing Federal troopers. Leaving the rolling fields of farmland behind, the Yankee cavalry began encountering that ubiquitous impediment of the rural South: stone walls. As the ground inclined steeply upward, Merritt's dragoons also ran into a steep ravine made even more impenetrable by thick strands of blackthorn shrubbery. Despite these obstacles, Merritt's skirmishers continued pressing the 9th Virginia Cavalry. "The advance soon drove in the enemy's skirmishers, and in turn was charged by the enemy's cavalry. The enemy dealt saber-blows and pistol-shots on every side," explained Merritt. "Friend and foe, mixed inextricably together," he continued, "rode on in this terrible carnage. . . . Each moment the fight grew fiercer, the dust and smoke and steam from the heated horses making the air dark and obscuring the vision."[55]

The 9th Virginia got the better of the hotly contested melee and forced the Yankees back. Merritt swung his regiment parallel to the St. James Church Road

---

53 Oakey, *History of the Second Massachusetts*, 11-12; Merritt, "Reminiscences," 287.

54 Merritt, "Reminiscences," 287.

55 Ibid., 287-288.

and advanced to the crest of Yew Ridge. As the 2nd U.S. cleared the ridgeline, the full fruit of the 9th Virginia's delaying tactics were revealed. "The charge, in its impetuosity, had carried everything before it," reported Merritt. "It bore up the hill, across the plateau, and to the crest on the other side. There were discovered in the valley below, fresh regiments of horse moving quietly towards the scene of our combat, anxious to strike us while we were in confusion." The 2nd North Carolina Cavalry drove forward to the right of the Church Road, and the 10th and 13th Virginia Cavalry regiments did so on the left. With the 6th U.S. and 6th Pennsylvania still climbing the slopes of Yew Ridge, Merritt and his men faced the advance of Lee's brigade alone.[56]

Urged on by the raucous baying of bugles and the curses of their officers, the veterans of the 2nd U.S. rallied on their guidons. The 10th Virginia struck the 2nd U.S. full on the front, while an oblique movement by the 2nd North Carolina skirted past the confused mass of fighting men and crashed into Merritt's flank. The charge broke Merritt's line and pushed his troopers back a half mile to where Whiting's reserves, the 6th U.S. and 6th Pennsylvania, were deployed. So suddenly had his regiment disintegrated that Merritt, accompanied by Lt. Paul Quirk, found himself cut off and in danger of capture.

The perilous moment etched itself with great clarity in Merritt's memory. Grimly re-holstering his empty revolver, he drew his saber. Distinguishing an enemy officer of high rank in the swirling dust, Merritt went for him and at saber point demanded the Rebel's surrender. "His reply was more forcible than courteous as, after a moment's surprise, he made a cut at my head with his saber. I partially parried the cut," he wrote years later. His head bloodied by the blow, Merritt realized that he and his lone companion had driven far into the Confederate ranks. "The Rebels . . . then commenced a rapid fire with their pistols and must have been surprised to see Lieutenant Quirk and myself, in spite of their firing and orders to surrender, ride safely back to the regiment."[57]

The identity of Merritt's assailant would later become the subject of much speculation. According to Merritt, "from a description of the officer who didn't surrender on this occasion," General Buford believed "that it was Colonel (later General) Wade Hampton." Although Hampton enjoyed a good tussle as much as any other Southern officer—many of whom shared a propensity for personal combat—he is an unlikely suspect, because as the battle unfolded his command

56 Ibid., 288-290.

57 Ibid., 289.

Wesley Merritt engages in a saber fight with Rooney Lee on Yew's Ridge at the Battle of Brandy Station. *Courtesy of Don Stivers*

had been withdrawn to counter Gregg's attack on the south side of Fleetwood Hill. The most likely possibility is Rooney Lee. Some historians, however, claim that, by that time, the son of Gen. Robert E. Lee had already been rendered *hors de combat* by a carbine bullet in the thigh.[58]

58 Ibid; Wittenberg, *The Battle of Brandy Station*, 158-159, 161-162. Respected cavalry historian Eric Wittenberg makes the argument that it was indeed Rooney Lee that faced off against Merritt. Early on in the battle for Yew Ridge, Wittenberg puts Rooney Lee at the head of Col. Richard L. T. Beale's 9th Virginia Cavalry. "About 4 o'clock in the afternoon Lee placed himself at the head of my regiment," recalled William L. Royall, "and gave the order to charge up the hill, he riding at the head of the regiment. . . . Lee did not hesitate an instant but dashed at the center of this line with his column of fours." Later, as Lee's brigade began to hound Buford's retreating troopers, he crested a small hill and "a bullet passed through his leg, in the moment of victory." Lieutenant Beale watched as Lee directed a soldier "to notify the next officer in command that he was wounded, [and] after passing his sword over to an orderly, he was assisted from the field."

As the 2nd U.S. struggled to reform, the 13th Virginia, which had taken little part in the fight on Yew Ridge, dismounted and took the Regulars under fire. Merritt dismounted his men as well, but failed to make any further progress "and, under orders, held the line we then had, for the remainder of the day." It had been a very long day, and the fighting gradually began to die out. By that time, Gregg had rallied his men and moved east to link up with Buford. The Rebel cavalry, now in possession of Fleetwood Hill, did not attempt to prevent this movement. As the two wings of the Federal cavalry came within supporting range of each other, Gregg rode to Pleasonton's headquarters and informed his commander that the Confederates were bringing up infantry from Culpeper Court House. Pleasonton decided that it was time to cut and run. "The operation of withdrawal was accomplished without interference, the enemy contenting themselves with looking on from a respectful distance," wrote Captain Oakey. "As we approached Beverly Ford, the First Regular Cavalry turned up." They were eager to join the fray, but "were too late for any of the fun." Pleasonton deployed them as mounted skirmishers to cover the withdrawal of the Federal cavalry back across the Rappahannock.[59]

By this time the sun was dropping low over the hard-fought hills. As the possibility of sudden death diminished, the men were better able to appreciate the grandeur of what was going on about them. "The sun had now set," recalled Captain Newhall, "but there was a mellow light on the fields, and the figures of Lord's troopers stood boldly out against the background of the yellow sky above the horizon. . . . There could be no prettier sight, and it was often recalled among us." Captain Oakey expressed the same thought when he marveled, "The scene at the fords was very picturesque. A lovely sunset shed its cool light over the long columns of cavalry winding their way toward the river, and the mounted skirmishers were thrown in bold relief against the brilliant sky."[60]

No general likes to admit that a battle was inconclusive. After all the bloodshed and sacrifice, there must be some positive result. In this case, both sides would lay claim to victory. Pleasonton would state that he had accomplished his mission and had fought the vaunted Rebel cavalry to a standstill. He would describe his move across the Rappahannock as a reconnaissance in force—nothing more than an attempt to find Lee's infantry and determine his intentions. Stuart would point to

59 Merritt, "Reminiscences," 288-290; Oakey, *History of the Second Massachusetts*, 14.

60 Frederick C. Newhall, "The Battle of Beverly Ford," in McClure, ed., *The Annals of the Civil War*, 144; Oakey, *History of the Second Massachusetts*, 14.

the fact that the Federal troopers had abandoned the field and returned to their side of the river.

"Thus ended one of the hardest fights and laborious day's work which was participated in by the Second Cavalry during the war," Merritt wrote glowingly. He would later claim that the actions of his regiment at Brandy Station were a major factor in his promotion to brigadier general. "While we had lost heavily, we had accomplished much," he recorded, but it had been worth it, "for from that day forth the prestige of the Confederate cavalry was broken, and its pre-eminence was gone forever."[61]

Not even the Confederates could deny this, and no less a personage than Henry B. McClellan, Stuart's adjutant general and the premier chronicler of the cavalry of the Army of Northern Virginia, acknowledged that, at Brandy Station, the momentum began to swing in favor of the Union cavalry. "One result of incalculable importance certainly did follow this battle," he wrote. "It made the Federal cavalry. Up to that time confessedly inferior to the Southern horsemen, they gained on this day the confidence in themselves and their commanders which enabled them to contest so fiercely the subsequent battle-fields of June, July, and October." Captain Oakey, who had fought with Buford on that long day, remembered, "After the long period of mismanagement, disaster, sacrifice, blood, and tears through which the Army of the Potomac had passed . . . the turning-point came, at last, in the brilliant conflict at Beverly Ford."[62]

Later that night Stuart ordered his headquarters tent to be pitched back atop the hill where it had originally stood. "But when we reached the place it was covered so thickly with the dead horses and men, and the bluebottle flies were swarming so thick over the blood stains on the ground," reported Major Blackford, "that there was not room enough to pitch the tents among them. So the general reluctantly consented to camping at another place." The history of the 6th Pennsylvania Cavalry depicts the marching columns of Union troopers just as night began to fall. "We slowly retired from the field, and again crossed to the north bank of the Rappahannock. Our return was in perfect order in four columns," it reads. "Never did anything appear to our eyes half so beautiful as our returning victorious

61 Merritt, "Reminiscences," 290-291.

62 McClellan, *The Life and Campaigns of Major-General J. E. B. Stuart*, 294; Oakey, *History of the Second Massachusetts*, 15.

cavalry force as they marched quietly and unmolested back again to the ground of their previous bivouac."[63]

You Can't Tarnish a Hero

The contemporary press and future biographers would vastly overplay Custer's role at Brandy Station. Simply put, they never got the story right. Despite the magnitude of fighting, which would prove to be the war's largest cavalry battle, Custer did nothing particularly spectacular on June 9, 1863. Like thousands of other troopers present on that field, however, he could rightfully claim to have done his duty honorably. For reasons undisclosed, however, the press and some of Custer's biographers decided to direct the spotlight squarely on him. The Battle of Brandy Station provided the fodder for a story that picked up momentum with each retelling. Armed with the greatest tool in an armchair historian's repertoire—20/20 hindsight—it soon became an established part of the Custer legend. More than a year after the battle, a correspondent for the *New York Tribune* would proclaim, "Future writers of fiction will find in Custer most of the qualities which go to make up a first class hero and stories of his daring will be told around many a hearthstone long after the old flag again kisses the breeze from Maine to the Gulf."[64]

One of the core premises of the Custer legend places him close to "Grimes" Davis at the moment of his death. According to this story, the stunned Custer quickly regains his senses, takes command of an obviously rattled regiment, and leads it forward against the resurgent Rebel cavalry. "Davis and Custer pointed their swords toward the string of heads along the stone wall," claimed Jay Monaghan in *Custer: The Life of General George Armstrong Custer*. "Come on boys," they shouted. "With the brigade behind them, they thundered across the field, broke the line, tore down and jumped the wall, [and] crashed through the woods beyond." According to Monaghan, Custer looked about for Davis and was dismayed to learn that the commanding officer had been killed and "the immediate command devolved on Custer." Rebel bullets were pelting the dangerously exposed Union troops from all sides. In fact, the road back to the safety of their lines was packed with Confederates. It was time to beat a hasty retreat, and Custer

---

63 Blackford, *War Years with Jeb Stuart*, 217; Gracey, *Annals of the 6th Pennsylvania Cavalry*, 164.

64 Gregory J. W. Urwin, *Custer Victorious: The Civil War Battles of General George Armstrong Custer* (Lincoln, NE, 1983), 36, 53.

might have made the "charge" to the rear, as "hacking and slashing with sabers, the Union men cut their way through."[65]

As of 1959, few comprehensive biographies of General Custer had been written, and Monaghan's account was about as balanced as a reader could get. Yet the legend as presented only adds to the aura surrounding the man, instead of helping us to more fully understand his soldierly qualities. *Favor the Bold*, a highly romanticized Custer biography by D. A. Kinsley, hit bookstores in 1967. The author's vivid imagination carried the story to a totally different level. At times Kinsley created entire conversations from bits of historical data. According to the biographer, crusty old Colonel Davis, a long-time comrade of Pleasonton, graciously turned over command of his brigade to Custer, understanding that the young man was about to be tested for bigger things. "A spectral glow shrouded the valley, causing many to shudder," he penned, more script-writer than historian, "and the sepulchral stillness was chilling, causing horses to champ and fuss. The sun was up, burning off the haze, and the moment of glory was nigh." Custer rode up to Davis and saluted him sharply with his saber. Behind the colonel stood 1,500 men "ready in extended order across the valley." Then Custer swept his broad-brimmed slouch hat from his head and, brandishing his saber, shouted out, "Buglers, sound the 'Advance'! He swung his steed about and rose to the trot. 'Come on boys! Give 'em the saber! Charge!'"[66]

In a more recent retelling, Custer commands all three regiments, cutting through the surrounding Confederates "in a smart saber charge that brought them out safely." Pleasonton is so pleased with Custer's "show of initiative that he mentioned him by name in his dispatches and sent him to deliver them to Hooker, together with a captured standard." Yet Frederick Whittaker, who could be expected to embellish a story to near farcical status, does not even mention this incident. In fact, he glosses right over the most momentous cavalry battle fought to that point in the war. Joseph Fought's heavily edited narrative contained in Marguerite Merington's *The Custer Story* makes no mention of Custer taking command from Davis, even by happenstance. Most convincingly, there is almost nothing from Custer himself—no familiar batch of heavy army parchment written in Custer's bold hand, with stories of leading a desperate charge against insurmountable odds. Even by Custer's standards that would have been stretching his participation more than a little too far. In 1996, Jeffry Wert finally put to rest the

65 Monaghan, *The Life of General George Armstrong Custer*, 127.

66 D. A. Kinsley, *Favor the Bold: Custer: The Civil War Years* (New York, 1967), 123.

stories of Custer assuming command at Brandy Station. "Other historians have repeated the story," he intoned, "but it is inaccurate."[67]

And that's the truth.

---

67 Urwin, *Custer Victorious*, 53; Wert, *Custer*, 78.

CHAPTER SEVEN

This Game Determines Who is the Best Man

THE BATTLE-TESTED MEN of the Cavalry Corps of the Army of the Potomac marched through Aldie Gap on June 17, 1863. They deployed onto the road net and spilled out into the magnificent fields beyond that rolled higher and higher until meeting the foothills of the Blue Ridge Mountains. Often overlooked by historians, the fight for the mountain passes after the battle of Brandy Station would be pivotal in the Cavalry Corps' development. Over the next few days, Pleasonton's troopers would brawl with Stuart's cavalry in a series of wide-ranging, free-flowing, take-whatever-break-nature-gives-you fights, with every level of command on both sides firmly focused on one objective: the gaps in the Blue Ridge Mountains.

In those contested fields, the young officers—many of them citizen-soldiers just as courageous, tactically gifted, and devoted to the Union as any Regular cavalry officer—would begin staking their claims to positions of command. Between that day and the surrender at Appomattox, many of those men would be gone. Some would be killed in action. Others would suffer horrible wounds, never to return to active duty. Many would end up in some of the South's most notorious prison camps. Still others would just fade away, their bodies crushed by disease or their faith ruined by the horrors they had witnessed.

The good majority would go on to make fine cavalry officers, bold and resourceful in combat. They had learned to care for the lives and comforts of their men in camp life and had become fiercely protective of the command's horse flesh. The quality of the leadership that rose to the top of the Cavalry Corps was such that Sgt. James Clark would one day elaborate: "Space will not allow the justice due them in this paper, but take one, a type, Rodenbough. . . . His case will illustrate the points for the others. What a superb, magnificent specimen of manhood—a right down royally good cavalryman, yet as graceful and accomplished, always as if bound by the social conventions of a drawing room, and as genial in greeting on all times and occasions as if a comrade with his playfellows."[1]

Both George Custer and Wesley Merritt passed through Aldie Gap on that sweltering day. Once across, Custer took the road to Ashby's Gap while Merritt headed north toward Snicker's Gap and into a warren of stone walls and fences, woodlands, and marshes. Custer embraced the saber while Merritt put his faith in a reliable carbine. Even as the Union cavalry rode toward the fight for the mountain passes, a long-running debate about the future of cavalry operations—begun on another continent entirely—would erupt again with arguments not of ink and paper, but of lead and steel.[2]

War in God's Country

To James Mercer, the spot where the Little River flowed out of the Bull Run Mountains seemed like the perfect place to build a mill. Mercer erected his first small mill in 1764 and named it for the Mercer family's ancestral home in Scotland: "Aldie." Over the years a thriving community had grown around the Aldie Mill, and in 1809 the millers moved into a spacious new building. As the mill flourished, so did the village, which found itself at the hub of three major toll roads. Once through the gap in the Bull Run Mountains, a traveler could opt to take either the

---

1   James Albert Clark, "The Making of a Volunteer Cavalryman," *Commandery of the District of Columbia, Military Order of the Loyal Legion of the United States* (November 6, 1907), 27-29.

2   Laurence D. Schiller, "A Taste of Northern Steel: The Evolution of Federal Cavalry Tactics 1861-1865," *North and South Magazine* (January 1999), Vol. 2, No. 2, 32. Often neglected by the government due to its much greater cost compared to infantry, cavalry was employed only sporadically during the American Revolution and the War of 1812. In fact, from 1821 to 1833, the army counted no mounted units in its order of battle. It was not until 1834 that a U.S. Army board led by Gen. Winfield Scott published the first official American manual of cavalry tactics—the "Scott Tactics." Due to the unique features of combat on the American frontier, traditional European cavalry tactics had to be heavily modified. The debate over these modifications would rage for the next 30 years, well into—and after—the Civil War. Broadly speaking, two major theoretical camps evolved, roughly corresponding to two of the traditional types of European cavalry. Advocates of the "hussar" model believed cavalry was best used in shock actions, with the mounted charge being the ultimate projection of cavalier might. The "dragoon" model saw the horse as providing much needed mobility for troopers, who would dismount to employ the enhanced firepower provided by breech-loading carbines. For more detail, see Eric J. Wittenberg's Foreword at the beginning of this volume.

Ashby's Gap Turnpike or the fork to the right and head northwesterly on the Snickersville Gap Turnpike.

The village itself is situated just west of the Bull Run Mountains, a craggy, low-lying range that runs parallel to the Blue Ridge chain. Aldie Gap cuts through to a valley of rolling hills that extend for 15 miles between the two mountain ranges. Middleburg is about two miles due west of Aldie Gap, and Upperville lies eight miles beyond that. Ashby's Gap is another five miles farther up the road. Once over Ashby's Gap, the Shenandoah Valley can be surveyed in all its splendor. If one follows the Snickersville Turnpike to the northwest, Snicker's Gap provides another way into the valley, about 14 miles north of Ashby's Gap. South of Aldie, Thoroughfare Gap cuts through the southern end of the Bull Run Mountains; during the Civil War, it provided the Manassas Gap Railroad access to the valley. Stuart placed the bulk of his forces to guard the Aldie cut while Rooney Lee's brigade, temporarily commanded by Col. John R. Chambliss, Jr., after Lee's wounding at Brandy Station, blocked the road at Thoroughfare Gap. If Stuart's cavalry was to seal the gaps through the Blue Ridge and deprive the enemy of knowledge of Robert E. Lee's movements, the fight would start at Aldie.[3]

Loudoun County, with its businesslike farm buildings and rich, fruitful soil, had never been trampled by contending armies. Writing to his wife shortly before he set the Army of Northern Virginia on its epic march into Pennsylvania, Gen. Robert E. Lee took a moment to reflect on the scene, not as a general, but as a Christian man. "I reviewed the cavalry in this section yesterday," he wrote, looking back sadly on that spectacular day, with his share of the guilt staring over his shoulder. "The country here looks very green and pretty, notwithstanding the ravages of war. What a beautiful world God, in his loving kindness to his creatures, has given us. What a shame that men, endowed with reason and a knowledge of right, should mar his gifts." In a few days, distant fields would be full of dead bodies awaiting burial, and many of the surrounding houses would overflow with the wounded from both sides. Dozens of dead, bloated horses would lie waiting for

---

3 After graduating West Point as a brevet second lieutenant in 1853, Chambliss spent less than a year teaching at the cavalry school at Carlisle Barracks before resigning his commission to return to his family's plantation in Hicksford, Virginia. From 1856 to 1861, he served Gov. Henry A. Wise as aide-de-camp and led a regiment of Virginia militia. When the war began, he accepted a commission as colonel of the 13th Virginia Cavalry and served under Maj. Gen. D. H. Hill south of the James River. After leading several operations guarding the Rappahannock crossings, he and his regiment were assigned to Rooney Lee's brigade, which he led after Lee's injuries at Brandy Station. Chambliss was promoted to brigadier general in December 1863 and was killed in the second battle of Deep Bottom on August 16, 1864.

collection and burning, the smell of putrefaction lying heavy in the air. Nothing of military value would be left behind by the Rebels.[4]

From the beginning of the war through the ceding of the field at Brandy Station, Confederates feasted on the remains of the well-supplied Yankee horsemen. Gradually, the Southerners discarded the heirloom shotguns given to them by their fathers and grandfathers as they rode away to war. The presentation sword for services to His Excellency George Washington had not been able to withstand even one good whack from a Model 1860 Light Cavalry Saber, and the cumbersome dragoon pistols were much more trouble than they were worth.

"After a while the government provided a saddle that helped the soreback horse very much," recalled Rebel Capt. John Lamb, "but many an old cavalryman remembers to this day how sore he was made by those saddles." The Rebels gratefully claimed new McClellan saddles branded with a "US" as well as bits, bridles, harnesses, and saddle bags. "An old Confederate carbine or sabre, such as were first issued to the cavalry, would be a curiosity now," remembered Lamb wistfully, as if each discarded piece of a family's history somehow diminished the South forever. But war is all about being practical:

> They began this exercise early in the war, and pursued it industriously until nearly every company was well supplied. . . . North Carolina and Virginia, met the brave mounted infantry . . . with arms and ammunition and saddles and bridles, and often horses, that were rich trophies of battle.[5]

Colonel Munford also recalled the practice of resupply from enemy stockpiles. Southern boys, he explained, "began to be dragoons, and before two years were out, were good ones too, for we had an abundance of carbine and pistol ammunition which we use without stint."[6]

One admiring Yankee wrote that when the Rebel cavalry decided to stand and fight,

> It was found impossible to contend mounted with them with the least chance of success, and as a matter of necessity the Union troopers were compelled to resort to dismounting

---

4 John Lamb, "The Confederate Cavalry: Its Wants, Trials, and Heroism," *Southern Historical Society Papers* (Jan.-Dec. 1897), Vol. 25, 362.

5 Ibid., 361.

6 Thomas T. Munford, "A Confederate Officer's Reminiscences," *Journal of the United States Cavalry Association* (September 1891), Vol. 4, No. 14, 288.

from their horses and fighting on foot. It must be admitted that we followed the lead of the Southerners in this respect, as they were the first to adopt dismounted fighting to any extent, and we were obliged to meet them in the same manner.[7]

Stuart's newly re-equipped troopers would need all of those new tools to block Ashby's and Snicker's gaps and keep prying Yankee eyes from observing the invasion columns of the Army of Northern Virginia. Lee's 50,000 hardened veterans rapidly marched north through the Shenandoah Valley on the other side of those passes. By June 10, Lt. Gen. Richard S. Ewell's Corps was well on its way to Winchester, its advance elements pushing hard for the Potomac in order to open both the crossing at Hagerstown and the way into Union territory.

The Federals' task consisted of marching boldly up either the Ashby's Gap Turnpike or the Snickersville Turnpike, wrest either or both of the gaps from Stuart's men, and report back to Hooker on any enemy movements on the western side of the Blue Ridge Mountains. The Union troopers started the mission already behind, as Pleasonton had let a week pass after his self-proclaimed victory at Brandy Station before resuming active operations. In the meantime, the Rebel cavalry had stolen a march, advancing swiftly up the east side of the Blue Ridge. Each Federal command knew from hard experience just how suddenly the Confederate cavalry could strike.

Every step west toward the gaps was one more God-given opportunity for Custer and Merritt to learn their trade in the fields around Aldie, Middleburg, and Upperville. In a couple of weeks Pleasonton would clean out the top of the cavalry's command structure like so much spindrift and promote Merritt, Custer, and Elon Farnsworth to the rank of brigadier general. These low-ranking officers had but a brief time in which to prepare, less than a fortnight to experience the bread-and-butter operations of cavalry warfare. Sir John Moore, a visionary British general from the era of the Napoleonic Wars, forewarned, "Our business, like any other, is to be learned by constant practice and experience; and our experience is to be had in war, not at reviews."[8]

---

7 Louis H. Carpenter, "Sheridan's Expedition Around Richmond, May 9-25, 1864," *Journal of the United States Cavalry Association* (November 1888), Vol. 1, No. 3, 302.

8 S. L. A. Marshall, *Men Against Fire: The Problem of Command in Future War* (New York, 1947), 15. Moore began his military career in 1776 in the American Revolution and fought against Napoleon before dying a soldier's death at La Coruña during the Spanish campaign in 1809. His innovative thinking led to the creation of the famed Rifle regiments, which fought unencumbered by traditional British line tactics. Recruits at his training facility in Shorncliffe Army Camp had to showcase their skills with the new, eight-grooved Baker rifle, which could

In addition to its education as a fighting force, the Union cavalry struggled to define its identity. During the combats at Aldie, Middleburg, and Upperville the Union cavalry would—once and for all—turn its back on European cavalry models and begin the creation of a uniquely American style of mounted operations. Custer and Merritt would not meet during any of the engagements of this campaign. Since each encounter with the enemy was unique, no two lessons learned were the same. It is here that their career paths began to diverge.

As of yet, no open friction can be discerned in their relationship, but within a year these two men would be contending tooth and nail for the very soul of the Cavalry Corps of the Army of the Potomac.

Toward the Passes of Glory

On June 12, Maj. Gen. Daniel Butterfield warned Pleasonton, "The general [Hooker] desires to know how far beyond Sulphur Springs and in what portion of the Valley your scouts have penetrated; what reports and what you know positively regarding enemy's movements in that direction. This is of importance, and information is desired as soon as possible." At the time, Pleasonton could provide no clue, and no answer.[9]

It took Pleasonton until June 15 to get his cavalry on the move, but once in motion, he proceeded with uncharacteristic alacrity. On that day, he reported to Hooker that Stuart had 15,000 men—typical of Pleasonton's frequent gross over-estimations of enemy numbers—at Upperville, and that Federal scouts had reported hearing gunfire at Winchester, the hub of the Shenandoah Valley's road net. Hooker urged Pleasonton to move toward the enemy, and again stressed the importance of continued, timely intelligence. "The commanding general relies upon you with your cavalry force to give him information of where the enemy is, his force, and his movements." Hooker's military career was at stake, and he kept urging Pleasonton to deliver. "Get us information. It is better that we should lose men than to be without knowledge of the enemy, as we now seem to be."[10]

---

put a ball through a target at 300 yards. Distinguished from other British troops in their unique green uniforms, they specialized in scouting and skirmishing ahead of the infantry. Moore's Rifle regiments were the forerunners of Civil War units like Berdan's Sharpshooters.

9 OR 27, pt. 3, 71.

10 Ibid., 114, 172.

For days Pleasonton had been tinkering with his command, reorganizing the corps into two divisions. Judson Kilpatrick's promotion to brigadier general was just the tip of the iceberg of Pleasonton's program, but the constant prodding from army headquarters to discern the enemy's dispositions forced him to postpone the full realization of his plans. Now leading the advance of the cavalry toward Aldie, Kilpatrick had 2,000 men under his command: the 2nd New York, 4th New York, 1st Massachusetts, and 6th Ohio Cavalry regiments, along with Capt. Ansol Randol's battery of horse artillery. Further to the south, Col. Alfred Duffié and the 1st Rhode Island Cavalry headed for Thoroughfare Gap, intending to cut through and swing north to link up with Kilpatrick at Middleburg. Once there, Duffié and his men barricaded themselves in the streets of Middleburg and sat forgotten and unsupported by a stressed-out cavalry headquarters. Skirting the old Manassas battlefields, Kilpatrick's column moved leisurely toward the distant mountains, shimmering blue-green in the noonday sun.

Wednesday, June 17, 1863, was hot and the sun unrelenting. The dense clouds of dust kicked up by the marching cavalry made it difficult to see the set of fours riding just ahead, and the horses required frequent watering. Merritt set forth simple rules for his troopers on the march. "Permit no man to leave the ranks mounted; Permit no horse to be watered, officer's or private's, save when all are watered."[11]

Unaware of these strict guidelines, Custer rode along with the 2nd U.S. Cavalry. "While on the march we came to a stream between the side of the road, in which a full battalion could water their horses at once," recalled an orderly on General Gregg's staff named Henry C. Meyer. "For some reason," continued the orderly sergeant, the irrepressible Captain Custer broke from the column:

[Custer] concluded to go in on the other side of the stream, riding in alone to allow his horse to drink. The water was deeper than he anticipated and his horse nearly lost its footing. However, when he got to our side, he urged his horse to climb out at a point where the bank was steep. In this effort he fell over backward, Custer going out of sight in the water. In an instant, however, he was up on his feet and the horse struggled out amid the shouts of the spectators, when, mounting his horse, the march was resumed. The dust at

11 Merritt, "Marching Cavalry," 73.

this time was so thick . . . in a few minutes, when it settled on his wet clothes and long wet hair, Custer was an object that one can better imagine than I can describe.[12]

Knowing the proclivities of the Regulars, it is unlikely that Custer escaped a full dose of the friendly razzing due any highfaluting staff officer who failed to follow the simple rules for watering his horse.

Stuart had moved his five brigades into the Loudoun Valley east of the Blue Ridge Mountains, and by mid-morning of June 17 had established his headquarters at Middleburg. Fitz Lee's brigade pushed farther east toward the strategic village of Aldie. Still commanded by Colonel Munford in Lee's absence, the 2,000-man force consisted of the 1st, 2nd, 3rd, 4th, and 5th Virginia Cavalry regiments and the five guns of Breathed's battery. The rest of Stuart's units shadowed Robert E. Lee's army along the eastern edge of the Blue Ridge.

Arriving in the vicinity of Aldie around noon, Thomas Munford began making preparations to camp for the night. As the troopers of his brigade settled down to feed and water their horses, a company of the 2nd Virginia Cavalry was detached to scout through Aldie Gap and establish a picket line on the other side of the Bull Run Mountains. Bringing up the rear, Col. Thomas Lafayette Rosser's 5th Virginia Cavalry continued riding along the road toward Aldie, where it intended to camp that evening. It was nearly 2:00 p.m., and none of the troopers knew that all hell was about to break loose. For the advancing Yankees, contact with the videttes of the 2nd Virginia came as an unpleasant surprise, as no Confederates were expected east of the Bull Run range.[13]

The 2nd New York Cavalry led Kilpatrick's advance, its van snaking lazily into the approaches of Aldie Gap. Shocked by the first crackle of Rebel carbine fire, the Federal troopers unsheathed their sabers and raced toward the enemy pickets, easily chasing the small force back to Aldie. "I met the pickets running in," reported

---

12 Henry C. Meyer, *Civil War Experiences Under Bayard, Gregg, Kilpatrick, Custer, Raulston, and Newberry, 1862, 1863, 1864* (New York, 1911), 33-34.

13 Tom Rosser and George Custer developed a close friendship while classmates at West Point. Rosser submitted his resignation two weeks before graduation in 1861, and rose quickly through the ranks of the Confederate Army. The two old friends would clash repeatedly throughout the war, their ongoing duel culminating in the battle of Tom's Brook on October 9, 1864, also known as the "Woodstock Races." The battle ended with a 10-mile chase in which Rosser lost all his personal possessions, along with a great deal of his reputation. After the war Rosser became a railroad man, and surveyed the railbed for the Northern Pacific as it cut its way through the heart of Indian territory. Custer and his 7th Cavalry provided security for Rosser's team, and the two men spent many a night under a tent fly reminiscing about their experiences during the war.

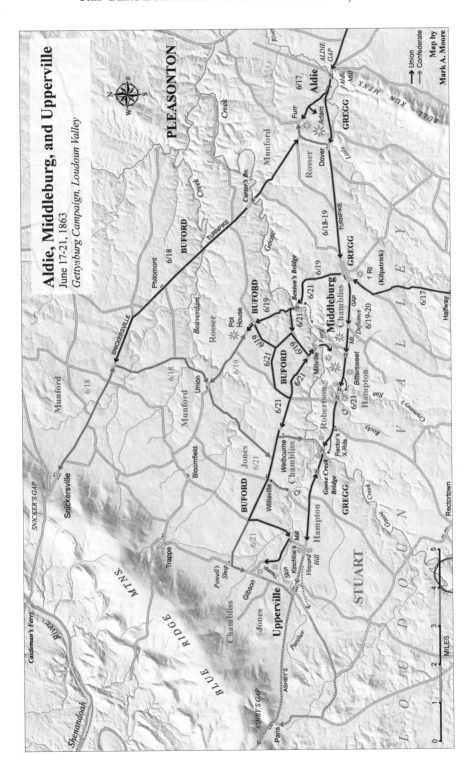

Aldie, Middleburg, and Upperville
June 17-21, 1863
Gettysburg Campaign, Loudoun Valley

Map by
Mark A. Moore

Rosser; the "Yankees were rapidly and closely pursuing them. I caused sabres to be drawn, and charged immediately, at the same time sending the information to the rear to the Colonel commanding. I drove the enemy upon his main body, which was in the town of Aldie." But Union troopers soon began to arrive in force and Rosser had no choice but to pull back, abandoning the intersection of the two pikes and taking up a position a half mile west on the Adam farm.[14]

Kilpatrick and his staff spurred forward to personally survey the field and ascertain the enemy's force. The new brigadier stationed himself on a small knoll behind the Snickersville Pike, where he was joined by Gen. David Gregg. Kilpatrick watched as Captain Randol's battery raced out of Aldie in a cloud of dust, clattered up the hill, and dropped trail across the road from him. Through the magnified lenses of his glass, Rosser's dispositions came into stark definition. The Adam homestead was just to the left of the Ashby's Gap Turnpike at the end of a dirt lane, just to the backside of a low-lying ridgeline that extended toward the Snickersville Pike. An orchard stood at the far end of the ridge.

The intervening land, with its plentiful drainage ditches and haystacks, provided the Rebels with a semblance of cover. Along this line Rosser stationed 50 sharpshooters under the command of Capt. R. B. Boston. One section of Breathed's battery unlimbered on a small elevation to the rear and west of the Adam farmhouse, and the other section deployed in the orchard. Rosser held the balance of his men in reserve, hidden from view west of the farmhouse. Soon the opposing batteries were engaged in a lively duel.

Kilpatrick's attack began with a series of disjointed advances by the 2nd New York Cavalry paralleling the Middleburg Road. Hampered by ditches and fences, the New Yorkers were easily dispersed by the accurate enemy fire of Boston's marksmen, "who were doing terrible execution in his [Kilpatrick's] ranks."[15]

In the meantime, the 6th Ohio Cavalry moved up the Snickersville Pike and swung into line to the west of the road. Things finally began to go right for the Federal troopers. "The enemy now showed considerable force," reported Rosser, "his flanks extending far beyond mine; on the left . . . [h]is dismounted skirmishers had pressed upon mine until their fighting had become desperate and close. Most of the horses of my dismounted men had been killed, and the enemy seeing that my

---

14 Thomas L. Rosser, "Colonel T. L. Rosser's Report of the Fight at Aldie," *Southern Historical Society Papers* (March 1881), Vol. 9, 119.

15 Ibid.

force was small . . . made a desperate effort to capture them, charging them in flank, right and left."[16]

Rosser responded to the threat with a countercharge by the balance of the 5th Virginia Cavalry. Smoke and fire engulfed both lines. In the meantime, galling fire from Randol's guns forced Breathed's right-hand section to retreat from the orchard to a ridge 500 yards to the rear. The Federal guns shifted their fire onto Rosser's line with devastating effect. "It became necessary for me to move," reported Rosser. Unfortunately, he "was compelled to take a position from which I could not support my line of skirmishers as well as before."[17]

Captain Boston fought grimly to hold his now untenable line, enjoined by Rosser "to hold his position at all hazards." The 6th Ohio gradually crept around Boston's left flank, and at the critical moment, Col. William Stedman "ordered a charge in line, and, passing the stack, captured all the enemy there, and I found in the next ravine a ditch . . . in which I found nearly 40 of the enemy, all of whom I captured." That was as far as they got, for Breathed's guns took advantage of the suddenly uncovered line and delivered a hail of grape and canister that took the starch right out of the Buckeyes. The Ohioans went to ground and held their position until dark, when Kilpatrick ordered the regiment to retire. Rosser wrote magnanimously of the stand made by Captain Boston: "The gallant and heroic manner in which Captain Boston and his men acted in this (one of the most vigorous cavalry fights I was ever engaged in) makes them the pride of their regiment."[18]

With that, the focus of the fighting shifted to the Confederate far left, where the absence of Rebels attracted the Union troopers like a shimmering beacon. Munford now began a mad scramble to shore up his exposed flank. In the early stages of the fight, he had managed to place a handful of sharpshooters behind a stone wall on the edge of the Furr farm, just north of the Snickersville Pike where it bent sharply from northwest to west. Colonel William Carter Wickham's 1st Virginia Cavalry shifted to the north of the Middleburg Road, freeing up the remnants of Rosser's 5th Virginia Cavalry and the fresh 4th Virginia Cavalry to move north along the Cobb House Road. Couriers were dispatched to track down the 2nd and 3rd Virginia, which had been on a foraging expedition on the far left and were unaware that the two armies were locked in a desperate struggle.

---

16 Ibid., 119-120.

17 Ibid., 120.

18 Ibid., 119-120; *OR 27*, pt. 1, 972.

As the Confederate forces began to filter into the area, one of Breathed's guns took up a commanding position from which it could enfilade the Snickersville Pike—close enough to lash it with canister. Two squadrons of Confederate sharpshooters hunkered down behind the stone wall on the north of the road, and the Little River and its tributaries secured the flanks. "Col. Munford now felt that his position was secure," wrote Maj. Henry B. McClellan of Stuart's staff. "The enemy must necessarily attack his front. The road by which it was approached was worn, as it ascended the hill, by deep gullies, which compelled an attack in column of fours and prevented the enemy from spreading out his front."[19]

The two lead squadrons of the 1st Massachusetts Cavalry headed straight into the ambuscade. The unsuspecting Union troopers took the bait, in the form of the 2nd Virginia Cavalry. "I immediately ordered one squadron into the road and we charged these men. They turned straight around and ran away," recalled Maj. Henry L. Higginson. "We reached the top of the hill, and the Confederates had stopped. . . . [Capt. Lucius M.] Sargent turned around in his saddle and made faces at them with his fingers, whereat they pursued us." It was already too late for the Yankees, who were well into the ambush. Up sprang the concealed Rebel sharpshooters, who promptly wrecked the two squadrons of the 1st Massachusetts.[20]

Seeing his comrades falling before the wall of smoke, fire, and flame, Capt. James Parsons led the rest of the 1st Massachusetts into the fray, only to face a counterattack by the 4th Virginia. "The fire was murderous, the charges and counter-charges were superb and grand," Maj. Charles Davis recalled of the scene. "The 1st Massachusetts Cavalry fought as brave men could fight to stem the tide that bore them back, until the whole right gave way upon this bloody field." Committed in piecemeal fashion, the 1st Massachusetts was butchered bit by bit. Captain Charles F. Adams, commanding one of the squadrons, stood helpless with rage. "My poor men were just slaughtered and all we could do was to stand still and be shot down, while the other squadrons rallied behind us," he lamented. Of the 294 men in the eight companies engaged in the action, the 1st Massachusetts suffered 198 casualties.[21]

---

19 McClellan, *The Life and Campaigns of Major-General J. E. B. Stuart*, 299.

20 Bliss Perry, *Life and Letters of Henry Lee Higginson*, 2 vols. (Boston, 1921), 1:197.

21 Benjamin W. Crowninshield, *A History of the First Regiment of Massachusetts Volunteers* (Boston, 1891), 477-479; Perry, *Life and Letters of Henry Lee Higginson*, 1:195.

To support the beleaguered Massachusetts troopers, Kilpatrick ordered the 4th New York Cavalry to charge. As the regiment lined up for the attack its commander, Col. Luigi Palma di Cesnola, rode at its rear, once again under arrest—this time for allowing his troopers to ride through the camp of a neighboring infantry regiment—and bereft of saber and pistol. Despite his questionable behavior, di Cesnola's courage was indisputable, and he shouldered his way to the front of his command. As the 1st Massachusetts scattered and broke for the rear, di Cesnola led his men forward to their left, where they encountered the same destructive fire from the Confederates. In a few moments, his troopers abandoned him and hightailed it to the rear just as the 1st Massachusetts had done.

When Kilpatrick learned of di Cesnola's gallant actions, he asked Pleasonton to release di Cesnola from arrest, and even went so far as to give the colonel his personal sidearms. Thus armed, the diminutive Italian count once again took his place at the head of his regiment and led them forward. But the New Yorkers, who had had enough, selected self-preservation over duty and refused to charge. Not even bothering to look over his shoulder to see if his men were following, di Cesnola charged the Rebels almost single-handedly and paid a steep price. Hit three times, he and his horse went down in a shower of gravel and dust, and he remained pinned under the animal's weight. The trapped di Cesnola was easy prey for the Rebels, a fitting end to a dismal week in which his faith and courage had been severely challenged.

The results were catastrophic. "The enemy, encouraged by the cowardly work of the Fourth New York," recalled Sgt. M. O. White of Company F, 1st Massachusetts Cavalry, "pressed hard upon our boys, closing in on our flanks, in fact hemmed us in for a time with little hope of escaping. Now Kilpatrick is seen dashing to the rear for other support, soon to return with the First Maine." Just as things seemed bleakest for Kilpatrick's crumbling blue line, Col. J. Irvin Gregg's brigade came up to the front and the Rebels broke off their attack. By 4:00 p.m. Gregg's command, composed of the 1st Maine Cavalry, the 10th New York Cavalry, the 4th Pennsylvania Cavalry, and the 16th Pennsylvania Cavalry, had extended into line.[22]

A Michigan newspaperman accompanying Kilpatrick's brigade reported on the moment. "Reserves were giving advantage to Stuart's redoubtable cavalry," read his account, "while Kilpatrick's body consisted largely of raw recruits, many of the regiments seeing service for the first time. Back and forth went the tide of

22 M. O. White, letter to the editor, *The First Maine Bugle* (April 1893), Vol. 3, No. 2, 77.

Much of the swirling action on the Union left flank took place in the form of thundering mounted charges. *Forbes Magazine*

battle, until a wavering, the moment preceding panic, came." Gregg ordered the 1st Maine to move forward to the front line, but the impetuous Kilpatrick pounded up to the regiment's commander, Col. Calvin S. Douty, and ordered him to charge. To the right the remnants of the 1st Massachusetts were streaming back down the Snicker's Gap Road. As the 1st Maine broke into a trot, the Southern sharpshooters rose as one and delivered a point-blank volley into the regiment's exposed right flank. All was bedlam! The battle smoke, thick and acrid, billowed high enough to hide the dead, dying, and wounded that littered the fields around the narrow dirt road.[23]

"Suddenly," observed the Michigan reporter, "a young officer of Pleasonton's staff came up at a gallop. Waving his broad-brimmed hat he shouted, 'Three cheers for General Kilpatrick.'" George Custer had made his dramatic entrance, and his

23 Merington, *The Custer Story*, 55.

subsequent actions, like Merritt's at Brandy Station, would significantly advance his career.[24]

Custer had first been spotted on the march to Aldie. "General Pleasonton, the corps commander, was represented at General Gregg's headquarters by one of his staff officers, Capt. George A. Custer," recalled Sergeant Meyer of the 24th New York Cavalry:

> He at once attracted the attention of the entire command. On that day he was dressed like an ordinary enlisted man, his trousers tucked in a pair of short-legged government boots, his horse equipments being those of an ordinary wagonmaster. He rode with a little rawhide riding whip stuck in his bootleg, and had long yellow curls down to his shoulders, his face ruddy and good-natured.[25]

With the charge blowing discordantly from a dozen bugles, the 1st Maine Cavalry—Kilpatrick, Douty, and Custer racing in the lead—counterattacked. In the space of a few seconds Douty was killed, two bullets smacking into his chest with meaty thumps. Kilpatrick's horse went down hard. Custer found himself all alone and far in front of a thundering, charging line of hell-bent-for-leather troopers, "outstripping the swiftest and a moment later . . . in the midst of the enemy." In the swirl of confused action, the clanging and clamor of saber strokes rang clearly over the hoarse shouts of men, the shrieks of wounded horses, and the barking of revolvers. For weeks prior, Custer had endured good-natured jibes about how much he looked like a Rebel. It worked to his advantage in the middle of that melee, surrounded as he was on all sides by gray-clad horsemen. "Cut off from my own men," he recorded, "I made my way out safely, and all owing to my hat, which is a large broad brim, exactly like that worn by the rebels. . . . The rebels at first thought I was one of their own men. . . . I then put spurs to 'Harry' and made my escape."[26]

The charge splintered Rosser's command and forced the Confederates to give up their ambush position behind the stone wall. As the sun began to sink below the horizon, the fight sputtered to a close. "The regiment gained the position," reported Col. Charles Smith, who took command of the 1st Maine after Colonel Douty's death, "secured our wounded, collected the trophies of the field, and were

---

24 Ibid.

25 Meyer, *Civil War Experiences*, 33.

26 Whittaker, *A Popular Life of George A. Custer*, 158-159.

George Custer was left in the lead when Col. Douty was killed and Gen. Judson Kilpatrick's horse hit the ground. *Frederick Whittaker, A Popular Life of Custer*

burying the dead when relieved just before dark." An amazed Munford described the damage his men had inflicted on Kilpatrick's never-say-die troopers. "I do not hesitate to say that I have never seen as many Yankees killed in the same space of ground in any fight I have ever seen, or on any battlefield in Virginia that I have been over." He added, "We held our ground until ordered by the major-general commanding to retire, and the Yankees had been so severely punished that they did not follow."[27]

Is "Every Man for Himself" in the Order Book?

When Colonel Duffié and the 1st Rhode Island Cavalry reached Thoroughfare Gap, they found it occupied by what looked to be a brigade of Confederate cavalry. "After a smart skirmish," reported Capt. George N. Bliss, "the rebels fell back. We then took the road to Middleburg, and, two miles out of the place, again encountered the rebel cavalry." The Federal troopers drove the enemy back once more; one of the Rebel pickets, however, managed to escape and sounded the alarm. Just as Jeb Stuart and his staff were settling down in Middleburg, about ready

27 OR 27, pt. 1, 979-980.

to call it a day, the picket rode by yelling at the top of his voice that the Yankees were coming up behind him. Quickly the Southern cavaliers jumped into their saddles and just barely escaped Duffié's troopers, who took possession of the town.[28]

As Duffié ordered the 1st Rhode Island to fortify the village, Alfred Pleasonton was writing another of his classic misleading reports, beginning with a verifiable fact followed by conjectures and extrapolations that no other officer had seen or even imagined. "I have a regiment in this (Thoroughfare) Gap, and as it has not yet reported, I am satisfied there are no troops in that vicinity." This report reached the Army of the Potomac's headquarters at 1:00 on the morning of June 18th.[29]

At 7:00 p.m., the Confederates launched their first attack, dashing down the road in a column of fours, "yelling and firing like demons." A messenger rode off to Kilpatrick with the news of the regiment's dire predicament. Protected by their barricades, the Rhode Island men waited in the dark. "Hold your fire" was the whispered order. "When the road was full in front of our line of carbineers, the order was given," recounted Captain Bliss. "'Fire!' and eighty carbines hurled death into the rebel ranks." The Rhode Islanders could not miss at that range. "Rider and horse went down in one confused mass; and those who were unhurt rushed wildly away from the scene of slaughter."[30]

The Confederate attacks persisted. Hard-pressed within the confines of Middleburg, Duffié's regiment dissolved into small units. Desperate groups of men used every trick in the book to evade the hunting Rebels. The rally point was two miles away from Middleburg, and not everyone made it. By dawn, fewer than 200 had reported to the rendezvous. "[We] waited for daylight, anxiously listening for the roar of Kilpatrick's guns. But the succor we hoped for came not," wrote Captain Bliss, "and at daybreak, the enemy were upon us. Our column was quickly placed in the road. And we were about to charge upon the rebels in our front when we discovered a rebel column coming down at a charge upon our rear."[31]

"Both charged simultaneously upon each other," reported correspondent Thomas M. Newbould of the *New York Daily Tribune.*

---

28 Frederic Denison, *Sabers and Spurs: The First Rhode Island Cavalry in the Civil War, 1861-1865* (Central Falls, RI, 1876), 233.

29 *OR* 27, pt. 1, 906-907.

30 Ibid., 234.

31 Denison, *Sabers and Spurs*, 235.

Yells, cheers and curses intermingled, ?rearms cracked, sabers gleamed, and horses rose upon their hind feet, borne upward by the pressure. . . . Each pushed through the ranks of the other, and turned to engage the nearest combatant. It was a thrust and parry or a pistol shot, and a run. . . . The Rebels at last ran."[32]

The desperate story of the 1st Rhode Island Cavalry made the front page of the *Tribune*, Horace Greeley's tabloid. "Stuart Surrounds the Rhode Islanders," blared the headline. "They Cut Their Way Out With Heavy Losses." The paper announced that 13 officers and 247 enlisted men had been killed, wounded, or were missing.[33]

Middleburg in the Middle

The casualty lists from Gregg's badly mauled division looked grim in the cold light of the morning of June 18. Pleasonton, of course, saw things through a much different lens and could not wait to forward the good news to his friend, Illinois Representative John Franklin Farnsworth. "The raid into Pennsylvania appears to be a fizzle," he bragged. "Yesterday we smashed Fitzhugh Lee's brigade considerable today your boys are away to the front on their old stomping grounds around him."[34]

In contrast to Pleasonton's rosy outlook, the orders from army headquarters, dated June 17, felt like a choke hold around his neck. "Do not advance the Main body of your cavalry beyond [Aldie] until further information is received of the movements of the enemy," dictated Butterfield. "Direct the force sent to Snicker's Gap to penetrate if possible into the valley. . . . The General feels the worth of

32 Andrews, *The North Reports the Civil War*, 412.

33 "Skirmishes Between the First Rhode Island Cavalry and the Enemy," *The New York Daily Tribune*, June 22, 1863.

34 Alfred Pleasonton to John F. Farnsworth, June 18, 1863, Alfred Pleasonton Papers, Library of Congress. When the war began, Farnsworth took a break from serving two terms in Congress and returned to Illinois to raise a regiment of cavalry, becoming colonel of the 8th Illinois Cavalry on September 18, 1861. As a brigade commander one year later, he grew close, both personally and professionally, to his commanding officer, Alfred Pleasonton. In November 1862, while running for a third term in Congress, Farnsworth received a promotion to brigadier general of volunteers, but he had to tender his resignation on March 4, 1863, in order to return to Washington. Once back in the capital, he made common cause with the Radical Republicans and continued to support his friend Pleasonton in his campaign of self-promotion.

reliable information in that direction and desires that you spare no labor to obtain it."[35]

Colonel William Gamble's brigade of John Buford's division took up the task, striking up the Snickersville Pike. Munford's brigade again contested the Union advance, digging in its heels even as Gamble came within sight of Snicker's Gap. Their stout resistance forced Gamble to give up his attempt to peek into the Shenandoah Valley, and he retreated all the way to Aldie with Munford's men snapping at his heels most of the way. At about the same time, Col. Irvin Gregg's brigade forayed from Aldie with the intention of occupying Middleburg. Here too, Confederate skirmishers made a tough go of it for the Union troopers; as a result, they did not reach the town until mid-afternoon. A few hours later Gregg decided to withdraw and camp about a mile and half east of Middleburg. As his command established its bivouac, a pounding thunderstorm moved into the area. Although filled with a lot of movement and sporadic fighting, the day turned out to be a disappointment for the Federals.

At 6:00 a.m. on June 19, Colonel Gregg's brigade departed its camps and rode along the Ashby's Gap Turnpike toward Middleburg. Before this host of 1,500 men could arrive, the Confederates abandoned Middleburg and fell back on their reserves to take up a defensive stance on the aptly named Mt. Defiance. There, the Rebels deployed about 3,200 men "strongly posted on the crest of a hill in the woods and behind stone fences." The land to the front, cultivated with thick yellow wheat, afforded not a scrap of cover for the attackers. The position extended several hundred yards on either side of the turnpike. The roadway narrowed considerably as it ascended to the crest, and any mounted attack would be constricted to a column of fours. Two expertly deployed batteries crouched on the hill, one on each side of the pike, stood ready to demolish Gregg's troopers with shot and shell. Rooney Lee's brigade under Colonel Chambliss occupied the northern portion of the line behind a stone wall along the front of the wooded hilltop while Beverly Robertson's 4th and 5th North Carolina cavalry regiments protected the southern approaches. "Our cavalry is really fighting infantry behind stone walls," complained Pleasonton after he conducted an inspection of the battlefield. "This is the reason for our heavy losses. One of the rebel infantry soldiers captured had 200 cartridges in his haversack." Fighting dismounted, the

35 Robert F. O'Neill, *Chasing Jeb Stuart and John Mosby: The Union Cavalry in Northern Virginia from Second Manassas to Gettysburg* (Jefferson, NC, 2012), 263.

Confederates dictated the tactics for this brawl. "The enemy," reported Irvin Gregg, "compelled me to do the same."[36]

Gregg moved the 4th and 16th Pennsylvania regiments to the south of the pike and, still afoot, the men began a steady advance across the open fields, only pausing every now and then to fire and reload. Two squadrons of the 10th New York dismounted on the north side of the road while the rest of the regiment sat their horses on the pike, hidden from sight and out of the line of fire. Gregg ordered Lt. William Fuller to unlimber his guns on a ridge west of Middleburg, about 1,000 yards from the Confederate lines; but he sensed the risk of another bloodbath like the ambush at Aldie a few days earlier and began to cast about for a backup plan.

At this time, Brig. Gen. David M. Gregg, Irvin's cousin, arrived on the field along with the brigades of Kilpatrick and Col. John Taylor. Shifting the Pennsylvania regiments still farther south, Gregg inserted a pair of companies from the 1st Maine next to the pike, while units of the 2nd New York and 6th Ohio rode north behind the 10th New York, extending the Federal right flank well beyond the Rebel front.

Irvin Gregg did not hold to the Kilpatrick school of cavalry tactics and refused to get his men killed for no purpose. He dismounted the Harris Light Cavalry (the 2nd New York) to stealthily make its way to the last occupied stone wall. Much of their approach was conducted at a crawl. The rest of the Union horsemen listened for the opening volleys from the Harris Light—the signal to advance through the gently swaying wheat. Suddenly the New Yorkers "appeared only a few rods in rear of the Confederates behind the wall, who, without warning, received a volley in their backs. They were at once in confusion and at that moment the bugle sounded the charge."[37]

The Yankees drove forward all across the line in a determined advance, their carbines spitting fire and smoke. South of the pike, the Pennsylvanians advanced at the double quick, and with the 1st Maine Cavalry thrown in for support, carried the position to their front "in gallant style." For a time the situation on the right side remained dicey. "I feared for a moment we would be repulsed," admitted Colonel Gregg, "but at this juncture the Tenth New York, under Major Avery, charging gallantly up the road in column, and the First Maine, Sixteenth and Fourth

---

36 OR 27, pt. 1, 911, 975.

37 Meyer, *Civil War Experiences*, 38.

Pennsylvania Cavalry pushing through the woods, the entire position was carried."[38]

But before this tidal wave could hit, the Confederates began to withdraw, giving up ground reluctantly and buying time for their other brigades to take up a new position on high ground about 500 yards to the rear. Stuart threw the 9th Virginia Cavalry into the center, buying time for him to extricate his artillery. "The attack was resisted for a long time, but when the enemy gained a considerable advantage on the Confederate right by a charge of dismounted men supported by two regiments of cavalry, Stuart withdrew," recalled Major McClellan. "This withdrawal was effected in good order, under the fire of the enemy's dismounted men and artillery, and no attempt was made to charge the retiring lines."[39]

Satisfied with his gains, General Gregg ordered a halt, flung forward a sheaf of skirmishers, and spent the rest of the day in a desultory exchange of gunfire with the enemy's skirmishers. Of Gregg's tactics a grateful Meyer would later write, "I think that Colonel Gregg's coolness and solicitude for the safety of his men, where, by the use of a little strategy a needless loss of life was saved, deserved recognition."[40]

Even as Colonel Gregg's brigade advanced through Middleburg to attack the Confederate positions at Mt. Defiance, General Buford sallied out of Aldie and cut to the north just before Middleburg in an effort to outflank the Rebel resistance. Buford's division crossed Goose Creek at Benton's Bridge. The few Rebel pickets that guarded the crossing did not even slow the Union column down. Leaving the bridge under the protection of two squadrons and a section of guns, Buford proceeded north until he reached the Pot house. There he deployed Gamble's brigade on some high ground that commanded the Old Pot House Road. Along that same road, Colonel Rosser rode with his much-reduced 5th Virginia Cavalry, supported by the 7th Virginia Cavalry of "Grumble" Jones's brigade.

Stuart had given Rosser specific orders: Delay the enemy but do not bring on a general engagement. While the 5th Virginia launched a series of diversionary attacks to Buford's front, the 7th Virginia tried to sneak around his right flank. Fortunately for Buford, a large portion of Gamble's brigade had been completely rearmed with the fast-loading Sharps carbine. The high volume of fire combined with a few loads of well-placed canister proved to be enough of a deterrent that

38 OR 27, pt. 1, 976.

39 McClellan, *The Life and Campaigns of Major-General J. E. B. Stuart*, 306-307.

40 Meyer, *Civil War Experiences*, 39.

Due to the nature of the ground, and the proliferation of stone fences, the maneuvers on the right flank were mostly dismounted. *LOC*

Rosser decided to go back from whence he came. While engaged in this ruckus, Buford received orders from Pleasonton to detach Major Whiting's Reserve Brigade to ride to the sound of the guns and join General Gregg's fight along the Ashby's Gap Pike.

The Reserve Brigade covered the two and one-half miles from the Pot house back to Goose Creek at a trot the whole way. Merritt's 2nd U.S. Cavalry probed for the enemy's flank and rear. Stuart had fallen back from the Mt. Defiance position and had taken up a new defensive position on the Bittersweet farm. Elements of Chambliss's brigade picketed the fords along Goose Creek. Merritt's advance had no sooner splashed across the ford on the Millville Road than Rebel couriers were racing south to inform Stuart of the enemy's presence on his left flank. A commanding knoll—soon to be known as "Battle Knoll"—dominated the crossing. "Within two miles of Middleborough," stated Merritt, "the brigade—the Second still leading— turned through an opening in a stone wall into an enclosed meadow, when it was suddenly attacked in flank and rear by a force of Rebel cavalry, which made a rapid dash to get possession of the stone wall surrounding the field."[41]

41 Merritt, "Reminiscences," 293.

According to Eugene J. Stocking of the 1st U.S. Cavalry, it was a very close affair. "Our regiment dismounted and made for a stone fence. The rebels seeing us, made for it at the same time, but we reached it before them. When they were within about five rods from us, we gave them a volley, and they turned and ran. We let them have our volley in the back." By 6:00 p.m. the fight was over except for occasional long-range shots by Rebel sharpshooters. As darkness embraced the field a severe thunderstorm burst over the area. Standing miserably by their saddled horses, the shivering troopers, "without our blanket or overcoats, and without supper," wiled away the night by digging "port holes through the fence, and got a few shots as they would crawl up to carry off their dead, as we supposed." Buford, meanwhile, moved back to Aldie, and on June 20 the Reserve Brigade moved to join him.[42]

That night the rest of Jones's brigade straggled into the Confederate lines and moved to the far left. Chambliss's brigade also deployed on the left, in support of Colonel Jones. Munford's command, having fought two heavy engagements in the past few days, shifted to the left as well, covering the approaches to Snicker's Gap. Hampton arrived the next day, June 20, and took up position on the Upperville Pike. Robertson's brigade was next to Hampton and covered Ashby's Gap. "Although Stuart's five brigades were now in position," Major McClellan pointed out, "the necessity of guarding the three roads by which the mountain passes might be approached compelled him to divide his command into as many parts."[43]

Though forced to give ground and retreat toward the gaps, Stuart had, for the most part, accomplished his mission by denying Pleasonton the ability to lay eyes on Lee's rapidly moving army. Hooker, on the other hand, believed Pleasonton's reports and informed Washington that he thought Lee had no intention of moving north of the Potomac. In reality, Lt. Gen. James Longstreet's First Corps now stretched along the Shenandoah Valley from just opposite Ashby's Gap in the south to Berryville in the north. At Williamsport, Ewell and his corps were poised to cross into Maryland at first light on June 21. Lieutenant General Ambrose Hill had already reached Shepherdstown on the north bank of the Potomac. The Union forces could not have been more ignorant or complacent. As the rain continued to fall throughout the morning of June 20, Pleasonton stopped to rest and regroup, for he had big plans for June 21.

42 Letter, Eugene J. Stocking to his parents, October 4, 1863, Eugene J. Stocking Papers, Michigan State University Archives, Lansing, MI.

43 McClellan, *The Life and Campaigns of Major-General J. E. B. Stuart*, 307.

The horses of the Cavalry Corps paid a great price for the continuous days of action. The course of the cavalry across the Loudoun Valley could be traced by following a grim trail of dead horses. Thomas M. Newbould of the *New York Tribune* followed the advance along the Ashby's Gap Turnpike. "Half a dozen dead horses are suddenly seen lying in the road, or in the fields nearby," Newbould wrote of the gruesome scene. "Their bodies have already begun to swell, and a few lie on their backs, with legs stiffly projecting in the air. Long streams of blood issue from their noses." As Jeb Stuart once said, "rough roads" could, for "want of adequate shoeing facilities," decimate a cavalry brigade.[44]

Brigadier General Rufus Ingalls, the Army of the Potomac's chief quartermaster, felt compelled to write Quartermaster General Montgomery Meigs that the cavalry had already incurred heavy losses among the horses. Moreover, those recently acquired from the remount depot were all unshod. To his credit, Ingalls had taken steps to provide forage, forges, farriers, and an adequate supply of horseshoes. "Will you please order a good supply of horses?" he implored Meigs. "Three or four thousand should be kept on hand and well shod, ready for issue." Ingalls followed up on June 20 with another missive to Meigs. "Please do all you can to have as many good horses ready as possible. It is most important," Ingalls urged. The repeated requests put him on a rocky slope, for Meigs was not known for keeping his temper on a leash, nor did he suffer slights against his department lightly.[45]

According to information received from a prisoner, the only Confederate force east of the Blue Ridge Mountains was Stuart's cavalry. "General Gregg and I both believe this to be the case, from all the information we can obtain," Pleasonton assured army headquarters. "I would, therefore, respectfully request that the general commanding permit me to take my whole corps to-morrow morning, and throw it at once upon Stuart's whole force, and cripple it up." Pleasonton also requested the addition of infantry to his depleted, worn-out horsemen who, "[f]or the last three days . . . have been constantly fighting, and have behaved splendidly, and are in the highest spirits and confidence."[46]

---

44 Andrews, *The North Reports the Civil War*, 412; OR 27, pt. 2, 689.

45 Ibid., pt. 3, 212, 230.

46 Ibid., pt. 1, 911.

Upping the Stakes at Upperville

On June 21, Pleasonton began his final effort to break through Stuart's screening cavalry and get a view at what was going on in the Valley. "So about nine in the morning it began, near Upperville," wrote Merritt, with "General David Gregg's division on the left, a force of infantry under General Meade in rear of the centre, and General Buford, with his trusted division, on the right." The infantry belonged to the superb brigade commanded by Col. Strong Vincent.[47]

If Pleasonton's cavalry, augmented by Vincent's infantry, could force its way well into Ashby's Gap, it would finally be able to observe the Shenandoah Valley and comply with Hooker's repeated entreaties to ascertain the whereabouts of Lee's army. But as Merritt would report, "The country being well adapted to defense, because of its hilly character and the long lines of substantial stone walls and heavy woods which covered it," would make cavalry maneuvers difficult for the Federals.[48]

Sometime during the early evening hours of June 20, Hooker's official approval of Pleasonton's plans arrived at cavalry headquarters. "Your dispatch of 12.30 p.m., of this date has been received and laid before the major-general commanding," wrote Dan Butterfield, "who authorizes you, in accordance with your request, to move tomorrow morning with your entire corps against the enemy's cavalry." Again the persistent requests for accurate intelligence inundated Pleasonton. "The commanding general is very anxious that you should ascertain, at the earliest possible moment," relayed Butterfield with a hint of annoyance showing, "where the main body of the Enemy's infantry are to be found at the present time, especially A. P. Hill's corps." Butterfield took one more opportunity to remind Pleasonton that the cavalry served as the eyes of the army. In his opinion, Pleasonton's heavy force should have no trouble driving in the Confederate pickets.[49]

---

47 Merritt, "Reminiscences," 294. New Harvard graduate Vincent joined the Erie Regiment of the Pennsylvania Militia at war's start. He was commissioned lieutenant colonel of the 83rd Pennsylvania , and took command of the regiment when its colonel died at Gaines' Mill. He contracted malaria on the Peninsula and did not return to the Army of the Potomac until December 1862. The following May he was promoted to brigade command when the previous commander resigned after Chancellorsville. He died heroically leading his brigade in the defense of Little Round Top on July 2, 1863, at Gettysburg. Boatner, *Civil War Dictionary*, 878.

48 Merritt, "Reminiscences," 294.

49 *OR* 27, pt. 3, 227-228.

At this early stage of the battle, Stuart made only a minimal effort to retard his foe. "A general engagement was not sought by me," he explained. "I preferred waiting for the arrival of the cavalry still in rear . . . and I confined my attention to procuring, through scouts and reconnoitering parties, information of the enemy's movements." Stuart deployed the troopers of Hampton's and Robertson's brigades approximately two miles west of Middleburg on the Bittersweet farm, on a long finger of high ground beginning south of the Ashby's Gap Turnpike. Major James F. Hart's battery held the center of the line straddling the pike, while the 1st North Carolina Cavalry and the Jeff Davis Legion stretched to the south. The 2nd South Carolina Cavalry and Cobb's Legion deployed to the north. To Hampton's left, Robertson stationed two regiments. He anchored his far-left flank on Battle Knoll, on the northern edge of the ridgeline at Bittersweet Farm; that same knoll had been fought over repeatedly a few days earlier. Kirk's Branch fronted the entire Rebel line, and Southern sharpshooters covered its fords and bridges.[50]

As General Gregg's force approached Kirk's Branch with Kilpatrick's brigade in the lead, the cavalry wheeled off the pike, extended into line, and threw out a screen of skirmishers to its front. While the troopers cleared the roadway, Lt. William Fuller's battery unlimbered just west of Mt. Defiance and engaged the Confederates in an hour-long artillery duel at a range of 850 yards. Under cover of the barrage, Colonel Vincent's infantry began to spread out to Kilpatrick's left. The 16th Michigan lined up next to the 4th Pennsylvania, with the 44th New York to its left, followed by the 20th Maine. The 83rd Pennsylvania, Vincent's old regiment, moved stealthily through a covering patch of woods, sweeping in a wide arc to outflank the 1st North Carolina. "The dismounted men of the enemy were in position on the south side of this road," reported Vincent, "behind a series of stone walls running at right angles with it, the cavalry in the fields, and a battery of six guns placed near the road on the left. A belt of woods some 200 yards marked their position." From this line they opened a brisk fire. Pleasonton ordered Vincent to advance his infantry, which, "moving in conjunction with the cavalry . . . drove them from this position to other stone walls immediately in the rear, dislodging them at each attack, until we pushed them across Crummer's Run."[51]

Custer's position on the field cannot be pinpointed with any certainty. As Pleasonton's favorite aide, however, the odds are good that the young captain delivered Pleasonton's orders to Strong Vincent. If so, Custer had a front row seat

50 Ibid., pt. 2, 689.

51 Ibid., pt. 1, 614.

to the ensuing combined movement of cavalry and infantry. "Again General Pleasonton directed the infantry to advance in greater force," reported Vincent. "At the same time I directed Captain Woodward, commanding Eighty-third Pennsylvania, to move rapidly through the woods to our left, keeping his force concealed, and, the instant he had passed the stone walls, to emerge and take the enemy in flank and rear." Just as Kilpatrick advanced his dismounted troopers, the 83rd Pennsylvania Infantry made its move past the end of the stone wall, burst out of the woods, and struck the exposed right flank of the Confederate line, crumbling it like a two-day old cookie. The Rebel position melted from south to north, and Hampton's men streamed from the field, leaving Robertson completely exposed and forced to retreat as well. "The movement was entirely successful," asserted Colonel Vincent in his report.[52]

A long day of fighting still lay ahead. Yet again the terrain came to the assistance of the Confederates, as a series of impassable, constricting streams forced Kilpatrick's mounted force to return to the main roadway. There, Hampton's marksmen used the maze of stone walls to their best advantage, pouring a galling fire into the Union troopers. Hart's battery continued to assail Kilpatrick's column until Fuller's guns came back into action and cleared the road. Vincent's men, meanwhile, continued their remorseless advance on the enemy flank.

Hampton had held up Kilpatrick's advance for two hours, more than enough time for Stuart to bring his widely scattered brigades to Hampton's aid from their positions covering the Snicker's Gap Pike. Retreating once more, Hampton began consolidating his position beyond Rector's Crossing and behind Goose Creek. Hart's battery had been reinforced, while Robertson's troopers took up a supporting position on the left of the line. The 1st South Carolina Cavalry took up a rearguard position in front of the crossing, but Vincent's indefatigable foot soldiers soon overwhelmed them. On Stuart's order, the Confederate troopers mounted and raced back across the stream. As the Federal forces prepared to renew the offensive, the opposing artillery began a spirited exchange.

Kilpatrick surveyed the center of the Union line from a position just off the pike. He had just witnessed the repulse of his old regiment, the 4th New York Cavalry; he now turned to Pleasonton and remarked off-handedly, "If I had the 1st Maine, they would go through." At the same moment, Pleasonton spotted the 1st Maine Cavalry moving into position. Pleasonton immediately ordered them to

52 Ibid.

report to Kilpatrick, whose subsequent orders to Col. Charles Smith for once lacked the usual Kilpatrick hyperbole. "Charge the town, drive out the enemy, and, if possible, get beyond." The regiment obeyed with gusto. "It was one of those bold dashes for which Kilpatrick had a special fondness," recalled Chaplain Samuel Hill Merrill. "His opinion of the First Maine was indicated by his request for their services on that occasion." To those nearby, Kilpatrick announced that the "First Maine would charge straight into hell if they were ordered to."[53]

Moving straight down the pike, they took off through Upperville and out into the valley beyond, running roughshod over a small howitzer the Confederates had placed in the middle of town. Here the Southern force unleashed its full fury. The Maine boys faltered and "after firing a few shots, scattered to the right and left," reported the 4th Pennsylvania's Lt. Col. William E. Doster, who then took matters into his own hands. "The fire of my regiment being too hot for him, the enemy wheeled, and I ordered a charge, which was obeyed most promptly and gallantly by both officers and men. The enemy were driven from the field, leaving a number killed, many wounded, and several prisoners in our hands."[54]

Strong Vincent wrote admiringly of his experience with the cavalry. "The charges of the cavalry, a sight I had never before witnessed, were truly inspiring, and the triumphant strains of the bands, as squadron after squadron was hurled at the enemy in his flight up the hills and toward the gap, gave me a feeling of regret that we, too, were not mounted and could not join in the chase." Pleasonton reported to Hooker that "[v]ery many charges were made, and the saber used freely, but always with great advantage to us."[55]

If Buford Cannot Do It, No One Can

Buford, meanwhile, was to push north from Middleburg as he had a couple of days before and turn the Confederate left flank at the bloody Battle Knoll. With the full force of his division, he planned to get across Goose Creek and dislodge the Rebels from their position on the northernmost point of the Bittersweet ridge line. As they departed Middleburg at 7:30 a.m., Buford's marching cavalrymen could discern the muted rumbling of the artillery duel at Bittersweet farm as Gregg pitched into Stuart.

53 Edward P. Tobie, *History of the First Maine Cavalry, 1861-1865* (Boston, 1887), 169.

54 *OR* 27, pt. 1, 984.

55 Ibid., 615, 912.

At Goose Creek, Buford encountered the first hitch in his plan of action, although it is hard to understand how such a well-prepared cavalryman could have failed to anticipate the obstacle. On June 16, the Army of the Potomac's chief engineer, Brig. Gen. Gouverneur K. Warren, released a cursory report on the conditions of the river crossings and fords in the projected area of operations. Regarding Buford's route of advance for the next few days, Warren observed that in the Goose Creek area, "[t]he crossings . . . are no material obstructions."[56]

That night, General Butterfield spoke with Maj. Gen. Julius Stahel, commander of the cavalry division protecting Washington, who was visiting army headquarters. Stahel painted an entirely different picture of the area; he had operated in those environs for some time and knew the area intimately, certainly much more thoroughly than Warren's once-over. "General Stahel informs me that all the country is full of roads," wrote Butterfield, and "that some difficulty may be found at little streams and bridges, and at Goose Creek, in crossing. The pioneers will have to be prepared to fix these places for the troops and trains."[57]

After the action of June 19, Capt. Myles Keogh, aide-de-camp to General Buford, forwarded a message to General Gregg, informing him on behalf of Buford "that by some mismanagement the bridge over Goose Creek, by which Major Whiting proceeded to connect with you to-day, is burned, and that, if the rain continues the creek will be hardly fordable for any one returning by that way." Keogh had been sent to look for Whiting, but there were Rebels everywhere, and "when he came toward New Lisbon he found the enemy in possession of the road in some force, in rear of Major Whiting."[58]

Now, two days later, Buford found it impossible to cross the creek, and was forced to make a wide detour. He sent Gamble's brigade to the south, hoping to discover the Confederate flank unanchored in some muddy field near Millville. Instead, as usual, Gamble found all the Rebels hunkered down safely behind stone walls. Every road was a muddy morass, and Gamble's column floundered under the near-marshy conditions. Eventually he called a halt and countermarched back to the destroyed bridge crossing. Having no other option, Buford's men soon

---

56 Ibid., pt. 3, 149.

57 *OR 27, pt. 3, 150.* Hungarian-born Stahel served in the Austrian army and later fought for Hungarian independence in Lajos Kossuth's Revolution of 1848. After the Hapsburgs crushed the movement, Stahel fled to Prussia, England, and finally the United States in 1859. Instrumental in recruiting the 8th New York Infantry, he accepted a post as its lieutenant colonel. *OR* 27, pt. 1, 150.

58 Ibid., 210.

forced the crossing and began moving on the Rebel flank. But the lost time would be paid for in blood. "All along the wounded and dead and the horses scattered on the road attest [to] the severity of the conflict and that the ground was hotly contested," recorded the regimental diarist of the 3rd Pennsylvania Cavalry.[59]

Once across the creek, Buford encountered increasing resistance as the full weight of the Confederate cavalry reached the field of battle. Colonel Lunsford Lindsey Lomax spurred his command ahead at a lively clip and managed to get ahead of Buford, who was advancing west along the Millville Road. The Confederates began taking potshots at Buford's column, forcing him to halt and send skirmishers to clear out the Rebels. As the Federals resumed the advance, the Reserve Brigade under Maj. Samuel H. Starr took the lead. The sound of the guns to the south indicated that the Confederates on the Ashby's Gap Pike were falling back.[60]

Dispatching the Reserve Brigade to move to General Gregg's assistance, Buford continued heading west with Gamble's command now in the van. A mile farther down the road, Lomax resumed his long-distance sniping. The tiresome process of dislodging the Rebels began anew. Horse artillery units unlimbered their guns and skirmishers advanced. But now the Confederate resistance grew in intensity since Chambliss's men had retreated as far as they could. Any further withdrawal would open the flank of Stuart's new line at Goose Creek Bridge to attack by Buford's division. The fight for the Millville Road gained importance and momentum.

In addition to Lomax's 11th and 12th Virginia Cavalry regiments, Chambliss now threw in the 9th Virginia Cavalry as well as a battery. Canister flayed the advance of Buford's division and his momentum gradually dissipated. "It became apparent that I had not succeeded in gaining the enemy's flank," Buford's report stated, though this was not from a lack of trying. "The column struck a brisk trot,

---

59 Brooke Rawle, *History of the Third Pennsylvania Cavalry*, 252.

60 By the beginning of the Civil War, Sam Starr had served in the U.S. Army for almost 30 years in the artillery, engineer, and infantry branches before transferring to the 2nd Dragoons in 1848. Known to his troopers as "Old Paddy" and "Old Nose Bag," he had a reputation as a fierce disciplinarian due to his enforcement of strict standards of behavior. He led the 5th New Jersey Infantry at Williamsburg and Fair Oaks, but lost his command after hitting a careless sentry over the head with the flat of his saber while profanely insulting the hapless soldier. Starr eventually returned to service in April 1863 with the 6th U.S. Cavalry and, as its most senior officer, subsequently replaced Major Whiting as commander of the Reserve Brigade. John Buford greeted his return with enthusiasm, as they had been good friends before the war.

but ran afoul of so many obstructions in the shape of ditches and stone fences, that it did not make fast progress, and got out of shape."[61]

At that moment Jones's brigade appeared from the north and struck Buford's attacking columns. Jones stationed four guns behind another of the ubiquitous stone walls, and they opened a withering fire on Buford's lead regiments. "The enemy then came up in magnificent style from the direction of Snickersville," reported Buford, "and for a time threatened me with overwhelming numbers. He was compelled, however, to retire before the terrific carbine fire which the brave Eighth Illinois and Third Indiana poured into him. As he withdrew, my rear troops came up, formed, and pressed him back to the mountains."[62]

One Confederate account confirms Buford's version of the battle. "In front bearing towards Upperville was a hill which they [the Confederates] aimed to reach and thence give battle to the enemy," wrote Capt. William N. MacDonald of the famed "Laurel Brigade" of Virginia cavalry. Buford was one step ahead of them and occupied the stone fence first. "The Federal dismounted squadrons with their carbines delivered successive volleys." The constricting walls on either side of the road trapped the Laurel Brigade in the Yankee kill zone. "Never was a brigade taken at greater disadvantage than in this engagement." Jones found it impossible "to get his regiments into any sort of formation, and the stone fences beyond in the fields occupied by the enemy furnished protection for his sharpshooters, who fired with deadly effect into the almost helpless Confederate masses."[63]

For the most part, however, Confederate accounts downplay the effects of the Federal cavalry's maneuvers. They claim that the 11th Virginia Cavalry soundly checked Buford's advance, buying sufficient time to reposition the guns and once again pound the foe. "Our cavalry having cleared our battery," reported Jones, "it played with fearful effect upon their men and horses. The punishment here inflicted, together with the difficulties of the ground, soon caused the enemy to abandon his intention of preventing a junction of our forces." Wade Hampton remembered the movements of his regiments being conducted as if they were on parade. "This series of charges," declared Hampton, "went on until all my regiments named had charged three times, and I had gained ground to the right and front of more than half a mile. At this moment the 2nd South Carolina Cavalry was

61 OR 27, pt. 1, 921.

62 Ibid.

63 William N. McDonald, *A History of the Laurel Brigade*, Bushrod C. Washington, ed. (Baltimore, 1907), 150-151.

brought up in good order from the rear, and under its protection I reformed my command, and retired in column of regiments, at a walk and without molestation."[64]

Nonetheless, by late afternoon the Federals were fighting to take Upperville. A fierce melee took place as both sides struggled desperately for supremacy of the surrounding fields. One of Stuart's horse artillerymen, whose guns hurled shells into the midst of the advancing Yankees with startling accuracy and tore huge rifts in their ranks, described the action. "Soon after the fight became general all over the field. . . . They quickly closed up and came at us again. They were certainly the bravest and boldest Yanks that ever fought us on a field."[65]

At last the Union horsemen drove the Rebels from Upperville. The entire Loudoun Valley now lay before Pleasonton's troopers, along with the entire array of Stuart's command. From his first contact, Stuart had planned to delay the enemy then retire en echelon, the movement covered by his batteries of horse artillery. "At no time," reported Major McClellan, "was the enemy able to cause any serious disorder in our ranks." Though it was getting late, the day's action was far from over.[66]

Across the entire front, the Union cavalry moved to the attack. "At four in the afternoon the enemy was subjected to the final charge from the entire command," wrote Merritt of the action. "The regular Brigade . . . made a furious charge into the midst of the enemy." The opposing forces fought the old-fashioned way: The two sides lined up across from each other then had at it. "They marched out with their red battle flag waving, and a number of men were gathered around it," recalled Eugene Stocking of the Reserve Brigade. Over the uproar Stocking could clearly hear the Rebel commander inspiring his troopers by telling "his men that they must fight for they had the Regular Brigade to deal with. . . . It was a hard fight for the time."[67]

Finally, Stuart called it a day. "After this repulse, which was not followed up, as the enemy's infantry was known to be in close supporting distance, I withdrew the command leisurely to the mountain gap west of Upperville," read his official account. "The day was far spent. . . . By night, part of Longstreet's corps occupied

---

64 McClellan, *The Life and Campaigns of Major-General J. E. B. Stuart*, 311-312.

65 George M. Neese, *Three Years in the Confederate Horse Artillery* (New York, 1911), 182-183.

66 McClellan, *The Life and Campaigns of Major-General J. E. B. Stuart*, 308.

67 Merritt, "Reminisces," 294; Stocking to his parents, October 4, 1863.

the mountain pass, and the cavalry was ordered farther back for rest and refreshment, of which it was sorely in need." As the exhausted Rebel horsemen settled in for the night, the ever-restless John Buford sent a party to climb to the top of the Blue Ridge Mountains to see what they could see. The scouts spied "a rebel infantry camp about 2 miles long on the Shenandoah, just below Ashby's Gap. The atmosphere was so hazy they could not make out anything more beyond." That night Pleasonton wrote a lengthy memorandum to army headquarters, finally detailing the disposition of Lee's army for Gen. Hooker. "Longstreet's corps . . . is now in the Shenandoah Valley. . . . The main body of the rebel infantry is in the Shenandoah Valley. . . . My opinion is, that Stuart's force is kept in our front as a blind until their main force is thrown across the Potomac."[68]

Despite its reported success, the charge by the Regulars at Battle Knoll on June 21 planted the seeds of another of those internal squabbles that repeatedly threatened to diminish the accomplishments of the Union cavalry. The quick-tempered Maj. Starr would not tolerate any snub to his authority. "At four in the afternoon the enemy was subjected to the final charge from the entire command," reported Merritt; "the Sixth, led by its gallant Major [Starr] . . . made a furious charge into the midst of the enemy, and was closely supported by the First Cavalry which engaged the enemy with the sabre." But in the heart of the action, the 2nd U.S. Cavalry had been pulled out of the attack and directed to support a battery that was in danger of being overrun by the advancing Confederates. Starr ordered a squadron of the 6th U.S. Cavalry, commanded by Capt. George C. Cram, to support the attack. That support failed to appear, however, and the irascible Starr made no bones about his displeasure. In fact, he accused Cram of disobeying his orders.[69]

In mitigation of his actions—or lack thereof—Cram described the exhausted condition of his command at that moment. Quite prepared to do its duty, the squadron found itself advancing "under an harassing artillery fire and over a long stretch of heavy and marshy ground, intersected by a most difficult ditch and terminating in a hill of plowed ground. . . . The enemy in large force awaited it." This movement fatigued the horses. "Most of the horses," he reported, were "so blown that it was impossible to bring or keep them for such a distance at a charging pace." The attack proved unsuccessful and the squadron dismounted, taking shelter behind one of the stone walls. Cram claimed that his soldiers had done all

68 OR 27, pt. 2, 691; Ibid., pt. 1, 912-913; pt. 3, 244.

69 Merritt, "Reminiscences," 294.

that could have been asked of them. "The men were exhausted and worn out by the recent imposition of incessant picket duty in their position near Middleburg," he recalled:

> They were taken from behind stone walls, which they had been guarding all night and the day before, mounted on horses as famished as themselves, and immediately marched with the column, and at the end of a fatiguing day were required to charge over ground almost impracticable in its nature.[70]

Once back in camp—his duties to Army, God, and Country fulfilled—Pleasonton wasted little time in returning to the political machinations that the war had interrupted. "I desire to inform the general commanding that the losses my command has sustained in officers require me to ask for promotion of good commanders," he wrote to Asst. Adj. Gen. Seth Williams. "It is necessary to have a good commander for the regular brigade of cavalry, and I earnestly recommend Capt. Wesley Merritt to be made a brigadier-general for that purpose. He has all the qualifications for it, and has distinguished himself by his gallantry and daring. Give me good commanders and I will give you good results." If there had ever been a clash of personalities between Merritt and Pleasonton during his short tenure on Pleasonton's staff, it must not have affected Pleasonton's opinion of Merritt as a fighter.[71]

Cut to the Chase

On Merritt's side of the battlefield, meanwhile, dismounted tactics predominated because of the broken terrain and the ever-present stone walls and fences. The Rebels repeatedly dismounted and to fight behind the cover offered by the thick walls, each rock matched to another by generations of farmers to mark the boundaries of their properties. A few days later on the morning of July 1 at Gettysburg, Buford would use those same dismounted tactics to their best effect. On McPherson's Ridge, two of his brigades, fighting on foot behind stone walls and wooden fences, worked to delay the advance of Maj. Gen. Henry Heth's

---

70 Carter, *From Yorktown to Santiago*, 93-94.

71 *OR*, pt. 1, 913.

infantry division just long enough to allow Federal infantry to arrive at the front and stave off what could have been a real disaster for the Union army.[72]

George Custer, on the other hand, had seen mounted action used effectively during the course of the campaign. He had hurled himself enthusiastically into the saber charge at Aldie, reaping a whirlwind of praise for his performance. That particular weapon, however, had lost its luster among cavalry leaders. "During the war many officers contracted a positive prejudice against the use of the sabre, and in some regiments, mostly Confederate, it was entirely laid aside, all charging being done with the pistol," wrote Frederick Whittaker. In the minds of many officers, the saber had two things working against it. Mastering the weapon took hard work and much practice. "The sabre is a weapon that requires constant practice to keep one's hand in, and our cavalry officers, as a class, are entirely deficient in that practice. Hence the contempt for the sabre inculcated by a class of men who simply could not handle it."[73]

"The other cause," wrote Philip St. George Cooke, "was that the sabre was seldom sharpened or kept sharp. As issued to the new troops, it is little better than a club." One officer told of his fruitless efforts to put an edge on a sword. "Sabres are issued blunt enough to ride on to San Francisco. The steel is hard. . . . The writer has stood at a grindstone turned by steam and tried to grind an Ames sabre for over an hour. He can testify that it is hard work, the hardest kind of work."[74]

To Whittaker the solution was simple, if costly to implement. "If ground while in soft temper, at the factory, the hardening temper subsequently received would leave them sharp, and easily kept so," he asserted, "if the War Department would simply require in all future contracts for sabres that they should be delivered, each sharp enough to cut a sheet of paper." As if there were not enough obstacles to proper saber maintenance already, cavalry soldiers never had enough grindstones.

---

72 The fields of Loudoun County abound in rocks, and local farmers built the stone walls as they cleared their fields for cultivation—thereby killing two birds with one proverbial stone.

73 Frederick Whittaker, *Volunteer Cavalry: The Lessons of a decade, by a Volunteer Cavalryman* (New York, NY, 1871), 60. Artist Alfred R. Waud's sketch of the charge at Aldie contributed to Custer's fame. He caught Custer looking back over his shoulder to see Kilpatrick crashing to the ground. Over his other shoulder, the slain Colonel Douty falls from his horse. Behind the officers charge the massed ranks of the bold Maine horsemen. Custer is at a full gallop, his saber brandished high. Waud would make a series of similar sketches over the next few years of the war, cementing Custer's image in the mind of the American public. See also, Whittaker, *Volunteer Cavalry*, 6.

74 Philip St. George Cooke, "Our Cavalry," in *The United States Service: A Quarterly Review of Military and Naval Affairs* (July 1879), vol. III, 329-330; Whittaker, *Volunteer Cavalry*, 7-8.

"If whetstones were furnished the men . . . a sabre issued sharp would be kept sharp. But as it is, the men cannot get them sharp." Thus, as both Cooke and Whittaker agreed, in a mounted charge "the soldiers lose confidence in the weapon, and prefer the revolver."[75]

Fighting with the carbine brought its own set of difficulties. To begin with, carbines were notoriously inaccurate when fired from horseback. Dismounting the command, however, reduced the strength of the firing line by a quarter, as every fourth man grabbed the reins of three other horses and took them back to some semblance of safety. The rifled musket in use by the Confederate infantry outmatched the short-barreled carbine in both range and reliability. The cavalry, wrote Cooke, had become "in battles and serious combats little better than a poor substitute for infantry,"[76]

On the field at Upperville, Custer witnessed Pleasonton's collaborative use of cavalry and infantry. Much like Merritt, Custer filed away everything he saw for future use, including the sight of a combined force of cavalry and infantry working successfully in tandem. Unlike many old-school cavalrymen, he did not envision his beloved hot-footing cavalry slowed down by clod-footed infantry support. Instead, he imagined them acting in concert with their own mobile carbineers, men from the same brigade, who could mount up and move quickly to help consolidate a victory. Now all he needed was a command of his own to provide a test bed for his theories.

---

75 Whittaker, *Volunteer Cavalry*, 7-8.

76 Cooke, "Our Cavalry," 331.

CHAPTER EIGHT

A Hussar is a Thing of the Past

THIN- FACED AND AUSTERE, with just enough whiskers to cover his gaunt cheeks, Governor Austin Blair of Michigan never underestimated the daunting effort required to assure the very survival of the Constitution of the United States. Even as President Lincoln called for a levy of 75,000 men to serve for a limited period of 90 days in 1861, Governor Blair was preparing for a protracted fight against the scourge of slavery. On May 7, he addressed both houses of the state legislature in an extraordinary session convened in Lansing. At the stroke of noon he took to the rostrum. His cadaverous features belied the steely determination of the practiced politician. The rumble of applause that had filled the chamber slowly stilled and he began to speak. Up in the packed galleries, the crowds pressed closer to the balcony railing so they could better see and hear what was transpiring. The Rebels had fired on Fort Sumter nearly a month earlier on April 12, and that was all that anyone could talk about.

The Michigan governor let everyone present know exactly what part his state would play in the war that would surely follow the bombardment of the bastion in Charleston Harbor. "I have summoned you together in extra session upon the most extraordinary occasion which has had existence since the formation of the Federal Government," he declared in his opening remarks without preamble, his words resounding in the high-vaulted chamber. "African slavery has dropped the mask and taken up arms. . . . Confederates in a pretended form of government, raises armies, besieges and takes a fortress . . . and makes its Wnal appeal to the arbitrament of battle." The choice was simple: Either abrogate the pact sealed with the blood of thousands during the Revolution or fight to preserve the Constitution!

Blair's message rung out clear and strong: "Liberty and Union, one and inseparable, now and forever."[1]

More importantly, he presented a plan to mobilize all of Michigan's assets in support of the new president. "This is to be no six weeks' campaign," he forewarned. "While I do not expect the grand result immediately, nor that it will be attained without great sacrifices, yet I cannot doubt the final issue." Three days later, by the unanimous vote of both chambers of the legislature, Governor Blair received carte blanche to raise as many as 100 companies of volunteers, to be organized into 10 regiments of 10 companies each. Ambitiously, he planned to outfit several cavalry regiments.[2]

Against this backdrop of patriotic fervor, the 1st Michigan Infantry received its regimental colors, designed by the women of Detroit. Within a week these loyal men were on their way to join the gathering host around Washington. Blair would not be deterred, and even as the authorities in the capital begged him to stop organizing so many units, seven more infantry regiments were rapidly clothed, equipped, and armed. The state also mustered three companies of United States Sharpshooters, whose commander, Col. Hiram Berdan, rejected any recruit "who cannot, at 200 yards, put ten consecutive shots in a target, the average distance not to exceed five inches from the center of the bullseye."[3]

By early September, the first two companies of horsemen traveled to St. Louis to become part of the 2nd Missouri Cavalry. The 1st Michigan Cavalry first assembled on September 13, 1861, at Camp Lyon near Detroit. The regiment left for Washington on September 29 with an enrollment of 1,144 officers and men under the command of Col. Thornton F. Brodhead. The 1st Michigan carried only sabers and revolvers, and as a result it established the proud reputation of being a "saber regiment."

The 5th Michigan Cavalry departed for Washington on December 4, 1862, in conjunction with Battery I of the Michigan Light Artillery. Mustered into the service in Detroit, the regiment listed 1,144 officers and men on the books. The commander was Col. Joseph T. Copeland, the former colonel of the 1st Michigan Cavalry. A shortage of arms and other supplies delayed their departure and when they could wait no longer, the Wolverines left for the capital only partially armed.

---

1 George S. May, *Michigan and the Civil War Years, 1860-1866: A Wartime Chronicle* (Ann Arbor, MI, 1964), 4, 95.

2 Ibid., 100-101.

3 Ibid., 14.

Colonel Copeland sent the horses ahead in four companies, each in the care of 10 men from each company. Lieutenant Samuel Harris led one of those details to Washington. "We made the trip to Washington without accident or incident of note," he wrote, and found an army unprepared to receive them. "There had been no provisions made for my men or horses," complained the irate Harris. "It was a bitter cold night and we suffered a good deal. . . . There was no rations for men or horses, no wood to keep us warm, or tents to shelter us from the cold wintry night."[4]

Congressman Francis W. Kellogg personally organized two regiments, the 6th Michigan Cavalry and the 7th Michigan Cavalry, both formed at Grand Rapids. The 6th Michigan numbered 1,229 officers and men under the command of Col. George Gray. The regiment departed Michigan on December 10, 1862, and, like their counterparts in the 5th Michigan, marched out only partially armed. Captain James Kidd had imagined riding off to war cheered by crowds lining the main street of downtown Grand Rapids. The city would be awash in red, white, and blue bunting, and the column of horsemen would parade through the riot of color and noise, with flowers cascading over them. The band would provide a suitable score, including some rousing Irish tunes from one of history's most ferocious warrior societies.[5]

Reality blew that reverie to bits early on a December morning with a rude shove and an exhortation to get moving. It was time for the 6th Michigan to march to the station and board trains for Washington. "It was like tearing asunder the ties of years," anguished Captain Kidd. "The scenes of our sojourn for a few months, where we had engaged in daily drills and parades, in the pomp and circumstance of mimic warfare, were to know us no longer." Under the stark silver moonlight of a cloudless winter sky, the command struck its tents, the horses were sent away under the care of details, and the quartermasters packed up their impedimenta. Like debtors in the night, the men slunk out of their camps while the good citizens of Grand Rapids were still slumbering in their beds. "When we left camp at 2 a.m., the streets were deserted," wrote Kidd disappointedly. "The town was wrapped in slumber. No sound was heard, except the tramp, tramp of the soldiers, and the roar

---

4 Harris, *Personal Reminiscences*, 11-12.

5 A native of Massachusetts, Kellogg moved to Grand Rapids in 1855 and served in the Michigan House of Representatives from 1857 to 1858. Although he organized the 2nd, 3rd, and 6th Michigan Cavalry regiments and held the colonelcy of the 3rd Michigan, he never took field command of any of the regiments.

of the river as it plunged over the dam, which only served to intensify the stillness."[6]

Some elements of the 7th Michigan Cavalry had already departed for Washington, but the last contingent reported for duty at Grand Rapids with an enrollment of 783 officers and men under Col. William D. Mann, previously a captain in the 1st Michigan Cavalry and a lieutenant colonel in the 5th Michigan Cavalry. The latecomers left for Washington on February 20, 1863, having each received a saber and a new Colt revolver; but they didn't receive their Burnside carbines until March 25, 1863. "Our departure was notable only in that but little attention was given to it," related Sgt. Asa B. Isham. "The papers merely mentioned the fact that we were ordered off to the seat of war."[7]

There's a Round Jammed in the Chamber

Colonel Joseph Tarr Copeland was a visionary with enough imagination to make him a maverick by any military standard. Forty-nine years old in 1861, Copeland had amassed enough political favors during his years as a justice of the Supreme Court of Michigan to get the lieutenant colonel's slot in the 1st Michigan Cavalry. Like many of his generation, the exploits of John C. Frémont's "mounted riflemen" during the Mexican War fascinated him. "[Frémont] was one of the most picturesque figures in America before the war," recalled James Kidd. Known as "The Pathfinder," Frémont's 1856 autobiography was widely read by boys with much "avidity. . . . The youthful imagination of those days idealized it into a *corps d'elite*, as it idealized Mexican war veterans, Marion's men, or the Old Guard of Napoleon Bonaparte." Colonel Copeland envisioned a modern version of the mounted rifleman, armed with the seven-shot repeating Spencer rifle.[8]

Copeland mustered out of the 1st Michigan Cavalry on August 29, 1861, to accept the colonelcy of his yet-to-be-organized regiment—in his mind already designated the 1st Michigan Mounted Rifles. Appointment in hand, he immediately visited the governor's office to request official permission to arm his regiment with

6   Kidd, *Personal Recollections*, 69, 70.

7   Asa B. Isham, *An Historical Sketch of the Seventh Regiment Michigan Volunteer Cavalry, From its Organization, in 1862, to its Muster Out, in 1865* (New York, 1893), 12.

8   Kidd, *Personal Recollections*, 31-32; John C. Fremont, *The life of Col. John Charles Fremont and his narrative of explorations and adventures, in Kansas, Nebraska, Oregon and California* (New York, NY, 1856).

the new repeating rifle. A veteran politician, Blair sensed the newsworthiness of this idea, if not its military value. He signed off on the order and sure enough the newspapers took up the story. "They will be armed with repeating rifles," marveled the *Detroit Free Press*, "and with a brace of pistols each, but no sword."[9]

If war is truly the mother of invention, the Civil War gave birth to a large family of innovations. Of all her brood, the ready-fire magazine and self-contained cartridge would have the most influence on the future development of small arms. Christopher Miner Spencer, a bright young man of 27 with a passion for guns, sired the "Horizontal Shot Tower" with his application for a patent for a lever-action rifle. A trooper loaded a Spencer by inserting a tubular, spring-loaded magazine with seven cartridges into the rifle's butt stock. Once that was done, he pulled down the trigger guard to drop the rolling breechblock and open the breech. The same motion ejected the spent round and chambered a fresh .56-56 caliber, rim-fired cartridge.

It was also a soldier's dream to clean. All he had to do was open the action by pulling down on the trigger guard, turn the rifle upside down, and wash and oil the mechanism and bore. Accessing the internal mechanism was as simple as removing a lever pivot screw, which dropped the whole assembly into the trooper's hand. Fully versed with the inner workings of the Sharps rifle, Spencer incorporated its best features into his design, going so far as to make sure that several of its internal components were interchangeable with those of the Sharps. Many regiments already had quite a few of the parts in their inventories.

The added allure of the Spencer rifle helped Copeland's new regiment reach its authorized recruiting limits by the end of July 1862. Unfortunately the rifles themselves, along with their ammunition and the rest of the necessary accouterments, were nowhere in sight. Colonel Copeland soon learned the harsh truth that to be an army maverick entailed a life of ordeal, disappointment, heartbreak, and rejection. The first hard lesson came from the army's chief of ordnance, Brig. Gen. James W. Ripley, who told Copeland to forget all that foolishness about the 1st Michigan Mounted Rifles and concentrate on organizing the 5th Michigan Cavalry, the regiment's official war department designation.

General Ripley held a deep bias against the Spencer Repeating Rifle Company and its primary product. He presented a list of objections as long as the chevrons

---

9 Wiley Sword, "'Those Damned Michigan Spencers: Colonel Copeland's 5th Michigan Cavalry and their Spencer Rifles," *Man at Arms Magazine* (September/October 1997), Vol. 19, No. 5, 27.

on a sergeant-major's sleeve. The weapon weighed in excess of 10 pounds when fully loaded, adding an extra burden to already heavily encumbered soldiers. The exorbitant cost counted against it as well. A Spencer cost $45 while most rifled muskets could be purchased for $18.00. Most importantly, in keeping with his crusade to standardize the types of ammunition used by the army, he was adamantly opposed to having to order the special cartridges needed for the Spencer's tubular magazine.

But the truly unforgivable sin was the Spencer Repeating Rifle Company's failure to deliver on an existing contract, which entailed the delivery of the first 500 rifles in March 1862, and an additional 1,000 every month thereafter. The aggressive delivery schedule would be difficult to meet by a fledgling company, but the navy's initial order for 700 rifles came close to sinking the entire venture. "It was the beginning of struggles and troubles," Spencer would tell his children. "The installation of the machinery, building a forging shop, making of tools, fixtures, gauges, and many special machines, and finishing the first of the Navy guns, all within a year, was a Herculean task." Needless to say, the company fell behind and came very close to being in breach of contract. General Ripley wanted nothing further to do with them.[10]

By then, sufficient hand-made prototypes existed for testing by any government agencies that may have needed such a weapon. The Spencer endured a wide variety of trials, including being buried in sand and immersed in saltwater for twenty-four hours. Regardless of the indignity, the weapon fired successfully. During the grueling process of over 100 test firings, the Spencer suffered only one misfire due to a faulty fulminate. R. A. Peirce, the Massachusetts chief of ordnance, gave the weapon a ringing endorsement: "for safety, durability, simplicity in construction, rapidity of firing and effectiveness, particularly at long range, the Spencer excels any other arm."[11]

George McClellan's chief of ordnance kept pestering him to purchase the 15-shot Henry rifle. Instead, "Little Mac" issued Special Order No. 311, which permitted the testing of the competing weapon. Even Abraham Lincoln tried out the new rifle, spending about an hour plinking away at a wooden board set at 50 yards. It was a "wonderful gun, loading with absolutely contemptible simplicity and ease with seven balls & firing the whole readily and deliberately in less than half a

---

10 William B. Edwards, *Civil War Guns* (Secaucus, NJ, 1962), 146.

11 Sword, "Those Damned Michigan Spencers," 24.

minute," remarked John Hay, one of Lincoln's secretaries who accompanied the president that night. "The President made some pretty good shots."[12]

Even more importantly for Copeland's project, a mounted man could load and fire the Spencer with one hand. The head of the three-officer board testing the Spencer, then-Capt. Alfred Pleasonton, deserves full credit for this discovery. With a cavalryman's instinct, Pleasonton soon figured out that a trooper could press the weapon under his right arm, then work the cocking lever with his right hand to eject the spent cartridge, cycle a fresh bullet, and bring the hammer back to a full cock. The trooper then simply raised his left "rein" hand to support the fore-stock and pulled the trigger with his right hand.

On November 22, 1861, the overly optimistic Pleasonton convened the board at the Washington Arsenal. "The Rifle is simple and compact in construction," the board reported, "and less liable to get out of order than any other breech-loading arm now in use." The board pronounced the Spencer to be "a very useful arm for the Mounted Service," and Spencer, a consummate salesman, would incorporate its ease of use into its list of many benefits. One of the company's catalogs stated that the repeater's "special aptitude for the Cavalry Service may be inferred from the single fact that but one hand is required to load and fire it." Though the Spencer had passed every test to which it was subjected—and had even received President Lincoln's personal endorsement—General Ripley steadfastly refused to give it his official sanction.[13]

In response, Copeland exerted a great deal of "personal effort and expense" to get the process rolling again. First, he appealed to Governor Blair for assistance, and then obtained a signed petition from Michigan's congressional delegation supporting the adoption of the rifle. Michigan's adjutant general, John Robertson, aggressively lobbied the war department, stating that the 5th Michigan already could have been in the field if it were not for their lack of long arms. Spitefully, Ripley told Robertson that his units would be equipped with 800 French rifles and 400 Sharps rifles. When he found out that Spencer had begun a limited production run, Copeland angrily rallied his allies to fight back. The secretary of war received multiple visits, and on November 26 Governor Blair wrote a letter to Maj. Gen. Henry Halleck, chewing him up one side and down the other. The governor bluntly demanded "the proper guns and accouterments." Maybe even President Lincoln

---

12 Edwards, *Civil War Guns*, 151-152.

13 Ibid., 146.

directly intervened, for on December 26, 1861, Ripley personally sent an order for 10,000 rifles to the Spencer Repeating Rifle Company.[14]

In fact, Ripley expedited the processing of Copeland's order. The colonel's persistence had indelibly etched itself on the mind of James Ripley, and once the tide had clearly turned in Copeland's favor, the general wrote directly to Copeland on October 18, 1862. Completely free of rancor, his letter officially granted Copeland "1,200 Spencer Repeating Rifles and 200 cartridges each per arm." Now that the contractor had filled the navy order, the ordnance department would forward the newly manufactured rifles to the cavalry in batches of five cases, each holding 20 rifles. Along with the rifles, the New York Arsenal would provide "1,200 sets of accouterments suitable for use with that arm by mounted men." On November 21, the ordnance department informed Copeland that the rifles had been inspected and would be "forwarded by fast passenger train tomorrow." Copeland and his well-placed supporters had won. Or so it seemed.[15]

Unfortunately, the fast passenger train carrying the 1,200 rifles supposedly sent by Ripley failed to arrive as promised. Due to the exigencies of the covert activities of Confederate partisans around Washington, the services of the long-delayed 5th Michigan Cavalry were now in demand. The regiment left immediately for Washington and missed the arrival of the Spencers by one day. They were armed only with a handful of sabers and a couple dozen Colt revolvers. Six days after the 5th's departure, the 6th Michigan Cavalry, likewise destitute of carbines, followed. "We find ourselves soldiers equipped with farmers' weapons [picks and brooms]," scoffed one of Copeland's troopers. Another man attested that "[a]bout forty men in each company had sabers and revolvers, but only a few of them [were] drilled well enough to have made an effective use of them."[16]

Records indicate that the shipment of Spencers did not depart Boston until December 2. Rather than being rushed to Detroit by train, they seem to have been shunted onto a wagon supply train, for the shipment took three days to arrive. Ironically, the press saw the regiment's rifles before the troopers did. "We have examined the new rifles supplied [for] the 5th Cavalry," reported an enthusiastic correspondent for the *Detroit Advertiser and Tribune* on December 6, "and without a doubt, it is the neatest weapon we have seen. . . . The specimens bought are the first

14 Sword, "Those Damned Michigan Spencers," 25, 27.

15 Ibid., 28.

16 Ibid., 30.

that have been manufactured, hence no regiment is armed so well [as will be] this regiment."[17]

The first 500 Spencers caught up with the regiment on December 27. At least one recipient was unable to hide his excitement. "We have received our rifles," he crowed in a letter, "and I tell you they are some[thing]." Another Michigan trooper confirmed his comrade's opinion of the Spencer. "They are really nice. They are breechloaders and take seven cartridges at a time. That means we can fire 8 shots before reloading. We also have a saber. There is not a regiment in Washington as well equipped as we are." The love affair of the Michiganders with their Spencers never diminished. "Our brigade has carried them since January, 1863. While in the Cavalry Corps, Army of the Potomac, [we] often . . . heard the cry, 'Lookout! there come those damned Michigan Spencers,'" recalled Wilson W. Wood, a veteran enlisted trooper with the 6th Michigan Cavalry. "There is no such arm on the face of the earth as a Spencer."[18]

It probably never entered Copeland's mind that he would end up with a surplus of Spencer rifles. He had ordered 1,200 of them for his projected muster of 1,000 enlisted men, giving him a few extra to cover any losses. He had not taken into account the astounding attrition rate that would thin the ranks of his units. Regimental returns for June 1863 show 734 enlisted men in the 5th Michigan and 582 in the 6th Michigan. From their inception, the regiments had lost men due to sickness, death, desertion, transfers, temporary postings, and promotions. In the end, the 5th Michigan's ordnance officer issued 900 rifles and had 300 rifles left over, still packed in their shipping crates. Lieutenant Colonel Freeman Norvell wrote to Governor Blair and put the bug in his ear that "the 6th [Michigan] has the prospect of being armed as ourselves with the Spencer rifle." Subsequently, five companies of the 6th Michigan received an average of 67 Spencers each.[19]

Slit from One Ear to the Other

Secretary of War Edwin Stanton disliked the bad news that continued to filter in from the fringes of Washington's defenses. He regarded the city's cavalry screen as little more than a sieve. As a result, on March 18 Maj. Gen. Samuel Heintzelman, commander of the city's defenses, found himself in a one-on-one, face-to-face

---

17 Ibid., 30.

18 Ibid., 30, 35-36.

19 Ibid., 31, 32.

meeting with Stanton, who was clearly in a foul mood. The resultant verbal skewering elicited a promise from the general to reorganize the cavalry department. Unfortunately, a mere shuffling of commands would not suffice to correct the situation. The Union cavalry regiments, operating haphazardly from defensive lines around Washington, were simply overwhelmed by their Confederate opponents.

The operations of the 1st Michigan Cavalry during the winter of 1862-63 typify the experiences of the stretched-out regiments far from the city's battlements. Fruitlessly the regiment patrolled its assigned sector north and west of the capital. Throughout the bitterly cold winter they scouted through Leesburg and Aldie and down into Loudoun County—soon to become known as "Mosby's Confederacy." No picket line was safe; no patrol went without attack. On January 9, near Brentsville, a raiding party of 20 Rebels jumped a party of six men led by Lt. George Maxwell. The rangers killed three of the Federals, and captured Maxwell and the other two men. Fortunately, the three were rescued the next day.[20]

On January 31 at Dranesville, Pvt. Dexter Macomber noted in his diary that his picket detail had been attacked by Mosby and two dozen of his men. Rumors swirled throughout the camps that over 20 men had been captured. Mosby, however, never claimed such a feat in the records of his command's activities. Macomber himself stated that only three men had been captured. In mid-February, the raiders ambushed a 45-man detachment, and in the ensuing running gun battle, the Union lost one officer and 17 men killed, wounded, or captured. One short-handed Union cavalry officer voiced a common and increasingly more strident complaint about the nefarious foe operating on the fringes of the cavalry screens. "If I had 1,000 more cavalry I could keep a column constantly in motion beyond our right flank, which would have a tendency . . . to render rebel raids less certain of success."[21]

On March 21, Heintzelman created a division composed of three brigades and assigned it to Maj. Gen. Julius Stahel. In turn, Stahel consolidated his various cavalry commands and posted them in a more aggressive posture on the southern side of the Potomac. Colonel Timothy Bryan of the 18th Pennsylvania Cavalry stepped forward to take command of the first brigade, relieving Col. Sir Percy Wyndham, who returned to the Army of the Potomac and command of the 1st

20 Robert F. O'Neill, *Chasing Jeb Stuart and John Mosby: The Union Cavalry in Northern Virginia from Second Manassas to Gettysburg* (Jefferson, NC, 2012), 61-62; OR 21, 750.

21 Dexter Macomber, Diary, January 31 and February 13, 1863, Clarke Historical Library, Central Michigan University (hereafter cited as CMU); OR 21, 750.

New Jersey Cavalry. The second brigade, headed by Col. Richard Butler Price, included the veterans of the 1st Michigan Cavalry, the 2nd Pennsylvania Cavalry, the 1st Vermont Cavalry, and a squadron of the 1st Ohio Cavalry.

The third brigade, composed of newly promoted Brig. Gen. Copeland's Michigan troopers, was organized on December 12, 1862. The idea behind its formation was that "a well-organized and efficient body of cavalry, as this may become, stationed in the vicinity of Fairfax Court House would be very useful both in repelling raids from the enemy's cavalry and making raids in return." On March 2, 1863, the 7th Michigan Cavalry augmented the brigade. "It was organized and will ever be known in history as a Brigade. Still it was more like a large Regiment," was how one veteran Michigan trooper described it looking back from 1903. "Almost invariably where one regiment was, the balance of them were in the immediate vicinity."[22]

With haunting eloquence, Lt. Daniel McNaughton of the 7th Michigan Cavalry put into words the feelings of the troopers of the Michigan Brigade. "I have never had occasion to regret my association with that splendid body of men. The comradeship of those old days, the friendships formed and fostered in those far-off years are the most cherished recollections of my later life," McNaughton wrote:

> I love to go back to those eventful times and linger along the pathway of those stirring scenes. I touch the wand of memory and I am with the old boys again. I am with them on the dusty, wearisome march, and share with them a soldier's couch, the covering being the clouds and the stars. I am with them again in camp and field, through mountain gap and over swollen rivers . . . with them in sunshine and cold. . . . Bravely and well they carried the old Flag through the night of tempest and storm . . . its brightened folds radiant in the sunlight of a hundred victories.[23]

Toward the end of June, the assignment to the brigade of the veteran and distinguished 1st Michigan Cavalry offered the three raw regiments of Michiganders a chance to observe "how real soldiers conducted and took care of themselves." Even a short week of camping next to these experienced soldiers proved highly beneficial, asserted Captain Kidd, "from whom by observation and

---

22 O'Neill, *Chasing Jeb Stuart*, 126-127; William O. Lee, ed., *Personal and Historical Sketches of and By Members of the Seventh Regiment Michigan Volunteer Cavalry 1862-1865* (Detroit, MI, 1990), *iii*.

23 Daniel McNaughton, "Reminiscences," in *Personal and Historical Sketches*, 74-75.

personal contact, much information was gained that proved of great value during the following months."[24]

Lieutenant Frank W. Dickerson of the 5th U.S. Cavalry noted the positive effect of the veteran horse soldiers on the volunteers. "The association of them with our men has taught them more than they could have learnt in a year's time if they had been alone," he wrote. "They have learned all the duties of a soldier by observing our men perform them in a soldier-like manner, also how to take care of themselves, to prevent sickness, and how to live like a soldier." But the double-edged relationship, recalled Lieutenant Dickerson, cut both ways. "The frequent association of our men with the volunteer cav'y . . . has done more towards demoralizing them, and destroying all principles of military rigor and discipline, than all defeats, disasters, or sufferings ever could," he wrote with concern. "With the volunteers, their carelessness, uncleanliness, familiarity with the lack of respect to officers, and superiors, and the lack of discipline generally, has had a tendency to impair somewhat the fine state of discipline we possessed before we were associated with them."[25]

Overall, reported Captain Kidd, the officers and men of his company felt more comfortable in their roles as cavalrymen. "The men had learned what campaigning meant," he wrote his father, "and, thereafter, knew how to provide themselves for a march, and how important to husband their rations so as to prevent waste at first and make them last as long as possible." According to Pvt. John N. Wilson of the 7th Michigan Cavalry, the work felt monotonous in the beginning. "[We] broke camp near Fairfax," he wrote, "picketing the railroad and scouting and patrolling the country for Mosby's guerrillas, so that the boys of the 7th in my squadron knew the country well and nearly every point on the railroad from Fairfax Station to Rappahannock." In the coming weeks, they would be so hungry they would be gnawing on their knuckles.[26]

The Confederate cavalry hammered the hapless Union troopers from two directions. On the one hand, Col. John Singleton Mosby's guerrilla raids increasingly wrought havoc and fear behind the Union lines. On the other, the surgically precise strikes of Jeb Stuart's hard-riding cavalry disrupted Federal

---

24 Kidd, *Personal Recollections*, 95-96.

25 Frank W. Dickerson to his father, February 17, 1863, letter 10, Frank W. Dickerson letters, GNMP.

26 Kidd, *Personal Recollections*, 96; John N. Wilson, "Passing Mosby's Pickets," in *Personal and Historical Sketches*, 138-139.

communications and raised Confederate spirits. The sight of Chambersburg, Pennsylvania, going up in flames imprinted itself indelibly on everyone's mind. Ranger James J. Williamson applauded the achievements of his compatriots in the Confederate cavalry. "The winter of 1863 . . . was a season of remarkable activity for the Confederate cavalry. Their bold and successful raids and daring attacks . . . furnished material for stories which read like the deeds of the heroes of romance."[27]

How quickly the fortunes of men can change. On March 23, the 5th Michigan Cavalry received the disappointing news that the regiment would be spending the remainder of the war in Washington. Trooper William Rockwell bemoaned the bad news. "[It is] one of the miserablest muddy Countrys in the world, it cannot be beat for mud, and dead horses and [Crows] in flocks of hundreds. Take it altogether it is a miserable place." Thankfully, the very next day the Michigan Brigade received orders to depart from Washington, although being soldiers they continued to grouse. "I suppose we are now to occupy the ground in which the guerrillas live and act," wrote Lt. Col. Ebenezer Gould, "& we are to commence picket and outpost duty in earnest." One trooper put it even more succinctly: "I suppose we will have to go out and chase them into their holes." He need not have worried. Mosby's Rangers came after the Michiganders.[28]

Known as the "Gray Ghost," Mosby had served with distinction under Jeb Stuart before beginning his independent operations in northern Virginia behind Union lines with but a handful of men. His small command grew both in size and in reputation until it officially joined Confederate service on June 10, 1863, as the 43rd Battalion of Virginia Cavalry. Although Mosby forced Federal officers to detach thousands of men to guard against his partisan attacks, many in the Confederate high command, including Robert E. Lee, questioned the effectiveness of Mosby's tactics. The leaders of Union regiments such as the 7th Michigan Cavalry vehemently disagreed with Lee's evaluation. "Mosby, with 200 men and one howitzer, attacked our train near Catlett's; guard fled; Mosby burned train," read Col. William D. Mann's report on May 30 after a typical hit-and-run raid. "Heard firing in camp and went in search. . . . Came up with Mosby in strong position 2 miles southwest of Greenwich and charged him. He gave us grape; boys never

27 James J. Williamson, *Mosby's Rangers: A Record of the Operations of the Forty-Third Battalion Virginia Cavalry* (New York, 1896), 17.

28 O'Neill, *Chasing Jeb Stuart*, 131.

faltered; took his gun. . . . Our loss, 4 killed, and 1 officer . . . and 7 enlisted men wounded."[29]

It was not just that men were being killed; men die in war every day. What really galled the men in blue was the manner in which Mosby's Rangers conducted their war. One particular incident made the tawdry nature of guerrilla warfare personal to the members of the 6th Michigan Cavalry. In one of those gun-and-run ambuscades, Private Foe had been killed instantly by a bullet to the chest. Some of the regiment's troopers later found Foe's body sprawled by the side of the road, completely stripped of clothes and dignity. "These are the kinds of men that Mosby commands," Captain Kidd remarked caustically in a letter to his father. "Our boys killed one rebel and wounded another so that we would be even if one of our men were not worth a dozen of these miserable 'Bushwhackers.'"[30]

The dead ranger was Bradford S. Hoskins, a former captain in the British army turned soldier of fortune. Hoskins kept a meticulous diary of his activities with Mosby's men; his last entry was written on May 25, 1863. A special correspondent for the *Philadelphia Inquirer* found the diary after Hoskins's death. The reporter took his time reviewing the papers before declaring, "His memorandums denote the activity and audacity of the Rebel guerrillas more clearly than they have ever been described before." Published under the headline "Ignoble End of an Adventurer," the narrative describes the Rangers' operations and "their long and wearisome marches and desperate raids upon our pickets, railroads and telegraph lines south into Washington." For instance, on May 10 they attempted to burn the Orange and Alexandria Railroad bridges over Kettle Run and Broad Run, but the fires did not take hold, which allowed the Union troops to extinguish them easily. The Rangers, however, did manage to cut the telegraph line. On May 17, Hoskins tells of an encounter with Yankee cavalry in which the Union lost two men killed, one lieutenant and five privates wounded, and four captured by the Rebels.[31]

The press pounced on the story from the beginning, and their calls for retaliation only served to heighten the fear of the local citizenry. "Hanging is certainly too good for these bushwhacking murderers," thundered the *New York Tribune*, "and it is to be hoped that an example will soon be made of this class of

---

29 Williamson, *Mosby's Rangers*, 67.

30 Eric J. Wittenberg, ed., *One of Custer's Wolverines: The Civil War Letters of Brigadier General James H. Kidd, 6th Michigan Cavalry* (Kent, OH, 2000), 32.

31 Horace Mewborn, *From Mosby's Command: Newspaper Letters and Articles by and About John S. Mosby and his Rangers* (Baltimore, MD, 2005), 13, 19-21.

part thief, part marauder, but no soldier." Almost inevitably, as Mosby's operations increased in notoriety, if not so much in tempo or scale, the attempts to capture him and his band expanded to include the civilian population that supported the bandits.[32]

"The impression seems to be that we are protected by them from the Yankees," wrote Mrs. Ida Dulany, who herself had quartered some of Mosby's men, "but I fear it is just the reverse for after every raid by Mosby's men there is retaliation by the enemy, in which the citizens suffer severely, as Mosby and his men must always get out of the way, seeing he is always out-numbered." Undoubtedly that retribution was sure to come. The 1st Michigan Cavalry in particular had become a holy terror to the locals. The major players who would administer this abominable punishment still waited in the wings, leaving the stage for their understudies to practice their craft.[33]

On May 21, General Hooker officially took off the kid gloves when, from his headquarters near Falmouth, he ordered Pleasonton to let the dogs of war loose. "The major-general commanding directs that you send Colonel Duffié with his command to clear out the bushwhackers and guerrillas in the country," he directed. "Colonel Duffié . . . will notify all the inhabitants that whenever any guerrillas or bushwhackers are found ranging around within their premises, their houses will be burned to the ground and their property confiscated." Untold numbers of homes, barns, and other buildings would be burned to the ground and lives ruined, leaving only the blackened fingers of stone fireplaces to mark the grounds of once flourishing farms and stately homesteads that had been passed down through generations.[34]

The Yankees referred to Mosby's men as killers, murderers, thieves, ravagers, and—most contemptuously—war profiteers. Later, the word "depredations" would serve to summarize the acts behind those names. An amused Mosby claimed full credit for the creation of the Michigan Cavalry Brigade. "What were called my depradations," he later gloated, "had caused another brigade of cavalry to be sent into Fairfax to protect Washington." Lieutenant Harris grew tired of the tasks required to respond to Mosby's shenanigans. "The most of our duty was to guard against raids by Mosby," he wrote, enduring the "usual hardships and pleasures of picket duty." The order to join up with Hooker in the middle of June could not

---

32 O'Neill, *Chasing Jeb Stuart*, 162.

33 Ibid., 158.

34 *OR* 25, pt. 2, 511.

have come at a better time. "The boys were wild with joy. They were tired of camp and picket duty and wanted more active work. They got all they wanted during the next few weeks."[35]

With diminishing vigor and enterprise, Stahel began to wear an air of defeatism. From the front he received continuous jabs from the Confederate cavalry and the other various partisan units operating in the area. From behind, Alfred Pleasonton and the war department stalked him mercilessly. Sometimes the little Hungarian would give a shrug of his shoulders and secretly admit to himself that perhaps the enemy just enjoyed superior tactics, better intelligence, and an encyclopedic knowledge of the area of operations.

Captain Elon J. Farnsworth possessed a little of his uncle's "political animal" instincts and wasted no time informing Congressman Farnsworth of the machinations taking place. "I think they are using him [Pleasonton] rather shabbily," he wrote, with a hint of Pleasonton's own xenophobia. "Yet Stahl does nothing. Now if you can do anything to get the cavalry consolidated and Stahl left out for God's sake do it. You hardly know or can imagine the bitter feeling that exists among the officers of this cavalry towards Stahl and those trying to set him & other Dutchmen up."[36]

Stahel's command suffered from the lack of a cohesive strategy, his troops scattered far and wide. They seemed to be always a step behind the Rebels. Occasionally its just time to call it quits and focus on something else, and Stahel had finally reached that point. Even if he were to capture or kill Mosby, it would only be a fluke, an accident of war for which neither side had prepared. It almost happened a few times and could happen again. Stahel knew that behind his back, Gen. Hooker was wondering why 6,100 cavalrymen were out chasing 200 brigands.

So, in essence, Stahel gave up on catching Mosby. He did so with the sure knowledge that he had given Pleasonton all the ammunition he needed to advance a long-held ambition. With Stahel removed, Pleasonton could take command of all

---

35 O'Neill, *Chasing Jeb Stuart*, 127; Harris, *Personal Reminiscences*, 17, 22.

36 Elon J. Farnsworth to John F. Farnsworth, June 29, 1863, Alfred Pleasonton Collection, GNMP. Farnsworth was the nephew of Congressman John F. Farnsworth of Illinois and the third of the "Boy Generals" soon to be promoted by Pleasonton. His impulsive streak led to his expulsion from the University of Michigan after a prank in which another student died. When the war began, Elon joined his uncle's newly formed 8th Illinois Volunteer Cavalry as a first lieutenant. Popular with the men, Farnsworth courted further controversy when he yanked a pastor in Alexandria, Virginia, from his pulpit for omitting a prayer for President Lincoln. Pleasonton later selected the young officer to serve on his staff; he subsequently became one of the ambitious general's favorite aides, as well as a useful conduit to his well-connected uncle.

three cavalry divisions. With a hint of Germanic gloom-and-doom, General Heintzelman, Stahel's commander, wrote in his personal diary that "I fear that he is trying to get my cavalry."[37]

Is Ambition Ever for the Good of the Service?

June 26, 1863, saw a rare lull in the action that felt like the proverbial calm before the storm. For a time, the rumble of the guns stilled, and the trappings of war were invisible. The dusty march of the 5th Michigan Cavalry and the trailing 6th Michigan Cavalry took them to the crest of a ridgeline, where they were "greeted by a magnificent scene." Many troopers remembered cresting that height and looking down on the picturesque town of Frederick, Maryland. As the sun fell low on the far horizon, they paused to take in the wonderment of nature. "A more enchanting vision never met human eye than that which appeared before us as we debouched from the narrow defile," related Captain Kidd, the moment frozen in time like a photograph:

> Thousands of acres of golden grain were waving in the sunlight. The rain of the early morning had left in the atmosphere a mellow haze of vapor which reflected the sun's rays in tints that blended with the summer colorings of the landscape. An exclamation of surprise ran along the column as each succeeding trooper came in sight of this picture of Nature's own painting.[38]

On a day like that, war can seem glorious indeed. For others, however, the arrival of the Army of the Potomac at Frederick merely underscored the deviltry of war. Private William Baird of the 6th Michigan did not remember June 26 as a moment of peace, but rather as the continuation of a nefarious war against the Confederate partisans—a war the Michigan regiments had been fighting since February. "After breakfast we fell into line and started our way passing through Frederick City Maryland," he recorded. That very afternoon, "the advance . . . had captured a Confederate spy, and made short work of him." The lynching, disguised as a military execution, followed a time-worn ritual. The culprit was mounted on a horse and led to a nearby apple tree. The executioners placed a noose around his neck, threw the loose end over a limb, and made it fast. Then the troopers led the

---

37 O'Neill, *Chasing Jeb Stuart*, 208.

38 Kidd, *Personal Recollections*, 115-116.

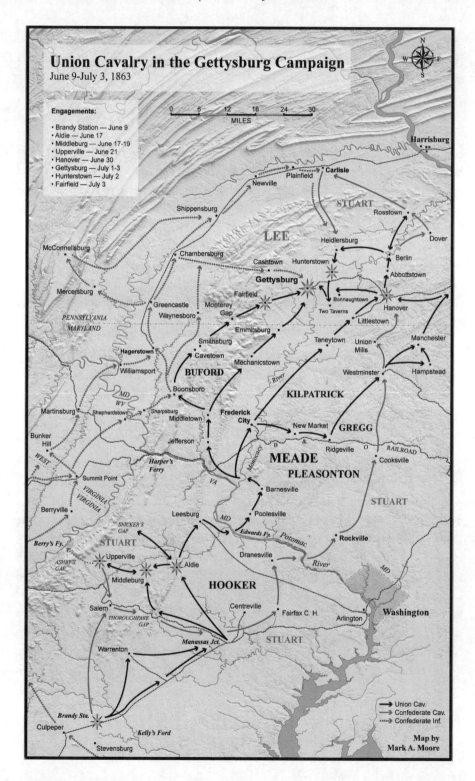

Union Cavalry in the Gettysburg Campaign
June 9-July 3, 1863

Engagements:

- Brandy Station — June 9
- Aldie — June 17
- Middleburg — June 17-19
- Upperville — June 21
- Hanover — June 30
- Gettysburg — July 1-3
- Hunterstown — July 2
- Fairfield — July 3

MILES

Map by
Mark A. Moore

horse "out from under him and left him hanging there, where he was hanging when we passed."[39]

On June 29 even the vaunted discipline of the Regulars fell apart. As the Reserve Brigade advanced toward Frederick, its march stalled when the cavalrymen columns encountered a traffic jam of wagons in the thoroughfares. With time on their hands, recalled Lt. Tattnall Paulding, the "men procured an abundance of whiskey.... There was a sad scene of drunkenness among our soldiers.... Whiskey was found abundantly, and for miles beyond the city the roadside was strewn with soldiers, both infantry & cavalry, dead drunk." The condition of the command was verified by another member of the 6th U.S. Cavalry, Pvt. Ram R. Knapp, who noted wryly in his diary, "Boys nearly all tight.... There has been more men drunk today than I ever saw before.... F[rederick] is full of drunk men. They are lying about outside of town like dead men on a battlefield. I think Gen. Whiskey conquered Gen. Meade for Meade lost the most men." In Paulding's decided opinion, "A heavy fine & imprisonment together with general confiscation should be the penalty for selling liquor to soldiers."[40]

In Frederick, the political generals of the Army of the Potomac gave in to their worst impulses in the wake of Joseph Hooker's resignation as commander of the army and Lincoln's appointment of Maj. Gen. George Gordon Meade as his replacement. Hooker had interposed the army between the enemy and Washington, moving north on a parallel axis to Lee's line of march. Pleasonton in particular saw Meade's promotion as an opportunity to further his ambitions. Behind Meade's back, Pleasonton sneered, "[He] had not that grasp of mind, when thrown into a new and responsible position, to quickly comprehend and decide upon important events." To Meade's face, he said whatever was necessary to ingratiate his way into the man's good graces. Pleasonton's peremptory treatment of Meade would come back to haunt him when Meade pulled him from the field and forced him to operate out of army headquarters. Pleasonton's duplicity rightfully infuriated Meade.[41]

39 William Baird, *Reminiscences*, 26-27, in Baird Family Papers, Bentley Historical Library, University of Michigan, Ann Arbor, MI.

40 Milgram, "The Libby Correspondence of Tattnall Paulding," 1,114; Ram R. Knapp, Diary, June 28, 1863, DeYoung Henry Collection, Western Michigan University (WMU), Kalamazoo, MI.

41 Alfred Pleasonton, "The Campaign of Gettysburg," in McClure, ed., *Annals of the Civil War*, 455.

Early on, Pleasonton had initiated an insidious campaign to unify the Union cavalry in the east into one corps composed of three divisions under his direct command—a command worthy of two stars. Pleasonton took advantage of this latest command transition to embark on a sweeping revitalization of the Cavalry Corps at the division and brigade levels. In order to elevate his own cadre of favored officers, he would need to eliminate the "foreigners," beginning with Maj. Gen. Julius Stahel. Colonel Percy Wyndham, the foppish, mustachioed Englishman, was already out of action due to his calf wound from the hard-fought battle of Brandy Station. Pleasonton's chopping block had more than enough room for the insufferable little Frenchman, Col. Alfred Duffié of the shattered 1st Rhode Island Cavalry, and the detestable Italian, Count Luigi P. di Cesnola.

In truth, the wartime performances of these officers never fully lived up to the puffed-up reputations that had pushed them up in rank and command responsibility. They may have looked good during war games, but they certainly could not match Alf Pleasonton at word games. For all of Pleasonton's faults, his gift for crafting a politically useful narrative rarely let him down. He possessed a dark talent for drafting lengthy documents without ever losing track of his objective from start to finish. Effortlessly, he could obfuscate throughout a document's length, turning every demand into a pleasantly worded request and reversing every fault and misstep into a sweet triumph.

Of all the letters he wrote to army headquarters, the one Pleasonton dispatched late on the afternoon of June 22 had the greatest impact on the evolution of the Cavalry Corps. It was Alfred Pleasonton at his worst *and* at his best. From his campsite he could see the contested fields of the fights around Aldie. "I would most respectfully and earnestly request that my force may be augmented by some regiments drawn from other commands, at least until I shall have been able to scatter or destroy the enemy's cavalry, which now so largely outnumbers me," he informed Brig. Gen. Seth Williams, the Army of the Potomac's adjutant general.[42]

On that day, Pleasonton began to unfold his carefully orchestrated plan to his chief proponent, abolitionist congressman John Franklin Farnsworth. The politician's nephew, Capt. Elon Farnsworth, then serving on Pleasonton's staff, acted as an intermediary between the two men. Barely disguised as military correspondence by virtue of Representative Farnsworth's brevet rank, Pleasonton's letters to his friend and congressional patron served mostly as an avenue for making an end-run around the war department. Farnsworth's political

---

42 *OR* 27, pt. 3, 259.

power would force Pleasonton's plan for control of all the army's cavalry on the hapless Army of the Potomac, on a reluctant Henry Halleck, and on an adamantly opposed Secretary of War Edwin Stanton.[43]

"My dear General," began Pleasonton. "Since you left us we have done some hard & splendid fighting, & altho' we have always been victorious against superior forces, it is at the sacrifice of many good men." Pleasonton continued with a side-long glance at getting his hands on some of Stahel's troops. "Our cavalry business is badly managed & will lead us into trouble unless speedily corrected—We have too many detachments—independent of each other—scattered over this country—while the rebels have their whole concentrated & ready to strike a heavy blow—at any moment."[44]

As he approached his closing, Pleasonton unmasked the true, vituperative nature of his character. "In justice to my soldiers I must ask for reinforcements; all the cavalry in Washington & Stahel's command should combine with this corps & [be] held for ready blows—not scattered about & frittered away on trifling objects." Any tone of civility disappeared from his discourse. "With regards to General Stahl he ranks me & if put over me [I] shall retire—as I have no faith in foreigners saving our Government or country," he wrote scathingly. "I conscientiously believe Americans only should rule in this matter & settle this rebellion. I care little for my own personal fortune until this war is settled, but the honor, reputation & welfare of my troops is very dear to me."[45]

In the end it all proved easier than he could have imagined. The receptive Meade readily approved his pitch for the addition of Stahel's men to his command. At a meeting on the morning of June 28, Pleasonton informed Meade of what he needed in order to make the reorganization work. "I would like to have officers I would name specially assigned to it, as I expected to have some desperate work to do," Pleasonton recorded. "The General assented to my request, and upon my naming the officers, he immediately telegraphed to have them appointed brigadier generals."[46]

Pleasonton had no qualms about using George Stoneman's well-known case of hemorrhoids to set him up for the kill. Stoneman, who had taken medical leave

43 Stewart Sifakis, *Who Was Who in the Civil War* (New York, 1988), 212.

44 Alfred Pleasonton to John F. Farnsworth, June 23, 1863, Alfred Pleasonton Collection, GNMP.

45 Ibid.

46 Pleasonton, "The Campaign of Gettysburg," 452.

on May 15, never returned to the Army of the Potomac. "Gen'l Stoneman, upon his return, finds that his rivals have been intriguing against him and have been trying to have him superseded in the command of the Cav[alr]y Corps," wrote Lt. Dickerson.[47]

Dickerson offered a behind-the-scenes look at Pleasonton's machinations in a chatty letter laced with insider tidbits to his father dated May 23, 1863. Hooker, he declared, tried to downplay the disaster at Chancellorsville by blaming the cavalry. The general's efforts included an already written order relieving Stoneman for incompetency. In a brazen Machiavellian move, continued Dickerson, the general also tried to remove Buford and Gregg. Thankfully, he continued, "the outside pressure of the army and the country was so great . . . that Hooker was obliged to back down and countermand his orders against the Cav[alr]y Corps."[48]

By that time Pleasonton had assumed temporary command of the corps in Stoneman's absence, thus acquiring a secure foundation for his future ambitions. Stanton opposed the idea of Pleasonton receiving permanent command of the corps, and it took a great deal of persuasion by Meade to make even the temporary promotion a reality. Although Pleasonton's elevation was never intended to be a permanent appointment, by late summer he formally replaced General Stoneman, who went on to command the newly formed Cavalry Bureau.

On June 28, 1863, the headquarters of the Army of the Potomac issued Special Orders Number 98, promoting Capts. George Armstrong Custer, Wesley Merritt, and Elon Farnsworth to the rank of brigadier general of U. S. Volunteers. Merritt received command of the Reserve Brigade of John Buford's 1st Cavalry Division. Custer and Farnsworth took over the brigades of Stahel's former command, now re-designated the 3rd Cavalry Division under Brig. Gen. Judson Kilpatrick. That same day, General Stahel was relieved of his command.[49]

---

47 Frank W. Dickerson to his father, May 23, 1863, letter 11, GNMP.

48 Ibid.

49 OR 27, pt. 3, 376.

CHAPTER NINE

The Stars Don't Shine on Just Anybody

FLUSH WITH HIS HEADY political victory, Pleasonton wrote a letter to his good friend, Rep. John Farnsworth, full of praise for his nephew, Elon. "Capt. Farnsworth has done splendidly," he commended; "I have serious thoughts of asking to have him made a brigadier-[g]eneral, what say you? I am sadly in want of officers with the proper dash to command cavalry-having lost so many good ones." Captain Farnsworth, on the other hand, seemed conflicted about the potential promotion when writing to his uncle. "I do not know that I ought to mention it for fear that you will call me an aspiring youth. I am satisfied to serve through this war in the line in my Regt. as a Capt. on Genl Pleasonton's staff, but I can do any good anywhere else of course 'small favors & c'." But the young officer's humility did not prevent him from asking the congressman to put in a good word for him with President Lincoln.[1]

That took care of one promotion—and a hefty reward for a powerful patron. Meanwhile, Pleasonton's efforts to place Wesley Merritt in charge of the Reserve Brigade had begun as early as June 22. The leadership vacuum at the top of the Reserve Brigade's chain of command required immediate attention. When Buford moved up to division command in May, Charles J. Whiting, the brigade's ranking major, succeeded him. Whiting's heroic leadership of the 5th U.S. Cavalry at Gaines' Mill had earned him a great deal of respect among the Regulars. Merritt

---

1   Alfred Pleasonton to John F. Farnsworth, June 23, 1863, GNMP; Elon J. Farnsworth to John F. Farnsworth, June 29, 1863, GNMP.

certainly recognized both the importance of Whiting's charge and the valor of the regiment's sacrifice. Whiting, however, lost his temporary command due to the return of Maj. Samuel "Paddy" Starr to the cavalry.[2]

Starr's tenure would be short-lived and fractious, even when compared to the low standards set by the officer corps of the Army of the Potomac. As one trooper in the 6th U.S. Cavalry noted, "The government made one of its characteristic mistakes in assigning Major Starr to the command of a cavalry regiment in time of war." His soldiers hated the crotchety old cavalryman, due in large part to the creative and humiliating punishments he visited upon them. These were "unlimited as to number and variety," recalled Sidney Morris Davis. One punishment consisted of making the culprit sit precariously astride a fence rail with his feet tied together under the rail and his hands tied behind his back. A horse's nosebag would be lowered degradingly over his head. "This original feature . . . won for Starr the appellation of 'Old Nosebag.'"[3]

Starr had so poisoned the brigade's morale that Pleasonton found it easy to remove even this senior officer of the "Old Army" with no undue repercussions. Pleasonton was not above taking advantage of an argument between Major Starr and Captain Cram, "a short consultation, gesticulating wildly all the while," declared one witness in disgust. "It was said among the men that he was denouncing the captain for disobedience of orders—which the latter, when the enemy had exhausted their strength . . . was to have attacked vigorously." Distraught, Lt. Tattnall Paulding wrote, "There is a great deal of complaint in the regt because of some remarks made by Maj. Starr derogatory to the character of the regt. & because the First Squadron was put on picket as punishment."[4]

It also helped that "Paddy" Starr's belligerent Irish temperament often led him to places on the front line best left to lower ranking officers. Not surprisingly, this earned him a wound at Upperville that forced him to relinquish command of the Reserve Brigade. Even without the injury, Starr's lackluster performance at Upperville sealed his fate. Pleasonton had already picked his successor. On June 29,

---

2 OR 11, pt. 2, 43. Whiting's failure to curb his criticism of civilian authorities led to his dismissal in November 1863, for using disparaging and impertinent words against the president of the United States. His reputation remained marred despite the restoration of his rank in 1866. *Cullum's Register*, 590.

3 Sidney Morris Davis, *Common Soldier, Uncommon War: Life as a Cavalryman in the Civil War*, Charles F. Cooney, ed. (Bethesda, MD, 1994), 420.

4 Caughey and Jones, *The 6th United States Cavalry*, 98; Milgram, "The Libby Prison Correspondence of Tattnall Paulding," 1,114.

One of the earliest photographs of Wesley Merritt as a brigadier general.

U. S. Military Academy Library

Pleasonton relieved Starr of command of the Reserve Brigade and returned him to regimental command. Just a few days later, at the head of the 6th U.S. Cavalry, Starr would make a series of disastrous decisions that would lead to his serious injury and captivity. His war days were almost over.

"On June 29," wrote Capt. Wesley Merritt, his 2nd U.S. Cavalry "went into camp at Mechanicsville [sic], where it remained for several days." Far from just lounging about, the Reserve Brigade spent the next few days actively "picketing, scouting and patrolling the roads through the mountains . . . keeping headquarters informed as to the movements of the enemy from Mechanicstown [Maryland]." Lieutenant Paulding considered it arduous duty, "for the road is very rugged, one passing through the rocky defiles over the Katoctin Mountains." The friendly faces of the Union supporters encountered on the march buoyed the spirits of the men. "The people were very kind to us," recalled Paulding. "Where I established my main reserve they opened a school house & set out a fine dinner for the men of my company." Paulding sent one company to Hagerstown, Maryland, "& there as all along the road was rec'd with great joy by the people."[5]

The Regulars easily transitioned to the long-established routines of professional, disciplined soldiers. Throughout the day, bugle calls regulated the camp's functions, starting with "Reveille" and "Roll Call" in the morning. "The military day began patriotically with the raising of the national and headquarters flags," remembered one witness. "The Color Sergeant with his enlisted men . . . took it to the flag staff where it was unfurled. . . . [They] were never indifferent to the honor." Guard mount, confirmed one veteran, "excepting reviews and dress parades . . . always appealed to the author as the most impressive of military services." Once the ceremony came to an end, the men fed and groomed their horses.[6]

Quite possibly on that last day of regimental command, Merritt strolled the horse line, his mind leaping ahead to the challenges of higher command to come. Despite his musings, after years of practice he never failed to note the condition of the horses and their trappings. He likely patted the flank of a horse here and stroked the muzzle of another there. There might have been one last caress at the end, with the running of a hand over the animal's back, providing tangible proof of its health

---

5 Merritt, "Reminiscences," 294; OR 27, pt.1, 943; Milgram, "The Libby Correspondence of Tattnall Paulding," 1,114.

6 Reynolds, *The Civil War Memories of Elizabeth Bacon Custer*, 119; Henry P. Moyer, *History of the Seventeenth Regiment Pennsylvania Volunteer Cavalry* (Lebanon, PA, 1911), 276.

and reinforcing his belief that the care of the horses was the bedrock on which cavalry operations were built—just as Phillip St. George Cooke had taught him.

After "Stable Call," the men prepared and ate their breakfasts, cared for the sick, and watered the horses. Fatigue parties swept through the camps "policing and cleaning the streets, stables, mess-tents, burying refuse matter, getting wood for the cooks, and whatever other similar duties were necessary," recalled one of the troopers. Whenever they met their commanding officer in the course of their duties, the interaction was marked by his personal touch and pleasant remarks to the men. James Clark later wrote admiringly of his commanding officer: "General Merritt . . . had that genial, though rather more reticent demeanor, and left his impress on us."[7]

Any regiment not actually engaged in routine business spent much of its time on the drill field. For hours, each regiment broke down into company formations and performed the evolutions of the school of the trooper. The men drilled by squads and by company, on foot and mounted. They practiced religiously with the traditional cavalry side arms: revolver, saber, and carbine. After an invigorating session of drill, a horseman with one of the Pennsylvania regiments recounted, "The recall from the drill ground . . . was welcomed by all, who, tired, dusty and hungry gladly repaired to camp to await the next and even more welcome of the various calls." That would be the call to dinner. Two hours later, the men returned to the drill field to focus on regimental movements that "were invariably directed by bugle notes and it was surprising how soon, both men and horses learned the meaning of the bugle sounds and became masters of the movements required of them."[8]

The long military day finally came to an end at 4:00 p.m., when the bugles sounded the assembly call for dress parade. Eagerly anticipating the call for supper, the men fell into formation before the regimental officers. "Dress Parade," opined one veteran cavalryman, "was the most imposing of all our military ceremonials. . . . The regimental band would strike up some familiar selection of marching music, and the respective companies would form on the color line, with the band on the right." The commanding officer and his staff took up a position 100 feet in front of the line while the company officers advanced five paces to the front of their respective companies. After the orderly sergeants made their reports, the

7   Moyer, *History of the Seventeenth Regiment*, 276; Clark, *The Making of a Volunteer Cavalryman*, 27.

8   Moyer, *History of the Seventeenth Regiment*, 277-278.

regimental adjutant read any orders that had been received from the various echelons of command.[9]

Dress parade on June 29, 1863, brought a major change for the 2nd U.S. Cavalry. "Pursuant to Special Orders No. 98, Headquarters Cavalry Corps," read the adjutant, "Brig. Gen. Wesley Merritt will report without delay to Brig. Gen. John Buford, commanding First Cavalry Division, for assignment." The stalwarts of the regiment greeted Merritt's promotion with a round of cheers. In spite of the hearty congratulations of his fellow officers, the moment certainly sounded a bittersweet note for Merritt, as he would have to leave behind his beloved dragoons.[10]

In the years following his arrival in Utah as a baby-faced lieutenant straight out of West Point, Merritt worked hard to earn the loyalty of the crusty dragoons. As a regimental commander he had proven his dedication to the regiment both in camp and on the battlefield. In camp, his troops could trust him with their welfare. On the battlefield, they emulated his cool demeanor under fire and his ferocious fighting temperament when close to the enemy. Together, they had grown as soldiers, and the dragoons would miss his daily presence in their lives.

So there stood Merritt, turned out in the regulation coat of a brigadier general of cavalry, the sixteen glistening buttons arranged in parallel columns of two, each of his shoulder straps bearing a single silver star shining on a black field. Although tall, good-looking, and clean-cut in a way that is now often described as "all-American," the Union army's newest field-grade officer still did his best to try and hide his youth behind a thin mustache that did absolutely nothing to make him appear older. In the early evening, with the heat of the day having dissipated, the flags fluttered overhead in the cooling breezes as the band played crisp and snappy tunes while parading back and forth in front of the regiment. There would be no melancholy tunes this day.

Perhaps a Union gunner best expressed Merritt's great satisfaction and contentment at that moment, intermingled with unselfish pride. "I have loved to be a soldier," explained Samuel J. Marks, Battery D, 2nd U.S. Artillery, attached to the 1st U.S. Cavalry Division. "The spirit of the soldier is chained, especially the regular who is supposed not to be influenced by feeling." To his wife he wrote, "You know that I am a soldier yet and cannot suppress . . . [that] which has burned in my chest

9 Ibid., 277.

10 OR 27, pt. 3, 376.

since I was a wee boy, for the first books in my hand were the lives of Wallace and Napoleon which lit the flame."[11]

Merritt turned over command of the 2nd U.S. Cavalry to Captain Theophilus Rodenbough and the ceremony ended. As the men marched off to their well-earned suppers, the officers of the regiment crowded around Merritt and offered him their heartfelt congratulations—and more than likely a few celebratory toasts from flasks and tin cups. Wesley Merritt was not a bad sort, and few said anything to the contrary. Captain Rodenbough described him as "a pleasant, handsome young fellow, wearing his rank with easy grace, and apparently possessing just the temperament for a cavalryman." Captain James Kidd later served in various command capacities under Merritt, and, for a time, offered high praise for the new brigadier, "a position for which he was peculiarly fitted by nature, by acquirements, and by experience. Modesty which fitted him like a garment, charming manners, the demeanor of a gentleman, cool but fearless bearing in action, were his distinguishing characteristics. He was a most excellent officer."[12]

Thirty years of service with Merritt gave George B. Sanford a unique perspective on the man's personality. "Gen. Wesley Merritt of the Reserve brigade was a young man of perhaps twenty-five or six years—tall, slender and intellectual looking," he described. "He had a constitution of iron, and underneath a rather passive demeanor concealed a fiery ambition." Lieutenant Colonel Eben Swift also served under Merritt for many years. "Merritt in his prime was the embodiment of force," he recalled:

> He was one of those rare men whose faculties are sharpened and whose view is cleared on the battlefield. His decisions were delivered with the rapidity of thought and were as clear as if they had been studied for weeks. . . . In him a fiery soul was held in thrall to will. Never disturbed by doubt, or moved by fear, neither circumspect nor rash, he never missed an opportunity or made a mistake.[13]

By the time of his promotion, Merritt's reputation had spread beyond the Regulars. One volunteer described him as a hands-on officer. "During the many

---

11 Samuel J. Marks to Carrie Marks, March 11, 1864, USAHEC.

12 Eric J. Wittenberg, "Merritt's Regulars on South Cavalry Field: Oh, What Could Have Been," *The Gettysburg Magazine* (January 1997), No. 16, 112; Kidd, *Personal Recollections*, 237-238.

13 Hagemann, *Fighting Rebels and Redskins*, 225; Swift, "General Wesley Merritt," 837.

hotly contested cavalry engagements, from Upperville and Aldie to Five Forks, he was not accustomed to view the progress of the battle from a distance, but plunged into the fray." Like Custer, Merritt felt that his presence at the front encouraged his men. "[He] would not hesitate to place himself at the head of a single squadron for a charge. . . . By his coolness and intrepidity in action, he won for himself an enviable reputation."[14]

Find Me a Star

On Sunday, June 28, 1863, Alfred Pleasonton summoned George Custer to his room at the City Hotel in downtown Frederick. The young captain neither knew nor cared whether he would receive a new mission or simply enjoy a fine dinner with the general. When Custer arrived, Pleasonton astounded his favored aide by announcing his appointment as a brigadier general in the U.S. Volunteers. Later, three weeks after Gettysburg, Custer finally found the time to write to Judge Isaac P. Christiancy, his old benefactor. "I was never more surprised than when I was informed of my appointment as a Brigadier General," he stated incredulously. "To say I was elated would faintly express my feelings. I well knew that I had reason to congratulate myself, I was but twenty-three years of age the youngest General in the U.S. army by more than two years."[15]

But political patronage brings an altogether different set of hazards than the battlefield. Although fearless in the face of the enemy, Custer worried about his prospective promotion and expressed his fears to Judge Christiancy. "If I fail to receive my confirmation from the Senate because I am not worthy to fill the position, well and good," he declared, "but I do not wish to be defeated in another manner. . . . I have tried and still endeavor to discharge my duty so as to merit the position conferred upon me."[16]

To make room for Custer, someone would have to go. Pleasonton had already made up his mind to get rid of Brigadier General Copeland of the Michigan Brigade, now attached to Kilpatrick's newly designated 3rd Cavalry Division. "Gen. Pleasonton's first act was to relieve Gen. Copeland," Custer told Judge Christiancy. "He asked me what he should do with me, I replied that I had but one

---

14 Wittenberg, *One of Custer's Wolverines*, 126.

15 Servacek, *Custer: His Promotion in Frederick, Maryland*, 31.

16 Ibid., 29.

request to make which was to assign me to the command of the Michigan brigade . . . My request was granted."[17]

The orders relieving him of his well-earned command shocked Copeland, especially since he was heavily engaged in the business of cobbling together the four Michigan regiments into a well-coordinated and disciplined fighting force. Fury quickly replaced his shock, and he loudly and abrasively let Pleasonton know of his displeasure. Relieved on the very "eve of Battle, in the face of the Enemy," Copeland protested, "[t]o have my command taken from me . . . is an indignity and disgrace that I should not and cannot quietly submit to." Pleasonton replied firmly that he had only accepted command of the Cavalry Corps on the "understanding that he should have the assignment of the commanding officers, and that he had selected officers known to himself and who were affiliated with him, and that while he intended no disrespect nor reflection on me, he must insist on giving the command to those best known to himself." Nevertheless, Copeland's attitude rankled Pleasonton, and Copeland soon found himself on his way to Annapolis, Maryland, and the career-ending command of a rendezvous depot for drafted soldiers.[18]

Unlike the nearly unanimous approval of Merritt's rapid promotion, there can be no doubt that Custer's equally astonishing ascendancy from staff captain to brigadier general of a volunteer cavalry brigade deeply offended the sensibilities of the officers of the Cavalry Corps. Joseph Fought, Custer's young aide, recalled that "all the officers were exceedingly jealous of him. Not one man but would have thrown a stone in his way to make him lose prestige. He was way ahead of them as a soldier, and that made them angry." Perhaps James Kidd, always perceptive and erudite, came closest to the heart of the matter. "Among regular army officers as a class he cannot be said to have been a favorite," he penned with some understatement. "The meteoric rapidity of his rise to the zenith of his fame and success, when so many of the youngsters of his years were moving in the comparative obscurity of their own orbits, irritated them." Elizabeth Clift Bacon—who would soon enter the picture full-time—expressed her jaundiced view of the situation much later in life. "Of course with my husband's success and rapid promotion," she explained, "the usual swarm of enemies presented him with maligning and falsehoods, and there were deprecations of his ability, which attacks

---

17 Ibid., 31.

18 Petruzzi, *Alfred Pleasonton's Civil Wars*, 20-21.

he tossed aside with the buoyancy [of] his temperament. . . . But it was no use. It is something few wives conquer."[19]

John Buford, whose military career had advanced at a snail's pace, definitely ranked among those disgruntled officers. When the newly renamed 2nd U.S. Cavalry arrived in Washington in October 1861, the unprepared Regulars found a city thriving on the business of war. Many of the regiment's officers had spent years perfecting their martial skills, largely unrecognized, on the far-flung reaches of the American frontier. Promotion had been agonizingly slow. Buford himself had waited 15 long, hard years before being promoted to captain. Yet everywhere he looked, he saw an army of men sporting newly minted epaulets of majors and colonels, each demanding the proper military courtesies from Capt. John Buford. Like an ugly stepsister, the 2nd Dragoons had come late to the ball. In a war increasingly dominated by the movement of infantry divisions and corps, the arrival of the Regular cavalry was but a drop in the bucket.

Two weeks later, Buford's raw feelings about Custer's promotion bubbled to the surface. On July 5 near Frederick, he ordered his men to hang several prisoners suspected of being spies. Abner N. Hard, a surgeon with the 8th Illinois Cavalry, wrote a fair summary of the well-documented event. "General Buford had been greatly annoyed by what he supposed were spies, or persons who had been allowed to enter camp under various pretexts," he noted. "Some he had arrested and sent to headquarters, who were there released." When confronted by "a committee of indignant citizens," Buford informed them that a spy had been sentenced by a drumhead court-martial to hang immediately. Amid cries of "Northern brute!" from outraged civilians, Buford told his officers "he was afraid to send [the spy] to Washington because he knew the authorities would make him a brigadier-general"—a pointed swipe at George Custer and Elon Farnsworth. According to Knapp, the body was still swinging from the tree the next day.[20]

Like everything else in Custer's life, the circumstances under which he received command of the Michigan Brigade gave birth to a number of apocryphal stories. Of course, Frederick Whittaker spun a thoroughly fictional yet entertaining tale, describing a weary Autie returning to headquarters after placing pickets during an all-night ride just 11 days after the fighting at Aldie:

19 Merington, *The Custer Story*, 60; Kidd, *Personal Recollections*, 130-131; Reynolds, *The Civil War Memories of Elizabeth Bacon Custer*, 49.

20 Eric J. Wittenberg, "And Everything is Lovely and the Goose Hangs High: Buford and the Hanging of Confederate Spies During the Gettysburg Campaign," *The Gettysburg Magazine* (January 1998), No. 18, 8; Moyer, *History of the Seventeenth Regiment*, 57; Knapp Diary, July 6, 1863.

He was greeted in the large tent, where the staff was wont to gather at night, by the salutations, "Hallo, general." "How are you, general?" "Gentlemen, General Custer." "Why, general, I congratulate you." "You're looking well, general." The greetings came from all quarters of the tent . . . [and] it was with some bitterness that he answered, "You may laugh, boys. Laugh as long as you please, but [I]will be a general yet, for all your chaff. You see if I don't that's all."

After a bit more ribbing, his friend George Yates "steered Custer to the table and pointed. 'Look on the table, old fellow. They're not chaffing,' he said with a smile." Sure enough, on the table "lay a large official envelope, and on it was written, 'BRIGADIER GENERAL GEORGE A. CUSTER, U. S. VOLS.'[21]

Although historians know for a fact that Custer received his appointment from Pleasonton in a private meeting, Whittaker can perhaps be forgiven for trusting his possible source for the story. The newly bereaved Libbie Custer consoled herself by recounting her husband's "own story of his promotion," somewhat brightening the solemnity of her extended widowhood. She felt a swelling in her heart when "those chaffing men gathered round him and in serious, very generous words, congratulated him." She retold the story so often that even she came to believe it.[22]

Merritt enjoyed a smooth transition to brigade command, which merely entailed a short ride from the camp of the 2nd U.S. Cavalry. Custer, on the other hand, faced two major challenges. First, he spent many of his earliest hours as a general adding the finishing touches to his new black velveteen battle outfit. Much can be said about the origins of that resplendent garment, but that is a tale for another time. Second—and possibly more importantly—he had to find and then join his far-flung 2nd Brigade of Kilpatrick's 3rd Cavalry Division on the march. "Kilpatrick's command was badly scattered," explained Kidd, describing the division's deployment across southern Pennsylvania. "A part of it including the First and the Seventh Michigan and Pennington's battery, was at Abbottstown a few miles north of Hanover; Farnsworth's brigade at Littlestown, seven miles southwest of Hanover."[23]

---

21 Whittaker, *A Popular Life of Gen. George A. Custer*, 162-163.

22 Reynolds, *The Civil War Memories of Elizabeth Bacon Custer*, 128-129.

23 Kidd, *Personal Recollections*, 125. Col. Charles H. Town commanded the 1st Michigan Cavalry. Colonel William D. Mann still headed the 7th Michigan Cavalry after beating out Custer for the post. Likewise, Colonel Alger commanded the 5th Michigan Cavalry instead of

Gathered about their campfires that night of June 29, the so-called Wolverines speculated amongst themselves, eagerly sharing what little they knew of their new commanding officer. It amounted to little, recalled Kidd. "Of him we knew but little except that he hailed from Monroe, Michigan, was a graduate of West Point, had served with much credit on the staffs of McClellan and Pleasonton, and that he, too, was a 'fighter.' None of us had seen [him]." Around the mess fires of the 1st Michigan Cavalry, soldiers asked, "Who is he, and what is he like?" The answer was, "No one knows, only they say he is a young sort of a fop in his looks, with long, golden, curly hair. Someone says he is a quick, nervous boy, and fights the fight before his opponent is ready."[24]

Long before dawn on June 29, Custer departed Frederick to find and join the Michiganders. He located them just in time to lead them in his first battle as a general officer. He spent all day in the saddle, traveling 45 miles from Frederick to Abbottstown, Pennsylvania, which he finally reached well after night had fallen. During the long ride, he gave much thought to setting up his brigade staff. Rather than fan the flames of resentment by bringing in staff officers from outside, Custer opted to make his appointments from among his fellow Michiganders. "Most of my husband's staff were friends or schoolmates of Monroe," recorded Libbie. "The boys with whom he was associated were his most valued friends and soon made gallant fearless soldiers under his leadership."[25]

Pleasonton issued orders for the movement of the Cavalry Corps toward Pennsylvania on June 29, commanding his three divisions to advance along four parallel roads. Buford's two brigades marched furthest on the left, passing through Boonsboro, Maryland, then traveling north along the western edge of South Mountain into Pennsylvania. At Monterey Pass, Buford would cut back through the mountains and bivouac at Fairfield. Merritt's Reserve Brigade would move up the Emmitsburg Road to hook up with Buford at Emmitsburg as soon as it was relieved of its duty of guarding the wagon train. Further east, Kilpatrick's 3rd Division moved directly along the Taneytown Road past Littlestown, then struck through Hanover en route to York. Gregg's 2nd Division protected the army's right flank, marching to Westminster while patrolling the Pennsylvania countryside

---

the ambitious young Custer. Colonel Gray led the 6th Michigan Cavalry. Battery M, 2nd U.S. Artillery, under Lt. Alexander C. M. Pennington, Jr., supported the brigade.

24 Kidd, *Personal Recollections*, 122-123; Eric J. Wittenberg and J. David Petruzzi, *Plenty of Blame to Go Around: Jeb Stuart's Controversial Ride to Gettysburg* (El Dorado Hills, CA, 2006), 72.

25 Reynolds, *The Civil War Memories*, 54.

toward York and Carlisle. The whereabouts of the enemy remained a complete mystery. Marching blind in that way, any of Pleasonton's units could stumble upon the Rebels at any time.

Going the Wrong Way on a One-Way Street

The violent cavalry clash at Hanover underscores the repeated failure of modern historians to fully understand both Custer's instinctive grasp of cavalry tactics and his combative personality, misconstruing and even denigrating his tactical virtuosity. Beginning with Hanover, historian after historian created a slate of events with absolutely no factual support, basing their subsequent conjectures on this shaky foundation. In the process, they painted a totally incorrect picture of Custer's first battle as a brigade commander. Rather than recognize the hard-nosed, bare-knuckles essence of the warrior within, some chose to erroneously perpetuate the romantic image of Custer, focusing on his fashion sense instead of his combat instincts.

The first of these fallacies appeared in 1951 with the publication of George A. Rummel, III's *Cavalry on the Roads to Gettysburg*. Rummel's extensive research produced the following record:

> On that Tuesday morning Brigadier General Kilpatrick again chose to travel in the vanguard of the division with General Custer and Colonel Town. . . . With Custer at the head of his brigade, the twenty-one troops from the two Michigan regiments quickly spread out along the main road running between Littlestown and Hanover.[26]

In the following years, learned writers and historians—men of impeccable credentials—would travel down the Hanover Road with George Rummel. The fiction that Custer had marched through Hanover with Judson Kilpatrick early on June 30 soon became the cornerstone of the historical analysis of Custer's performance that day. In 1979, Stephen Z. Starr sparked a resurgence in the study of the Army of the Potomac's understudied Cavalry Corps with his massive tome *The Union Cavalry in the Civil War*. "Kilpatrick had also marched for Hanover that morning, coming from the west. Custer's brigade had already marched through the

---

26 George A Rummel, III, *Cavalry on the Roads to Gettysburg: Kilpatrick at Hanover and Hunterstown* (Shippensburg, PA, 2000), 167.

town," explained Starr. "Farnsworth was in the process of doing so when J. R. Chambliss' brigade of Stuart's command arrived from the south."[27]

In 1986, Edward G. Longacre lent his considerable reputation to the fight at Hanover in *The Cavalry at Gettysburg*, his tactical study of campaign's mounted operations . "Judson Kilpatrick entered Hanover at the head of Custer's 1st and 7th Michigan. He set up a command post at a local home," explained Longacre, reinforcing the vivid, yet wholly inaccurate, narrative. "Custer's horsemen . . . trooped through the town. In Centre Square the line of riders temporarily halted to partake of gifts, ranging from buttermilk to cigars, handed up by the townspeople. The men ate and drank in the saddle, even as they went out the York Pike to Abbottsville."[28]

In actuality, Kilpatrick rode with Farnsworth's 1st Brigade through Hanover. Arriving at the head of his division, Kilpatrick set up a temporary headquarters in the home of Jacob Wirt. As the "dirty, bedraggled and unshaven" troopers of Farnsworth's brigade marched into Hanover they were met by a rejoicing citizenry. "Flags waved everywhere," recalled Capt. Henry C. Parsons of the 1st Vermont Cavalry. "Bells were ringing. Hundreds of school children stood in the market square singing songs of welcome. . . . Matrons and maidens and children ran with bread and milk, beer and pretzels. . . . It was a scene perhaps unsurpassed in all the marches of war."[29]

Neither Custer nor the units of his new command enjoyed the festivities taking place in the choked streets of Hanover. Perhaps the best antidote to the false narrative can be found by pinpointing the actual locations of Custer and the various units of the Michigan Cavalry Brigade. At dawn on June 30, Custer rode out with half of his brigade from Abbottstown, some distance to the north of Hanover. The 7th Michigan led the way, followed by Pennington's battery and the 1st Michigan in the rear. Unfortunately, the authorization to transfer the Michigan Brigade from the Department of Washington to Kilpatrick's new division caught the 5th and 6th

---

27 Starr, *The Union Cavalry in the Civil War*, 1:428.

28 Edward G. Longacre, *The Cavalry at Gettysburg: A Tactical Study of Mounted Operations During the Civil War's Pivotal Campaign, 9 June-14 July 1863* (Lincoln, NE, 1986), 173.

29 Farnsworth's brigade consisted of Maj. John Hammond's 5th New York Cavalry, Lt. Col. Addison W. Preston's 1st Vermont Cavalry, Col. Nathaniel P. Richmond's 1st West Virginia Cavalry, and Lt. Col. William P. Brinton's 18th Pennsylvania Cavalry. Lt. Samuel S. Elder's Battery E, 4th U.S. Artillery provided support; Wittenberg and Petruzzi, *Plenty of Blame to Go Around*, 77.

Michigan Cavalry regiments far afield from the new brigade headquarters in Abbottstown.

Both regiments had marched by separate roads from Frederick straight north to Emmitsburg. On June 28, General Copeland, still in command of the brigade at this point, accompanied Col. Alger's 5th Michigan as it marched from Emmitsburg to Gettysburg, where the Rebels had just slipped out of town. Colonel Alger learned from a couple of captured stragglers that Lee's army intended to stab deep into Pennsylvania. When Copeland's command arrived, it found an atmosphere of revelry. "Such demonstrations of joy as we witnessed," avowed Alger, "made by the good people of Gettysburg upon our arrival, it has never been my privilege to witness, either before or since; they almost literally covered my soldiers with flowers. How little they realized the terrible scenes that were to be enacted near their homes so soon thereafter." The 5th Michigan Cavalry rode back to Emmitsburg when Buford's 1st Division arrived to relieve them on the 29th. There they received the news that Copeland had been relieved, and Alger took temporary command of the brigade.[30]

Both regiments moved out that evening for an all-night trek to Littlestown, planning to march to Abbottstown the next day to rejoin the rest of the brigade. Early on the 30th, the exhausted troopers arrived at Littlestown. "We were plodding our weary way along, sleeping in the saddle," Kidd wrote of the exhausted, worn-out command. At every halt, the bone-tired troopers dismounted and collapsed at their horses' feet, reins in hand, falling into a "profound slumber." Only the clomping of "the horses' hoofs moving in front served to arouse the riders." At Littlestown sometime during the night or pre-dawn morning, Lt. Samuel Harris of the 5th Michigan spotted his new brigade commander and his escort of two buglers. "At this time a flaxen-haired boy rode up to me and asked where the Michigan Brigade of Cavalry was," Harris reminisced, "It was the boy who less than two months before had asked our officers to sign a petition to have him appointed colonel of our regiment. My eye caught the star on his shoulder."[31]

June 30 would be another long day for the troopers of the two regiments. "The early morning hours," recalled Kidd, "were consumed in scouring the country in all directions, and information soon came to the effect that Stuart was moving toward Hanover. . . . The Sixth remained in the town until a citizen came running in, about

---

30 Robertson, *Michigan in the War*, 578.

31 Kidd, *Personal Recollections*, 124-125; Harris, *Personal Reminiscences*, 28.

noon, reporting a large force of the enemy, about five miles out to Hanover." At this point, the deadly work began in earnest.[32]

Just outside of town, Alger's men engaged in a running gun battle with Fitzhugh Lee's troopers, who seemed to be everywhere. As the 6th Michigan approached Hanover, the troopers left the road and cut across a wheat field toward a crest to their front. As they topped the hill a heavily supported section of Lee's artillery took them under fire. "Colonel Gray," wrote Kidd, "seeing that the force in front of him were preparing to charge, and aware that one raw regiment would be no match for a brigade of veteran troops, made a detour to the left, and sought by a rapid movement to unite with the command in Hanover." The growing confidence of the troopers caused one Michigander to grouse that the regiment "was obliged to skedaddle not very creditably to our Col[onel]." Their misplaced confidence evaporated as the withdrawal turned into a "mad flight for safety."[33]

Trooper John B. Kay lost everything of sentimental value after "[we] were ordered to throw off everything to speed our flight." Of those desperate moments he wrote, "Oh what a loss I have met with! . . . But thank God I have not lost my life yet, though the Balls whistled close & shells burst near me He has kept me under the shadow of his wing. I have felt it." As the regiment galloped hell-bent for leather to the safety of Kilpatrick's line, Maj. Peter A. Weber stayed behind with two companies to delay the enemy. "Right gallantly was this duty performed," lauded Kidd. "Three charges upon the little band were as often repulsed by the heroic Weber, and with such determination did he hold to the work, that he was cut off and did not succeed in rejoining the regiment until about three o'clock the next morning." Unfortunately, Major Weber would have little time to enjoy his enviable reputation as a soldier.[34]

Meanwhile, once in sight of Hanover, Custer spurred his horse ahead of the 1st and 7th Michigan and sought out Kilpatrick for his first conference with his new commanding officer. Kilpatrick, Farnsworth, and Custer pulled down a large-scale map of the York area from the wall of Jacob Wirt's study, laid it on a table, and clustered around it. Kilpatrick explained that Custer's mission was to proceed north to York and establish the whereabouts of Jubal Early's division. Satisfied that they had gleaned as much information as possible from their study of the map and

---

32 Kidd, *Personal Recollections*, 125-126.

33 Ibid., 127; Longacre, *Custer and His Wolverines*, 135.

34 John B. Kay to his parents, July 6, 1863, John B. Kay letters, Bentley Historical Library, University of Michigan; Kidd, *Personal Recollections*, 127-128.

interrogation of the locals, Custer and Kilpatrick mounted their horses and rode out to intercept Custer's marching column.

Farnsworth turned his attention to the 5th New York Cavalry, which was "resting in a line extending from Frederick Street, through Center Square, and a short distance down Abbottstown Street. The troopers were being fed by the patriotic citizens." Captain William Parker Wilkin of the 1st West Virginia Cavalry recalled the festivities. "We were received with lively demonstrations of joy. . . . Flags and handkerchiefs were waved, patriotic songs were sung, and it seemed a time of general rejoicing." At the north end of town, the van of the 1st West Virginia started to wend its way slowly up the Pigeon Hills, a series of steep rises just three miles north of Hanover. Just behind them, the 1st Vermont Cavalry still struggled to escape the revelry which clogged the streets of Hanover. To the south units of the 18th Pennsylvania Cavalry, the brigade's rear guard, began to approach the town.[35]

After studying the lay of the land and the positions of his units, Kilpatrick galloped off to the head of the northbound column with his staff in tow. He failed to hear the first pop-popping of gunfire far to the south, where elements of the 18th Pennsylvania Cavalry had suddenly encountered a small detachment of troopers from the 13th Virginia Cavalry of Col. John R. Chambliss's brigade.

On June 29, Stuart's command, consisting of the three brigades of John Chambliss, Wade Hampton, and Fitzhugh Lee, had moved through Westminster, where scouting parties of the 4th Virginia Cavalry clashed with the 1st Delaware Cavalry. Stretched out on the road between Westminster and Union Mills, Stuart's five-mile-long column took a well-deserved breather from the rigors of war. The two columns spent the night a mere 11 miles apart. The next morning Stuart, with the help of a Rebel sympathizer familiar with the area's roads, turned onto the Old Hanover Road, a dirt track that cut cross-country to Hanover. Chambliss' brigade led the Confederate advance, followed by the artillery and Hampton's command. Lee's brigade swung out to the left flank.

Believing that he only faced a regiment of Union troopers protecting a wagon train, Chambliss ordered the 13th Virginia to charge. "No one seemed to dream how sadly the scene was to be changed in a few minutes. While our column was out in the streets Stewarts' [sic] cavalry, from under cover of a piece of woods, opened on us with artillery, and at the same time charged on our rear." The Rebel attack

---

35 Wittenberg and Petruzzi, *Plenty of Blame to Go Around*, 79; William Parker Wilkin, letter to his wife, *The Athens* [OH] *Messenger*, August 13, 1863.

surprised Farnsworth's entire command, including Captain Wilkin. "A desperate hand to hand conflict ensued. In a few minutes the street was filled with dead and wounded of both armies."[36]

At about 10:30 a.m., near the intersection of the Abbottstown Road with the York Road, Kilpatrick ordered the column to dismount, take a break, and give Farnsworth's men a chance to catch up with them. Lieutenant Stephen A. Clark of the 1st Vermont Cavalry remained stuck in Hanover. "We were having a grand jubilee on loyal soil," he reported, "when all of a sudden, like a clap of thunder from a clear sky, came the report of artillery and small-arms fire in our rear." At this point Kilpatrick finally heard the throaty reverberations of artillery fire, jumped into the saddle, and headed for Hanover as fast as his horse could take him. Cresting the ridgeline on the Pigeon Hills, Kilpatrick slowed his headlong charge just long enough to take in the unfolding drama below.[37]

"The impetuous charge of the enemy," reported Capt. John W. Phillips of the 18th Pennsylvania Cavalry, "brought some of their troops in the midst of our men, and hand-to-hand contests were had with the sabre." As the mounted action intensified, Chambliss moved his artillery into position on a high ridgeline south of Hanover. Shot and shell soon rained down on Farnsworth's command, still mired in town.[38]

The firestorm of artillery caught many of the citizens of Hanover out in the open, innocent folks who had turned out to see their boys in blue and make them welcome. Slow to realize the meaning of the bursting shells, the crowd stood momentarily still as comprehension, panic, and fear all set in at the same moment. Then everybody started running. "The sudden surprise had a strange effect upon the people who at first did not realize what had happened," remarked Charles B. Thomas of the 5th New York Cavalry. The civilians had never heard "the fierce rebel yell," and as it grew louder and louder, the Confederate horsemen burst into the town square. Alarmed, Thomas watched as "the women and children fled in terror from the scene, seeking shelter within their homes. What a change! In less time than it takes to tell it, the streets were full of live Rebels."[39]

36 William Parker Wilkin, letter to his wife, *The Athens* [OH] *Messenger*, August 13, 1863.

37 Wittenberg and Petruzzi, *Plenty of Blame to Go Around*, 83.

38 Ibid., 86.

39 John T. Krepps, *A Strong and Sudden Onslaught: The Cavalry Action at Hanover, Pennsylvania* (Orrtanna, PA, 2008), 44.

The action continued to escalate. "The attack was determined and fierce," Kilpatrick reported to his superiors, "the main and side streets [of Hanover] swarmed with rebel cavalry. The Eighteenth Pennsylvania was routed." Farnsworth, displaying the tactical aptitude that justified his promotion to brigadier general, quickly turned the other regiments of his command around and jumped into the fray. Charge and countercharge roiled through Hanover. One Vermont trooper bragged in his diary, "General Farnsworth had wheeled us into line and with lightning speed charged the rebel foe driving them in hot haste before us."[40]

Dead, dying, and wounded soldiers and horses of both sides littered the streets of the town. As the Confederates fell back to the shelter of their position on Rice Hill, Kilpatrick arrived in Hanover and took up position in the Central Hotel. As he leaped from his saddle, the beast he had ridden nearly to death collapsed under him. Custer, in the meantime, had reached his command and turned the men around, rapidly approaching the battlefield. Arriving in Hanover ahead of his regiments, Custer consulted quickly with Kilpatrick and then began to deploy his troops as they arrived. What follows is the real story of Custer's first fight and the lessons he learned from it.

Kilpatrick ordered Custer to place the division's two batteries on high ground just north of Hanover, straddling the Carlisle Pike, with Pennington's Battery M west of the road and Elder's Battery E to the east of it. They soon had the Confederate guns on Rice Hill under an accurate fire. The 7th Michigan deployed as dismounted skirmishers in the field to the front of the batteries and to the left of Hanover. The 1st Michigan took up position in support of Pennington's guns, while elements of the 1st Vermont backed up Elder. As the troopers of the 7th Michigan maneuvered into their assigned positions, Custer and Kilpatrick climbed up to the belfry of St. Matthew's Church for a birds-eye view of the action. From this advantageous position, Custer detected the approach of the harried 6th Michigan Cavalry through his glass. It would be noon before the disorganized men of the 6th Michigan reformed behind the railroad tracks.

A lull fell over the field as the opposing division commanders brought up reinforcements and rearranged their lines in preparation for continued combat. Farnsworth, taking command of the situation in the town proper, ordered his regiments to pull back into Hanover and construct barricades across the streets. His men feverishly overturned wagons and piled hay bales, crates, fences, and anything else that offered a modicum of protection to form rudimentary

40 OR 27, pt. 1, 992; Wittenberg and Petruzzi, *Plenty of Blame to Go Around*, 93.

breastworks. On the Confederate side, Hampton finally got his troopers up and deployed them astride the Baltimore Pike, anchoring his line on the right with a battery of four guns at Mt. Olive Cemetery. "The confederate line of battle," stated Kidd, "could be distinctly seen on the hills to the south of town." The two sides were immersed in their final preparations until nearly two o'clock in the afternoon.[41]

Custer came down from his perch in the church belfry and, after finally introducing himself, ordered Colonel Gray to dismount his men and prepare to move against Chambliss's brigade. The 5th Michigan made its appearance about this time and deployed into line of battle. Ostensibly, the primary target was the enemy battery on Rice Hill, but an even more important objective lay in keeping the Hanover-Littlestown Road open as a line of communications back to the Army of the Potomac.

As Gray's dismounted command began working its way through the wheat fields and pastures to its front, a solitary horseman cantered along the line. Custer had finally taken charge of his brigade. "As the men of the Sixth, armed with their Spencer rifles, were deploying forward across the railroad into a wheat-field beyond, I heard a voice new to me, directly in rear of the portion of the line where I was," detailed a "riveted" James Kidd in his first impression of the man who would captivate him for decades. The newly minted brigadier rode from company to company, giving orders "in clear, resonant tones, and in a calm, confident manner, at once resolute and reassuring."[42]

Kidd could not help but notice the customized uniform, and at first believed the newcomer to be a staff officer. "[His] appearance amazed me if it did not for the moment amuse me," but it soon became "apparent that he was giving the orders, not delivering them, and that he was in command of the line." Captain Kidd described Custer's ensemble, eccentric even by the lax uniform standards of the day. "He was clad in a suit of black velvet," he began,

> elaborately trimmed with gold lace, which ran down the outer seams of his trousers, and almost covered the sleeves of his cavalry jacket. The wide collar of a blue navy shirt was turned down over the collar of his velvet jacket, and a necktie of brilliant crimson was tied in a graceful knot at the throat, the long ends falling carelessly in front. . . . A soft, black hat with wide brim adorned with a gilt cord, and rosette encircling a silver star, was worn

---

41 Kidd, *Personal Recollections*, 128.

42 Ibid.

Brigadier General George Armstrong Custer in his signature black velveteen battle uniform, taken sometime in September 1863.

National Photo Institute, Smithsonian Institute Library

turned down on one side giving him a rakish air. His golden hair fell in graceful luxuriance nearly or quite to his shoulders, and his upper lip was garnished with a blonde mustache.[43]

Many in the Army of the Potomac scoffed at the flagrantly exotic costume. Colonel Theodore Lyman of General Meade's staff spoke for many when he wrote, "This officer is one of the funniest looking beings you ever saw, and looks like a circus rider gone mad!" Lyman conceded, however, that Custer's "aspect though highly amusing, is also pleasing, as he has a very merry blue eye, and a devil-may-care style."[44]

Under Custer's direct command, the regiment began a stealthy approach to the Confederate positions. A long ridge that ran parallel to the Littlestown Road covered part of the three-quarter-mile skirmish line. At some points, the men dropped to their hands and knees, crawling through the wheat fields and underbrush. Outraged citizens later claimed that several acres of wheat had been trampled and destroyed. Arriving at the designated position, the entire line stood up and on command let loose a well-aimed volley at the battery's support troops, who melted away under the withering fusillade. The Michiganders quickly chambered another round and took aim at the gunners. Although much too cumbersome for traditional cavalry carbine action, the Spencer rifle offered one great advantage: better-than-average accuracy at long range. It did not take long to silence the enemy's fire.

43 Ibid., 129. To this day, the origins of Custer's singular battle outfit remain shrouded in mystery and controversy. Any investigation of the subject would likely require a chapter of its own.

44 George R. Agassiz, ed., *Meade's Headquarters 1863-1865: Letters of Colonel Theodore Lyman from The Wilderness to Appomattox* (Boston, 1922), 17.

Realizing the danger to his battery, Lee acted quickly to salvage the situation. Moving the main portion of his men forward, he dislodged the 6th Michigan from its commanding perch and forced it back to its original position. Custer met the retreating troopers and ordered Colonel Gray to reform the regiment and retake the initiative. Advancing as far as the knoll, the four Spencer-armed companies of the 6th Michigan went to ground and began a desultory, long-range fire that occupied Lee for the balance of the day.

Just before dark, Lee made one last attempt against Custer. Moving past the right of the 6th Michigan, Lee struck down the Littlestown Turnpike but ran into the 5th Michigan, which had taken up a protective position at the village of Pennville. At the intersection of the Littlestown Pike and the Westminster Road, "my regiment had its first serious encounter with the enemy," reported Alger. "Towards evening the enemy attacked me in quite a large force. I charged him, driving him some distance, dismounted my command and fought him on foot, killing and capturing quite a number. My loss was severe."[45]

Stuart began pulling out that evening. Denied direct access to the rest of the Army of Northern Virginia through Hanover, he had no choice but to begin a circuitous trek that would take him east to Jefferson, north to Dover, and then west in a wide arc toward Carlisle, which he reached late on the evening of July 1.

After dark, the two Union regiments fell back to Hanover, finally uniting the Michigan Cavalry Brigade under Custer for the first time. After apprising Custer of the activities of his regiment, Colonel Alger also briefed him on the effects of the Spencer repeater on his tactics. "It is proper here to state," he informed Custer, "that my regiment was armed with the Spencer rifle, being the only regiment in the brigade, and I think in our division, then provided with that weapon. Consequently I was then and afterwards required to do very much fighting on foot."[46]

Custer and Alger hit it off instantly. Kidd described Alger as "the ideal soldier. Tall, erect, handsome, he was an expert and graceful horseman." Unlike Custer, Alger "was scrupulous to a degree about his dress. His clothes fitted, and not a speck of dust could be found on his person, his horse, or his equipment. . . . As a battalion commander Colonel Alger had few equals and no superiors." Alger soon became Custer's right-hand man. Of their relationship Kidd wrote, "In all the battles of that eventful campaign, whenever they were associated together,

45 Robertson, *Michigan in the War*, 578.

46 Ibid.

wherever the one wanted a man tried, true, trained and trustworthy, there he would put the other."[47]

During the battle of Hanover, Custer gained his first inkling of how the superior firepower of the Spencer repeater would impact the cavalry tactics to be used by his command. Custer's unique tactics relied on the presence of the Spencer in the hands of the 5th Michigan Cavalry and part of the 6th Michigan Cavalry. After more experience with the Spencer, Custer made his opinion known directly to the inventor in a May 1864 letter in which he gave the weapon unstinting praise. "Dear Sir, Being in command of a Brigade of Cavalry which is armed throughout with the Spencer Carbine and Rifle, I take pleasure in testifying to their superiority over all other weapons," he wrote. "I am firmly of the opinion that 1500 men armed with the Spencer carbine are more than a match for 2500 armed with any other firearm. I know this to be true from actual experiment."[48]

47 Kidd, *Personal Recollections*, 54-55, 383.

48 Edwards, *Civil War Guns*, 155.

CHAPTER TEN

If You Can't Find Glory at Gettysburg

ON JUNE 29, 1863, AN OFFICER in Cobb's (Georgia) Legion Cavalry, part of Wade Hampton's brigade, rode into Hunterstown, Pennsylvania, with 85 men and "occupied the town and threw out strong pickets on all the roads . . . east and south." It was a dandy day to be a Confederate horse soldier. Sitting astride spirited if rather hungry and tired steeds, they cantered in perfect formation down the main street. Red, white, and blue bunting festooned the local hotel in preparation for the upcoming Fourth of July festivities. The residents began to gather but seemed fearful.[1]

Just days earlier, a column from Maj. Gen. Jubal Early's division had marched up the turnpike from Gettysburg to York and torched Gulden's Station, just two miles away from Hunterstown. "It was the only act of vandalism committed," reported C. E. Goldsborough of the *Philadelphia Record* in a postwar article on the Battle of Hunterstown. "No one ever knew why it was done. There was of course a good deal of excitement and apprehension among the people."[2]

Crossing into northern territory did indeed bring out the worst in some of the Rebels. "We are paying back these people for some of the damage they have done us, though we are not doing them half as bad as they done us. We are getting up all

---

1   C. E. Goldsborough, "The Hunterstown Fight: A Civil War Engagement of Which Little is Known," *The Philadelphia Record*, September 15, 1901. The officer is identified only as "Captain Crawford" in the sources consulted for this book.

2   Ibid.

the horses, etc., and feeding our army with their beef and flour, etc.," wrote Confederate trooper William S. Christian to his wife, his heart still aching over the earlier destruction of their home by Northern ravagers. Much to his disgust, there were "strict orders about the interruption of any private property by individual soldiers. Though with these orders, fowls and pigs and eatables don't stand much chance."[3]

On July 1, the rumble of distant artillery "could be distinctly heard in the fight at Gettysburg, five miles south," recalled a reporter for a Philadelphia paper, "and the Confederates informed the citizens that a big battle was raging, although no unusual concern manifested."[4]

The growing volume of gunfire acted as a magnet and pulled heavy columns of Confederates toward the crossroads town. Communiqués from higher echelons confirmed the rumors of heavy fighting. "The whereabouts of our army was still a mystery," reported Jeb Stuart, "but, during the night, I received a dispatch from General Lee . . . that the army was at Gettysburg and had been engaged on this day (July 1) with the enemy's advance. I instantly . . . gave orders to the other brigades, with a view to reaching Gettysburg early the next day and started myself that night."[5]

The long march soon came to an end for Stuart's weary troopers. The van of his column reached Brinkerhoff Ridge, a piece of high ground just north of Gettysburg, on the evening of July 2. Finally having rejoined the army, Stuart rode off in search of General Lee. Wade Hampton's cavalry brigade brought up the rear, halting a mile to the south of Hunterstown "when orders came from General Stuart that it should move up, and take position on the left of our infantry," reported the South Carolina general. "Before this could be accomplished, I was notified that a heavy force of cavalry was advancing on Hunterstown, with a view to get in the rear of our army."[6]

That same day, Captain Crawford informed the local citizenry "that 'Jeb' Stuart's cavalry would soon pass through the town and all who desired to see them should come up to the square. The crowd gathered and the head of Stuart's command soon appeared." There is little doubt that Stuart's picturesque mounted

---

3 William S. Christian to his wife, June 28, 1863, in Henry Steele Commager, ed., *The Blue and the Gray: The Story of the Civil War as Told by Participants* (New York, 1950), 595.

4 Goldsborough, "The Hunterstown Fight."

5 OR 27, pt. 2, 697.

6 Ibid., 724.

men, four brigades strong, paraded through Hunterstown at their preening best and took their sweet time in passing.[7]

"After the Confederates had passed through the town, there was a great deal of activity manifested by the pickets." Custer's scouts soon picked up the scent. The trail left by Stuart's columns was undeniable. "About 4 or 5 o'clock, a picket came dashing into the town from the turnpike on the Hanover road and called out 'The Yankees are coming!'" The firing of the pickets was long past the point of being sporadic. The Rebels, under Crawford, marshaled in the town square.[8]

As Beautiful a Piece of Ground for Killing

On that same 1st of July agony clouded Judson Kilpatrick's mind. His kidneys were killing him after his "heroic" ride of the previous day. Ignobly his pain prevented him from mounting, much less sitting on a horse, and he ended up trundling along in one of the division's ambulances. Likewise, his command basically took the day off from the rigors of the war. Although scouting parties maintained contact with Stuart's strung out, exhausted columns, they reported that the Confederates were in no mood for a fight. Altogether the 3rd Cavalry Division marched a little under 20 miles before going into camp in the vicinity of East Berlin. From there Kilpatrick contacted Cavalry Corps headquarters and apprised Pleasonton of the division's encounter with Stuart.

Content with the knowledge that he had Stuart to his front and the Army of the Potomac to his rear, Kilpatrick considered his job finished. Misled by erroneous reports of a strong enemy infantry force approaching from the north, he informed Pleasonton, "I made no further attempts to intercept Stuart's command. . . . I have gone into camp at Hanover. My command will be in readiness to move again at daylight to-morrow morning. We have plenty of forage, the men are in good spirits, and we don't fear Stuart's whole cavalry." Worried that Kilpatrick did not understand the big picture, Pleasonton dispatched his chief of staff, Lt. Col. Andrew J. Alexander, to establish communications with Kilpatrick. Alexander also carried orders for Kilpatrick to rejoin the army in the vicinity of Gettysburg as soon

---

7   William C. Storrick, "William C. Storrick Provides Interesting History of Cavalry Battle at Hunterstown and Suggests Erection of Suitable Marker."

8   Goldsborough, "The Hunterstown Fight."

as possible. Stubbornly committed to his own plan, however, Kilpatrick remained in Hanover until the following day.[9]

The march of Kilpatrick's column on the 2nd of July lacked energy; the men and the horses simply worn-out. A back country road helped guide the lethargic division to the Baltimore Pike, which the long column followed south to the York Pike. Farnsworth's brigade led the way as the command turned westward to New Oxford before swinging north to Hunterstown and beyond. A courier from cavalry headquarters finally located Kilpatrick with orders to retrace his march up the York Pike to near Abbotstown. From that position, he could protect the army's right flank and rear simultaneously. Kilpatrick promptly turned his column around and moved on, with Custer's brigade now its lead element. The 6th Michigan led the advance and soon made contact with enemy pickets. "A moment later cavalry came dashing at full speed into the town, firing as they came at the fleeing pickets with their carbines," wrote reporter C. E. Goldsborough. "Crawford's men retreated up over the hills to the west."[10]

The regiment continued through the town and emerged into the clearing beyond. The majestic fields of the J. Felty farm to the west and the J. G. Gilbert farm to the south came into view. From the crest of Felty-Tate Ridge the ground sloped gradually into a cultivated valley. Just as the land began to rise on the far side, a tree line extended off to the right of the Gettysburg-Hunterstown road, which ran straight as an arrow until it approached the end of the tree line, then made a gradual turn to the right and was lost to sight behind the woods. Sturdy wooden fences flanked the road on both sides. It was impossible to tell what lay behind that cover, unlike the Union boys riding in plain sight. "The advance encountered a heavy force of Confederate cavalry," Kidd recorded. "A mounted line was formed across the road, while there were dismounted skirmishers behind the fences on either side." Custer reported to Kilpatrick that the "woods [were] swarming with rebels."[11]

Both sides deployed just one mile apart. "It began with Custer ordering elements of the 6th and 7th Michigan cavalry regiments to dismount and move south on foot beyond and below the ridge along both sides of the Hunterstown Road," reported the *Gettysburg-Adams Newsletter*. The Michiganders moved through the light cover provided by the tall golden wheat. Marksmen slid unseen into

---

9   OR 27, pt. 1, 987.

10   Goldsborough, "The Hunterstown Fight."

11   Wittenberg, *One of Custer's Wolverines*, 47; Goldsborough, "The Hunterstown Fight."

Though no one ever questioned his courage, his cavalier attitude to the lives of the men under his command soon earned him the sobriquet "Kil-cavalry."

Library of Congress

hidden positions, their view of the killing field unobstructed. In the middle of the line stood an "enormous Pennsylvania bank barn west of the road." Lieutenant Pennington's Battery M of the 2nd U.S. Artillery rumbled up behind it for cover and unlimbered its pieces, the barrels of the guns barely poking over the crest of

Felty-Tate Ridge. The 7th Michigan dismounted on the other side of the road and moved surreptitiously into the wheat.[12]

The Confederates saw it as just another rearguard action, protecting Stuart's move to Brinkerhoff Ridge. It suited them not to fight; they held their line and dared the Yankees to attack. At the first crackle of gunfire Custer spurred back to the road and ordered Capt. Henry Thompson to charge the enemy to his front. "All was ready, and Thompson was preparing to charge," recorded Frederick Whittaker, "when to everyone's surprise, the boy general flashed out his long Toledo blade, motioned to his staff to keep back, and dashed out in front of Co. A with the careless laughing remark, 'I'll lead you this time, boys. Come on!'" With Whittaker one never knows whether the events occurred exactly as narrated, but in this case Custer indeed led Company A down that road.[13]

"Away he went at a gallop. . . . The men raised a short yell of delight and followed him. Down the road in a perfect cloud of blinding dust went the boy general, in front of that single company." Custer, Thompson, and the men of Company A crashed into the rear guard of Cobb's Legion. In the confined space of the narrow roadway, hemmed in on both sides by rail fences, the combatants squared off in a hand-to-hand melee.[14]

"I was in the front and came near being killed," remembered Confederate H. E. Jackson, astonished at his survival. "General P. M. B. Young came flying down the pike, hat in hand, with your men in close pursuit, firing at him constantly. He ordered a charge, and the two lines rushed at each other and had a hand-to-hand conflict." Horses reared while men cursed and shouted. Sabers clanged as cap and ball revolvers crackled continuously. Men hacked or shot each other from their saddles, and slowly the Confederates began to give way. Then from around a bend in the road more of Hampton's troopers joined the fray.[15]

Allen Rice of the 6th Michigan left a vivid account of the July 2 action at Hunterstown. "We went down through a wheat field in front of the battery towards a barn," he wrote to a friend. "We had nearly reached the barn before our men came up the road as tight as they could have come and the Rebs mixed all in with them, cutting and slashing and firing their pistols at our men's heads." Company C

---

12 Troy Harman, "Hunterstown: North Cavalry Field of the Battle of Gettysburg," *Preserve, The Gettysburg-Adams County Newsletter* (Winter 2006), Vol. 30, No. 2, 3-4.

13 Whittaker, *A Popular Life*, 173.

14 Ibid.

15 H. E. Jackson, "Battle of Hunterstown," *Confederate Veteran* (September 1899), 415.

of the 6th Michigan rushed dismounted into the line to support the battery, "and had scarcely got into position when the Rebels made a desperate attempt to drive us back and capture our Battery," wrote Pvt. William Baird. The bold Rebels rode right up to and over the smoking barrels of the battery. "Everyone that reached the guns was hewn down with the saber or shot to death with Revolvers." Baird admired the tenacity of his enemies. "The Rebels made a desperate effort to carry this point."[16]

Back on the road, it was too late to disengage from the now superior Rebel force. Custer and his stalwarts "were received with a rattling fire of carbines, more efficacious than common, and the next moment down went the general, horse and all, in the road, the animal shot stone dead." A Confederate trooper spotted Custer struggling to escape from under the dead horse, raised his saber, and charged at the dazed general. Just in the nick of time Pvt. Norvill F. Churchill, one of Custer's orderlies, aimed his revolver and fired, blasting the luckless Rebel from his horse. Reaching down, Churchill grabbed Custer's arm and hauled him onto the back of his saddle. Churchill yanked his horse around and retreated down the road up which the Yankees had advanced just minutes earlier.[17]

Thompson's men frantically sought to disengage from the overwhelming force of gray-clad horsemen. "Custer came back . . . with about as many rebs mixed up with them as there was members of Company A," remembered Pvt. Nathan H. Green of Company D, 6th Michigan Cavalry, "all cutting and slashing as best they knew how." Even then, Custer was not fully out of danger. "Our old general came near having his head off," was how orderly Allen Rice described the close-call, "for there was a Reb right behind him with his saber raised to cut him down when one of the men that in the wheat field drawed a bead on him and that was the last of mr Reb."[18]

"In the valley between," one witness grimly watched as the "fierce hand-to-hand fight ensued across the J.G. Gilbert and J. Felty Farms. . . . So caught up in the chase were the Georgians that they fell like a hungry mouse right into the trap, which was released on them as soon as the Union troops cleared the waiting crossfire." Rebel trooper H. E. Jackson found himself the sole survivor of that deadly vortex of Yankee fire. "Pretty soon your men whirled and retreated, and for several paces, the blue and gray were mixed up, knocking, cutting and shooting

---

16 Allen Rice, "Eyewitness to War: Letter by Allen Rice, 6th Michigan Cavalry," 29.

17 Whittaker, *A Popular Life of Gen. George A. Custer*, 173.

18 Wittenberg and Petruzzi, *Plenty of Blame to Go Around*, 173; Rice, "Eyewitness to War."

each other," he recounted. "Finally we ran into your dismounted men, who were on both sides of the road, and into a large barn on the left. Every door and window was a blaze of fire, and every man who was with me fell."[19]

"I threw the Phillips Legion and the Second South Carolina as supporting forces on each flank of the enemy," wrote Wade Hampton in his after-action report. "The charge was most gallantly made, and the enemy were driven back in confusion to the support of his sharpshooters and artillery, both of which opened on me heavily." That was as far as the Confederates got.[20]

"The dismounted men on the right of the road," reported Kidd, "kept up such a fusillade with their Spencer carbines, aided by the rapid discharges from Pennington's battery, that he was driven back in great confusion." From the left side of the roadway the dismounted 7th Michigan poured fire into the exposed enemy flank. In the swirling cloud of dust, smoke, and fire it was impossible to distinguish friend from foe. "There was a company behind us and they fired on us from one direction and it was a great wonder we was not all killed," orderly Rice asserted vehemently in a letter home, "for the Rebels were firing on us from one direction and our men from the other and I tell you the shots came in on us like hail stones." One trooper fell, struck down by fire from his own men, "but by good luck there was no one else hurt."[21]

Finally, Hampton rounded up some guns, brought them forward, and a furious artillery duel commenced. "The shot and shell would come crashing along," attested Sgt. James H. Avery, "tearing up the earth, or demolishing a tree or building." One shell burst in the midst of Pennington's battery, disabling a gun and killing four horses. But Pennington gave as good as he got, killing one Confederate gunner and wounding 15 others. "The roar of guns ceased with darkness," recalled Avery, "and the guards were placed on the line to keep watch in the still hours of the night."[22]

Bodies littered the field, bathed luridly in the light of the moon. Those troopers who escaped sentry duty rolled themselves to sleep on the ground, without shelter,

---

19 Harman, "Hunterstown," 4; Jackson, "Battle of Hunterstown," 415.

20 *OR* 27, pt. 2, 724.

21 Wittenberg, *One of Custer's Wolverines*, 47. Kidd is incorrect in his statement as the Michiganders were not yet equipped with Spencer carbines, but rather the Spencer rifle, and only the 5th and 6th Michigan had them. Rice, "Eyewitness to War."

22 Eric J. Wittenberg, ed., *Under Custer's Command: The Civil War Journal of James Henry Avery* (Washington, DC, 2000), 34.

keeping their weapons close at hand. The night of July 2-3 passed peacefully, though quickly, for the men, "[m]any of whom were to awake for the last time on earth in the early dawn." The attacking Confederates had suffered heavily, and one Southerner reported that his regiment had lost six officers in the charge.[23]

In later years, some historians concluded that Custer had set up an elaborate ambush using Company A—and his own person—as the bait to draw the Rebel horsemen into the trap. "Custer had arranged the perfect trap, but how to lure Confederate cavalrymen into it required another step," read one report. "Custer used Co. A as a small shock force to establish contact with the southern troopers. After hitting them hard to get up their ire, he retreated intentionally drawing them back north to the prepared ambush waiting east and west of the Hunterstown Road at Felty's barn."[24]

This analysis may give Custer too much credit. It is fair to say that he did a good job deploying his horsemen and his artillery to take every advantage of the features of the landscape. As usually, he demonstrated his personal courage by leading the charge down the road, so "tightly flanked on both sides of the road with post and rail fences, it was impossible for more than one company to move at a gallop."[25]

Later in life, in one of his "I-told-you-so" moments, Pleasonton stated that he had pointed out this flaw to Custer on several occasions, but his young protégé never changed his ways. For, above all else, Custer was a new brigadier, cloaked with the invincibility of youth and trying to establish a legacy, not just for himself, but for the Michigan Cavalry Brigade. "Custer lost his life in not doing what I told him to do," Pleasonton reproached his former aide. He had urged Custer to keep his traditional place in the line; let the troopers fight the fight. "Don't be so anxious to fight yourself—fight your command." Without any real authority to back his claim, Pleasonton told his interviewer, "That is what he did with the Indians. He was so anxious to fight himself that he lost his command and got killed."[26]

23 Ibid.

24 Harman, "Hunterstown," 4.

25 Ibid.

26 Styple, *Generals in Bronze*, 120.

He is a Ray of Sunshine

Stuart finally reported to Lee on the afternoon of July 2, following his eight-day absence. If he had harbored any thoughts of repeating his glorious ride around McClellan's army during the Peninsula campaign, they were dashed when he met Lee on Seminary Ridge. Frostily, Lee reprimanded Stuart. "Well General Stuart, you are here at last." In addition to Lee and Stuart, only two other officers were privy to the facts of the meeting: Col. Charles Marshall, Lee's military secretary, and Maj. Andrew R. Venable of Stuart's staff, neither of whom ever divulged what transpired during that meeting.

Stunned by Lee's chastisement, Stuart now moved his exhausted command to cover Ewell's left flank, where it recuperated and refitted. Despite the controversies that would swirl around Stuart's ride to Gettysburg, it is to Lee's credit that his "confidence in General Stuart was unlimited, and his admiration for him deservedly great." Stuart, nonetheless, felt duty bound to atone for Lee's perceived failure of Stuart's foray into enemy territory.[27]

Typical of a freewheeling cavalryman, Stuart could not resist the urge to scope out any opportunity for future operations. On the assumption or knowledge that Lee would continue to hammer at the Union defenses on Cemetery Ridge, he sought a position from which he could not only cover Ewell's left flank, but which would also provide a chance for redemption. Stuart marched his semi-rested command several miles along the pike running from Gettysburg to York to high ground known as Cress Ridge. Though unaware of Lee's future tactical decisions, Stuart remained optimistic of his chances. His aim, recounted H. B. McClellan, was "if opportunity offered, to make a diversion which might aid the Confederate infantry to carry the heights held by the Federal army."

From this commanding ground, Stuart realized he could completely control "a wide plain of cultivated fields stretching towards Hanover on the left, and reaching to the base of the mountain spurs among which the enemy held position." The salient feature was a large wooden barn on the Rummel farm. Turning onto a forested country lane, Stuart moved his troopers ahead, setting the stage for the battle that was to come on East Cavalry Field.[28]

The strength of Stuart's command has been the subject of considerable debate. On the afternoon of July 2 it was aggregated into four brigades under Brig. Gens.

---

27 Freeman, *Lee's Lieutenants*, 3:139; Wittenberg and Petruzzi, *Plenty of Blame to Go Around*, 201.

28 McClellan, *Life and Campaigns*, 337.

Fitz Lee, Wade Hampton, Albert G. Jenkins (led by Lt. Col. Vincent Witcher), and Col. John Chambliss. Two batteries of horse artillery moved with the column while two others remained in Gettysburg to replenish their ammunition. Cavalry historian and Gettysburg expert J. David Petruzzi claims Stuart's force numbered 6,109 men. Petruzzi's fellow historian and occasional co-author, Eric J. Wittenberg, however, maintains Stuart rode into battle with a combined force numbering 4,800. The latter figure is roughly supported by Jeffry Wert, who avers that Stuart had just over 5,000 men. Whatever the actual number, it was "the main strength and flower of the Confederate cavalry, led by its most distinguished commanders."[29]

Meanwhile, at the Union cavalry's headquarters, a series of blunders, miscommunications, and miscues—symptomatic of the haphazard way Pleasonton ran his staff operations—were coming together in a manner that would dictate the course of events that unfolded on both East Cavalry Field and South Cavalry Field during the battle's third day. It all began, simply enough, with the withdrawal of Buford's cavalry from its position on the Army of the Potomac's left flank on July 2. Buford's two brigades, commanded by Cols. William Gamble and Thomas Devin, had thrown out a line of outposts to cover Maj. Gen. Daniel E. Sickles' III Corps, and their videttes covered the road from Emmitsburg. "What, then, was the surprise of Sickles," recounted one eyewitness, "to see of a sudden all the cavalry withdrawn, leaving his flank entirely exposed?" Sickles's strident complaints went directly to Meade, who, somewhat surprised, replied that it had not been his intent to withdraw all of the cavalry, and that he would rectify the situation immediately. Buford's troopers never did return to their positions covering Sickles.[30]

Appalled at the lack of cavalry on Sickles's left flank, Meade fired off a communiqué to Pleasonton. "The major-general commanding," wrote Meade's chief of staff, Daniel Butterfield, just after noon on July 2, "directs me to say that he has not authorized the entire withdrawal of Buford's force from the direction of Emmitsburg and did not so understand when he gave the permission to Buford to

---

29   J. David Petruzzi and Steven A. Stanley, *The Gettysburg Campaign in Numbers and Losses: Synopses, Orders of Battle, Strengths, Casualties, and Maps, June 9-July 14, 1863* (El Dorado Hills, CA, 2012), 150-151; Eric J. Wittenberg, *Protecting the Flank: The Battles of Brinkerhoff's Ridge and East Cavalry Field, Battle of Gettysburg, July 3, 1863* (El Dorado Hills, CA, 2013), 55, 164; Jeffry Wert, *Gettysburg: Day Three* (New York, NY, 2001), 260; William Brooke Rawle, "The Cavalry Fight on the Right Flank at Gettysburg," *The History of the Third Pennsylvania Cavalry* (Philadelphia, 1905), 302.

30 *OR* 27, pt. 1, 131.

go to Westminster, that the patrols and pickets upon the Emmitsburg road must be kept on as long as our troops are in position." In a follow-up note, Meade again stressed the necessity "that a force should be sent to replace it, picketing and patrolling the Emmitsburg road. He understood that all your force was up."[31]

Surprised by Meade's vehemence, Pleasonton put together a sketchy plan to remedy the situation. About 1:45 p.m. on July 2, he ordered General Gregg to detach a regiment of his 2nd Division "to picket the left of our line." His orders the previous day to Gregg lacked the usual civility in tone for which military correspondence is famous. "General: Major-General Meade is disappointed in the movement of your division to Westminster," began Pleasonton without any preamble. "Your instructions required two brigades and a battery to move by Carters to Westminster. No report has been received from you whether they did or not. Please state what routes you took in the march to Westminster, and for what reasons, that a reply can be made to the major-general commanding the army." Pleasonton was beginning to get a bit jittery.[32]

This was a high-handed manner in which to treat the likes of David Gregg, and it displayed a rudeness that had never been present in their relationship. When Meade realized that Pleasonton was proposing to send a single regiment to perform the duties that had been attended to by two brigades, he exploded. Summoning Pleasonton to his headquarters, Meade verbally chastised Pleasonton for his obstinacy. "At least one of the trips he had seen Pleasonton make in and out of army headquarters had as its purpose to deal with a major tactical blunder," recorded one onlooker. Pleasonton's relationship with Meade was beginning to unravel.[33]

After this latest tongue lashing, the rattled Cavalry Corps commander ordered Kilpatrick's division to "move to the left of our line and attack the enemy's right and rear with [your] whole command and the Regular Brigade." But Meade had used the occasion for more than one purpose. He also made known to Pleasonton his concerns over the position of the cavalry on the army's right flank. "The general commanding is fearful of the enemy obtaining possession of the ridge on the Baltimore turnpike . . . which is the right of General Slocum's position, and wishes you to place a force of cavalry and battery, to hold that position, to the right of the

31 Ibid., pt. 3, 490.

32 Ibid., 469;

33 Petruzzi, *Alfred Pleasonton's Civil War*, 29.

Brigadier General McMurtrie Gregg was one of the most experienced division commanders of the Army of the Potomac's Cavalry Corps. He is credited with ordering Custer to remain on East Cavalry Field despite direct orders from Kilpatrick to move Custer's brigade to the southern side of the field.

Library of Congress

road facing Gettysburg. This point is so important that it must be held at all hazards."[34]

Only hours earlier Pleasonton had been busy plotting reconnaissance patrols and demonstrating a rare and even aggressive attitude. "You will, therefore, hold your force at Hanover Junction," he had commanded Gregg then, "keeping up communication with our infantry at Hanover, and send out a small force to scout toward York and Carlisle as well as Berlin, to get the earliest information of the enemy. . . . Let your reports be sent in quickly, if you have to employ horses of the country to do it." But now, mere hours later, his latest missive to Gregg underscored his fall from grace, as it was evident that Pleasonton had been relegated to merely passing on Meade's concerns to Gregg. He dictated an insipid note, copies of which he sent to the three division commanders and Merritt, each starting with "the major-general commanding directs me to order you to fall back," and ending, as if tutoring recalcitrant children, "The cavalry will dispute every inch of the ground." In effect, Pleasonton had lost tactical control of his cavalry because of his own ineptitude.[35]

Gregg, who was not docile like Pleasonton, disagreed vehemently with Meade on the importance of a position so close to the Union infantry. On July 1, he had been in a wicked fight with the 2nd Virginia Infantry of the "Stonewall" Brigade on the road to Hanover, to the east of Gettysburg, where it climbed to the crest of Brinkerhoff Ridge. Control of the stone wall along the ridgeline had gone back and forth, but Gregg's troopers finally prevailed. As darkness overtook the field, squadrons from the 10th New York and 3rd Pennsylvania held the battleground. He assessed the enemy's intentions and concluded that the Confederates would continue their attempts to gain entry to the Union rear on July 3. Pleasonton, his relationship with Meade rapidly cooling, was in no position to override his commander's wishes; all he could do was reaffirm Gregg's instructions to position himself closer to the infantry lines around the Baltimore Pike. "I then requested the aide-de-camp to return to General Pleasonton," wrote Gregg, committing to paper his most adamant disapproval, and "[s]tate to him that I regarded the situation on the right of our army as exceedingly perilous." With its vital crossroads in the rear of the army, the area needed to be covered "by a sufficient force of cavalry." If not,

34   OR 27, pt. 1, 992; Ibid., pt. 3, 502.

35   Ibid., 469, 470.

Gregg despaired, "it would be to invite an attack upon our rear with possible disastrous results."[36]

It was a decision that seriously upset Gregg's naturally gruff disposition. He had spent most of the morning of July 2 arguing that it would be more advantageous to protect the army's flank from a position at the Hanover-Low Dutch Road intersection. Gregg decided to disobey his orders. He solidified his connection to the infantry with Irvin Gregg's brigade, then moved out of his positions on the Baltimore Pike with the balance of his division. Colonel John B. McIntosh's 3rd Brigade took the lead toward the Hanover Road, en route to the Low Dutch Road. Pleasonton realized that the only way to placate Gregg was to promise him the use of one of Kilpatrick's brigades. Unbeknownst to General Kilpatrick, Pleasonton had approved the temporary transfer of one of the 3rd Division's brigades to Gregg's division. One of Gregg's staff officers was dispatched immediately to the last known location of the 3rd Division. On his arrival, the officer found that Kilpatrick, with Farnsworth's entire brigade, had already departed around 8:00 a.m. for the southern end of the Union lines. Only the brigade of Brig. Gen. George Custer remained.

Custer Deploys the Michigan Cavalry Brigade

Kilpatrick's division left Hunterstown just before midnight on July 2. Custer's Michigan Cavalry Brigade took the lead, cutting cross-country past the York Pike and the Hanover Road, before reaching Two Taverns, well in the rear of the Union army. By that time, the men and horses were beyond fatigued. "I also remember well that weary night march, which lasted until the first streaks of dawn had begun to appear in the east," recounted Kidd. The spent command, having been in constant motion day and night since June 29, dropped on the spot. "Never were the experiences of a single night less calculated to prepare soldiers for the tremendous duties of the succeeding day," opined Kidd. Yet, on the morning of July 3, they were "ready and willing to do their part in the great conflict that was impending."[37]

Majors Luther S. Trowbridge and Noah Ferry of the 5th Michigan Cavalry shared their thin blankets, curled up on the ground, and were lulled to sleep by the

---

36 Eric J. Wittenberg, *Protecting the Flank*, 48.

37 Eric J. Wittenberg, ed., *At Custer's Side: The Civil War Writings of James Harvey Kidd* (Kent, OH, 2001), Kindle edition; Wittenberg, *One of Custer's Wolverines*, 48.

booming of artillery. So used to the sound were they that they didn't awaken until General Kilpatrick himself roamed through their camp around 7:00 a.m. "Come on boys turn out, turn out," he called out in "a sharp but pleasant voice. . . . 'We are all going in today and we are going to clean 'em out! I couldn't find Custer so thought I'd just turn you out myself.'" Kilpatrick's prodding was rather unnecessary, for by then a steady roll of artillery fire, and the annoying ebb and flow of crackling musketry had the Michiganders out of their bedrolls; the noise "brought every man to his feet, to mechanically buckle on his arms, for the fray. Nor had we long to await orders . . . and soon all were ready, the last thoughts of home indulged and stern reality before us." Thus, Custer's command was ready to go next, and just waiting to hear that Farnsworth had cleared the road, whereupon the van of the Michigan Cavalry Brigade would swing onto the road and follow in the tracks of its sister brigade. In fact, this had already happened, for according to Custer, "My column was formed and moved out on the road designated."[38]

At that moment, recalled Custer, "a staff officer of Brigadier-General Gregg, commanding 2nd division ordered me to take my command and place it in position on the pike leading from York [Hanover] to Gettysburg, which position formed the extreme right of our line of battle on that day." Luther Trowbridge thought this was a brilliant move. "With the instinct of the true soldier, anticipating serious trouble on that flank from Stuart's cavalry. . . . Sagacious soldier! Most fortunate order!" applauded Trowbridge, for "on that flank, this day, is to be made a desperate attempt to turn Meade's flank, which, if successful, may work dreadful mischief for the Army of the Potomac." Instead of going left on the Baltimore Pike and following Farnsworth, Custer turned the Michigan Brigade to the right and cut cross-country to the designated position.[39]

Just as at Hanover, Custer's actions during the cavalry battle at Rummel's farm have been misinterpreted. For many, the crux of the matter rested with Gregg's decision to keep Custer's brigade on the firing line in the army's rear. This directly countermanded Kilpatrick's orders for Custer to move his brigade south. Many participants, as well as future generations of historians, downplayed Custer's role and heap the credit and glory onto Gregg's shoulders. Many would like to believe

---

38 Luther S. Trowbridge to John B. Bachelder, March 5, 1886, in David Ladd and Audrey Ladd, eds., *The Bachelder Papers* (Dayton, OH, 1994), 2:1219; Wittenberg, *Under Custer's Command*, 34-35; Robertson, *Michigan in the War*, 582.

39 Robertson, *Michigan in the War*, 582; Luther S. Trowbridge, "The Operations of the Cavalry in the Gettysburg Campaign," *The Michigan Commandery, Military Order of the Loyal Legion of the United States* (Dearborn, MI, 1888), 9-10.

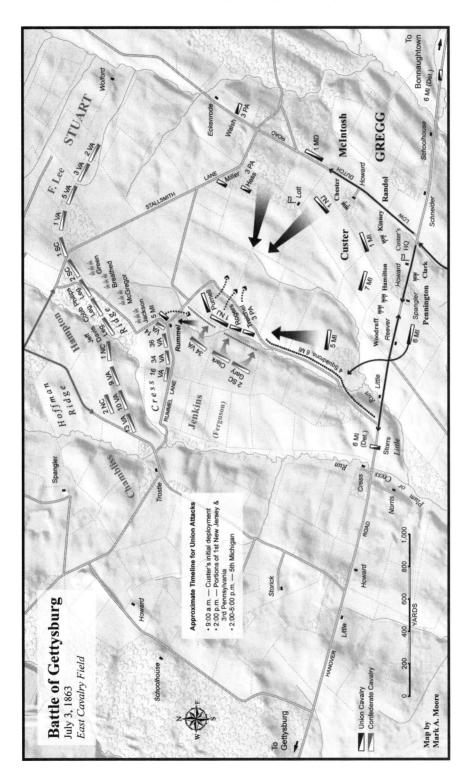

Battle of Gettysburg
July 3, 1863
East Cavalry Field

Approximate Timeline for Union Attacks
• 9:00 a.m. — Custer's initial deployment
• 2:00 p.m. — Portions of 1st New Jersey & 3rd Pennsylvania
• 2:00–5:00 p.m. — 5th Michigan

Union Cavalry
Confederate Cavalry

Map by
Mark A. Moore

that Custer's contribution to the victory was his reckless charge at the head of the 1st Michigan Cavalry troopers, when they launched themselves into the heart of the Confederate cavalry and brought it to a standstill. That is the story that has been promulgated for over 150 years. This interpretation unfairly slights Custer and demeans the sacrifices made by his men. To truly understand how the battle developed, it is necessary to go back to 7:00 a.m. on July 3 and Kilpatrick's peremptory awakening of the exhausted Michigan Brigade.

Custer, accompanying the 6th Michigan Cavalry and Pennington's Battery M, reached the intersection of the Low Dutch Road and the Hanover (York) Road well ahead of Gregg's command. The alacrity of Custer's movement to the spot designated by Gregg's staff officer surprised the 2nd Division's commanding officer. Gregg's specific orders were to protect the infantry's right flank with his mounted division. Gregg's intuition concerning the enemy's movements was about to be confirmed, however, for Union infantry from Maj. Gen. Oliver Otis Howard's XI Corps, observing from atop Cemetery Hill, spotted enemy troops on the north side of the Union battle line. Though only glimpses of Rebels could be seen through the trees, the roiling clouds of dust above the treetops were enough to indicate that a major movement of cavalry was in the works. Gregg had already begun sliding his brigades toward the Hanover Road.[40]

Custer's reported on the deployment of his brigade, a movement that began shortly after eight that morning and was over by 9:30 a.m. Informed speculation fills in some of the gaps. For instance, we can place the arrival of the van of Custer's column at the Hanover-Low Dutch Road intersection at no later than 9:00 a.m. The distance from Two Taverns, where the brigade had slept, to the intersection of the Hanover-Low Dutch Roads, is less than three cross-country miles—an inconsequential distance for a disciplined marching column of cavalry. Custer's obedience to Gregg's order required nothing more than reversing the march of the column. No indication of the order of march is provided, but we can safely assume the 6th Michigan, followed by Battery M, led the advance. It follows that the 5th Michigan was next in column, as these two regiments had begun forming a tight association based on their possession of the Spencer rifles. The 7th Michigan was next in line, and the 1st Michigan brought up the rear.

---

40 Colonel Gregg's brigade maintained contact with the Rebel infantry and would miss the battle at Rummel's farm. At the crucial moment in the attack on Culp's Hill, Gregg's troopers became hotly engaged with the enemy's infantry and were credited with preventing a brigade of Rebel infantry from participating in the assault.

Custer made his headquarters at the home of George Howard, conveniently located at the intersection of the two roads. The position offered an unparalleled view of the glories of Pennsylvania's agricultural abundance, including thick and high golden wheat. Brinkerhoff Ridge, a mile and a half to the southwest, loomed over the field. "Upon arriving at the point designated, I immediately placed my command in a position facing toward Gettysburg," reported Custer of his deployment of the 6th Michigan. This was the squadron of Maj. Charles E. Storrs, recalled Captain Kidd, which "was sent out to the left and front of Custer's position, soon after the brigade arrived upon the ground. He remained there several hours and was recalled about noon . . . to take position with the troops on the left of the battery." Storr's squadron took up a position bordering the eastern bank of Cress Run. "At the same time," reported Custer, "I caused reconnaissances to be made on my front, right and rear, but failed to find any considerable force of the enemy."[41]

Like two tendrils, detachments of the 6th Michigan, under the command of Maj. Peter Weber, had worked their way up on opposite sides of the battlefield. On the right side, a detachment of 50 men moved up the Low Dutch Road, struck off down a small country lane, and concealed themselves in the woods near the Lott farm barn. From their position they had a nearly unobstructed view of the vast cultivated fields to the west. The other side of the field was defined by two trickles of water, Little Run and Cress Run, their positions marked by the thin lines of trees along their banks. Just to the north, Cress Ridge began its ascent, shielding secrets Custer as yet knew nothing about. The area remained quiet for several hours, though exactly how long remains an open question.

The Rebel cavalry had managed to maneuver into position on Custer's right flank, where the wooded promontory of Cress Ridge afforded them excellent concealment. Albert Jenkins's brigade, under Lt. Col. Vincent Witcher, led Stuart's march. Stuart was anything but satisfied with the outfit. "My command was increased by the addition of Jenkins' brigade," he later reported, "who here in the presence of the enemy allowed themselves to be supplied with but 10 rounds of ammunition, although armed with the most approved Enfield musket." After Jenkins came Chambliss's veteran brigade, followed by the two batteries of Capts. William H. Griffin and Thomas E. Jackson, and then Hampton with a section of guns from Green's Louisiana Battery. Fitzhugh Lee's brigade brought up the rear of the column. Stuart intended to move Jenkins and Chambliss "secretly through

---

41 Robertson, *Michigan in the War*, 582; Kidd, *Personal Recollections*, 142.

the woods to a position, and hoped to effect a surprise upon the enemy's rear." The commanding high ground of Cress Ridge afforded Stuart a bird's-eye view of the "wide plain of cultivated fields stretching to Hanover, on the left, and reaching to the base of the mountain spurs, among which the enemy held position."[42]

The 5th Michigan's Major Trowbridge insisted Custer was aware of Stuart's movement. Custer "had sent out scouting parties which gave him timely notice of the approach of the enemy." Stuart, however, had no idea there were any Union forces in the immediate vicinity. "There was nothing apparently to oppose his [Stuart's] march," concluded Trowbridge, "Not a man . . . was to be seen through all those beautiful fields. In fact, Custer had already positioned his command (in accordance with General Gregg's orders) on the Hanover-to-Gettysburg road. At this early hour Custer was the senior officer present on the field and conscious of the gravity posed by the threat of Stuart's force moving into the rear of the Union army. He determined to hold his position until the arrival of reenforcements from Gregg's division—a flagrant disregard of Kilpatrick's orders to move south.

For many decades, historians and students of the war have believed it was Gregg who set the tone for the battle of East Cavalry Field. In fact, Custer— through his aggressive actions before Gregg's arrival—was the true instigator of the success about to enjoyed by the Union cavalry. The two like-minded generals— years apart in age and experience—essentially disobeyed orders and kept their respective commands exactly where they were most needed at the moment Fitz Lee and Wade Hampton were moving in their direction.[43]

In his official report, Custer observed that "[e]verything remained quiet until 10 a.m., when the enemy appeared on my right and opened upon me with a battery of six guns." This short simple sentence is but the first in a series of confusing, and often contradictory, accounts. Custer's reference to 10:00 a.m. as the time when serious action commenced on this part of the Rebel cavalry raises questions.[44]

If Gregg received the warning around noon that Confederate cavalry was on the move, then the first sighting of the enemy had to have been was close to 10:00

42 OR 27, pt. 2, 697.

43 Trowbridge, "The Operations of the Cavalry in the Gettysburg Campaign," 10-11.

44 Robertson, *Michigan in the War*, 582. Many years later, James Kidd latter suggested the possibility that the time was the result of a simple typographical error. "A possible solution of this difficulty has come to my mind," ruminated Kidd. "It is this. That Custer originally wrote '1 o'clock' and that in copying the '1' and '0' were mistaken for 10 and o'clock added." Kidd, *Personal Recollections*, 142. Custer never retracted or corrected the time issue, and Kidd's explanation was more of a sop to his comrades of the 2nd Division than anything else.

a.m. If Howard's initial report was true, and if the report followed the established protocol, it probably made its way to the commanding general's headquarters, which would probably pass it on to cavalry headquarters as the proper arm to initiate any action. The distance from Howard's position on the northwest corner of the Union line to Pleasonton's headquarters was but one mile, but the distance was strewn with the detritus of war, confusion, and the always-recalcitrant staff officers with which couriers were forced to deal. A messenger from Pleasonton's headquarters faced a three-and-a-half-mile trip—more if he had to skirt scouting Confederates—to reach Gregg. We know a courier had been dispatched from Howard directly to David Gregg. That route would have been shorter, but with the added danger of the proximity of Rebel infantry. If all this activity consumed, say, an hour and a half, the original sighting was perhaps 10:30 a.m.

Stuart's plan was to travel two and one-half miles along the York Pike before veering south onto a narrow country lane, which was sure to act as a bottleneck but would put Stuart's entire command behind the covering woods of the Stallsmith and Rummel farms. Scouts and advance parties were on the move early, prowling ahead on the path the column would take. They were good at what they did, using the forested lane and covering woods to stay hidden from prying Yankee cavalry.

The intrepid Major Weber had been scouting the Union front and flank since 9:30 a.m., his parties ranging far along Cress Ridge to where they could see the open country beyond. And they saw plenty. Later, sitting side by side on their horses, Weber would tell Kidd, "I have seen thousands of them over there. The country yonder is full of the enemy." It was about ten o'clock in the morning. Several testimonials backing this claim, principally those of Russell Alger, Luther Trowbridge, Peter Weber, and James Kidd. There is therefore little doubt that Custer, upon hearing Weber's report, redeployed his brigade to face the threat from the north and began offensive operations shortly afterward.[45]

"At 10 a.m. our brigade, being on the right of the army, the enemy's cavalry under General Stuart appeared in our front," verified Colonel Alger. "I was ordered to dismount my regiment and attack him, which I did, driving him back about a half a mile and into a thick wood." Each regiment was positioned on the field by Custer as they arrived to meet the new threat posed by "the enemy [that] appeared on my right and opened upon me with a battery of six guns." Custer left two guns and one regiment in position, facing toward Gettysburg. "I shifted the remaining portion of my command, forming a new line of battle at right angles to

45 Kidd, *Personal Recollections*, 146.

my former line," he reported. The remainder of the brigade was brought into position at right angles, to face the enemy near Rummel's farm. "I was enabled to make my dispositions with complete success," he announced. By the time Custer had finished his dispositions, a series of interconnected events was about to come together to impact the subsequent movements of the Union cavalry under General Gregg. Custer did not underestimate the value of Weber's intelligence. James Avery was with the 5th Michigan as it deployed into line on the right of Little Run. "Arriving at the point assigned to us, Colonel Alger dismounted the regiment to fight action front, and left," Avery recorded. "We deployed in a heavy line, then advanced toward a fence which ran along the edge of a wheat field, in front of a piece of timber. As we advanced through the wheat field, the rebs poured volleys into our lines."[46]

The Confederate artillery, from its spectacular positions on Cress Ridge, soon found the range of Custer's new line, "and were pouring solid shot and shell into my command with great accuracy." At that moment, two sections of Pennington's Battery M galloped up in a spray of dust and gravel, unlimbered, and quickly went into action. "I ordered them to silence the enemy's battery, which order, notwithstanding the superiority of the enemy's position, was successfully accomplished in a very short space of time," reported a satisfied Custer. "Pennington's return fire," wrote an admiring Kidd from his position protecting the guns, "was so fast and so accurate that Griffin was speedily silenced and compelled to leave the field." Taken in conjunction, Custer's movements are clear indicators that as early as 10:00 a.m., he—like General Gregg—had already determined that he was going to disobey the orders issued to him by his own division commander. Custer, declared Kidd, "was reluctant to leave his post— knew he ought not leave it. He had already been attacked by a fire from the artillery in position beyond the Rummel buildings."[47]

In quick succession, several important events took place. The first was the arrival of Kilpatrick's orders reiterating Custer's instructions to rejoin the division. "At 12 o'clock an order was transmitted to me from the Brigadier-General, commanding the division," Custer acknowledged, "[d]irecting me, upon being relieved by a brigade from the Second Division, to move with my command and form a junction with the First brigade on the extreme left." Gregg, too, received the same missive from Pleasonton and reluctantly ordered McIntosh's brigade to

---

46 Robertson, *Michigan in the War*, 578, 582-583; Wittenberg, *Under Custer's Command*, 35.

47 Robertson, *Michigan in the War*, 582; Kidd, *Personal Recollections*, 141, 144.

move toward Custer's positions. About this time, scouts sent Custer reports of the huge dust clouds being kicked up by an enemy cavalry column moving toward the Federal right flank. Colonel McIntosh had spurred ahead to Custer's position on the George Howard farmstead, northwest of the crossroads, and consulted with the young brigadier. Custer cheerfully warned McIntosh that "I think you will find the woods out there . . . full of them." McIntosh, a no-nonsense soldier described as "a born fighter, a strict disciplinarian, a dashing leader, and a polished gentleman," apparently did not want young Custer's assistance. He certainly did not appreciate Custer's wry sense of humor. Once McIntosh's brigade arrived, Custer was "prepared to execute the order" to move to the south.[48]

Around 10:00 a.m., McIntosh received orders to move his command to the position it had occupied the previous day. "Between 9 and 10 o'clock on the morning of the 3rd 'to horse' was sounded and we were again in the saddle," noted Capt. William Miller of the 3rd Pennsylvania. "Retracing our steps, we resumed our position on the right, but with a more extended line, while McIntosh moved to and halted at the crossing of the Low Dutch and Hanover roads." Custer's brigade was stationed to the right of the 3rd Pennsylvania, and slightly to its front. McIntosh's command went into camp for three hours. Finally, "after some delay McIntosh moved forward to relieve Custer, who had been ordered to report to his division commander (Kilpatrick) in the vicinity of Round Top."[49]

McIntosh's meeting with Custer had been perfunctory and cool. He seemed to indicate that he was eager to get Custer, who outranked him, out of his way. Custer's light-hearted warning about the Rebel concentrations in the woods was not taken seriously. Having been there the day before, and having "looked well over the ground," McIntosh was determined that "as soon as the Michigan Brigade had withdrawn from the field," he was going "to ascertain what force was in his

---

48 Robertson, *Michigan in the War*, 583; Wert, *Custer*, 92; Boatner, *Civil War Dictionary*, 533-534. Colonel John Baille McIntosh was commissioned a second lieutenant in the 2nd U.S. Cavalry in 1861, promoted to first lieutenant, and transferred to the 5th U.S. Cavalry—Custer's outfit. He fought at White Oak Swamp, South Mountain, and Antietam, was promoted to colonel of the 3rd Pennsylvania, and led it at Kelly's Ford and Chancellorsville. Later that year, he was severely hurt in a fall from his horse, and would be wounded in the leg (which would require its amputation) at the Battle of Third Winchester on September 19, 1864. McIntosh soldiered on in the Regular Army after the war and retired in 1870 with the rank of brigadier general.

49 William E. Miller, "The Cavalry Battle Near Gettysburg," in Johnson and Buel, eds., *Battles and Leaders*, 3:401. One of the maps accompanying Luther Trowbridge's article, "The Operations of the Cavalry in the Gettysburg Campaign," which was read before the Michigan Commandery on October 6, 1886, shows McIntosh's brigade of 1,400 saber arms deployed between the Baltimore Pike and the Hanover Road.

front without waiting to be attacked." He had no clue what was out there, and Custer, who apparently thought his cheery warning was enough, did not venture any further information. "At that time there was no picket firing," reported McIntosh, "Everything was perfectly quiet." Under these conditions, and after his men broke camp, McIntosh commenced the deployment of his brigade.[50]

Then it was just a matter of waiting for McIntosh's men to occupy the positions staked out by the Michiganders. As soon as McIntosh's brigade hove into sight, the jig would be up. The situation would escalate from insubordination to outright disobedience, for Custer was not going to withdraw and leave Gregg to fill that gaping hole of a line with two battered brigades. That was when the second providential occurrence took place. "Then there was a lull," remembered James Kidd. "I cannot say how long it lasted, but, during its continuance, General Gregg arrived and took command in person." Custer reported to Gregg immediately. "Before I had left my position, Brigadier-General Gregg, commanding the Second Division, arrived with his entire command," a much-relieved Custer later recorded. "Learning the true condition of affairs in my front, and rightly conjecturing that the enemy was making his dispositions for vigorously attacking our position Brigadier-General Gregg ordered me to remain in the position I then occupied." Of course, in Custer's report it all sounds so cut and dried. In reality, it was a moment of the highest drama.[51]

The weather had turned from hot to torrid. "All around the sun beat down at a fearful rate," wrote William Baird of the 6th Michigan, "and the heat of the surroundings was extremely hot. The Heartbeat was hot and strong the blood seemed to boil." Out on the left flank, Colonel Algers' troopers complained that "men and horses are suffering very much for water." The two generals met near where Custer had unlimbered his guns. Both men were probably exhausted, the strain of the situation particularly telling on the older soldier. Gregg was fully decked out in the frock coat of a brigadier general and sported a full beard; Custer was probably sweating profusely under his heavy velveteen battle jacket, and his lank golden curls framed his florid features. He informed Gregg that "I think you will find the woods out there full of [Confederates]."[52]

---

50 William Brooke Rawle, "The Right Flank at Gettysburg," in McClure, ed., *Annals of the Civil War*, 477; John B. Bachelder, "Stuart's and Gregg's Cavalry Engagement, July 3, 1863," in David L. Ladd and Audrey J. Ladd, eds., *The Gettysburg Magazine*, Vol. 16, 105.

51 Kidd, *Personal Recollections*, 144; Robertson, *Michigan in the War*, 583.

52 Baird, *Reminiscences*, 31; Wittenberg, *Protecting the Flank*, 52, 61-62.

For a moment, Gregg pondered his options. "The importance of successfully resisting an attack at this point, which, if succeeded in by the enemy, would have been productive of the most serious consequences, determined me to retain the brigade of the Third Division until the enemy were driven back." The decision was quick in coming, recounts historian Eric J. Wittenberg, whose impeccable primary sources record the exchange between the two. "Say you never got the message," Gregg reportedly told Custer. "I need you here." Both men were sticklers for military protocol. "I will only be too glad to stay, if you will give the order," Custer replied to Gregg. The order was given. Gregg later wrote that "General Custer, commanding the brigade, fully satisfied of the intended attack, was well pleased to remain with his brigade."[53]

The third factor in the equation was the enemy. As Stuart had feared, the loss of surprise had cost him dearly, for the Federals responded with the "corresponding movement of a large force of [their] cavalry." As he attempted to improvise, fate continued to give Stuart the back of the hand. Believing that Hampton and Lee were fully up, he summoned them to a point atop the ridgeline. Neither general made the meeting. There would be no opportunity for Stuart to point out the salient features as he saw them. Hampton claimed that he never received the message; Lee was heavily engaged and deemed it inappropriate to leave the field at that moment. The direction of the battle to follow would be in the hands of the Confederate brigade commanders on the field, and not in Stuart's, as he had lost the ability to influence the command decisions affecting the movement of his troops. Stuart's chief of staff Henry McClellan lamented that Hampton and Lee did not get to see what Stuart saw. "The roads leading from the rear of the Federal line of battle were under his eye and could be reached by the prolongation of the road by which he approached. Moreover, the open fields . . . admitted movement in any direction."[54]

Stuart's inability to communicate his vision of the coming battle to his brigade commanders was the first kink in his plans, and the choices open to his division began to dwindle dramatically. He later admitted that he "would have preferred a different method of attack, but I soon saw that entanglement by the force of circumstances narrated was unavoidable." This "force of circumstances" was the inexplicable, perhaps unintentional, appearance of Confederate cavalry to the front of the shielding woods. Stuart had taken every care to place Jenkins's and

---

53 OR 27, pt. 1, 956; Wittenberg, *Protecting the Flank*, 62.

54 OR 27, pt. 2, 697; Ladd and Ladd, "Stuart's and Gregg's Cavalry Engagement," 98.

Chambliss's brigades and some of his horse artillery on Cress Ridge, hidden from view on the ridge's heavily wooded front side; Hampton and Lee had taken up position to the left, a belt of woods screening their presence from the enemy outposts. The Confederate position stretched from the Rummel farm, "extending opposite the Federal front and a mile from it, and being screened by two patches of woods between Rummel's and Stallsmith's farms. . . . The ridge occupied by Stuart commanded a large area of cultivated fields." It was a shock to Stuart when troopers from Hampton's and Lee's brigades had "debouched into the open ground, disclosing the movement." Battle could no longer be avoided, and Stuart "determined to make the best fight possible."[55]

It is uncertain how long the lull in the action lasted, but it had seemed like hours. Perhaps at this particular moment David Gregg saw those same qualities in Custer that other great soldiers had seen, or would see, in him. "I knew Custer as a soldier when he was a brigade and division commander under Pleasonton and Sheridan," attested Jacob L. Greene, who served as Custer's adjutant-general in the Michigan Brigade:

> Those who knew the estimate in which those great commanders held him—the tasks they committed to his soldierly intelligence and comprehension, his fidelity and skill—need no reminder that in nothing of all their dependence upon and confidence in him did he ever fail in letter or spirit . . . He was true as steel. He was depended upon for great things because he was dependable.[56]

Henry Meyer of Gregg's staff found the whole situation ironic and could not believe the change that had taken place in just two short weeks. Meyer had last seen Custer when he had taken a tumble into a stream during a routine horse watering. Now, wrote Meyer, appreciating the irony of it all, "It therefore happened that the man they refused to have as their colonel was sent to be their general, and under his leadership the Michigan cavalry brigade became famous." But there were many who saw matters differently.[57]

---

55 OR 27, pt. 2, 697-698; *History of the Third Pennsylvania Cavalry*, 317.

56 Cyrus Townsend Brady, *Indian Fights and Fighters* (New York, NY, 1904), 392.

57 Meyer, *Civil War Experiences*, 49.

There Was No Middle of the Road

The lull had not been wasted by the 5th Michigan, as Custer had advanced a skirmish line further up the timberline that bordered Little's Run. Lieutenant Colonel Alger commanded two battalions, under Majs. Noah Ferry and Luther Trowbridge. Both units were armed with Spencer rifles. A portion of the 6th Michigan remained in its original morning position on the Hanover Road at the crossing of Cress Run, where it guarded the left flank and protected Pennington's guns. The 5th Michigan, recalled Captain Kidd, "moved briskly forward towards the wooded screen behind which the enemy was known to be concealed. In this movement the right of regiment was swung well forward, the left somewhat 'refused,' so that Colonel Alger's line was very nearly at right angles with the left of Stuart's position." Ferry's battalion was on the left; Trowbridge's was on the right.[58]

The Confederates also made good use of the lull by moving Jenkins's Brigade onto the Rummel farm. Jenkins was wounded on July 2 and his second in command, Col. Milton J. Ferguson, was not present on July 3. This left the 34th Battalion of Virginia Cavalry's Lt. Col. Vincent A. Witcher, as senior officer present, in command. Armed with Enfield rifles and their 10 precious rounds, some of his men took up sniping positions by cutting loopholes in the sides of the Rummel barn. The structure could not accommodate the entire battalion, so the rest of the men deployed next to the 14th and 16th Virginia regiments behind a long fence running in front of the Rummel farmhouse. Witcher, wrote one historian, "was never so happy as when in the thick of battle as he rode at the head of his battalion in battle charge." He was certainly in the thick of it now.[59]

As the accuracy of the Rebels' long-range rifles began to tell, the Rummel farm buildings drew the attention of Pennington's two sections of three-inch rifled guns. At this propitious moment, Battery E, 1st U.S. Artillery, attached to Gregg's division and commanded by Lt. Alanson M. Randol, arrived and took up position along the Low Dutch Road, stretching to the Lott house. Pennington's two sections remained where they had first unlimbered, on the left along the Hanover Road. "General Gregg stationed himself near his batteries, where he could see the field and direct the battle," wrote Henry C. Meyer. "Both were famous batteries. In this engagement the fire of these batteries, especially Pennington's was remarkably

58 Kidd, *Personal Recollections*, 145.

59 Wittenberg, *Protecting the Flank*, 63. The 14th and 16th Virginia were part of Jenkins's brigade, and thus also led by Witcher on July 3.

accurate, compelling the enemy at times to shift their guns, and contributed in no small measure to our success." For once, the often contrary accounts of the Michiganders and the Pennsylvanians are in rare agreement. "Pennington and Chester soon silenced the Confederate battery," wrote Capt. William Miller, "and finding Rummel's barn filled with sharpshooters, who were picking off our men, they turned their guns on it and drove them out."[60]

Unfortunately, driving the Rebels from the cover of the barn forced them out into the open, and they chose to move to the attack. "As the Fifth Michigan advanced from field to field and fence to fence, a line of gray came out from behind the Rummel buildings and the woods beyond. A stubborn and spirited contest ensued." Custer thrust Alger's regiment even farther forward with orders to "maintain their ground at all hazards." It was an unnecessary order, according to Custer, for Alger and his squadron commanders had "made such an admirable disposition of their men behind fences and other defenses." Safely ensconced behind stout fences, they took aim on the 1,200 troopers of Col. John R. Chambliss's brigade. As an onlooker noted, the Rebels then came on arrogantly, "with perfect confidence of success." The first volley crashed from the Michigan ranks at 100 yards. Over the din of the guns, the Confederate officers urged their men forward. "Now, for them before they can reload," cried one officer. With a Rebel yell, the entire enemy line surged forward to the attack. This was when the 5th Michigan dropped the hammer on them—seven times. When the powder smoke cleared, the field to their front was strewn with the dead and dying. The remnants, recalled one Wolverine, ran "faster than they came." James Avery was on the firing line, and he wrote, "When we were ordered forward, we dashed ahead and with such a fire from our Spencers, that the rebs were quickly dislodged and driven back, where we held them for some time, continuing a heavy firing all the time, effectively checking their advance, which they undertook several times."[61]

---

60 Meyer, *Civil War Experiences*, 49-50; Miller, "The Cavalry Battle Near Gettysburg, 3:402. By the time Brooke Rawle's article was published (1879), Pennington's battery had been neatly shoved out of the picture. "Captain Randol, upon coming on the ground, placed a section of his battery of three-inch light ordnance guns, under Lieutenant Chester, in position, well to the front," wrote Brooke Rawle, the blinders of history fixed firmly around his eyes, "and opened upon it. Shell after shell struck the building, soon compelling the enemy to abandon it. . . . By the accuracy of their firing and superior range, Randol's guns soon silenced the enemy's battery on the crest beyond Rummel's, near the crossroad, and Pennington's, some guns in position more to our left." *Annals of the Civil War*, 478.

61 Kidd, *Personal Recollections*, 145-146; Robertson, *Michigan in the War*, 583; Sword, "Those Damned Michigan Spencers," 23; Wittenberg, *Under Custer's Command*, 35.

From his position supporting the batteries, Kidd had a beautiful view of the action. "Alger's men with their eight-shotted carbines, forced their adversaries slowly but surely back," he wrote, "the gray line fighting well and superior in numbers, but unable to withstand the storm of bullets. It made a final stand behind the strong line of fences, in front of Rummel's and a few hundred yards out from the foot of the slope whereon, concealed by the woods, Stuart's reserves were posted." Noted Civil War historian and firearms expert Wiley Sword called this action "a unique occurrence. The use of the Spencer repeating rifles at Gettysburg was exclusive to the 5th and 6th Michigan; there were no other units armed with that weapon in the battle. As such, it was among the most significant 'weapons events' of the entire war."[62]

During that "stubborn and spirited contest," however, it did not take long for a man armed with a repeating firearm to burn through a cartridge box full of ammo, and Alger's line soon fell ominously silent, as whatever ammunition remained, was carefully hoarded. "Thus we held the line until mid-day, when we were ordered to mount, and the regiment fell back to where our horses were." "Colonel Alger," recalled Custer with admiration, "held his ground until his men had exhausted their ammunition" until he was "compelled to fall back on the main body. The beginning of this movement was the signal for the enemy to charge." According to Avery, the Union troopers barely made it to their horses. Custer was in their midst, lending support. "[He] rode in front of our troops, and with his flag in one hand, and his sabre in the other, ordered us forward, and with a cheer, the brigade rushed to meet the charging rebs." But the Rebels were obstinate that day. They retreated in confusion, but rallied, and "came again, only to be repulsed a second and third time." Avery's heart thumped with unit pride. "Never did men do better fighting than did ours that day, and they won lasting honors, for they defeated the enemy, at every point."[63]

Gregg recalled that by that time, "the skirmishing became brisk on both sides, and an artillery fire was begun by the enemy and ourselves." It was in the open fields in front of the Rummel farm, in front of a fence lined with Rebel sharpshooters, that William Brooke Rawle's contention that Custer had long since begun his movement to withdraw clashed openly with James Kidd's argument that Custer never intended to give up the positions he had established at 10:00 a.m., and

---

62 Kidd, *Personal Recollections*, 146; Sword, "Those Damned Michigan Spencers," 23-24.

63 Kidd, *Personal Recollections*, 146; Wittenberg, *Under Custer's Command*, 35, 37; Robertson, *Michigan in the War*, 583.

was just not holding his ground, but moving forward on the offensive. The diametrically opposed nature of these and other perspectives of the battle, and the ensuing debate they engendered, are difficult to correlate. Read a dozen accounts, and you will get a dozen different stories.[64]

The 3rd Pennsylvania and the 1st Maryland, in columns of squadrons, had taken up positions to the right of Custer's line in an open field near the Lott farm. An extensive wooded area offered concealment from the prying eyes of the Confederates. One hundred and fifty men of the 1st New Jersey were detailed to cut across the wheat fields, towards Little's Run, where Custer's picket line was formed. Cavalry historian Edward Longacre's research shows that "[Custer's] forward most pickets remained in position much longer, for Major Beaumont, whose lst New Jersey McIntosh had selected to replace them, was slow to appear." Beaumont claimed to have a sudden illness, a malady, some smirked, that afflicted him whenever battle was imminent. McIntosh replaced him with Maj. Hugh H. Janeway, "an officer of more fortitude." It was said of the 19-year-old firebrand Janeway that he had more battle scars on his body, "as years on earth." In his rage, McIntosh yelled out, "Damn them, bring them up at a gallop!" In quick time the regiment came forward.[65]

One moment, everything was peaceful and calm in the fields surrounding Gettysburg. Colonel J. J. Blackford of Stuart's staff meandered through the Confederate lines, sent by his commander to gauge the mood of the men. "All was as quiet as if there was not a soldier within a hundred miles," he reported in amazement, "and the country looked so calm and beautiful, dotted over with thrifty farms, that it was hard to realize that nearly a quarter of a million men were met together to settle their 'difficulty' upon 'the field of honor.'" Suddenly and without forewarning, recorded one trooper with the 3rd Pennsylvania, "[t]he very ground shook and trembled, and the smoke of the guns rolled out of the valley as tho there were thousands of acres of timber on fire." Such was the discord between Kidd and Brooke Rawle that they couldn't even agree upon what hour the thunderous barrage against Cemetery Hill began. According to Brooke Rawle the 1st New Jersey was cutting across the field to relieve the picket line of the 5th Michigan. "The Third Pennsylvania . . . and First Maryland were drawn up in close columns of squadrons in a clover field west of the Lott house, awaiting developments," he remembered. "While in this position, and a few minutes after

64 OR 27, pt. 1, 957.

65 Longacre, *The Cavalry at Gettysburg*, 225.

one o'clock, the tremendous artillery firing which preceded Longstreet's attack began." Safely out of range, the officers and men, "while allowing the horses to graze," gathered to spend time gawking "with astonishment upon the magnificent spectacle."[66]

Like McIntosh's men, the troopers of the Michigan Brigade were taking their ease, the horses munching on the clover, "when suddenly there burst upon the air the sound of that terrible cannonading that preceded Pickett's charge. The earth quaked. The tremendous volume of sound volleyed and rolled across the intervening hills like reverberating thunder in a storm. It was then between one and two o'clock." Kidd places it closer to 2:00 p.m., based on the testimony of Major Storrs of the 6th Michigan, who was commanding a squadron that "was sent to the left and front of Custer's position." Storrs's command moved up well in rear of the 5th Michigan and stayed in this position for several hours, when it was recalled to support the guns of Pennington's battery. "He is positive it was later than twelve," wrote his regimental mate; "He states that the first shot was not fired until sometime after his recall, and he is sure it was not earlier than two o'clock." And, as if on cue, Stuart's guns, carefully hidden in the woods of Cress Ridge, opened on the Union troopers in the valley below.[67]

---

66 Blackford, *War Years with Jeb Stuart*, 233; Longacre, *The Cavalry at Gettysburg*, 225; Brooke Rawle, *The Right Flank at Gettysburg*, 477.

67 Kidd, *Personal Recollections*, 142, 145.

CHAPTER ELEVEN

Merritt Finds Mediocrity

EVERY OFFICER REMEMBERS HIS first command, and Wesley Merritt was no exception. The poignancy of June 30, 1863, that had so affected Merritt would stay with him for the rest of his life.

These were the men he had lived and interacted with on a daily basis. Their welfare had been entrusted to him; their families depended on him. In many a desperate fight, with Merritt leading from the midst of his men, as was his wont, they had forged a bond. "Every day and many nights we marched and countermarched, through good weather and bad, over mountains and through woods, subsisting as best we could on army rations, when it was possible to obtain it, or 'living off the country.'" It was, wrote Merritt, "a precarious living at best." On June 30, he would make his last entry as commander of the 2nd U.S. Cavalry, bringing the account of his tenure with the regiment to an official end. Wistfully, he wrote from the perspective of one who was still *with* the 2nd U.S., but no longer *of* it. The regiment had been in camp for little more than a day when it was ordered to embark "upon a month of even more active service than it had seen up to this time—a month of daily marches and almost daily engagements." By its end, only a remnant would report to the monstrous cavalry depot at Giesboro in order to "recruit its numbers and strength for the future of the war."[1]

Events were occurring so fast that it was becoming difficult to tell where one campaign ended, and another started. In fact, the *Official Records* lump the period from Brandy Station through Aldie, Middleburg, and Upperville, and on to

---

1 Merritt, "Reminiscences," 294-295.

Gettysburg and beyond, under the single heading of "The Gettysburg Campaign." When Merritt took command of the Regulars, the brigade consisted of the 1st U.S. Cavalry (Capt. Richard S. C. Lord); 2nd U.S. Cavalry (Capt. Theophilus F. Rodenbough); 5th U.S. Cavalry (Capt. Julius W. Mason); 6th U.S. Cavalry (Maj. Samuel H. Starr); and the 6th Pennsylvania Cavalry (Maj. James H. Hazeltine). Following their performance at Brandy Station, Buford had praised the 6th Pennsylvania to Pleasonton: "These men did splendidly yesterday; I call them now the Seventh regulars." From Buford it was the ultimate compliment. Altogether, Merritt fielded a force of 52 officers and 1,650 men. From this force, two companies of the 6th U.S. Cavalry were posted to headquarters, as were small detachments from the other four regiments.[2]

Though many descriptions of John Buford stress his genial personality, he was a tiger on the prowl when crossed. On June 30, the most important thing on his mind was why the highly trained Regulars were wasting their time guarding a wagon train, far in the rear of the army. Just prior to the fateful encounter on the Chambersburg Pike outside Gettysburg, he demanded that the Reserve Brigade be relieved from its duties in the rear and returned to his division. In a sharp message to Pleasonton, Buford stressed the urgency of the situation. He had arrived in Gettysburg at approximately 11:00 a.m. on June 30, and "found everybody in a terrible state of excitement on account of the enemy's advance upon this place," adding drolly, "accounts of which are greatly exaggerated." Buford angrily told Pleasonton that his command was played out. "I can't do much now," admitted the quintessential man of action. "My men and horses are fagged out. I have not been able to get any grain yet. It is all in the country, and the people talk instead of working. Facilities for shoeing are nothing. Early's people seized every shoe and nail they could find."[3]

But it was the absence of the Regulars which irritated Buford most of all. "The Reserve Brigade, under General Merritt, is at Mechanicsville with my trains," he wrote, adding querulously, "I have many rumors and reports of the enemy advancing upon me from York." Buford felt this put him at a disadvantage, as he had "to pay attention to some of them, which causes me to overwork my horses and men. I can get no forage nor rations, am out of both." Following up on fresh intelligence of the enemy's movements, he sent another communique to headquarters 10 minutes later. "His pickets . . . are in sight of mine," reported

2 Wittenberg, "Merritt's Regulars on South Cavalry Field," 112.

3 *OR* 27, pt.1, 923.

Buford. Ewell's entire corps was rumored to be on its way across the mountains from Carlisle. Buford continued to hammer away at his need for the Reserve Brigade. "When will the reserve be relieved, and where are my wagons?" he queried. "I have no need of them, as I can find no forage."[4]

Like Rats in a Trap

Major Samuel H. Starr was not a happy regimental commander. The order announcing the promotions of Merritt, Custer, and Farnsworth had been followed by one removing Starr from brigade command and placing him at the head of the 6th U.S. Cavalry. He had been a soldier for as long as he could remember, and he could remember at least as far back as 1832. Now, Pleasonton's choice of young Capt. Wesley Merritt to command the brigade Starr had led briefly did not sit well with him. The brigade was his by right, by seniority, and by every rule in the army. From Merritt's perspective as well, it was going to be a troublesome relationship. On June 30, the silver star still shiny and new on his shoulder straps, Merritt went out of his way to meet with the officers of his command, over which many of whom he had been politically promoted.

He established the standards he expected in the care of the command's horses, applying a stricter measuring stick to the officers. "In the preparation and start, as well as in the smallest details of the march," Merritt informed them in his serious but agreeable manner, that "the closest supervision of the Commanding Officer must be exercised. . . . As soon as the 'General' sounds, one or more troop officers should repair to the troop grounds and superintend the details of everything till the march begins." Once he explained the process for marching cavalry, Merritt would brook no excuses, would tolerate no failure. But the officers seemed to have bought into his program, for it appeared they all supported him, even when he told them the bad news in Special Orders 99 from cavalry headquarters. "One brigade and battery with trains to march . . . to Mechanicstown," it read, "where it will encamp for the night, protecting the rear, and bringing up all stragglers." The Reserve Brigade was going to move.[5]

Protecting the slow, heavily laden wagons in the rear was an odious task for a unit of veteran soldiers. The resources of the brigade would be stretched for over 20 miles, from Mechanicstown all the way to Hagerstown. "The road is very

---

4 Ibid., 923-924.

5 Merritt, "Marching Cavalry," 72; OR 27, pt. 3, 400.

rugged, one passing through rocky defiles over the Katoctin mountains," one trooper recalled, though the men were somewhat ameliorated by the joy of the populace at their appearance. According to Lt. Tattnall Paulding, "The people were very kind to us . . . and where I established my main reserve they opened a school house & set a fine dinner for the men of my company." Company G had advanced to Hagerstown, where it was met with enthusiasm, and "there as all along the road was recd with great joy by the people." The next day, the brigade marched leisurely to Emmitsburg.[6]

They had already missed the first two days of the war's largest battle, ingloriously guarding the rear, while the intrepid brigades of Cols. William Gamble and Thomas Devin attained historical immortality. The tactics Buford employed in his legendary stand at Gettysburg would set the standard for future cavalry operations. According to Eric Wittenberg, who has studied Buford for over 30 years, his "most important legacy lay in the successes of the Cavalry Corps of the Army of the Potomac." "It was during the Gettysburg campaign that the Union horsemen first took on Jeb Stuart's vaunted cavaliers and fought them as equals. Their fighting at Brandy Station, coupled with Buford's perfectly executed delaying action at Gettysburg, demonstrated what these volunteer horse soldiers could accomplish with good leadership."[7]

For days, the pace of the Reserve Brigade had been dictated by the slow-moving transports. Frustrated cavalrymen rained curses down on the drivers, whose heavily laden wagons could move no faster. But finally, on July 3, the order had come through relieving the Reserve Brigade of the burdensome, albeit traditional, cavalry duty of guarding the supply trains. "In compliance with orders received from corps headquarters," reported Merritt, "I marched with the brigade about 12m. to attack the enemy's right and rear, and annoy, while the battle was progressing on the right." The rattle of gunfire was far in the distance, and the orders to march to the south of Gettysburg had no wording, or tone, to indicate rapidity of movement. It was not an order that, in Merritt's view, required undo exertion of the horses. Merritt had already established a pace for his troopers: "Easy campaign marches of from ten to fourteen miles per day, are good in preparing both horses and men for forced marches," Merritt would advise. "Without this preparation, a command will not be able to make the marches, either

---

6 Milgram, "The Libby Correspondence of Tattnall Paulding," 1,114.

7 Eric J. Wittenberg, *"The Devil's to Pay": John Buford at Gettysburg* (El Dorado Hills, CA, 2014), 196.

campaign or forced, and an attempt to accomplish even a portion of the distances mentioned must result in the destruction of a cavalry command through disabling or killing the horses." Private Samuel James Crockett, of Company A, 1st U.S. Cavalry, did not remember any sense of urgency on that march. "We (Reserves) had been lying on the left of the main road between Emmitsburg and Gettysburg near a creek till afternoon," he recalled. "We countermarched to Emmitsburg and moved out on a dirt road toward the west soon turning to northward and soon after crossing a narrow deep creek."[8]

It should have been a time of flying to the sound of the guns; it should have been a time to let the horses canter—perhaps even gallop—for brief periods. It should have been a time to marshal all one's forces, and with regimental colors and company guidons whipping in the wind, attack the enemy. But instead, en route to Gettysburg, at one of the mandated rest stops, a series of unusual events occurred, resulting in Merritt frittering away his force.

A local farmer passed inform on to Merritt that a large Confederate wagon train was on the move from Cashtown to Fairfield with the obvious intent of passing through one of the gaps in the Cumberland Valley. As Tattnall Paulding put it, "a citizen was speaking to Gen. M. of a large wagon train that had been encamped all night at Fairfield without guard of any strength." In a chummy way, observed Paulding, the local imparted some homespun wisdom, saying that if Merritt acted, there was "a right smart chance for you'ns to capture it, the soldiers are all over the big fight." Some of the men doubted the truth of the intelligence. The local was "a rebel spy," asserted trooper Heinrich G. Mueller, and had "informed some of our officers that this train was only guarded by mounted infantry. A farmer from the neighborhood of Fairfield was secured to pilot the command to its destination."[9]

Perhaps the young brigadier was swayed by the enthusiasm of his men, for one trooper recalled that "all was excitement, and you will not wonder when you imagine capturing a hundred wagons laden with spoils for confiscation, and the plundering and destruction of the same." Merritt decided to detach Major Starr with four squadrons of the 6th U.S. Cavalry, approximately 400 men, to capture the wagon train. The rest of the brigade would cover the endangered right flank.

8 OR 27, pt. 1, 943; Merritt, *Marching Cavalry*, 75; Samuel J. Crockett to John B. Bachelder, December 27, 1882, in Ladd and Ladd, eds., *The Bachelder Papers*, 2:916.

9 Milgram, "The Libby Correspondence of Tattnall Paulding," 1,114-1,115; Caughey and Jones, *The 6th United States Cavalry*, 103; Heinrich G. Mueller, "An Account of the Reunion of the 6th U. S. Cavalry," publishing information unknown.

"About mid-day, 'To Horse' was sounded & we were informed that the Brigade was to attempt the capture of the train at Fairfield," recalled Paulding. "The balance of the brigade was to move upon the road between Fairfield & Gettysburg to keep off any supports which might be sent from Gettysburg by the enemy." At some point, an impatient Kilpatrick, desperate for men in Custer's absence, went looking for Merritt. The chances Kilpatrick found him were good, as Merritt decided to abandon the 6th's tenuous flank and move further north to Gettysburg. Starr's squadrons continued to advance deeper into enemy territory. This decision would prove disastrous, for instead of finding a small escort, Starr ran into Confederate Gen. "Grumble" Jones's brigade, and to his mortification, no Union cavalry was in supporting range.[10]

Merritt was headed north with the remainder of his brigade when, quite unexpectedly, Capt. Ulric Dahlgren of General Meade's staff arrived with Meade's written orders for Merritt to assign 100 of his men to Dahlgren for the latter's raiding and reconnaissance activities. Merritt detached these men from the 6th Pennsylvania, leaving him with just 1,500 men after Dahlgren's departure. Then came the unanticipated orders from Pleasonton to get his act in gear and move to Gettysburg. With this sudden burst of activity, and events moving at an even faster pace, the timing of the 6th U.S. Cavalry's departure for Fairfield was now viewed differently by men who were still judging the qualities of their new commanding officer. To many, it was a separate operation that had been decided upon and set in motion before the arrival of Pleasonton's orders. In his after-action report, in reference to the 6th, Merritt uses the term, "In the meantime," disingenuously implying that the fight at Fairfield, and the one that would take place on what came to be known as "South Cavalry Field," were part of the same plan to "annoy" the enemy.[11]

Though participants gave different estimates of the length of the march to Fairfield (from five to 11 miles), most of their accounts agree that the squadrons covered the distance in about an hour. It was an eerie ride. Starr led the whole way, with the farmer keeping a talkative pace next to him. According to one trooper, "[t]he man seemed somewhat excited emphasizing his conversations by gestures with a rawhide which he held in his right hand," while "Starr looked as gloomy as usual, not in the least partaking of the stranger's animation." Part of the march took

10 Caughey and Jones, *The 6th United States Cavalry,* 104; Milgram, "The Libby Correspondence of Tattnall Paulding," 1,115.

11 *OR 27,* pt. 1, 943.

them through Fairfield Gap, the road thrown into gloom by the surrounding woods, and hauntingly silent in the absence of the Rebels. "We saw no signs of the enemy's cavalry or pickets on the road," reported Paulding, "except on a mountain side a mile from the road there seemed to be a small picket post." Major Starr was truly vexed, but he was still enough of a soldier to stop the command as it debouched out of the gap, a mere two miles away from Fairfield. There, Starr detached a squadron under the leadership of someone even more dislikeable than himself, Capt. George C. "Damn" Cram of the 6th U.S. Cavalry, to follow along the bed of an unfinished railroad that intersected the road. Curving northward, the bed skirted the edge of the mountains that defined the Fairfield valley's western side. Sixty men were now following the grading.[12]

As the remaining four squadrons entered Fairfield, one thing became very evident. "Arriving at Fairfield we found no train," an outcome that Paulding had feared throughout the ride into the unknown, "but a few wagons which had been at the neighboring barns had left the town a few moments previous to our entering." Lieutenant Balder's squadron was thrown forward to search for the wagons, which they found galloping for their lives up the valley on the Fairfield-Orrtana road. The chase was on! And then suddenly, it wasn't. Private Mueller remembered that, "[w]hen about two and one-half miles beyond Fairfield, on the Cashtown road and, at the James A. Marshall farm, the regiment encountered the Seventh Virginia Cavalry." This was not, contrary to popular belief, a chance encounter.[13]

One Federal trooper had joked about ransacking 100 wagons, but he had visions of them lined in a neat row, ripe for the picking. The wagons were there alright, but they were scattered all over the Pennsylvania countryside foraging for food and any other supplies useful to the Confederates. A picket line had been established outside Cashtown in the direction of Fairfield to provide support for the foraging parties. At around one o'clock, Sgt. T. J. Young of Company G, 7th Virginia, commanding one of the picket details, reported that an out-of-breath, nearly panic-stricken forage master approached on the run from Fairfield, where his post had been "guarding the wagon train, which was two or three miles in the rear of Lee's Army." The man, Sergeant Young informed his officer, "came running into camp and said the Federals were after him." Young continued: "[The]

---

12 Davis, *Common Soldier, Uncommon War*, 427; Milgram, "The Libby Correspondence of Tattnall Paulding," 1,115.

13 Milgram, "The Libby Correspondence of Tattnall Paulding," 1,115; Mueller, "An Account of the Reunion of the 6th U. S. Cavalry," 3.

Sixth and Seventh Regiments both had orders to mount, and almost in an instant started in the direction from which the forage master came. . . . We had gone but a short distance, when we met a squad of about thirty Federal cavalrymen, who turned and ran through a lane with post and rail fence on each side." The Confederates were in overwhelming force, and the detachment turned tail and ran, with the 7th Virginia hot on its trail.[14]

Back down the Fairfield-Cashtown road, Major Starr, as befitting a disagreeable old veteran of the frontier, had made the decision to stand and fight. He had chosen his position well; he was perched on a low ridge, his left flank protected by a steep wooded eminence called Mary's Hill; half a mile to the right of the road, a wooded ridge ran north to south, blocking any flank movement from that side. He dismounted part of his command and deployed one group along an apple orchard that topped the length of the small rise. The second group was arranged behind a stout post and rail fence to the right of the road, just ahead of magnificent fields of golden wheat swaying in the gentle breeze. The rest of the men were mounted in column along the road. "My Squadron was ordered by Maj. Starr to be dismounted & into a field on our right," wrote Lieutenant Paulding of the regiment's position. "After my men were posted behind a fence by which they were to act, I saw the enemy in great numbers forming beyond us." With the Rebels piling up in numbers, Starr looked to his right, and saw a mere 60 men lining 100 yards of the fence line; 60 more sought covered positions in the apple orchard, stretching 100 yards to the left of the road. Two hundred men remained mounted in the road.[15]

In the orderly fashion of Pennsylvania farms, the landscape was criss-crossed with every variety of fence known to man, and the 7th Virginia was left with no recourse but to charge straight down the fenced-in lane. The Confederates "[m]oved up at a charge, and found the enemy strongly posted," reported Lt. Col. Thomas Marshall, commanding the 7th Virginia, "a portion of their line in the lane, and their other forces disposed on either flank." With the charging columns held in place by the heavy fencing, the Rebel flanks proved too tempting a target to ignore for long. "They opened a galling fire upon us, driving us back and killing and wounding a good many," recalled one eyewitness. Captain William N. McDonald, Jones's ordnance officer, recalled the "terrible fire from the flanking squadrons.

---

14   Paul N. Shevchuk, "'Cut to Pieces': The Cavalry Fight at Fairfield, Pennsylvania, July 3d, 1863," *The Gettysburg Magazine*, No. 1 (July 1989), 12-13.

15   Milgram, "The Libby Correspondence of Tattnall Paulding," 1,115.

The failure of the Seventh . . . was clearly due to fire from the . . . men on the flanks, who being unmolested, shot with deadly effect into the charging column." The flying lead was simply too much to bear, and the troopers of the 7th Virginia broke for the rear, streaming directly past an outraged "Grumble" Jones. "The leading men hesitated," General Jones groused, "the regiment halted and retreated, losing more men than a glorious victory would have cost had the onset been made with vigor and boldness. . . . The 6th Virginia Cavalry was next ordered to charge."[16]

Beside himself with rage and intent on leading the charge himself, Jones stormed to the front of the 6th Virginia, which was positioned on a ridge, listening to an address by its commander, Maj. C. E. Flourney. Years later, E. H. Vaughn recalled the scene: "Over yonder, we met the Seventh Virginia coming back in great confusion, many of them being wounded," he wrote. Chew's Battery occupied positions on both sides of the road. It was a moment for an uplifting speech, and Major Flourney delivered. "Men, I want every one of you to do his duty; the men that you will meet are worthy of your steel; it is the Sixth Regulars, the best regiment the Yanks have," he shouted. "This rekindled some of our fire," vouched Vaughn, "for we did not feel very good after seeing the condition the Seventh was in."[17]

The lane down which the 7th Virginia had charged was littered with "many killed and wounded on the battle-field," wrote Private Mueller, little realizing that the worst was yet to come. Major Starr's years of experience were screaming that it was time to go. "Unexpectedly, from a little knoll beyond, Clue's [Chew's] Virginia battery opened fire, and the 6th Virginia Cavalry charged down on the 6th U. S. Cavalry," Mueller recalled. Starr began to pull his troops back to their held mounts. "Very soon recd an order from Maj. Starr to withdraw my men as he was about to charge & would be driven back," wrote Paulding in one of his last entries as a free man. But it was far too late. "They being dismounted, and having deployed in fighting the Seventh Virginia Cavalry, were taken at a great disadvantage, as most of them were unable to reach and remount their horses," wrote Mueller in stark, sparse prose, "and, as a result, it became a desperate hand to hand struggle . . . and many were the instances where our men fought with desperation until death, rather than surrender."[18]

Tattnall Paulding also remembered that harrowing effort to escape. The command was exhausted, and "before they could reach the horses our men who

16 Shevchuk, "Cut to Pieces," 15-16; OR 27, pt. 2, 752.

17 Mueller, "An Account of the Reunion of the 6th U. S. Cavalry," 5.

18 Ibid., 3-4; Milgram, "The Libby Correspondence of Tattnall Paulding," 1,115.

had charged were repulsed & the enemy closely following [and] using the saber mercilessly." Paulding did not get far, and the remainder of his fascinating diary recounts his subsequent journey south and captivity in Richmond's notorious Libby Prison. Confederate recollections like those of Pvt. John Opie of the 6th Virginia, were similar. "The boys rode, sabre in hand, right into the Sixth Regulars," Opie wrote, "sabring right and left as they went. . . . A great many of the enemy were knocked from their horses with the sabre, but succeeded in escaping through the tall wheat, which had not yet been harvested." One wisecracker noted that the Yankees' "running qualities were fully equal to their fighting."[19]

As the Union squadrons disintegrated, many of the troopers attempted to escape using the cover of the wheat fields. Some made their way into town, where they were hunted down in the alleys and streets. "Damn Cram," to his credit, had ridden to the sound of the guns and charged the enemy's right. Within minutes, his small command had been nearly encircled. Lieutenant Nicholas Nolan left vivid testimony of the ferocity of the Confederate attack in his official report. "Finding the enemy in force, I gradually fell back in the direction of Mechanicstown, where I found the regiment." There he heard the distressing news that most of the officers were dead, wounded, or missing. Over 290 of the enlisted men were *hors d'combat*, along with 292 horses. In the swirling mêlée, Starr, who was the last man off the field, suffered a saber slash to the head and a bullet-shattered arm in quick succession. His arm was later amputated. Lieutenant Balder refused to surrender and, surrounded by Rebels, had been gunned down; he died later that night.[20]

At the entrance to Fairfield Gap, with their bloodlust satiated and Jones grumbling about a possible Federal trap, the Confederates gave up the chase. The 6th Virginia, declared Jones, "did its work nobly, assailing and completely routing one of the best United States regiments, just flushed with victory." Closing out his report on the fight, Jones wrote with the greatest of satisfaction, "The Sixth U. S. Regular Cavalry numbers among the things that were." Sadly, observed Sgt. Samuel Crockett of the 1st U.S. Cavalry, Jones was not engaging in hyperbole. "The 6th US is cut to pieces," he wrote in his diary. "There are less than a hundred of them left." The pitiful remnants were assigned to Corps Headquarters. Officially, the regiment had lost a total of over 240 men: six killed, 28 wounded, and 208 captured, who "went into a horrible captivity, where one-half of them left their bones bleaching at

---

19 Milgram, "The Libby Correspondence of Tattnall Paulding," 1,115; Shevchuk, "Cut to Pieces," 21, 23.

20 Ibid., 25.

Belle Isle and Andersonville." By comparison, Jones' 1,600-man brigade reported losses of 58 killed, wounded, and missing. As Nolan's remnants rejoined the Reserve Brigade that evening, there could be no denying that it had all been a terrible misadventure.[21]

In 1888, on the 25th anniversary of the battle, the survivors of the 6th U.S. Cavalry met in a reunion held at Fairfield, at the very spot where "the blood of a great many of our comrades sprinkled [the] streets and fields." The guest of honor was E. H. Vaughn, formerly of the 6th Virginia Cavalry, who went over the field with the old troopers, and explained the battle from the perspective of the other side. Dimmed by the passage of the years, old animosities buried deep, the former foes finally looked each other in the eyes, and Vaughn grudgingly reflected on how tough a fight it had been. "We defeated you, that is true," he said by way of tribute, "but harder fighting we never did, nor heavier losses never suffered than on this field—in short it was a victory by defeat."

Pride, however, is a double-edged sword, recalled Heinrich Mueller. "Ask a member of the Sixth U. S. Cavalry about Fairfield, and you will see his eyes gleam; he knows he gave his regiment and Fairfield a place in the history of his country, of which neither he nor the citizens of Fairfield, need be ashamed—that is the secret of his love for this beautiful valley." They visited the graves of their comrades at the German Lutheran Seminary, many of them marked only "Unknown, Sixth Cavalry." Wiping away tears, Mueller spoke for others when he said, "none but a soldier can know the thoughts that filled our hearts."[22]

Go West Young Man . . . But Go Fast!!

Some men claim to see beyond the ken of most men. If this clarity of vision turns out to be true, the man is acclaimed and pronounced a genius. Should that vision be blurred, or should he have to grope his way forward blindly, the use of the word "delusional" would not be amiss. Then there are men like Judson Kilpatrick, who could have brilliant cycles of lucidity, only to have them marred by whiplashing storms of temper and emotion. With the mercurial Kilpatrick, it could happen, literally, in the twinkling of an eye. It happened to him at South Cavalry

---

21 Ibid., 30; Samuel James Crockett, Diary entry, July 3, 1863, copy on file, Park Library and Research Center, GNMP; Mueller, "An Account of the Reunion of the 6th U. S. Cavalry," 6; Shevchuk, "Cut to Pieces," 27, 28.

22 Mueller, "An Account of the Reunion of the 6th U. S. Cavalry," 5, 6, 8.

Field at Gettysburg, and when it was all said and done, he would never regain the respect of the men under his command. It had not taken long for those under his command to learn the essence of the man. The sobriquet of "Kil-Cavalry" that he had earned was apt. "He had begun to be a terror to his foes," wrote James Kidd disgustedly, describing a man who had broken the most fundamental of trusts between the men and officers and their commander—that their lives mattered; that their sacrifices had meaning. "There was a well-grounded fear that he might become a menace to friends as well," wrote Kidd, in a startling reversal of his initial impression of Kilpatrick:

> He was brave to rashness, capricious, ambitious, reckless in rushing into scrapes, and generally of expedients in getting out, though at times he seemed to lose his head entirely when beset by perils which he, himself, had invited. He was prodigal of human life, though to do him justice he rarely spared himself.[23]

General James Wilson, who had served in the same cadet company as Kilpatrick at the Military Academy, was hard put to explain the contradictory nature of the man. "I had known him well at West Point, and had come to regard him highly as an officer of energy, ability and patriotism," wrote Wilson, attempting to give a balanced portrayal of someone who simply defied balance. "No enterprise was too dangerous to appall him, no odds too great to deter him from the charge."[24]

The chronology of events is not at the root of the controversies surrounding the fight on South Cavalry Field; in fact, it probably is not even in dispute. The disputes begin with Gen. Alfred Pleasonton at cavalry headquarters, who, having been chained there by Meade, had nothing better to do than dictate orders. "At 8 a.m.," recalled Kilpatrick, "[I] received orders from headquarters Cavalry Corps to move to the left of our line and attack the enemy's right and rear with my whole command and the Regular Brigade." Most analyses of what transpired on that field end with Kilpatrick's reputation besmirched. The basis of the controversies is simple: Either Kilpatrick had a plan, or not. It is easy to say that Kilpatrick's actions were mindless, but the truth is that he always had some semblance of a plan, a method to his madness. If he did not have a plan, he never would have been able to justify his subsequent actions. If there had been a plan, and if it made military sense,

---

23 Kidd, *Personal Recollections*, 164.

24 Wilson, *Under the Old Flag*, 1:368-370.

Brigadier General Wesley Merritt in his dress uniform. *Library of Congress*

well then, that is a different animal altogether. According to Capt. H. C. Parsons of the 1st Vermont Cavalry, there was a plan. "Kilpatrick's orders were to press the enemy, to threaten him at every point, and to strike at the first opportunity," he asserted. "If he could bring on a battle . . . and break the lines on the mountain, Meade's infantry on Round Top would surely drive them into the valley, and then the five thousand cavalry in reserve could strike the decisive blow."[25]

Kilpatrick always believed that "had our infantry on my right advanced at once when relieved from the enemy's attack in their front, the enemy could not have recovered from the confusion into which Generals Farnsworth and Merritt had thrown them, but would have been rushed back, one division on another, until, instead of a defeat, a total rout would have ensued." Confederate accounts agree with the gravity of the situation and seem to concur with Kilpatrick's assertion that decisive action on the Union left flank could have produced credible results. "That General [James] Longstreet also felt the gravest anxiety as to the result of the fighting on this flank is evidenced by the fact that he rode hastily over from the center," recounted Brig. Gen. Evander M. Law, "and with the most marked expression of relief in his tone and manner, warmly congratulated me on the manner in which the situation had been handled."[26]

It is clear that General Longstreet's main concern was the vulnerability of the Army of Northern Virginia's right flank. The southern end of the army's line thus became the responsibility of Maj. Gen. John B. Hood's infantry division. Hood, however, had been seriously wounded by shell fragments during the early minutes of the attack on the afternoon of July 2. Command of his division passed to Law, its senior brigadier, who struggled the rest of that afternoon with the wider scope of his new responsibilities over exceedingly difficult terrain. His work as a brigade commander suffered as a result, and his regiments became separated and advanced across the rough ground terrain without a clear understanding of what was expected of them or their ultimate objective. As a result, Law's brigade was committed piecemeal into the fighting and chopped to pieces in the process. The regimental histories of this command resonate with the legendary names of the

---

25 OR 27, pt.1, 992; H. C. Parsons, "Farnsworth's Charge and Death," in Johnson and Buel, eds., *Battles and Leaders*, 3:393.

26 OR 27, pt. 1, 993; "General Law's Account," Participants Accounts, Farnsworth's Folder, General Farnsworth's Death.

areas over which they fought, including Slaughter Pen, Devil's Den—known to the Rebels as "The Gorge"—and the Round Tops.[27]

That evening, the northern part of Law's line was anchored on a slope near the Rose Woods, which dropped precipitously down Houck's Ridge to the lunar landscape of Devil's Den. Only a skirmish line accompanied the dead. Jerome Robertson's Texas Brigade picked up the line on the lower slopes of Big Round Top and ran across the ascent to unite with Law's Alabama command, which was now under Col. James L. Sheffield. The Alabamians comprised the right flank of the entire Virginia army. In the blackness of the night, Law's Rebels began to dig in with an urgency that belied their exhaustion. From a short way up the mountain, Law's men clearly heard the sound of axes, picks, and shovels. The Yankees were also entrenching. None of this boded well for the next day's action. "The light of the next morning disclosed the fact that the Federal troops in front of us had improved their time in the same way," reported Law.

While his men labored, Law did his best to rearrange his lines for the morrow. He knew his men had come within a hair's breadth of carrying the Yankee positions, but he had been shocked by the cost. The cries of the wounded made it impossible to get much if any real sleep that night. "It was an awful scene," shuddered Pvt. John Anderson in a letter to his wife, "to see and hear the shrieks and groanings of the poor dying soldiers on my right and on my left and before me and behind and all around." It was no different across the lines, where one Pennsylvanian recorded that "many had received severe and painful wounds, and their ceaseless cries for help, breaking upon the stillness of the night, sent a thrill to the heart of many a brave soldier." [28]

Convinced that his battered command would not be able to retake the offensive on the morning of July 3, Law was doing his best to prepare to hold his ground. What he saw was alarming. Early that morning, the ground extending from the base of Round Top to the Emmitsburg Road was covered by only three companies of the 47th Alabama. Their skirmish line extended west in order to keep the Emmitsburg Road under surveillance. As the morning progressed, a squadron of the 1st South Carolina Cavalry under Col. John L. Black, along with two Blakely Rifles of the Washington Light Artillery under Capt. James F. Hart, marched down

---

27 Evander M. Law, "The Struggle For 'Round Top,'" in Johnson and Buel, eds., *Battles and Leaders*, 3:326.

28 Ibid.; Morris M. Penny and J. Gary Laine, *Struggle for the Round Tops: Law's Alabama Brigade at the Battle of Gettysburg* (Colonial Heights, VA, 1999), 107.

the Emmitsburg Road. The cavalry and guns deployed into line at the David Curran house, where sharpshooters took up positions in the second-floor windows. Law reinforced his flankers with the 1st Texas, which he pulled from his main line. The savvy Texas veterans posted themselves behind a stone wall and were soon busy fortifying it with wooden fence posts and rails.

Just the day before, Colonel Black had been personally introduced to General Longstreet by no less a personage than Gen. Robert E. Lee. When queried by Longstreet as to the composition of his command, Black "told him I had a good battery, Hart's, as good as there was in the army, which was true." Black added, however, that he also had "some detachments of good cavalry & some hash picked up of whom I knew little." Law described this outfit as "100 men who had been gathered up from the medical trains, most of them partly disabled and only a part mounted." They were, he decreed, "the 'ragtag and bobtail' of the hospital and wagon trains, which proved to be a nuisance rather than a benefit." In the end, Colonel Black felt much respect and gratitude for his makeshift command. "Their behavior was very gratifying to me in this charge as they were improvised. If I had had 100 of my own men and officers. I would have felt sure of their behaving well but this mixed command did more than well."[29]

Everyone present at Gettysburg remembered where they were and what they were doing at the moment the thunderous opening artillery salvo signaled the beginning of the charge by Pickett, Pettigrew, and Trimble against the center of the Union lines. To strengthen the main attack, Lee had withdrawn troops from both of Evander Law's already tenuous flanks, and Law was concerned about how he was going to use his remaining troops. When the historic barrage began, he thought of little else, becoming, like all those not in the line of fire, an enthralled spectator. Looking north up the valley toward Gettysburg, Law viewed "one of the most magnificent battle-scenes witnessed during the war." He added, "The hills on either side were capped with crowns of flame and smoke. . . . Dense clouds of smoke settled over the valley, through which the shells went hissing and screaming on their errand of death."[30]

During the bombardment, Law detected the approach of Kilpatrick's lead regiments and initiated a series of countermoves that completely stymied whatever

29 Eleanor D. McSwain, ed., *Crumbling Defenses, or Memoirs and Reminiscences of John Logan Black, Colonel, C. S. A.* (Macon, GA, 1960), 37-38, 42; Law, "The Struggle For 'Round Top,'" 3:327; Evander M. Law to John B. Bachelder, June 13, 1876, *The Bachelder Papers,* 1:495.

30 Law, "The Struggle For 'Round Top,'" 3:327.

grand design Kilpatrick might have planned. Any understanding of just how thoroughly Evander Law outwitted the Federals on July 3 must start with a review of his actions at the close of July 2. It is the only way to comprehend the calamity that befell the lamented Farnsworth and his hard-charging band of daredevils. Reviewing Law's actions also sheds much-needed light on the inability of Wesley Merritt's brigade to turn the Confederate right flank, which prevented them from running amok in the open fields behind Rebel lines. As we shall see, the Union side of the story was so tainted as to render it unreliable. We must look to the perspective of the Confederate decision makers, for sometimes the best view for a war chronicler to take is that of the forces marshaled across the battle lines.

Farnsworth's brigade had left Two Taverns shortly before 8:00 a.m. and skirted south then west of the Round Tops. By then, Kilpatrick had discovered that the Michiganders had been side-tracked by Pleasonton. He informed the corps commander that he was reluctant to attack without Custer's men, and he pressed Pleasonton for more help. No doubt, the old schemer already knew that Custer had been waylaid and sent to Gregg's division. There was no "mistake" about it; Kilpatrick would have to await Merritt's arrival. Reluctant to commit to the attack with only Farnsworth's 1,900 saber arms, the normally aggressive Kilpatrick was forced to dawdle away his time in ascertaining the enemy's strength and dispositions. The waiting game did nothing for his hair-trigger equanimity. Farnsworth's lone brigade approached the battlefield from the south, massing in a heavy stand of timber that extended from the base of the Round Tops west toward the Emmitsburg Road.

Farnsworth's brigade finally shook out into line shortly after 1:00 p.m., beginning just southwest of the Round Tops, extending west, and crossing Plum Run. The 1st Vermont took up station on the right, the 1st West Virginia occupied the center, while the 18th Pennsylvania anchored the left flank. Elder's battery was man-handled through a heavily wooded slope to the crest of a rocky piece of high ground just behind the cavalry's battle line. The 5th New York, hidden in a ravine, was held back to support the battery. As the columns deployed into line, the massive barrage meant to prepare the way for Pickett began with two signal guns followed by the thunderous roar of the massed Confederate batteries.

The seasoned veterans of the 1st Vermont, in the van of Farnsworth's march, immediately pushed their 3rd Battalion (Companies A, D, K, and M) forward in skirmish order. The Vermonters made contact with the enemy skirmish line around noon and moved rapidly to engage the Confederate positions near the southwestern base of Round Top. "Soon after the Regiment struck the enemy's skirmish line, my battalion of four companies was dismounted," reported Maj.

John W. Bennett of the 1st Vermont. "The Confederates in my immediate front were slowly forced back to their main line at the very base of 'Round Top.' The battalions continued to press forward, creeping from rock to rock, until the groans and moans of the wounded in the opposing lines were heard with equal distinctness."[31]

From the center of the battlefield at Cemetery Ridge, the roar of combat ebbed and flowed, "and the awful musketry that soon followed had mostly died away, indicating the failure of Pickett's efforts to break our lines." Captain Parsons recalled an "oppressive stillness after the day's excitement." Taking advantage of the respite, Parsons rode to the brow of a nearby hill, from which he had a panoramic view of the field. "Directly in front of us opened the valley toward Gettysburg, with its wheat-fields; at the right, and less than half a mile distant, rose Round Top," he described, awed by the terrain. "Projecting from the Round Top was a hill . . . [whose slopes] were covered with immense granite boulders."[32]

James Longstreet, who had been watching the developing situation with extreme trepidation, left the center of his line, where he had been directing his corps' efforts to support Pickett's Charge, and rode to Law's side. The centerpiece of his defense line, Law explained, were his guns, even "[t]hough two of my batteries had been withdrawn to take part in the grand artillery attack that preceded General Pickett's fatal charge on Cemetery Ridge." Law, thankful for what assets he had rather than regretful of what he had lost, added, "I still had at my disposal twelve pieces of splendid artillery, and these I arranged in such a way as to command thoroughly every part of the line threatened by the Federal cavalry." These were the guns on which Kilpatrick fixated. Captain Henry Clay Potter of the 18th Pennsylvania recalled, "[He] wanted to have the enemy battery charged and captured, believing it to be unprotected." Kilpatrick initiated a series of reconnaissances, and the reports were almost identical in their observations. One averred "that the ground was not feasible for cavalry and that the enemy guns were on a hill behind a high stone wall in a very strong position."[33]

---

31 John W. Bennett, "Account of the 1st Vermont Cavalry at Gettysburg," Participants Accounts, Farnsworth's Folder, General Farnsworth's Death.

32 Bennett, "Account of the 1st Vermont Cavalry at Gettysburg"; Parsons, "Farnsworth's Charge and Death," 3:393

33 "General Law's Account"; Henry Clay Potter, "Personal Experiences of Henry Clay Potter, Captain, 18th Pennsylvania Cavalry, in the Battle of Gettysburg."

Merritt Gives It a Shot

The situation for the Confederates went from serious to precarious when Merritt's advance up the Emmitsburg Road was detected by Rebel outposts. This forced Law to withdraw Brig. Gen. George "Tige" Anderson's Georgia brigade from his line and shift it to a position straddling the Emmitsburg Road. As Merritt's troopers went into line, five regiments—possibly as many as 1,200 veteran infantrymen—took up corresponding positions to their front. Merritt reported that "[t]he 'Sixth Pennsylvania,' having the advance of the brigade, was the first of the cavalry to become engaged. The men were dismounted and pushed forward to meet the infantry line of the enemy. The 'Second' soon entered the field, and the engagement increased in fury." The 1st U.S. Cavalry, moving to the right of the 2nd U.S. Cavalry, cemented its right on the Emmitsburg Road. "[We] moved out on a dirt road toward the west soon turning northward and soon after crossing a narrow, deep creek, came in on the left of the First West Virginia, of Farnsworth's brigade," wrote Sgt. Samuel J. Crockett of the 1st U.S. in his diary. "This was a narrow country road; we dismounted near a schoolhouse in the woods to the left and moved on foot through the woods to support or relieve the Sixth Pennsylvania. who were about half way across a wide open field."[34]

From his vantage point at the edge of the woods, Crockett was able to clearly see the salient features of the ground: "The wide open fields which sloped from us (the woods) down to near the centre of the field" gave way to "an abrupt rise to the woods." It was in these woods, posted behind rail fences, that the Confederates awaited Merritt's attack. The Pennsylvanians were out in front, in skirmish formation. According to Crockett, the "1st were formed in a heavy one and passed through them at a run and into and through their line of battle." The 5th U.S. Cavalry went in on the left. If Kilpatrick took notice of the absence of the 6th U.S. Cavalry, he said nothing about it. Merritt's units straddled the Emmitsburg Road and advanced across open fields of wheat and corn. "It is risking little to say," opined an officer in the 6th Pennsylvania, "on the whole Confederate line at Gettysburg, there was hardly a point so well guarded by the enemy when Merritt's little brigade . . . came up this way from Emmitsburg." Some of the officers present contended that it was excellent ground to deliver a mounted charge and were mystified by the orders to go in dismounted. Sergeant Crockett rendered a more

---

34 Merritt, "Reminiscences," 295; Samuel J. Crockett to John B. Bachelder, December 27, 1882, *The Bachelder Papers*, 2:916.

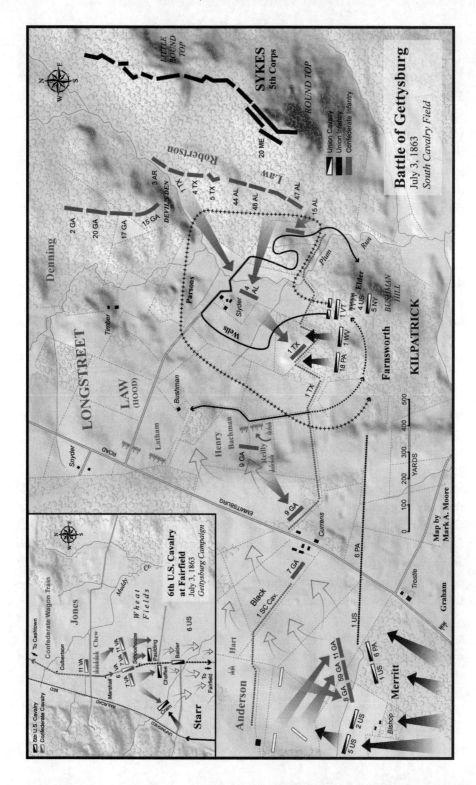

Battle of Gettysburg
July 3, 1863
South Cavalry Field

Map by
Mark A. Moore

realistic view: "The country was so woody & fences so high that both sides fought dismounted," he recorded.[35]

Behind the heavy fire of carbines, Merritt's men forged ahead. "We soon whipped their cavalry and drove it near a mile to their reserves," recalled Crockett, until "checked by a large force of the enemy, who, behind the stone walls of a house and its fences in our front, was pouring a shower of bullets on the advancing cavalry." Unable to punch his way through despite pushing the enemy back, Merritt began to extend his left flank in an attempt to sidle around the end of the Confederate right. He ordered a section of Capt. William M. Graham's battery brought up, and the accuracy of its fire soon cleared the sharpshooters from the Curran farmhouse. The enemy, reported Merritt, was "driven from one cover only to find and take possession of another in the rear." As the 5th U.S. tried to go around the flank, the 6th Pennsylvania struck straight up the Emmitsburg Road, supported on the left by the 1st U.S., and on the right by the 2nd U.S. "And thus the work continued, each regiment of the brigade doing its part nobly." Captain Hart, posted with his guns in the middle of the Emmitsburg Road, and keeping a hawk-eye on Merritt for the slightest movement that would lead to a forced retirement, recalled the cavalry's maneuvers. "Here a considerable skirmish occurred with the Federal Cavalry. Our line was too short, and a Federal column extended across the road by the Kern house, and enveloped our right completely, penetrating some distance to our rear. I was then retired."[36]

Evander Law's worst-case scenario was coming true. "This stretching process continued until I became fearful that it might be easily broken by a bold cavalry attack." Just in the nick of time, however, Law arrived at the endangered point with the first of Anderson's Georgia brigade. Personally taking command of the situation, he led the 9th Georgia to the attack. "When we arrived," reported Capt. George Hillyer of the 9th Georgia, "the enemy was nearly at the battery. Passing through from behind the guns, with a yell, the regiment charged the enemy in the open field, scattering and chasing them away in a moment, killing and wounding a number and capturing several horses." Colonel Black, his guns temporarily silenced, watched as the Alabama regiments "springing up poured a murderous fire into their left flank." It was an absolutely stunning move, perfectly timed and

---

35 Crockett to John B. Bachelder, 2:916; "Address of Col. Fredric C. Newhall," *Dedication of the Monument of the Sixth Penna. Cavalry on the Battlefield of Gettysburg* (Philadelphia, 1889), 21; Samuel J. Crockett, Diary entry for July 3, 1863.

36 Samuel J. Crockett, Diary entry for July 3, 1863; Merritt, "Reminiscences," 295; James F. Hart to John B. Bachelder, March 3, 1885, in Ladd and Ladd, eds. *The Bachelder Papers*, 2:1216.

professionally executed. "A whole Rgmt of Infantry rose at once in a wheatfield and gave us a volley," recalled one of the lucky survivors. "We knocked their colors down several times but our little squadron not more than 70 men could not hold their own against so many though everyone fought like a tiger. We had to fall back and then the rebel cavalry followed. The balls came like hail."[37]

The rest of the Rebel brigade, whooping and hollering, then rushed to join the 9th Georgia. The 11th Georgia passed behind the 9th and moved to block the charge of the 5th U.S. Cavalry. "The detachment," reported Maj. Henry D. McDonald, commanding the 11th Georgia, "reached the flank just as the enemy's dismounted cavalry succeeded in turning the same, driving our cavalry force before them. . . . I ordered a charge of the entire force, which was promptly made. The enemy was repulsed with loss and driven in confusion several hundred yards to a point far beyond our flank." On the Union side, Sam Crockett reported the same rough treatment of the 1st U.S. Cavalry. "We were driven back by a charge on our right flank and rear," he recorded. The regiment fell back to the woods and rallied, but the rest of the day was a fizzle. A weary Crockett wrote in his journal, "This was our last position. We did no fighting there but after dark moved (somewhere)."[38]

With Merritt's thrust beautifully parried, Law halted his pursuit and consolidated his positions. The Rebel flank was now formidably manned by three regiments of veteran infantry and three batteries of artillery. Captain Fredrick Newhall of the 6th Pennsylvania described this line as having "that confident look of being here to stay . . . and either Merritt called a halt, or Law brought him to a stand, just as you may happen to fancy the report of one or the other." After a two-hour gun battle, the combatants settled just outside of effective range, and though the guns continued to bang away at each other sporadically, a lull settled over the opposing lines. "After waiting behind a stone wall a good while for the rebels to come, Gen. Merritt sent us orders to mount and come to the batteries as the rebel infantry was advancing in great force," continued Crockett. That night, "Our dismounted men were steadily firing on them all the time. Three brigades of rebels came in sight but none charged the battery. At night we withdrew."[39]

37 "General Law's Account."; *OR* 27, pt. 2, 400; John L. Black to John B. Bachelder, March 22, 1886, *The Bachelder Papers*, 2:1242; Samuel J. Crockett, Diary entry for July 3, 1863.

38 *OR* 27, pt. 2, 402; Samuel J. Crockett to John B. Bachelder, December 27, 1882, *The Bachelder Papers*, 2:916.

39 "Address of Col. Fredric C. Newhall," 21; Samuel J. Crockett, Diary entry for July 3, 1863.

In the opinion of Captain Newhall, the lesson of Merritt's fight against Law was simple: "A brigade of infantry backed by an army in position, will stop, if it wishes to, a brigade of cavalry outside the lines of its own army, devoid of support, and simply moving against the enemy's flank." To their credit, "neither Merritt nor the men under him had the least idea of breaking through Lee's right, alone and unsupported." Evander Law spent the rest of the day putting out brush fires along the length of his extended flank. "Being relieved for the present at least from the pressure of Merritt's Brigade on my right, and having reduced the length of the line to more manageable dimensions," he wrote, "I turned my attention to that part of the line threatened by Farnsworth's Brigade. . . . I did not have long to wait."[40]

Covered in Glory, Buried Without a Shroud

Controversy surrounds the Kilpatrick-Farnsworth confrontation prior to the latter's ill-fated charge at South Cavalry Field. The event is filled with so much human drama and pathos that historians are almost duty-bound to examine it in exquisite detail. The urge here is to resist that method and stick to the facts that are germane to the theme, i.e., the extent to which the actions of Farnsworth's brigade affected the operations of, and results earned by, Merritt's brigade.

This must be recognized as a pivotal event in the growth of the Federal cavalry; its ramifications were deeply felt, and the shock of its losses were long-lasting. It went far beyond just the tabulation of killed, wounded, and missing. It is the melodramatics of the moment which hold sway. Both Farnsworth and Merritt had received their attack orders from Kilpatrick, a man harboring the pre-battle belief that if he could break through what he supposed was a thin line of defenders on the far right of Lee's army, he would wreak havoc amongst the ammunition and supply trains of the Army of Northern Virginia. Somewhere in the recesses of Kilpatrick's often erratically brilliant military mind was a vision of two brigades, acting in unison, attacking a thin line of skirmishers, which early in the day might have been a scratch force at best. The way would be paved for military glory. Alas, nothing went as planned, for Merritt arrived late in the afternoon. By then, the Confederates had augmented their line, and, more disastrously, Kilpatrick's attacks had been delivered piecemeal. The vagaries of the terrain fronting each brigade were a major factor in their uncoordinated nature. Additionally, the topography of the land in front of Farnsworth was already presenting a slew of problems.

40   "Address of Col. Fredric C. Newhall," 21; "General Law's Account."

With respect to the possibility of a charge, Captain Potter said, "Nothing more was said about it until about four o'clock when we were getting a very severe and uncomfortable shelling." With the roar of battle on Cemetery Ridge providing a loud but familiar backdrop, "[t]he conversation continued for a long while and in a quiet and friendly manner until about the height of Pickett's charge which I think was about 3:30 or 4 P. M." By then, Merritt's attack had moved into the fields west of the Emmitsburg Road, and Kilpatrick had become impatient with the progress of Farnsworth's attack. He galloped right past Captain Parsons, who noted that Kilpatrick was "showing great impatience and eagerness for orders." Finding nothing but negativity at the point of the charge, Kilpatrick lapsed into a frosty silence. Major Charles E. Capehart of the 1st West Virginia Cavalry was one of the many who voiced his opinion in his after-action report. "I cannot fail to refer you to the defensive position the enemy had availed themselves of, which is one that above all others is the worst for a cavalry charge" he wrote, in reference to the high stone fences, concluding that the "whole ground over which we charged was very adverse in every particular, being broken and uneven and covered with rock."[41]

Farnsworth turned to Maj. John W. Bennett and exclaimed in a voice of the doomed, "Major, I do not see the slightest chance for a successful charge." New to command, and perhaps not yet ready to flagrantly defy his superior's orders even though they would result in the apparently useless deaths of so many of his men, Farnsworth decided to urge Kilpatrick to reconsider his decision. It was the wrong moment to approach Kilpatrick, who had finally woken from his torpor to realize that his plan was starting to fall apart before it had even gotten started. He could see his moment slipping away. On the left, Merritt's attack had already pushed far into the fields to the right of the Emmitsburg Road; the perfectly dressed skirmish line of the Regulars, blue and solid, stood out against the background of cultivated fields and pastures. Merritt's and Farnsworth's attacks were supposed to support each other, but east of the road, Farnsworth's command had not yet moved. The normally abrasive Kilpatrick was beyond "annoyed, not to say angered." He realized that it was imperative that the Rebel infantry to his right be prevented from marching to reinforce the troops opposing Merritt, or the enemy would simply keep extending his line, and prevent Merritt from turning his flank. Kilpatrick could already see Rebel infantry marching at quick step toward the endangered flank. And just like the snap of a hypnotist's fingers brings the mesmerized subject

---

41 Potter, "Personal Experiences"; Parsons, "Farnsworth's Charge and Death," 3:393; *OR 27*, pt.1, 1,018-1,019.

back to the real world, the whole tenor of their discussion changed. Finished with the extended conversation, Kilpatrick leaned in toward Farnsworth, and in a low, menacing voice said, "Farnsworth, if you don't charge that Battery, I will."[42]

Elon Farnsworth, recalled Captain Parsons, "was courage incarnate, but full of tender regard for his men, and his protest was manly and soldierly." His entreaties fell on deaf ears, for Kilpatrick, in his bull-headed Irish way, had already determined his course of action. Wearing his frustration openly, Kilpatrick unleashed his vitriol on Farnsworth. "Do you refuse to obey my orders?" he declared in a confrontational voice, his normally florid complexion now a dangerous shade of red. "If you are afraid to lead this charge, I will lead it!" Realizing that the die had been cast, Farnsworth replied, as he turned away, "General, if you order the charge I will lead it, but you must take the awful responsibility . . . [but] he said 'I will obey your order.'" This done, Farnsworth trotted back to where his regiments were preparing for the attack and informed his stunned commanders that Kilpatrick had ordered the brigade to go in.[43]

Lieutenant Colonel Addison W. Preston recalled that "[t]he contest for the possession of this hill was most desperate. . . . The opposing forces were now completely intermingled, and the contest became a hand-to-hand one, in which our sabers were effectually used." Captain Parsons described it as "a swift, resistless

---

42 "Account of Major John W. Bennett, 1st Vermont Cavalry"; Jeffry D. Wert, "All the Powers of Hell Were Waked to Madness," *America's Civil War Magazine* (July 2002), 5; Potter, "Personal Experiences."

43 Parsons, "Farnsworth's Charge and Death," 3:394; The Farnsworth-Kilpatrick confrontation and subsequent attack was one of the most highly charged and controversial episodes of the Civil War. Three Union officers claimed to have been present at that moment or close enough to hear it. The first was Capt. Henry C. Parsons of the 1st Vermont Cavalry. "I was near Kilpatrick when he impetuously gave the order to Farnsworth." (Parsons, "Farnsworth's Charge and Death," 3:393.) The others were Capt. Henry C. Potter of the 18th Pennsylvania and Maj. John Bennett, also of the 1st Vermont. Both of their accounts are in the files of Gettysburg National Military Park. Bennett was adamant that "[o]nly three persons were present during this interview, and I made the third." Potter maintained that he, too, was within hearing distance. A word of caution concerning Captain Parsons is in order. He returned to his regiment in February 1864, having spent more than six months recuperating from his Gettysburg wounds. When he reported to regimental headquarters, he was informed that he faced "unspecified charges," and was allowed to resign his commission as of January 4, 1864. The extent to which this incident colored Parsons's views of the confrontation and battle is unknown. According to Parsons, Farnsworth objected at once to Kilpatrick's orders. "General, do you mean it? Shall I throw my handful of men over rough ground, through thick timber, against a brigade of infantry?" an incredulous Farnsworth supposedly asked. For a thorough and authoritative treatment of this episode, see Wittenberg, *Gettysburg's Forgotten Cavalry Actions.*

charge over rocks, through timber, under close enfilading fire." A dazed bugler from Company I of the 1st Vermont, Joe Allen, likened it "to getting into a hornet's nest." Farnsworth was conspicuous for his gallantry during the doomed charge, as was Col. William Wells, who somehow managed to get through unscathed. Not so Farnsworth. Two days later, his body was found just after the second fence, riddled with bullets, surrounded by the bodies of his comrades. The shoulder straps with their single star, given to him personally by Pleasonton, had been cut off. Colonel William C. Oates of the 15th Alabama Infantry was one of many who left an account of Farnsworth's unfortunate end. According to the Alabama officer, one of his men, carbine in hand, had dashed forward and confronted the wounded officer, "who still grasped his pistol and was trying to rise, 'Now you surrender!'" Farnsworth replied, "'I will not do it,' and placing the pistol to his own head, shot his brains out."[44]

So, by the end of this hard day's work, what had Kilpatrick, Merritt, and Farnsworth accomplished? They certainly had wasted an awful lot of lives for very little tangible reward. In all, Kilpatrick's attack had killed 67 men, another 20 had been wounded, and 35 more had been taken prisoner. Kilpatrick's grandiose plans that envisioned cavalry overrunning the enemy's rear were predicated on two brigades acting in tandem: the one on the right drawing and holding the enemy, and the second extending west, finding the soft edge of the Confederate flank, and turning it. But then, in a battle in which it could be said that every minute was crucial, Merritt failed to adapt his plan to the day's march. Rather than change its tempo to that of a forced march, Merritt's brigade continued at a leisurely pace in order to acclimate the men and horses to the rigors of campaigning after extended time spent guarding the wagon trains.

It was certainly no more than an hour's hard ride from their position in the rear to South Cavalry Field, and what might have been possible at 1:00 p.m. was much more difficult, and likely impossible, just two hours later when Merritt reportedly arrived on the field west of the Emmitsburg Road. Merritt's part in the operation, originally conceived as a sweep around the enemy flank, morphed into what trooper Crockett described as "a ruse intended to make the rebels believe that the

---

44 OR 27. pt. 1, 1,013; Parsons, "Farnsworth's Charge and Death," 3:395; Account of Joe Allen; William C. Oates, "Gettysburg: The Battle on the Right," *Southern Historical Society Papers*, Vol. 6 (July-December 1878), 182.

real point of attack was there while it really was on the extreme right. . . . If it was a ruse it succeeded."[45]

In the end, Kilpatrick's sins were not deemed that significant. Unlike many of his contemporaries who were killed, maimed, succumbed to disease, or suffered the privations of the Rebel prison camps, Kilpatrick lived through the war.

45 Crockett, Diary entry for July 3, 1863.

CHAPTER TWELVE

Charges of Madness; Charges of Grandeur

CAPTAIN WILLIAM MILLER WROTE that "Gregg's troops were not so favorably situated"; they were "[o]ccupying a line . . . through an open country . . . in full view of the enemy." Custer became alarmed. "The enemy had obtained correct range of my new position, and was pouring solid shot, and shell into my command with great accuracy," he reported. The 1st and 7th Michigan, which had been taking their ease in a clover field, were quickly mounted, and retired out of range of the guns. It is, perhaps, this rearward movement that gave rise to the assertion by many that Custer's brigade had started its march south to Kilpatrick. In the meantime, Custer continued to feed the 5th Michigan, along with some squadrons from the 6th Michigan, toward the Rummel farm. "Custer, eager for the fray," recalled Miller, "extended the left of the line along Little's Run with a portion of the 6th Michigan, dismounted."[1]

It was 2:00 in the afternoon—two full hours after Custer had received his recall orders—and the 1st New Jersey had finally begun its own move toward the enemy. "McIntosh, who well understood Stuart's tactics, and had correctly discerned his position, dismounted the lst New Jersey and moved it forward . . . in the direction of Rummel's," stated Miller. His statement verified the actual time that Major Janeway led the 1st New Jersey up the Low Dutch Road to the Lott farm. Dismounting his men, Janeway pushed out of the woods and into the open fields ahead. As they broke from cover, Lt. Col. Vincent A. Witcher's detachment of Virginians opened on their flank, forcing the 1st New Jersey to adjust its "line to

---

1 Miller, "The Cavalry Battle Near Gettysburg," 402, 403; Robertson, *Michigan in the War*, 582.

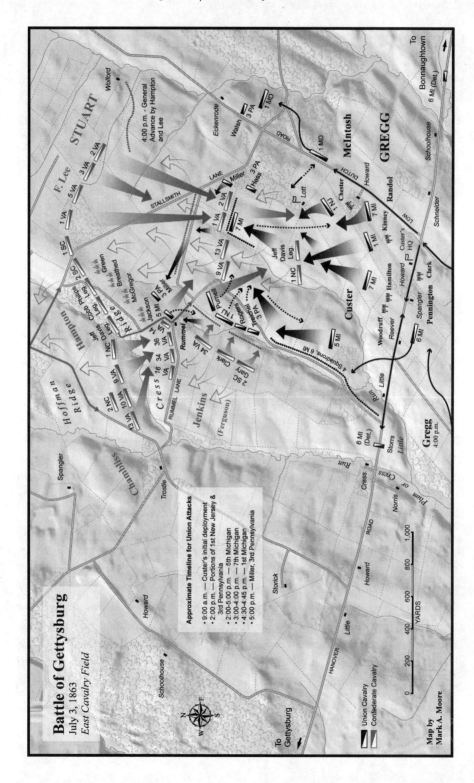

Battle of Gettysburg
July 3, 1863
East Cavalry Field

Approximate Timeline for Union Attacks

- 9:00 a.m. — Custer's initial deployment
- 2:00 p.m. — Portions of 1st New Jersey & 3rd Pennsylvania
- 2:00–5:00 p.m. — 5th Michigan
- 3:00–4:00 p.m. — 7th Michigan
- 4:30–4:45 p.m. — 1st Michigan
- 5:00 p.m. — Miller, 3rd Pennsylvania

Map by
Mark A. Moore

Union Cavalry
Confederate Cavalry

YARDS
0   200   400   600   800   1,000

correspond with that of their antagonists, and firing began. At the same time a Confederate battery appeared on the top of the ridge and commenced shelling." Lieutenant Brooke Rawle, his regiment poised to join the attack, watched as the 1st New Jersey reached "a fence running parallel with that occupied by the enemy . . . and immediately became hotly engaged." The battle for Rummel's farm was growing in fits and spurts, as the opposing commanders began to augment their skirmish lines with more support.[2]

The Rebels struck first. "They had not long been in position before under a vigorous fire from their skirmishers, a considerable body of the enemy made a resolute advance upon them," detailed Reverend Henry R. Pyne, the chaplain of the 1st New Jersey. "From behind the stone walls, taking advantage of every ditch and little inequality in the surface of the ground, the dismounted cavalry poured forth the contents of their carbines." The sanguinary fire not only halted the Rebels in their tracks; it actually pushed them back. Lieutenant Hermann Schuricht of the 14th Virginia commented on the volume of fire. "My company was ordered to the extreme right on the slope of a hill," he recalled. "Our opponents poured a rain of bullets and shells on us." Janeway now showed why he was a cut above the average officer. "Refusing to dismount in spite of the storm of bullets constantly whistling over our men," wrote an awestruck Pyne, "Janeway rode from end to end of his line of skirmishers, encouraging, warning, and directing its every portion—showing here as on many another field a coolness and bravery that made him a marked man among men."[3]

Inspired by Janeway's courage, the Jerseymen jumped the fence in their front and advanced on the enemy in bursts, cheering at every charge. McIntosh now committed the 3rd Pennsylvania to the fight. Two squadrons, under Capts. Charles Treichel and William W. Rogers, moved rapidly to Little's Run and took up position to the left of the 1st New Jersey. Two more squadrons of the 3rd, commanded by Capts. James J. Walsh and Frank W. Hess, moved along the Low Dutch Road, passed Lott's farmhouse, and broke out into the open on the right of the 1st New Jersey. "It will thus be seen," Captain Miller recalled, "that the 3rd Pennsylvania was divided—one-half being on the left of the line, whilst the other occupied the right." The remainder of the regiment, including Brooke Rawle's and

2 Miller, "The Cavalry Battle Near Gettysburg," 402; Brooke Rawle, *History of the Third Pennsylvania Cavalry*, 274.

3 Henry R. Pyne, *The History of the First New Jersey Cavalry* (Trenton, NJ, 1871), 164; Hermann Schuricht, "Jenkins' Brigade in the Gettysburg Campaign," *The Richmond Dispatch*, April 5, 1896.

Miller's commands, took up position along the edges of the woods north of the Lott house.[4]

After splashing across Little's Run, Treichel and Rogers cut squarely across the line of advance of the 5th Michigan, which was maintaining its position near the Rummel farm buildings. Custer then advanced the 6th Michigan and extended his line further to the left. Brooke Rawle remembered that "four squadrons of the Sixth Michigan went into position dismounted along Little's Run . . . so as to cover the Hanover Road, the remainder of the regiment supporting them." Tree-shrouded Cress Ridge loomed menacingly over their left shoulders. On the Confederate side, Stuart stacked his right flank with troops. Chambliss's two regiments were kept mounted. Jenkins's two regiments, armed with the long-range but cumbersome Enfield rifle, dismounted, and joined the fence line, which was longer than that of the Federals. As a result, the Confederate attack was poised to sweep past the Union left flank.[5]

In every hurricane there is an "eye of the storm," an area of false calmness contained by the furies that lie beyond. Similarly, in every battle there is a lull, a moment before all hell breaks loose; when life is cheap, and death is gruesome. Scattered, disorganized units were put back in fighting trim, and the men caught a breather. Some made a last cup of coffee. Others may even have had time to jot down that final mortal thought. Both Kidd and Brooke Rawle remembered that moment vividly; it was one of only a few things the two men agreed upon. "Then there was a lull," recalled Kidd. "I cannot say how long it lasted, but . . . the troopers were dismounted, standing 'in place rest' in front of their horses." Colonel McIntosh claimed to have arrived at Custer's position around 1:00 p.m. According to Brooke Rawle, "Everything was quiet at this time." Custer informed McIntosh that it was a deceptive calm. The enemy, Custer told him, "was all around, and that an attack might be expected at any moment." That was when McIntosh ordered the 1st New Jersey to move into a patch of woods on the Low Dutch Road. Facing to the northwest and the Rebel positions, the Jerseymen were, at last, going into action.[6]

And finally, as this portion of the drama that was the battle of East Cavalry Field lurched towards its conclusion, we come to the crux of the matter; the

4 Miller, "The Cavalry Battle Near Gettysburg," 402.

5 Brooke Rawle, *History of the Third Pennsylvania Cavalry*, 275.

6 Kidd, *Personal Recollections*, 144-145; Brooke Rawle, *History of the Third Pennsylvania Cavalry*, 273.

moment when all the forces that had been collecting haphazardly, at this point in time and space, clashed in mortal combat. Left behind was not just a field of dead and maimed men and horses, but a legacy of rancor and discord between two men who had fought proudly under the Stars and Stripes. "There is a great deal of luck in war," expounded Capt. William W. Blackford of Jeb Stuart's staff. "Circumstances sometimes seem to combine, for or against, in a way that sets at naught all calculations, and at the Battle of Gettysburg half a dozen things may be enumerated, any one of which might have given us the victory if we had been 'in luck' at the time."[7]

Gregg arrived on the field, probably between noon and 1:00 p.m., took command of all the cavalry and artillery present, and established his headquarters in the Lott farmhouse. After their meeting had broken up, Custer went back to the business of fighting his brigade, and as only the 5th Michigan was engaged at the time, he had spent his time with the forward elements of that regiment. He had witnessed the opening gambit, in which Alger's men had "successfully repel[led] the repeated advances of a greatly superior force." Custer attributed this success to the Spencer repeating rifle, "which, in the hands of brave, determined men, like those composing the 5th Michigan cavalry, is in my estimation, the most effective fire-arm that our cavalry can adopt." Custer, still at the front with the 5th Michigan, was thoroughly engrossed watching the fight that McIntosh's men were putting up. John Bigelow, a bugler with the 5th, later wrote that the volume of carbine fire was "absolutely without intermission." But this could only last so long, and eventually troopers on both sides slowed down their tempo of fire. In fact, the 34th Virginia, their 10 rounds fired away in a brief flurry, was nearly out of ammo, and had begun to pull out of the firing line. As Jenkins's men pulled back, recorded Brooke Rawle, the "center of our line advanced and occupied the enemy's line of fences near the farm buildings.[8]

Suddenly, the roar of horse artillery was heard from the Confederate side. Breathed's and McGregor's batteries, their ammunition replenished in Gettysburg, had finally joined the fight. By that time, the 1st New Jersey and 3rd Pennsylvania were running desperately low on ammunition. The 1st New Jersey stayed gamely at the fence line. Chaplain Pyne wrote that "for more than a hundred yards the First Jersey pushed their little line, and at last, with ammunition exhausted, they still held

---

7   Blackford, *War Years with Jeb Stuart*, 230.

8   Robertson, *Michigan in the War*, 583; John A. Bigelow, "Draw Saber, Charge!" *The National Tribune*, May 27, 1886; Brooke Rawle, *History of the Third Pennsylvania Cavalry*, 275.

their ground facing the rebels with revolvers." Not until the last ball had been fired did they withdraw; then they ran for their lives! As the New Jersey troopers attempted to leave the firing line, bursting shells sent them diving for cover. "Breathed and McGregor opened with redoubled violence. Shells dropped and exploded among the skirmishers," recalled James Kidd, "while thicker and faster they fell around the position of the reserves." This proved too much for the 1st New Jersey, and Major Janeway "rode back to the reserve, and reported to Major Beaumont the condition of his men, requesting ammunition and reinforcement. At Major Beaumont's request, Colonel McIntosh ordered another regiment to take the place of the First Jersey."[9]

McIntosh had prepared for just such an eventuality, and had posted the 1st Maryland in reserve, near the Lott house. The 1st Maryland, however, was not where it was supposed to be. Without informing his brigade commander, General Gregg had taken it upon himself to move the regiment. "Of Colonel McIntosh's Brigade," Gregg admitted, "one of these, the 1st Maryland, was placed by me at the intersection of the Low Dutch and Hanover Road as to guard the flank." According to Gregg, the 1st Maryland did not participate in the battle. Exasperated and sick as a dog, McIntosh reportedly "gave way to tears and oaths." This is rather perplexing, as the Reverend Pyne later told a rather odd story. "That regiment halted a hundred yards to the rear of the line where the Jerseymen were stationed, and would not advance any further, while the latter resisted every effort to move them back," he noted. "Even Colonel McIntosh failed to get the relieving regiment up through the tremendous fire to the position of the First Jersey; old soldiers as they were."[10]

In the face of McIntosh's inability to withdraw his men, Custer decided to act. "It was not long thereafter, when General Custer directed Colonel Alger to advance and engage the enemy," recounted Captain Kidd. "The Fifth Michigan, its flanks protected by a portion of the Sixth Michigan on the left, by McIntosh's brigade on the right, moved briskly forward towards the wooded screen behind which the enemy was known to be concealed." Alger's dismounted men struck off across the wheat field, "along a fence which intersected the field lengthwise running at right angles to the skirmish line." A dismounted regiment from Fitz

9   Pyne, *The History of the First New Jersey Cavalry*, 164-165; Kidd, *Personal Recollections*, 148

10   David McMurtrie Gregg, "The Second Cavalry Division of the Army of the Potomac in the Gettysburg Campaign," *Commandery of the State of Pennsylvania, Military Order of the Loyal Legion of the United States*, (Philadelphia, 1907), 11; Longacre, *The Cavalry at Gettysburg*, 230; Pyne, *The History of the First New Jersey Cavalry*, 165.

Lee's brigade suddenly appeared out of nowhere to support the Confederate skirmishers and opened a brisk carbine fire on the exposed 5th Michigan, taking it completely by surprise. From his ringside seat on the far edges of the Lott woods, Brooke Rawle watched as the Rebels made "a terrific onslaught along the line. Treichel's and Rogers' squadrons of the Third Pennsylvania, and that portion of the Fifth Michigan which had reached their line, held the ground stubbornly."[11]

Major Luther Trowbridge, in the thick of the bedlam, did not have the luxury of a ringside seat. His is a vivid account of a vicious fight, marked by tragedy. "In the afternoon came the work for us, which cost us the life of our dear [Noah] Ferry and cast a deep gloom over the regt.," he intoned, sorrow still heavy on him; "I can assure you the bullets flew thick as hail around us. I had some narrow escapes." Spencer rifles ate ammunition at a prodigious rate, and the moment finally came when none was left, precipitating Alger's command to "fall back to our horses. As we were falling back the Rebs came out of the woods in clouds and advanced with yells and shouts." The 5th Michigan was swept away like so much chaff. Attempting to stop the rush to the rear, Major Ferry called to his troopers, "Rally boys! Rally for the fence!" Reportedly, he had picked up a discarded Spencer, and fired several shots at the enemy. A few seconds later he crumpled to the ground, an enemy bullet through his head. The Rebels kept on coming, baying like coon dogs on a game trail, the scent of victory strong in the air. The 5th Michigan was paying a hard price for its stubborn stance, reckoned Jeb Stuart; his men "had piled more dead and wounded men and horses on as little space as he had ever seen on any field." It was a desperate moment, wrote a shaken Miller. "The short supply of ammunition of the 5th Michigan having by this time given out, and Maj. Noah H. Ferry, who was in command of the line, having been killed," he wrote, "the whole line was driven in." Seeking to capitalize on this opportunity, Fitz Lee deployed the 1st Virginia for the attack.[12]

Captain Miller recalled that a "lull in the firing now ensued, during which Custer's brigade returned." The respite proved short-lived. "A calm now ensued that indicated a storm, and soon the storm came off to my front and right," he wrote. The Confederate cavalry paraded out of the sheltering woods, beautifully

---

11 Kidd, *Personal Recollections*, 145; Brooke Rawle, *The History of the Third Pennsylvania Cavalry*, 275; Brooke Rawle, "The Right Flank at Gettysburg," 479.

12 Luther S. Trowbridge, letter, recipient and date unknown, 4-5; David M. Cooper, *Obituary Discourse on the Occasion of the Death of Noah Henry Ferry of the Fifth Michigan Cavalry, Killed at Gettysburg, July 3, 1863* (New York, 1863); Scott C. Cole, *34th Battalion Virginia Cavalry* (Lynchburg, VA, 1993), 52; Miller, "The Cavalry Battle Near Gettysburg," 403.

aligned in columns of squadrons, moving at a stately walk. The batteries on both sides opened in a roar. The Union guns "did splendid work, tearing large gaps in their column and slaughtering many of their men and horses. They moved right along, as if nothing was occurring, and with determination that bespoke business."[13]

The entire Federal line was buckling, merely waiting for one more push to send it scampering for the rear. Fitz Lee prepared to finish the job. The rearward movement of Colonel McIntosh's squadrons was more than enough to convince the Rebel command to believe "it a symptom of retreat," recounted Brooke Rawle, and the Southerners moved to the attack once more. It had become impossible for McIntosh to relieve Custer's men in their advanced positions. His 1st New Jersey had originally been sent to relieve the 5th Michigan. Thereafter, the 3rd Pennsylvania had been fed piecemeal into the fight, and, despite its huge expenditure of ammunition, had little to show for it. Now both regiments were vulnerable, and any support from the rest of their brigade was too far away to make any significant contribution. The 5th Michigan was also in deep trouble. They had been in action most of the day and were running low on Spencer cartridges, and then they were ordered in to relieve the regiments that had been sent to relieve them.[14]

In the middle of an open wheat field, the 5th Michiganders, scrabbling for cartridges from their many dead and wounded comrades, got caught in a hail of bullets. Though one account stated that they had held their ground "stubbornly," a more telling version by one of the Pennsylvanians claimed that the regiment had "acted badly and came near breaking our whole line." They were accused of trampling through McIntosh's strained skirmish line, seeking their held horses in their rush to escape the charging Rebs. At this inopportune moment, a colonel from another regiment took Trowbridge to task, and, "thinking we were giving ground immediately made a great fuss." These fears were allayed when Trowbridge "told him we were not falling back because we were beaten, but because our ammunition was gone, and we wanted to get back to our horses. That satisfied him." Colonel Alger was not the kind of soldier who lost control of his men. "We fell back, not as good a line as we would have done later on," admitted Major Trowbridge, "but deliberately and without disorder or confusion." The troopers

13 Miller, "The Cavalry Battle Near Gettysburg," 402; Brooke Rawle, *History of the Third Pennsylvania Cavalry*, 306-307.

14 Brooke Rawle, "The Right Flank at Gettysburg," 479.

ran to their horses and did what came natural to any cavalrymen: they mounted up and prepared to give or receive combat.[15]

A Fence in the Path to Glory

Throughout this chaos Alger kept his legendary cool, and, recalled bugler John Bigelow, "order[ed] me to go and say to Custer that a regiment can charge mounted, around our left, with a good show for success . . . Custer and staff [were] soon found." James Kidd, speaking at the dedication of the Michigan Memorial on East Cavalry Field in 1890, recalled that "Gregg, seeing the necessity for prompt action," ordered the 7th Michigan forward. Just then, remembered Capt. George Armstrong, a "good looking young officer rode out toward us, waving his hand, and in a pleasant tone of voice called out, 'Bring on your 7th now.'" Even Brooke Rawle testified to Custer's military perspicacity: "The Seventh Michigan . . . was just then coming on the field from the direction of the Reever house in column of fours. . . . Custer, who was near, also saw the emergency, ordered close column of squadrons to be formed at the gallop, and advanced with it to meet the attack." According to Kidd, "Squadron succeeded squadron until an entire regiment came into view, with sabers gleaming and colors gaily fluttering in the breeze." It was a splendid sight, he remembered:

> As the regiment moved forward, and cleared the battery, Custer drew his saber, placed himself in front and shouted: "Come on you Wolverines!" . . . There was no check to the charge. The squadrons kept up in good form. Every man yelled at the top of his voice.[16]

Units of the 1st New Jersey, 3rd Pennsylvania, and 5th Michigan were scattered throughout the field in front of the charging 7th Michigan. As the thundering columns approached, they scampered to get out of the way. "Just at this time the 7th Mich came on the field led by Gen. Custer in person charged the

---

15 Ibid.; Brooke Rawle, *History of the Third Pennsylvania Cavalry*, 306-307; Luther S. Trowbridge to John B. Bachelder, Feb. 19, 1886, in Ladd and Ladd, eds., *The Bachelder Papers: Gettysburg in Their Own Words* (El Dorado Hills, CA, 2020), 2:1207.

16 Bigelow, "Draw Saber, Charge!"; James H. Kidd, "Address at the Dedication of the Michigan Monument Upon the Field of Gettysburg," *Journal of the United States Cavalry Association*, Vol. 4, No. 12 (March 1891), 58; Brooke Rawle, *History of the Third Pennsylvania Cavalry*, 276; George A. Armstrong, "At the Battle of Gettysburg," in William O. Lee, ed., *Personal and Historical Sketches of and by Members of the Seventh Regiment Michigan Volunteer Cavalry 1862-1865* (Detroit, 1901), 155; Kidd, *Personal Recollections*, 148-149.

advancing rebels," recalled an awed Major Trowbridge. "Almost entirely out of ammunition we rallied and advanced with a thrilling shout for Michigan." In abject horror, bugler Bigelow watched the 7th begin a wide swinging movement to the right. "Vainly I yell as we gallop that the left is open, but to the right he cannot break," wrote Bigelow, still excited by the wild abandon of the charge 23 years after the battle, and "I urge them to go to the left." But the charge was developing too fast, and in the uproar of combat, Bigelow's shouted entreaties went unheeded. "First at a slow trot, then at a double quick, then the charge," rued Captain Armstrong, "[w]e went over the hill at a break-neck charge, down into the pithole of death."[17]

"On this day he [Custer] wore a small cap," wrote Sgt. Henry Meyer of Gregg's staff, and "after the fighting had been in progress for some little time, Custer took off his cap [and] placed it in his saddle-pocket." The general led the 7th Michigan in its wild charge, "his yellow hair flying and his uniform making him a conspicuous object." Now, far out ahead of the charging 7th, Custer saw what Bigelow had been hollering about. "The mistake is now clearly seen. Thirty rods more and we are on the rebel works—works and barriers too strong for horses to scale." Of this part of the action, Custer would report, "The ground over which they had to pass was very unfavorable, but despite all obstacles this regiment advanced boldly to the assault, which was executed in splendid style, the enemy being driven from field to field, until our advance reached a high and unbroken fence, behind which the enemy was strongly posted."[18]

From the head of the pack, Custer witnessed the strength of the Rebel position. "The Seventh dashed into the open field and rode straight at the dismounted line. . . . Custer led the charge half-way across the plain, then turned to the left; but the gallant regiment swept on under its own leaders, riding down and capturing many prisoners." Despite small successes, the charge threatened to become a tactical mistake. "We crashed against the stone wall, which withstood us, breaking our columns into jelly and mixing us up like a mass of pulp," wrote Armstrong. Shocked by the miscommunication, Bigelow lamented, "But bravely the troopers ride to the death. Officers and men all try to get over. 'Tis too bad they cannot! The rebels are too strong and too securely posted for the troopers. Hand to

---

17   Luther S. Trowbridge to J. Allen Bigelow, date unknown, GNMP, 5-6; Bigelow, "Draw Saber, Charge!"; Armstrong, "At the Battle of Gettysburg," 155.

18   Meyer, *Civil War Experiences*, 49-50; Bigelow, "Draw Saber, Charge!"; Robertson, *Michigan in the War*, 583.

hand the fight is going on either side of the barriers. The bugle rings the rally and the charge." The Michiganders' failure to push past the post and rail fence in the initial charge turned it into "an impassable barrier." Instinctively, the onrushing squadrons spread out along the fence line, "and pluckily began firing across it into the faces of the confederates, who . . . began to collect in swarms upon the opposite side.[19]

The fire from the Confederate line was unremitting. "The Rebels with their guns poked through the fence as they lay securely behind the wall," wrote Captain Armstrong, "were raking our helpless column with their deadly fire." Some of the braver officers jumped from their saddles. "Throw down the fence!" they ordered. The stout fencing proved difficult to bring down amid the heavy fire. With the unflappability of life-long hunters, the Rebels gleefully opened on the exposed cavaliers. Undeterred, the 7th Michigan passed through the holes and out into the open, plowed land beyond. Clouds of smoke scudded across the two fence lines. The fire, spurting unabatedly from both sides, flashed luridly in the gloom of the closeup fight. Armstrong said both men and horses struggled to clear the fencing, but eventually "through the gap in the fence our brave boys went pell-mell, their horses jumping the wall and at them we went every man for himself." It was a stubborn fight, and the enemy "recoiled and withdrew only as we cut or shot them down or rode over them. We withdrew and reformed our broken ranks and shattered companies." In some places along the fence, the dead and wounded were stacked like cordwood. Custer, once again, took the lead, and bypassing the charnel house at the fence line, pounded off for the Rummel farm and charged the Rebel line one more time. "Before it the Confederates at once fell back," wrote Kidd. There, another fence stymied their advance. The Yankees were within 250 yards of the Rebel batteries, but the veteran gunners "were pouring canister into the charging column as fast as could be fired."[20]

Bigelow was totally lost in the adrenaline-pumping madness of battle. "Custer is a host. The men are all heroes," he wrote in his exuberant style. "They stand face to face. The rebels are as brave as they. It is yelling, shooting, swearing, cutting, fight, fight—all fight. The ranks are being rapidly thinned. Horses and men are being shot down like dogs. They have us in a fix. The advantage is all on their side."

19 Isham, *Seventh Michigan Cavalry*, 23; Armstrong, "At the Battle of Gettysburg," 155; Bigelow, "Draw Saber, Charge!"; Kidd, *Personal Recollections*, 149.

20 Armstrong, "At the Battle of Gettysburg," 155; Bigelow, "Draw Saber, Charge!"; Kidd, *Personal Recollections*, 150-151.

In the tumult of the assault, Custer's horse went down, and when he looked up, he was staring into the muzzle of a Rebel gun. Custer later regaled Henry Meyer with the tale of his escape. "I heard him remark after the fight," wrote Meyer, "that he would have been captured except for the fact one of his buglers caught a horse for him and held off the man who wanted him to surrender."[21]

Major Trowbridge was appalled. "Go to left," he had said. "Go to the left!!" But the untested 7th Michigan had moved to the right, where he had told them there was little chance of success, "squadron after squadron breaking upon the struggling mass in front, like the waves of the sea upon a rocky shore, until all were mixed in one confused and tangled mess." In retrospect, Captain Armstrong thought, going back a second time was one charge too many. The regiment would get no closer to the thundering Rebel batteries than they were right then, and they were still more than 200 yards away. For all the "cutting, slashing and shooting them down," said Armstrong, an inkling of disaster started to take hold. The Rebels "were too heavy and sullen for us and stood their ground so desperately that as before we were compelled to withdraw over the wall a second time, badly broken and cut up." When another Confederate regiment appeared and moved to the charge, Armstrong informed Custer that enough was enough. "Yes, I know it," Custer answered, recognizing the further futility of a continued attack. "We must get back under the guns."[22]

Stuart began to feel the momentum of the fight swinging his way. "I ordered forward the nearest cavalry regiment quickly to charge this force of cavalry," he later reported. "It was gallantly done, and about the same time a portion of General Fitz. Lee's command charged on the left, the First Virginia Cavalry being most conspicuous." What the Confederate cavalry leader did not yet know was that he had lost the last vestige of control he would exert in the battle, for his pursuing troops soon outpaced their commanders. "In these charges," continued Stuart in his official report, "the impetuosity of those gallant fellows, after two weeks of hard marching and hard fighting on short rations, was not only extraordinary, but irresistible. The enemy's masses vanished before them like grain before the scythe." The charge of the 1st Virginia took the regiment right up to the fence line, where "both regiments then fought face to face across the fence with their carbines and

21 Bigelow, "Draw Saber, Charge!"; Meyer, *Civil War Experiences*, 50.

22 Trowbridge to Bachelder, Feb. 19, 1886, 2:1207; Armstrong, "At the Battle of Gettysburg," 155-156.

revolvers, while a scorching fire centered upon the First Virginia from either flank."[23]

Hampton, too, had ordered in reinforcements. As the 7th Michigan crumbled away from the fence, it was struck in the flank by portions of the 9th and 13th Virginia, "and assisted the First Virginia to pass the fence, whereupon the Seventh Michigan gave way." From his position on the left flank, Alger decided it was time for the saber, his decision made easy by the fact that the 5th Michigan was out of ammunition. "We rallied and advanced with a thrilling shout for Michigan," voiced Trowbridge. At this point, the battlefield was a free flow of men and horses. The fighting was growing more fast-paced as the early morning dismounted action gave way to the mounted combat that characterized the battle in the afternoon. It was an untenable position. "Past the Rummel buildings, through the fields, almost to the fence where the most advanced of the Seventh Michigan had halted, Trowbridge kept on," reported Captain Kidd. "But he, too, was obliged to retire before the destructive fire of the confederate cannon, which did not cease to belch forth destruction upon every detachment of the union cavalry that approached near enough to threaten them." As Trowbridge's battalion was retiring, it was struck in the flank by a mounted charge of the 1st Virginia. By that time, Colonel Alger had mounted the second battalion. "A few moments later the balance of the regiment was engaged, and the enemy checked and driven from the field," he reported. Just as obstinately, the Rebels rallied, and came back across the field "in still greater numbers."[24]

It is hard to pinpoint when the fight turned into a rout for the 7th Michigan. One minute they were holding off the 1st North Carolina and the Jeff Davis Legion; the next they were struck in the flanks, and almost dismembered. As the 7th's shattered remnants fled the field, they streamed past Colonel McIntosh, who "fairly frothing at the mouth," implored them, "For God's sake, men, if you are ever going to stand, stand now, for you are on free soil." They ignored his pleas as they rushed in confusion for the rear. Recalled one 6th Michigan trooper, "The 7th Michigan made a charge and got all cut to pieces," which he attributed to the fact that "it was the first charge they ever made and they made awful work." That it was an unsoldierly withdrawal was attested to by many. "The 7th are too badly

---

23 OR 27, pt. 2, 698; Brooke Rawle, *History of the Third Pennsylvania Cavalry*, 276.

24 Brooke Rawle, *History of the Third Pennsylvania Cavalry*, 276; Trowbridge to Bigelow, date unknown, GNMP, 5-6; Kidd, *Personal Recollections*, 152; Robertson, *Michigan in the War*, 578.

demoralized to help us," verified Bigelow, who said the undisciplined rush to the rear scarred the regiment: "Their charge ruined them in their own eyes."[25]

As the men of the 1st Virginia gave chase, they became strung out in the pursuit, and were "exposed to a terrific fire from the two batteries in front and the skirmish lines on the flanks. . . . It was more than even the gallant First Virginia could stand, and it was compelled to fall back on its supports." Reduced to mere spectatorship, Stuart lamented, "Their impetuosity had carried them too far, and the charge being very much prolonged, their horses already jaded by hard marching, failed under it." It seemed like the perfect time for a lull. "Then, as it seemed, the two belligerent forces paused to get their second breath," wrote Kidd from his vantage point. "Up to that time, the battle had raged with varying fortune. Victory, that appeared to perch first on one banner, and then on the other, held aloof, as if disdaining to favor either. . . . Gregg forced the fighting, putting Stuart on his defense, and checkmating his plan to fight an offensive battle."[26]

Charge! Charge!! Who Said That?!

Around 4:00 p.m., the Confederate cavalry inexplicably debouched into the open field. Like Stuart, Wade Hampton had noticed that his two regiments were badly overextended. "In their eagerness they followed him too far, and encountered his reserve in heavy force," reported Hampton, who spurred forward in an attempt to bring order out of chaos. His presence had the opposite effect, and much "to my surprise I saw the rest of my brigade . . . charging." All who witnessed the Confederate maneuvers were enthralled and remembered the sight for the rest of their days. Still awed years later, James Kidd wrote, "Squadron after squadron, regiment after regiment, orderly as if on parade, came into view, and successively took their places." Brooke Rawle recalled that "with sabres drawn and glistening like silver in the bright sunlight, the spectacle called forth a murmur of admiration." Though born in 1866, Capt. James G. Harbord put the moment into perspective in the *History of the Third Pennsylvania Cavalry*: "Now the Plumed Cavalier brought out his last reserves, the superb brigades of Hampton and Fitz Hugh Lee. . . . It was the moment for which cavalry wait all their lives—the opportunity which seldom

---

25 Meyer, *Civil War Experiences*, 50-51; Rice, "Eyewitness to War"; Bigelow, "Draw Saber, Charge!"

26 Brooke Rawle, *History of the Third Pennsylvania Cavalry*, 277; OR 27, pt. 2, 698; Kidd, *Personal Recollections*, 152-153.

comes—that vanishes like shadows on glass." From his position near the Lott house, Captain Miller witnessed the entire panoply as the Confederates emerged into the open from the woods near the Stallsmith farm, and described their movements in breathtaking detail. "A grander spectacle than their advance has rarely been beheld. They marched with well aligned fronts and steady reins. Their polished saber blades dazzled in the sun." The Federal batteries loosed a thunderous barrage, and the Rebels were met by a hurricane of exploding shell, and whip-sawing canister. Entire sections of the ranks disappeared. "Closing the gaps as though nothing had happened, on they came," Miller wrote, admiring the soldierly qualities of his enemy. "As they drew nearer, canister was substituted by our artillerymen for shell, and horse after horse staggered and fell. Still they came on."[27]

The Federal artillery continued to blast away at the onrushing Confederate cavalry. According to Brooke Rawle, Lt. James Chester, Battery E, 1st U.S. Artillery, "put charge after charge of double canister into their midst, his men bringing it up to the guns in armfuls. The execution was fearful, but the long rents closed up at once." To Chester's left, Pennington's Battery M was still thundering away at the enemy from a position on a small knoll, a few rods in front of the Spangler house. His guns were firing "with frightful regularity, as fast as he could load." The lanky Lieutenant Pennington was standing calmly by his guns. At this time, Chester's Battery E passed to the extreme right of the line, the cannoneers nudging each other as they saw the man of whom it was said, "the smoke of battle is to him as zephyrs are to lovers." The battle smoke was thick that day. But the most chilling description was left by Daniel Townsend, who lent his expertise on the mechanics of death by projectile. "Our guns being in position we loaded with shrapnel," he recounted clinically. "The first round the shells exploded at the edge of the woods in rear of the line of rebel cavalry that was formed four deep at that part of the field. On firing the next round the pieces were set so that the shells exploded in front of the line which resulted in dismounting, killing and wounding several."[28]

Even as they staggered under the fire of the batteries, the Confederates were driving the 7th Michigan like sheep back onto their own guns. "They got into pretty

---

27 OR 27, pt. 2, 725; Kidd, *Personal Recollections*, 153; Brooke Rawle, *History of the Third Pennsylvania Cavalry*, 277, 300, 319.

28 Brooke Rawle, "The Right Flank at Gettysburg," 481; Kidd, *Personal Recollections*, 154; Bigelow, "Draw Saber, Charge!"; Townsend, Diary, June 1863, 46.

close quarters," admitted Townsend, and "they fell back right in front of our guns we were deterred from firing." Frantically, the gun crews shouted to the 7th Michigan to split around their pieces and clear their line of fire. Townsend wrote that "[i]t was almost too late for us to do anything as the enemy were upon us." Finally, the 7th cleared the guns, and Battery E went back into action. "We fired the rounds of canister that were in the guns and loaded up again regardless of General Gregg's order not to do so, as he was laboring under a great deal of excitement [due to] the sudden transformation of things, from victory to defeat," recalled Townsend. One more charge was rammed down the barrels of the smoking muzzles. It was at that moment "our support of cavalry came bounding over the fields at a furious rate." It was the 1st Michigan.[29]

Colonel Charles Town and his veteran regiment had been held in reserve for just such an eventuality. And no, Gregg did not give the order to charge to Colonel. Town personally; he probably didn't even know where the 1st Michigan was, for the crafty old warriors had hidden themselves, out of the line of fire, in a small ravine. According to Bigelow, Gregg had given him the orders, to be conveyed to Colonel Town, to make the charge. "To the right [of the battery] a little I find Col. Town and the 1st Mich. Cav.," related Bigelow, who seems to have been everywhere on the field. Despite his high level of excitement, Bigelow remembered his encounter with Col. Town verbatim. To Bigelow's rushed entreaties, Town responded with aplomb. "Keep cool, Bugler, keep cool! Come along and tell me the whole situation." The orders were simple enough: Stop the enemy cavalry at all costs. Tuning in his saddle, Town bawled out, "Attention, 1st Mich. Cavalry!" His sickly commands were barely heard over the exultant shouts of the Rebels, now confident of victory.[30]

Just then, recalled Kidd, "Custer dashed up with similar instructions, and as Town ordered sabers to be drawn, placed himself by his side, in front of the leading squadron." That moment, frozen in time, could only be described as poignant. With the utmost military formality, Custer also ordered Town to attack. "Col. Town, the Seventh Cavalry has broken; I shall have to ask you to charge the rebels." The gallant Town, who was dying of tuberculosis and was so weak he had to be strapped to his saddle, enjoined his men, "Remember men; be steady, be calm, be firm! Think of Michigan! Forward!" In quick succession, he gave the command to draw sabers, forward march, trot, charge. Soon, the 1st Michigan was at a full

---

29 Townsend, Diary, June 1863, 47-48.

30 Bigelow, "Draw Saber, Charge!"

"Come on You Wolverines!" *Courtesy of Cowan's Auctions*

gallop. By all accounts, Custer was way out in front, saber pointing to the enemy. "He is bareheaded and glorious. His yellow locks of hair are flying like a battleflag," read one account.[31]

The batteries were in a parlous situation, and a panicked lieutenant in one of Pennington's sections was laboring to limber up his guns and make his escape. Pennington was never going to cede his ground. Addressing his faltering battery, he ordered them to drop their trails. It was no time to run, and he ordered his cannoneers to load their pieces with double shots of canister. "All four of the guns were fired point blank . . . into the face of the rebs," stated Lt. Samuel Harris of the 5th Michigan. "This iron hail storm was more than they could stand." The Rebel columns began to break to the right in an effort to escape the deadly fusillade. The last discharge coincided with the forward movement of the 1st Michigan, elements of which crossed in front of their artillery's line of fire. "Without doubt several of the boys of the First Michigan were killed and more wounded by our own battery," lamented Harris, "but it was absolutely necessary to break that charge at any cost,

31 Kidd, *Personal Recollections*, 154; Bigelow, "Draw Saber, Charge!" Many modern Civil War artists, including Don Troiani and Mort Künstler, have immortalized this moment. Künstler's version is a two-piece work that depicts the two charging lines just before they clashed.

for if it succeeded there were no Union troops between the rebels and our ammunition trains."[32]

Neither man nor beast could long withstand the terrible fire of the Union artillery. Brooke Rawle described the unfolding action: "Staggered by the fearful execution of the two batteries, the men in the front of the Confederate column drew in their horses and wavered. . . . Custer, seeing the men in the front ranks of the enemy hesitate, waved his saber and shouted, 'Come on, you Wolverines!' and with a fearful yell the First Michigan rushed on, Custer four lengths ahead." Kidd picks up the story at this point. "With ranks well closed," he began,

> with guidons flying and bugles sounding, the grand old regiment of veterans, led by Town and Custer, moved forward to meet the host, outnumbering it three to one. First at a trot, then the command to charge rang out, and with gleaming saber and flashing pistol, Town and his heroes were hurled right in the teeth of Hampton and Fitzhugh Lee.[33]

Captain Miller, too, had a ringside seat to the charge of the 1st Michigan. The two charging columns met each other at full speed, with "a crash, like the falling of timber. So sudden and violent was the collision that many of the horses were turned end over end and crushed their riders beneath them." Colonel Alger also marveled at the scene: "I do not believe it had its equal during the war, if ever." Methodically, amid the continuous clatter of revolvers and the angry clanging of sabers, Custer's Michiganders plunged deeper into the Confederate formation. Far from the action, his regiment thrust into a supporting role for Pennington's battery, Kidd thrilled at the panorama to his front. "Then it was steel to steel. For minutes—and for minutes that seemed like years—the gray column stood and staggered before the blow. . . . Town's impetuous charge in front went through it like a wedge, splitting it in twain, and scattering the confederate horsemen." In the swirling dust and battle smoke, Custer's horse went down; it was the third mount he had ridden to death. He quickly jumped into the saddle of a rider-less horse and continued to press further into the crowd of Rebels.[34]

Under orders to hold his position, Captain Miller fretted as the situation degenerated into a hand-to-hand mêlée. From his position atop a small knoll, he

---

32 Harris, *Personal Reminiscences*, 36.

33 Brooke Rawle, "The Right Flank at Gettysburg," 481-482; Kidd, *Personal Recollections*, 154.

34 Miller, "The Cavalry Battle Near Gettysburg," 404; Robertson, *Michigan in the War*, 578; Kidd, *Personal Recollections*, 155.

"had an elegant view of all that was going on." There was no doubt in his mind that "Stuart was too heavy for Custer, and unless some diversion was made all would be lost, i.e. we would be whipped like the d_____." Sitting his horse next to Miller, Brooke Rawle agreed with his assessment. In his later years, he would enthusiastically recommend Miller for the Medal of Honor. "Captain Miller and I saw at once that unless more men were sent against the enemy the Michigan regiment would be swept from the field." Scattered across the farmlands by the ebb and flow of battle, other aggressive Union officers sensed the same thing, and grabbed the initiative.

As the 1st Michigan speared into Hampton's brigade, scattered Union troopers initiated a series of sharp blows at the exposed Confederate flanks, slowly turning the momentum of battle in their favor. In quick succession, an attack by McIntosh and his headquarters company struck the left front of the Confederate column. A detachment of 21 men, under Capt. Walter Newhall, slammed into the Rebel right flank, penetrating nearly to Hampton's center. Simultaneously, a squadron of the 1st New Jersey assaulted the opposite flank, and hacked a path to Hampton, who nearly lost his head to the saber slashes of one of the Jerseymen. He was forced to leave the field. Colonel Alger, meanwhile, had remounted parts of his regiment. For the fourth time that day, he advanced to the attack, throwing the weight of his command against the Rebel right.[35]

Miller, whose "men were restive to get their fists in," informed Brooke Rawle that he was about to disobey his orders and attack the enemy. His men beat him to the punch. They let loose a volley of carbine fire at near pointblank range, then drew their sabers and leaped to the attack. The Pennsylvanians "struck the left flank of the enemy's column pretty well towards its rear . . . [and] drove well into the column and cut off its rear and forced it back in the direction whence it came." General Gregg later complimented the 3rd Pennsylvania's role in the action. "During the engagement," he wrote, "a portion of this regiment made a very handsome and successful charge upon one of the enemy's regiments." He was, however, equally laudatory of the 1st Michigan: "The advantage . . . was soon wrested from the enemy by the gallant charge of the First Michigan. . . . This regiment drove the enemy back to its starting point. . . . Defeated at every point, the enemy withdrew to his left."

The Confederates engaged the 3rd Pennsylvania in a desultory skirmish for the rest of the day. Stuart finally withdrew behind his horse artillery and slipped away at

---

35 Brooke Rawle, *History of the Third Pennsylvania Cavalry*, 307, 311.

dark. "At this time," wrote Gregg, "I was at liberty to relieve the [Second] Brigade of the Third Division, which was directed to join its division."[36]

A hard rain began to fall.

36 Ibid., 307, 312; OR 27, pt. 1, 957.

EPILOGUE

One Man's Word is as Good as Another's

NEITHER JAMES H. KIDD nor William Brooke Rawle was a champion of truth. Their narratives of the battle, driven mostly by unit pride, differed like a jagged coral reef separating the calm waters of a tropical lagoon from the frothing waves of the open ocean. The two men continued to duel with words the merits of their respective brigades "long after the bones of the slain have turned to dust."[1]

On March 26, 1886, Brooke Rawle got into a cavalry vs. infantry squabble when he took umbrage at an infantry officers' remark denigrating the role of the mounted arm. "You state that the gallant Cavalry fight by the troops under Gregg on the right flank was of no importance to the result of the battle," he began, before offering to correct the infantry officer's contentions by sending him a copy of his speech at the dedication of the Cavalry Monument on East Cavalry Field in October 1884. "This," he added, "will give you a concise account of our fight." Perhaps he realized early on that it was a losing battle. "I think that at any rate you should at least give us the credit of being of some assistance. Surely in that fight there was glory enough for all who were engaged, and plenty to spare." This, coming from a man who would spend much of his postwar career scrabbling for just a little bit more of that glory.[2]

1 Whittaker, *A Popular Life of George A. Custer*, 158.

2 William Brooke Rawle to unknown recipient, March 26, 1886, William Brooke Rawle Papers, Archives, Historical Society of Pennsylvania, Philadelphia.

Brooke Rawle disparaged, through his writings, speeches, and lectures, the part played by the Michigan Brigade in the battle. His opinion of the Michiganders was patronizing. "It was a splendid body of men," he wrote obsequiously, but "its ranks were much fuller than those of the other cavalry brigades, and the greater part of it was fresh from pastures green." This was a thinly veiled reference to the Michigan Brigade's lack of combat experience. Brooke Rawle contended that Custer's command had begun to pull back, and McIntosh's men had moved to the fight. McIntosh's Jerseymen and Pennsylvanians should have had the honor of opening the contest, and to them the deeds of glory should have been accorded. He made these arguments in a lengthy explanation written for an article that was eventually published in *The Annals of the Civil War*.[3]

By the time his article appeared, its wording had changed considerably. "Upon notifying Custer of the orders to relieve him," argued the author, "McIntosh inquired as to his picket line and the position and force of the enemy. Nothing was said as to any previous firing, and everything was quiet at the time." Brooke Rawle's accounts differ in yet another way, for he steadfastly maintained that when McIntosh finally approached Custer at 1:00 p.m. on July 3, "he found the latter in position, facing Gettysburg near the junction of the Bonaughtown and Salem Church Roads, and covering them. In his official report, Custer mistakes the names of the roads on which he held position." Brooke Rawle's *History of the Third Pennsylvania*, published in 1905 and based on a speech he gave just a few years after his article in *Annals*, does not contain this information. By the time McIntosh finally arrived on the field, Custer had accomplished his redeployment of the Michiganders to face the threat posed by the appearance of the Confederate cavalry and had been in action for hours.[4]

Brooke Rawle placed the blame for this predicament on the old-fashioned ideas that regulated interaction with the members of the press. "The neglect with which this portion of the battle has been treated is due, in a great degree, to the want of that self-assertion which was not uncommon among the officers of our Cavalry Corps," he argued, alluding to the cadre of officers who had served in the "Old Army." These men, such as George Stoneman, Philip St. George Cooke, David Gregg, and even the revered John Buford, all "enforced a rule that no newspaper correspondent should be quartered with the staff of his division." "The Second Cavalry Division, moreover, was not a favorite among the newspaper

---

3 Brooke Rawle, *History of the Third Pennsylvania Cavalry*, 269.

4 Brooke Rawle, "The Right Flank at Gettysburg," 476-477.

correspondents. None of them were attached nominally to its staff, nor allowed in its camps, or among its men—for its commander saw the mischief which they worked." Brooke Rawle excelled at criticizing with a velvet glove. Gregg, for example, he blamed for "his modesty and retiring disposition to stand in the way of his claiming for himself and his division the laurels to which they are entitled." This character flaw, he continued, allowed others with overweening ambition to steal "the glory which he had rightly earned, well knowing that no public denial would come from him."[5]

Not content with pointing an accusatory finger at General Gregg, Brooke Rawle took a full swing at George Custer. "And finally, General Custer . . . forwarded independently an official report of the movements of his command, which, in some of its statements, is not entirely ingenuous," he concluded after an exhaustive litany of the wrongs done to McIntosh's 3rd Brigade. "In the account referred to, he has taken to himself and his Michigan Brigade alone, the credit which, to say the least, others were entitled to share."

They were harsh words from a bitter man, but "blowing the bugle" for the 3rd Pennsylvania sometimes brought out a combative side in Brooke Rawle that often put him at odds with some of his many correspondents. One such letter of reply was written by Reverend George W. Beale, of the 9th Virginia Cavalry. On October 9, 1884, Beale cautioned Brooke Rawle on his barbed commentaries. "In my humble judgement there was enough of courage, prowess and heroism displayed among the soldiers on each side to permit their actions and achievements to go down to history without the distortion of error or the perversion of partisan prejudice," he lectured, his words deeply rooted in the many war stories he had heard in the two decades since the war ended.

Beale wasn't finished:

> It has ceased with me to be a matter of wonder that participants in a battle often differ very widely in their impressions of what occurred around them. . . . All tend to create conflicting opinions and contradictory accounts of the same action. Men who are on the same side and

---

5   Ibid., 468; Henry P. Moyer, *History of the Seventeenth Regiment, Pennsylvania Volunteer Cavalry*, 201. Buford's successor to the command of the 1st Division also promulgated this practice, wrote Moyer. "General Wesley Merritt, who succeeded him after the lamented death in December 1863, adhered to the same rule. It could hardly be expected that long descriptions of cavalry engagements with big 'scare lines' for headings could appear under such an existing state of things."

in the same regiment frequently, in all honesty, widely disagree as to the same incident or event of a battle.[6]

The Michiganders, of course, retorted that Brooke Rawle got the story all wrong. "It is reported in several histories, and stoutly maintained by some officers of high rank, that Custer moved off the field in obedience to that order and was turned back by General Gregg whom he met as he was moving away," wrote an angry Maj. Luther Trowbridge. "Such was not the case.... Doubtless such an order was given, for Custer mentions it in his report." These very facts were vouchsafed by James Kidd. "It has been claimed, and General Gregg seems to countenance that view, that Custer was withdrawn and that McIntosh, who was put in his place, opened the fight, after which Gregg brought Custer back to reinforce McIntosh. So far from this being true, it is quite the reverse of the truth," he recorded emphatically. "Custer did not leave his position. The battle opened before the proposed change had taken place, and McIntosh was hurried in on the right of Custer."[7]

Does It Really Matter?

Who ordered who to do what would remain a bone of contention between the Michiganders and Gregg's boys for the remainder of their lives. Some accounts attribute Colonel Town orders to charge directly to Gen. Gregg. Some of Custer's actions were already being debated, but the controversy over who ordered the charge at East Cavalry Field should not be one of them. For his own part, Custer was magnanimous in his praise of Gregg.

In the end, who actually gave the orders is irrelevant. The only fact that counts is that at the moment of truth, Custer was out in front of his troops shouting over his shoulder and exhorting them to the attack. "Come on, You Wolverines!" No such controversy existed among the rank and file of the Michigan Brigade. Kidd spoke for one and all when he wrote, "If, at Gettysburg, the Michigan cavalry

---

6 Brooke Rawle, "The Right Flank at Gettysburg," 470; David L. Ladd and Audrey J. Ladd, eds., *John Bachelder's History of the Battle of Gettysburg* (Dayton, OH, 1997), 750.

7 Trowbridge, "The Operations of the Cavalry in the Gettysburg Campaign," 11-12; Kidd, *Personal Recollections*, 140-141.

brigade won honors that will not perish, it was to Gregg that it owed the opportunity, and his guiding hand it was that made the blows effective."[8]

For their part, some of the Pennsylvanians would remember Custer fondly. The charge, recalled one officer, was "the finest thing I witnessed during nearly three years" of war. Completely overshadowed in significance by the epic Pickett-Pettigrew-Trimble charge against Cemetery Ridge that same afternoon, the Union cavalry's defeat of Jeb Stuart's cavalry on the fields of the Rummel farm would have to wait for decades before being recognized as the decisive and far-reaching action that it was. The reason for this, claimed Brooke Rawle, was because "[s]o fierce was the main engagement, of which the infantry bore the brunt, that the 'affairs' of the cavalry have almost passed unnoticed, yet on the right flank there occurred one of the most beautiful cavalry fights of the war."[9]

In his battle report, Custer lavished the veteran troopers of the 1st Michigan with praise. "I cannot find language to express my high appreciation of the gallantry and daring displayed by the officers and men of the 1st Michigan Cavalry," he wrote. "They advanced to the charge of a vastly superior force with as much order and precision as if going on parade; and I challenge the annals of warfare to produce a more brilliant or successful charge of cavalry." The cost had not been light. For the Wolverines under Custer, glory would never come cheap. His brigade lost 542 men, including nine officers and 69 men killed. Kidd gave conflicting testimony in his *Personal Recollections of a Cavalryman*, writing that "Custer's brigade lost one officer (Major Ferry) and 28 men killed." Yet, in the "Roll of Honor" appended to the end of Kidd's manuscript, he listed 54 Michigan men by name as having been killed in action on July 3. *Fox's Regimental Losses* only provides casualties for 1st, 5th, and 7th Michigan regiments, stating that the brigade lost 31 killed, 121 wounded, and 77 missing, for a total of 229. The Michiganders wore their "Red Badge of Courage" proudly.

In 1903, one former Wolverine told an appreciative throng of members of the Cavalry Brigade Association, "The War records show, and it is officially admitted, that the Custer Michigan Cavalry Brigade sustained the highest percentage of loss of killed of any mounted Brigade in the service in the War of the Rebellion, where its record of killed was 528 and a total loss from all causes of 1575 officers and

---

8 Kidd, *Personal Recollections*, 138.

9 Longacre, *Custer and His Wolverines*, 152; Brooke Rawle, "The Right Flank at Gettysburg," 468.

men." Earning the reputation for high casualty rates would always haunt these "grand old warriors," for you can bury only so many of your friends.

Transcending the bloodletting was the bond of love, comradeship, and respect that had grown between the brigade and their "Boy General." In Kidd's view, Gettysburg "gave great renown to the name of Custer as a general of brigade." Kidd dove deeper into its legacy:

> It was that fight that brought fame to the Michigan brigade, all due to his matchless leadership and its own prowess. It was that fight which but five days after the date of his commission, proved the wisdom of Custer's promotion from captain to brigadier general. It was that fight . . . that started him on his career of success—a success unbroken till the sun of the confederacy went down at Appomattox.[10]

General Charles King, who Kidd described as "a cavalry officer with a brilliant record in the army of the United States" and a fine reputation as a writer, described the fight as perceived by the Northern reading public. "And so, just as Gettysburg was the turning point of the great war, so, to my thinking, was the grapple with and overthrow of Stuart . . . the turning point of Gettysburg," he editorialized, his language forceful and eloquent. "It was Custer and the Wolverines who flew like bull dogs straight at the throat of the foes; who blocked his headlong charge; who pinned him to the ground while like wolves their comrade troops rushed upon his flanks."[11]

---

10 Robertson, *Michigan in the War*, 583. In fairness to Custer, it should be pointed out that his report was not "forwarded independently," but rather submitted "in compliance with instructions received from the headquarters of the 3rd division." In the opening sentence of the report, he states clearly, "I have the honor to submit the *following report of the part taken by my command* in the engagements near Gettysburg, July 3d, 1863 [emphasis added]." He felt sure that there were many more colonels and generals who would be trumpeting the achievements of their commands. Custer probably never envisioned General Gregg would not do so. Kidd, *Personal Recollections*, 155; William F. Fox, *Regimental Losses in the American Civil War, 1861-1865* (Carmel, IN, 1996), 440; *Articles of Association and Roster of Survivors of Gen'l Custer's Michigan Cavalry Brigade Association-Meeting, September 10, 1903* (Detroit, 1903), 24; James H. Kidd, *Historical Sketch of General Custer, Reprinted from Ceremonies Attending the Unveiling of the Equestrian Statue to Major General George Armstrong Custer* (Monroe, MI, 1978), 17-18.

11 Kidd, *Personal Recollections*, 158-159.

When Monuments Become Battlefields

In 1879, the state of Michigan moved to formalize the role played by its soldiers in the Civil War. Senator R. B. Robbins introduced a bill proposing that the Office of the Adjutant General compile, file, and publish a record of the "services of Michigan regiments, batteries and companies in the late war."

Colonel Russell A. Alger was routinely asked to provide reports detailing his regiment's activities during the Gettysburg Campaign. Much to Alger's chagrin, not one of those reports was included in the War Department files.

James Kidd faced a similar dilemma. The available reports, he complained, were "meager, some misleading. The Michigan regiments seem to have been peculiarly unfortunate in this regard. I was unable to find in the War Records office in Washington the official report, written in 1863, of a single one of the commanding officers, covering the operations of the Gettysburg campaign." Even more interesting was the fact that not a single one of Custer's official reports made it into the files. In 1881, the state authorized the printing of 30,000 copies of the compiled reports and *Michigan in the Civil War* appeared in print the following year. Custer's full Gettysburg report was included.[12]

A monument to the cavalry fight at Rummel's farm was dedicated on October 15, 1884. Almost six years later on June 12, 1890, a monument to the Michigan Cavalry Brigade was dedicated to the praises of Kidd. Not to be outdone, a monument to the 3rd Pennsylvania was dedicated on September 5, 1890, with Brooke Rawle as the keynote speaker. By this time, Kidd and Brooke Rawle were bitter enemies, and the battle lines on what had taken place that July 3 day fully drawn.[13]

Of utmost importance to the Michiganders was their unwavering loyalty to their esteemed Custer, who they had followed into the cauldron of battle. "He has been weighed by the men, and where he was found wanting he overbalances and swells by another element," was how bugler John Bigelow caressed the cherished memory of a young Custer relaxing in the midst of his men sitting on logs, the steady beat of a rainstorm tattooed on their hooded heads. He continued:

---

12 Robertson, *Michigan in the War*, 3.

13 Kidd, "Address at the Dedication od the Michigan Monuments," 42.

He is sitting upon a log just now, and we gather around him. He is cracking jokes with the rough troopers as familiarly as Artemus Ward would offer his umbrella to a young Shakeress.

"An orderly rides up, asks for Custer, and hands him his orders," continued Bigelow. And then the moment is over. "One minute, and the bugle rings out 'To Horse!' 'Tis a relief from waiting in the rain."[14]

The chase after Lee's beaten Army of Northern Virginia has begun.

14   John A. Bigelow, "Flashing Sabers: Chasing Lee's Columns After Gettysburg," *The National Tribune*, November 10, 1887.

Bibliography

NEWSPAPERS

Athens [OH] *Messenger*

Detroit Advertiser and Tribune

Frank Leslie's Illustrated Magazine

Gettysburg Times

Hanover [PA] *Evening Herald*

Harper's Weekly, 1864-77

National Tribune

New York Herald

New York Times, 1861-95

New York Tribune

Philadelphia Inquirer

Philadelphia Record

Richmond Daily Dispatch

Richmond Enquirer

Richmond Times

Savannah Register

The [NYC] *Independent*

Washington Evening Star

Washington Post, 1883-1910

GOVERNMENT SOURCES

Atlas to Accompany the Official Records of the Union and Confederate Armies. Washington, DC: United States Government Printing Office, 1891-95.

The War of the Rebellion: A Compilation of the Official Records of the Union and Confederate Armies. 128 volumes in 3 series. Washington, DC: United States Government Printing Office, 1889.

McClellan, George Brinton. *Report of the Organization of the Army of the Potomac and of Its Campaigns in Virginia and Maryland*. Washington, DC: United States Government Printing Office, 1864.

"Report of Major General A. Pleasonton, to the Committee on the Conduct of the War," included in Vol. 2 of *Supplemental Report of the Joint Committee on the Conduct of the War, in Two Volumes*. Washington, DC: United States Government Printing Office, 1866.

MANUSCRIPT SOURCES

Central Michigan University, Clarke Historical Library, Mount Pleasant, MS

Macomber, Dexter. Diary

Archives, Cincinnati Historical Soc., Cincinnati, OH

Hannaford, Roger. Papers

Christopher Densmore Collection, Getzville, NY

Townsend, Daniel. Diary

Archives, Gettysburg National Military Park, Gettysburg, PA

Allen, Joe. Account

di Cesnola, Louis P. Letter of March 10, 1863

Crockett, Samuel James. Diary, July 3, 1863

Dickerson, Frank W. Letter of May 23, 1863

Donlon, Michael. Letter to his brother, Aug. 8, 1863

Goldsborough, C. E. "The Hunterstown Fight: A Civil War Engagement of Which Little is Known"

Harman, Troy. "Hunterstown: North Cavalry Field of the Battle of Gettysburg." *Preserve Newsletter*, Vol. 30, No. 2, Winter 2006

Marks, Samuel J. Letter of April 26, 1864

Mueller, Heinrich G. "An Account of the Reunion of the 6th U. S. Cavalry"

Participants Accounts, Elon Farnsworth's Folder

Bennet, John W. "General Farnsworth's Death"

Law, Evander M. "Gen. Law's Account"

Potter, Henry Clay. Personal Experiences

Robertson, Albert Clark

Storrick, William C. "William C. Storrick Provides Interesting History of Cavalry Battle at Hunterstown and Suggests Erection of Suitable Marker"

Trowbridge, Luther S. Letter to J. Allen Bigelow, undated

Handley Library, Winchester, VA

Allen Tischler Collection

Morey, William C. Diary

Parry, Henry. Letters

Smith, Howard M. Diary

Tischler, Allen L. "Merritt and Averell 'Go In!'"

——. "The Final Charge at Winchester, September 19, 1864"

Encyclopedia Virginia, Charlottesville, VA

Bruce, Philip Alexander. "History of the University of Virginia, 1819-1919"

Duke, Jr., R. T. W. Recollections

Minor, John B. Diary, February 28-March 7, 1865

Strickler, Sarah A. G. Diary, March 2-10, 1865

Archives, Historical Society of Pennsylvania, Philadelphia, PA

Brooke Rawle, William. Papers

Carpenter, Louis H. "Letters from the Field, 1861-1865"

Meade Family Papers

Jefferson County Museum, Charles Town, WV

Chew, Robert Preston. Papers

Manuscripts Division, Library of Congress, Washington, DC

Pleasonton, Alfred. Papers

Pleasonton, Alfred. Letter to John F. Farnsworth, June 18, 1863

Shriver, Adam. Papers

Smith, Howard M. Diary, September 19, 1864

Massachusetts Historical Society, Boston, MA

Crowninshield, Caspar. Letters

Archives, Michigan State University, Lansing, MI

Stocking, Eugene J. Papers

The National Archives and Records Administration, Washington, DC

RG 94, General Wesley Merritt Papers Collection, Records of the Adjutant General's Office, 1780-1917

Platt, George C. Medal of Honor file

RG 94, Records of the Adjutant General's Office. 1780-1917

Archives, Rauner Special Collections Library, Dartmouth College Library, Hanover, NH

Woodbury, Eri. "The Civil War Papers of Eri Woodbury"

United States Army Heritage and Education Center, Carlisle, PA

Civil War Miscellaneous Collections:

Marks, Samuel B. M. Papers

Michigan Historical Collections, Bentley Historical Library, University of Mich., Ann Arbor, MI

Baird Family Papers

Comte, Victor E., Letter to his wife, Elise, July 7, 1863

Kay, John B. Papers

Kidd, James H. Papers

Archives, Michigan Historical Center, Michigan Department of State, Lansing, MI

Williams, Frederick D. Michigan Soldiers in the Civil War, 1998

Archives, Virginia Historical Society, Richmond, VA

Brooke, St. George Tucker. "Autobiography"

Early, Jubal A. Letter to H. B. McClellan, February 11, 1878

Phillips, John Wilson. Diary

DeYoung Henry Collection, Western Michigan University, Kalamazoo, MI

Knapp, Ram R. Diary

PUBLISHED SOURCES

"A Horror of the War. How General Custer Hung Some of Mosby's Men." *Southern Historical Society Papers*, Vol. 25, March 1897.

Adams, Charles Francis. *Charles Francis Adams, An Autobiography, 1835-1915*. Boston: Houghton, Mifflin Company, 1916.

Agassiz, George R., ed. *Meade's Headquarters 1863-1865: Letters of Colonel Theodore Lyman from The Wilderness to Appomattox*. Boston: Atlantic Monthly Press, 1922.

Alexander, Edward Porter. *Military Memoirs of a Confederate: A Critical Narrative*. New York, NY, 1907.

Allan, W. "'Lee's Invasion of Pennsylvania'—A Reply to General Longstreet." *The Century Magazine*, Vol. 34, May-October, 1887.

Allen, Stanton P. *Down in Dixie: Life in a Cavalry Regiment in the War Days, from the Wilderness to Spotsylvania*. Boston: D. Lathrop Company, 1893.

Articles of Association and Roster of Survivors of Gen'l Custer's Michigan Cavalry Brigade Association-Meeting, September 10, 1903. Detroit: N.P., 1903.

Arnold, Abraham K. "The Cavalry at Gaines' Mill." *Journal of the United States Cavalry Association*, Vol. II, No. 7, December 1889, 355-363.

Athearn, Robert G. "The Civil War Diary of John Wilson Phillips." *The Virginia Magazine of History and Biography*, Vol. 62, No. 1, January 1954.

Averell, William W. "With the Cavalry on the Peninsula," Robert U. Johnson and Clarence C. Buel, eds., *Battles and Leaders of the Civil War*, 4 vols. (New York, 1884-1889).

Bayard, George D. *History of the First Reg't Pennsylvania Reserve Cavalry, From Its Organization, August, 1861, to September, 1864.* Philadelphia: King and Baird, Printers, 1864.

Beach, William H. *The First New York (Lincoln) Cavalry, From April 19, 1861 to July 7, 1865.* New York: The Lincoln Cavalry Association Press, 1902.

Beale, G. W. *A Lieutenant of Cavalry in Lee's Army.* Boston: The Gorham Press, 1918.

Beale, Richard L. T. *History of the Ninth Virginia Cavalry in the War Between the States.* Richmond: B. F. Johnson Publishing Co., 1899.

Beck, E. W. H. "Letters of a Civil War Surgeon." *Indiana Magazine of History*, Vol. 27, No. 2, June 1931.

Blackford, W. W. *War Years with Jeb Stuart.* Baton Rouge: Louisiana State University Press, 1992.

Boudrye, Louis N. *Historic Records of the 5th New York Cavalry.* Albany, NY: J. Munsell, 1874.

Bowen, J. R. *Regimental History of the First New York Dragoons. Three Years of Active Service in the Great Civil War.* Privately published, 1900.

Boynton, Edward C. "History of West Point; its Military Importance during the American Revolution, and the Origin and Progress of the United States Military Academy." *The North American Review*, Vol. 98, Issue 203, April 1864.

Brewster, Charles, "Captured by Mosby's Guerrillas." *War Papers and Personal Reminiscences, 1861-1865. Military Order of the Loyal Legion of the United States*, Vol. 1. St. Louis: Becktold & Co., 1892.

Brooke Rawle, William. "Further Remarks on the Cavalry Fight on the Right Flank at Gettysburg." *The Journal of the United States Cavalry Association*, Vol. 4, No. 13, June 1891, 157-160.

————. "The Cavalry Fight on the Right Flank at Gettysburg." *History of the Third Pennsylvania Cavalry,*

Sixtieth Regiment Pennsylvania Volunteers, in the American Civil War, 1861-1865. Philadelphia: Franklin Printing Company, 1905.

————. "The Right Flank at Gettysburg," in *The Annals of the Civil War. Written by Leading Participants North and South*, edited by Alexander Kelly McClure. Philadelphia: Times Publishing Co., 1879.

Brooks, Ulysses R. *Butler and His Cavalry in the War of Succession, 1861-1865.* Columbia, SC: The State Co., 1909.

Brown, J. Willard. *The Signal Corps, U. S. A. in the War of the Rebellion.* Boston: U. S. Veteran Signal Corps Association, 1896.

Bryant, Edwin Eustace. *History of the Third Regiment of Wisconsin Veteran Volunteer Infantry, 1861-1865.* Madison, WI: The Veteran Association of the Regiment, 1891.

Burr, Frank A., and Hinton, Richard J. *Little Phil and His Troopers: The Life of Gen. Philip H. Sheridan.* Providence, RI: J. A. & R. A. Reid, 1888.

Butler, M. C. "The Cavalry Fight at Trevilian Station," in *Battles and Leaders of the Civil War*, edited by Robert U. Johnson and Clarence C. Buel. 4 vols. New York: Century Publishing Co., 1884-89.

Cadwallader, Sylvanus. *Three Years with Grant. As Recalled by a War Correspondent.* New York: Alfred A. Knopf, 1955.

Carpenter, Louis H. "Sheridan's Expedition Around Richmond, May 9-25, 1864." *Journal of the United States Cavalry Association*, Vol. 1, No. 3. Leavenworth, KS: Ketcheson & Reeves, November 1888, 300-321.

Carson, Janet, ed. *A Cavalryman Under Custer '64-'65: Reminiscences of the Civil War.* Transcription of unpublished diary, in Flora Johnson, ed., *E. M. Johnson's Reminiscences of The War*, 1933, 23-24.

Carter, William H. *From Yorktown to Santiago With the Sixth U. S. Cavalry.* Austin, TX: State House Press, 1989.

————. "The Sixth Regiment of Cavalry." *The Maine Bugle*, Camp 3, Call 4, October 1896.

"Ceremonies of the Unveiling at Front Royal, Va., September 23, 1899, of the Monument to Mosby's Men," *Southern Historical Society Papers*, Vol. 27, January-December, 1899.

Chamberlain, Joshua Lawrence. *The Passing of the Armies: An Account of the Final Campaign of the Army of the*

Potomac, Based Upon Personal Reminiscences of the Fifth Army Corps. New York: G. P. Putnam's Sons, 1915.

Cheney, Newell. *History of the Ninth Regiment, New York Volunteer Cavalry*. Poland Center, NY: Martin Mere & Son, Stationers, 1901.

Chester, Henry Whipple. *Recollections of the War of the Rebellion: A Story of the 2nd Ohio Volunteer Cavalry, 1861-1865*. Wheaton, IL: Wheaton History Center, 1996.

Cilley, J. P. "Up the Shenandoah Valley and On to Appomattox." *The First Maine Bugle*, Campaign 3, Call 1. Rockland, ME: Tribune Co., Printers, January 1893.

Claudy, C. H., ed. *Anson Mills: My Story*. Washington, DC: Press of Byron S. Adams, 1918.

Clark, James Albert. "The Making of a Volunteer Cavalryman." *Commandery of the District of Columbia, Military Order of the Loyal Legion of the United States*, November 6, 1907.

Colston, Frank M. "Recollections of the Last Months in the Army of Northern Virginia." *Southern Historical Society Papers*, Vol. 38, January-December, 1910.

"Constitution and By-laws of the U. S. Cavalry Association." *Journal of the United States Cavalry Association*, Vol. 1. Leavenworth, KS: Ketcheson & Reeves, 1888, 121-125.

Cooke, John Esten. *Wearing of the Gray, Being the Personal Portraits, Scenes & Adventures of the War*. New York: E. B. Treat & Co., 1867.

Cooke, Philip St. George. "Our Cavalry." *The United Service: A Quarterly Review of Military and Naval Affairs*, Vol. III, July 1879. Philadelphia: Lewis R. Hamersly & Co., 22, 330-346.

———. "The Charge of Cooke's Cavalry at Gaines's Mill." *The Century Magazine*, Vol. 30, No. 5, September 1885, 777-779.

Cooper, David M. *Obituary Discourse on the Occasion of the Death of Noah Henry Ferry of the Fifth Michigan Cavalry, Killed at Gettysburg, July 3, 1863*. New York: John F. Trow. 1863.

Cox, William R. "Major-General Stephen D. Ramseur: His Life and Character." *Southern Historical Society Papers*, Vol. 18, January-December, 1890.

Crawford, J. Marshall. *Mosby And His Men: A Record of the Adventures of That Renowned Partisan Ranger John S. Mosby*. New York: G. W. Carleton & Co., Publishers, 1867.

Crockett, Samuel J. Letter to John B. Bachelder, December 27, 1882, in *The Bachelder Papers: Gettysburg in Their Own Words*, edited by David L. Ladd and Audrey J. Ladd. 3 vols. Dayton, OH: Morningside, 1994.

Crowninshield, Benjamin W. *A History of the First Regiment of Massachusetts Cavalry Volunteers*. Cambridge, MA: The Riverside Press, 1891.

Cummings, W. G. "Six Months in the Third Cavalry Division Under Custer." *War Sketches and Incidents, Iowa Commandery, Military Order of the Loyal Legion of the United States*, Vol. 1. Wilmington, NC: Broadfoot Publishing Company, 1994.

Curry, W. L., ed. *Four Years in the Saddle: History of the First Regiment Ohio Volunteer Cavalry*. Columbus: Champlin Printing Co., 1898.

Custer, Elizabeth B. *Boots and Saddles, or, Life in Dakota with General Custer*. Norman, OK: University of Oklahoma Press, 1961.

———. *Tenting on the Plains or General Custer in Texas and Kansas*. Norman, OK: University of Oklahoma Press, 1994.

Davies, Henry E. *General Sheridan*. New York: D. Appleton and Co., 1895.

Davis, George B. "The Operations of the Cavalry in the Gettysburg Campaign." *Journal of the United States Cavalry Association*, Vol. 1, No. 3, November 1888, 325-348.

Davis, Sidney Morris. *Common Soldier, Uncommon War: Life as a Cavalryman in the Civil War*. Edited by Charles F. Cooney. Bethesda, MD: SMD Group, 1994.

DeGraff, Henry. "Recollections," in *Personal and Historical Sketches and Facial History of and by Members of the Seventh Regiment Michigan Volunteer Cavalry 1862-1865*, compiled by William O. Lee. Detroit: Ralston, 1901, 79-80.

De Jomini, Henri. *The Art of War*, translated by G. H. Mendell and W. P. Craighill. West Point, NY: 1862.

Denison, Frederic. *Sabers and Spurs: The First Regiment Rhode Island Cavalry in the Civil War, 1861-1865*. Published by the First Rhode Island Cavalry Veteran Association. Central Falls, RI: Press of E. L. Freeman & Co., 1876.

DePeyster, John W. *The Decisive Conflicts of the Late Civil War*. New York: MacDonald & Co., 1867.

"Diary of Capt. R. E. Park." *Southern Historical Society Papers*, Vol. 1, May 1876.

Douglas, Henry Kyd. *I Rode with Stonewall: Being Chiefly the War Experiences of the Youngest Member of Jackson's Staff from the John Brown Raid to the Hanging of Mrs. Surratt.* Chapel Hill, NC: University of North Carolina Press, 1943.

Douthat, Robert William. "Service with the Virginia Army." *Confederate Veteran.* No. 36, 1928.

Early, Jubal A. *Jubal Anderson Early, CSA, Autobiographical Sketch and Narrative of the War Between the States.* Philadelphia: J. B. Lippincott, 1912.

——. *War Memoirs.* Bloomington, IN: Indiana University Press, 1960.

——. "Winchester, Fisher's Hill and Cedar Creek," in *Battles and Leaders of the Civil War,* edited by Robert U. Johnson and Clarence C. Buel. 4 vols. New York: Century Publishing Co., 1884-89.

Eaton, H. E. to Elizabeth Bacon Custer, July 20, 1896. Copy in the author's collection.

Eckert, Edward K. and Amato, Nicholas J. *Ten Years in the Saddle: The Memoir of William Woods Averell, 1851-1862.* San Rafael, CA: Presidio Press, 1978.

Farley, Joseph P. *West Point in The Early Sixties.* Troy, NY: Pafreats Book Company, 1902.

Farrar, Samuel Clarke. *The Twenty-Second Pennsylvania Cavalry and the Ringgold Battalion 1861-1865.* Pittsburgh: Twenty-Second Pennsylvania Ringgold Cavalry Association, 1911.

Finch, S. M. to the Buford Memorial Association, April 9, 1894. *Proceedings of the Buford Memorial Association.*

Fisher, W. H. "First and Only Two Days' Picket Duty During My Term of Service." William O. Lee, ed. *Personal and Historical Sketches of and By Members of the Seventh Regiment Michigan Volunteer Cavalry 1862-1865,* Detroit: Ralston, 1901, 86-88.

Ford, Worthington Chauncey, ed. *A Cycle of Adams Letters.* 2 vols. Boston: Houghton-Mifflin, 1920.

Fry, James B. "McClellan and His 'Mission.'" *The Century Magazine,* Vol. 48, Issue 6, October 1894, 931-946.

Gallaher, D. C. "Closing Scenes of War in the Shenandoah Valley." *Confederate Veteran,* Vol. 31, No. 1, January 1923.

"General McClellan's Change of Base." *North American Review,* Vol. 141, No. 347, October 1885, 335-345.

"General Ramseur Fights and Dies for His Country," in *The Blue and the Gray: The Story of the Civil War as Told by Participants,* edited by Henry Steele Commager. New York: Bobbs-Merrill Company, 1950.

"Generals in the Saddle." *Southern Historical Society Papers,* Vol. 19, January 1891.

Gillespie, Samuel L. *A History of Company A, First Ohio Cavalry, 1861-1865.* Washington Court House, OH: Press of Ohio State Register, 1898.

Glazier, Willard. *Battles for the Union.* Chicago: Dustin, Gilman & Co., 1875.

——. *Three Years in the Federal Cavalry.* New York: R. H. Ferguson & Company, Publishers, 1872.

Gordon, John Brown. *Reminiscences of the Civil War.* New York: Charles Scribner's Sons, 1904.

Goss, Lee. "Why Don't You Hide Behind a Tree?" in *Battles and Leaders of the Civil War,* edited by Ned Bradford. New York: Appleton-Century-Crofts, Inc. 1956.

Gracey, Samuel L. *Annals of the Sixth Pennsylvania Cavalry.* Philadelphia: E. H. Butler & Co., 1868.

Grant, Ulysses S. *Personal Memoirs of U.S. Grant.* 2 vols. New York: Charles L. Webster & Co., 1885-86.

Greenleaf, William L. "From the Rapidan to Richmond." *War Papers of Vermont, and Miscellaneous States' Papers and Addresses, Military Order of the Loyal Legion of the United States.* Wilmington, NC: 1994.

Gregg, David McMurtrie. "The Second Cavalry Division of the Army of the Potomac in the Gettysburg Campaign." Read before the Pennsylvania Commandery of the Military Order of the Loyal Legion of the United States, May 1, 1907. Philadelphia: 1907.

Greiner, H. C. *Gen. Phil Sheridan as I Knew Him: Playmate-Comrade-Friend.* Chicago: J. S. Hyland, 1908.

Grimsley, Daniel A. *Battles in Culpeper County, Virginia, 1861-1865.* Culpeper, VA: Raleigh Travers Green, 1900.

Hall, Hillman, ed. *History of the Sixth New York Cavalry (Second Ira Harris Guard) Second Brigade, First Division, Cavalry Corps, Army of the Potomac, 1861-1865.* Worcester, MA: Blanchard Press, 1908.

Hall, William P. "Use of Arms, Mounted." *Journal of the United States Cavalry Association,* Vol. 1, No. 1. Leavenworth, KS: Ketcheson & Reeves, March 1888, 34-37.

Hamlin, Augustus C. "Who Recaptured the Guns at Cedar Creek?" in *The Shenandoah Campaigns of 1862 and 1864 and the Appomattox Campaign, 1865, Papers of the Military Historical Society of Massachusetts*, Vol. 6. Boston, MA: 1907.

Hampton, Wade. "General Hampton's Report of the Battle of Trevylian's Depot." *Southern Historical Society Papers*, Vol. 7. Richmond: Southern Historical Society, 1879.

"Hanging of Mosby's Men," *Southern Historical Society Papers*, Vol. 24. Richmond: Wm. Ellis Jones, Printer, 1896.

Hard, Abner. *History of the Eighth Cavalry Regiment Illinois Volunteers during the Great Rebellion*. Aurora, IL: Privately published, 1868.

Harris, Moses. "With the Reserve Brigade, Part 1." *Journal of the United States Cavalry Association*, Vol. 3, No. 8. Leavenworth, KS: Ketcheson & Reeves, March 1890, 9-20.

———. "With the Reserve Brigade, Part 2." *Journal of the United States Cavalry Association*, Vol. 3, No. 10. Leavenworth, KS: Ketcheson & Reeves, September 1890, 235-247.

———. "With the Reserve Brigade, Part 3." *Journal of the United States Cavalry Association*, Vol. 3, No. 11. Leavenworth, KS: Ketcheson & Reeves, December 1890, 363-370.

———. "With the Reserve Brigade, Part 4." *Journal of the United States Cavalry Association*, Vol. 3, No. 12. Leavenworth, KS: Ketcheson & Reeves, March 1891, 3-26.

Harris, Samuel. *Personal Reminiscences of Samuel Harris*. Chicago: The Rogerson Press. 1897.

Harrison, William H. "Personal Experiences of a Cavalry Officer." *Pennsylvania Commandery of the Military Order of the Loyal Legion of United States*, Vol. 1, Feb. 1866-May 1903.

———. "Reminiscences—Deep Bottom to Winchester," in *From Everglade to Canyon with the Second United States Cavalry*, compiled by Theophilus F. Rodenbough. Norman, OK: University of Oklahoma Press, 2000.

Hitchcock, W. H. "Recollections of a Participant in the Charge." *The Century Magazine*, Vol. 30, No. 5, September 1885.

Hoffman, Elliott W. *History of the First Vermont Cavalry Volunteers in the War of the Rebellion*. Baltimore: Butternut & Blue, 2000.

Hotchkiss, Jedediah. "Virginia," Vol 3. *Confederate Military History*, 12 vols. Atlanta: Confederate Publishing Co., 1899.

House, William Edward. "In Shenandoah Valley, 1864," in *Personal and Historical Sketches of and By Members of the Seventh Regiment Michigan Volunteer Cavalry 1862-1865*, edited by William O. Lee. Detroit: Ralston, 1901, 117-120.

Howard, McHenry. *Recollections of a Maryland Confederate Soldier and Staff Officer Under Johnston, Jackson, and Lee*. Baltimore: Williams and Wilkins Co., 1914.

Hyde, Bill, ed. *The Union Generals Speak: The Meade Hearings on the Battle of Gettysburg*. Baton Rouge: Louisiana State University Press, 2003.

Imboden, John D. Fire, "Sword and the Halter." *The Annals of the Civil War: Witten by Leading Participants North and South*. New York, Da Capo Press, 1994.

———. "The Retreat from Gettysburg," in *Battles and Leaders of the Civil War*, edited by Robert U. Johnson and Clarence C. Buel. 4 vols. New York: Century Publishing Co., 1884-89.

Isham, Asa B. *An Historical Sketch of the Seventh Regiment Michigan Volunteer Cavalry*. New York: Town Topics Publishing Co., 1893.

———. "Through the Wilderness to Richmond." *Military Order of the Loyal Legion of the United States, Ohio Commandery*, September 8, 1884. Cincinnati: Peter G. Thomson, Publisher, 1884.

Jackson, H. E. "Battle of Hunterstown." *Confederate Veteran*, September 1899.

James, C. F. "The Battle of Sailor's Creek." *The Richmond Dispatch*, March 29, 1896, in *Southern Historical Society Papers*, Vol. 24, 1896.

Kidd, James H. "Address at the Dedication of the Michigan Monument Upon the Field of Gettysburg." *Journal of the United States Cavalry Association*. Vol. 4, No. 12. Leavenworth, KS: Ketcheson & Reeves, March 1891, 40-63.

———. *Historical Sketch of General Custer, Reprinted from Ceremonies Attending the Unveiling of the Equestrian Statue to Major General George Armstrong Custer*. Monroe, MI: Monroe County Library Systems, 1978.

———. *Personal Recollections of a Cavalryman with Custer's Michigan Cavalry Brigade in the Civil War*. Ionia, MI: The Sentinel Press, 1908.

———. "The Michigan Cavalry Brigade in the Wilderness." *Michigan Commandery, Military Order of the*

Loyal Legion of the United States, Vol. 1, October 1886-April 1893. Detroit: Winn & Hammond, Printers, 1893.

King, Will C. *Campfire Sketches and Battlefield Echoes of 61-65*. Springfield, MA: King, Richardson & Co., 1888.

Kipling, Rudyard. *American Notes*. Boston: Brown and Company, 1899.

Ladd, David L. and Ladd, Audrey J., eds. *The Bachelder Papers: Gettysburg in Their Own Words*. 3 vols. Dayton, OH: Morningside Press, 1995.

Ladd, David L. and Ladd, Audrey J., eds. *The Bachelder Papers: Gettysburg in Their Own Words*. 3 vols. El Dorado, CA: Savas Beatie, 2020.

Lamb, John. "The Confederate Cavalry: Its Wants, Trials, and Heroism." *Southern Historical Society Papers*, Vol. 25, January-December, 1897.

Law, Evander M. "The Struggle For 'Round Top,'" in *Battles and Leaders of the Civil War*, edited by Robert U. Johnson and Clarence C. Buel. 4 vols. New York: Century Publishing Co., 1884-89.

Lee, William O. "Introductory, The Michigan Cavalry Brigade (Custer's Cavalry)," in *Personal and Historical Sketches and Facial History of and by Members of the Seventh Regiment Michigan Volunteer Cavalry 1862-1865*, edited by William O. Lee. Detroit: Ralston, 1901, iii-ix.

Lloyd, Harlan P. "The Battle of Waynesboro," in W. H. Chamberlin, ed. *Sketches of War History, 1861-1865, Papers Prepared for the Ohio Commandery of the Military Order of the Loyal Legion of the United States*, Vol. 4. Cincinnati: The Robert Clarke Company, 1896.

Lloyd, William P., ed. *History of the First Pennsylvania Reserve Cavalry*. Philadelphia: King & Baird, Printers, 1864.

Loeser, Charles. "Reminiscences of the Civil War," in *From Everglade to CaZon with the Second Dragoons*, edited by Theophilus F. Rodenbough. New York: Van Nostrand and Company, 1875.

Long, Armistead Lindsay. "General Early's Valley Campaign." *Southern Historical Society Papers*, Vol. 18, January-December, 1890.

Longman, Arthur. "Reminiscence," in *Personal and Historical Sketches and Facial History of and By Members of the Seventh Regiment Michigan Volunteer Cavalry 1862-1865*, edited by William O. Lee. Detroit: Ralston, 1901, 258-259.

Longstreet, James. *From Manassas to Appomattox*. Philadelphia: J. B. Lippincott, 1896.

———. "Lee's Right Wing at Gettysburg," in *Battles and Leaders of the Civil War*, edited by Robert U. Johnson and Clarence C. Buel. 4 vols. New York: Century Publishing Co., 1884-89.

Lothrop, Charles H. *A History of the First Regiment Iowa Cavalry Veteran Volunteers*. Lyons, IA: Beers & Eaton, Printers, 1890.

McCall, John T. "7th Tennessee—Battle of Falling Waters." *Confederate Veteran*, No. 6, 1898.

McClellan, George B. "The Peninsular Campaign." *Battles and Leaders of the Civil War*, 4 vols., Robert U. Johnson and Clarence C. Buel, eds. New York, 1884-1889.

———. "Now We Shall Save the Country," in *Battles and Leaders of the Civil War*, edited by Ned Bradford. New York: Appleton-Century-Crofts, Inc., 1956.

McClellan, Henry B. *The Life and Campaigns of Major-General J. E. B. Stuart: Commander of the Cavalry of the Army of Northern Virginia*. Boston: Houghton, Mifflin & Co., 1885.

McClure, Alexander Kelly, ed. *The Annals of the Civil War: Written by Leading Participants North and South*. Philadelphia: Times Publishing Co., 1879.

McDonald, William N. *A History of the Laurel Brigade*, Bushrod C. Washington, ed. Baltimore: Sun Job Printing Office, 1907.

Meade, George Gordon, ed. *The Life and Letters of George Gordon Meade, Major-General United States Army*. 2 Vols. New York: Charles Scribner's Sons, 1913.

Merrill, Samuel H. *The Campaigns of the First Maine and First District of Columbia Cavalry*. Portland, ME: Bailey and Noyes, 1866.

Merritt, Wesley. "Cavalry: Its Organization and Armament." *Journal of the United States Cavalry Association*, Vol. 23. Leavenworth, KS: Ketcheson & Reeves, 1912/1913, 845-853.

———. Correspondence with the publishers of *The Century Magazine*. Century Company Records. Copies on file in Mss. and Archives Section, New York Public Library.

———. "Discussion of Lieut. Schenck's Paper." *Journal of the United States Cavalry Association*, Vol. 1, No. 3. Leavenworth, KS: Ketcheson & Reeves, November 1888, 412-413.

——. "Life and Services of General Philip St. George Cooke." *Journal of the United States Cavalry Association,* Vol. 8, No. 29. Leavenworth, KS: Ketcheson & Reeves, June 1895, 79-92.

——. "Marching Cavalry." *Journal of the United States Cavalry Association,* Vol. 3, No. 11. Leavenworth, KS: Ketcheson & Reeves, December 1890, 71-78.

——. "Reminiscences of the Civil War," in *From Everglade to Canyon with the Second Dragoons,* edited by Theophilus F. Rodenbough. New York: Van Nostrand and Company, 1875.

——. "Sheridan in the Shenandoah Valley," in *Battles and Leaders of the Civil War,* edited by Robert U. Johnson and Clarence C. Buel. 4 vols. New York: Century Publishing Co., 1884-89.

——. "Some Defects of Our Cavalry System." *The United Service,* Vol. 1, Oct. 1879, 557-561.

——. "The Appomattox Campaign." *War Papers and Personal Reminiscences, 1861-1865. Papers Read Before the Commandery of the State of Missouri, Military Order of the Loyal Legion of the United States,* Vol. 1. St. Louis: Becktold & Co., 1892.

——. "The Army of the United States." *Harper's New Monthly Magazine,* Vol. 80, No. 476, March 1890, 490-509.

Meyer, Henry C. *Civil War Experiences Under Bayard, Gregg, Kilpatrick, Custer, Raulston and Newberry 1862, 1863, 1864.* New York: Privately printed, 1911.

Michigan Soldiers and Sailors Individual Records. Lansing, MI: Wynkoop, Hallenbeck, Crawford Co., 1915.

Minor, Kate Pleasants. *An Author and Subject Index to the Southern Historical Society Papers,* Vols. 1-38. Richmond: Virginia State Library Bulletin, Vol. 6, Nos. 3, 4, July and October, 1913.

Mitchell, Frederick W. "An Irish Lieutenant of the Old Second Dragoons." War Papers.

Commandery of the District of Columbia, Military Order of the Loyal Legion of the United States, Volume 4, No. 77, November 3, 1909.

Moore, James. *Kilpatrick and Our Cavalry: Comprising a Sketch of the Life of General Kilpatrick, with an Account of the Cavalry Raids, Engagements, and Operations Under His Command, from the Beginning of the Rebellion to the Surrender of Johnston.* New York: W. J. Widdleton, 1865.

Morgan, W. H. *Personal Reminiscences of the War of 1861-5.* Lynchburg, VA: J. P. Bell Company, Inc., 1911.

Mosby, John S. *The Memoirs of Colonel John S. Mosby.* New York: Little, Brown and Company, 1917.

——. "Stuart's Ride Around the Union Army in the Gettysburg Campaign." *The Century Magazine,* Vol. 34, May-October, 1887.

Moyer, Henry P. *History of the Seventeenth Regiment, Pennsylvania Volunteer Cavalry.* Lebanon, PA: Sowersa Printing Co., 1911.

Mulligan, Abner B. *"My Dear Mother and Sisters": Civil War Letters of Capt. A. B. Mulligan, Co. B, 5th South Carolina Cavalry-Butler's Division-Hampton's Corps, 1861-1865.* Spartanburg, SC: Reprint Co., 1992.

Munford, Thomas T. "A Confederate Officer's Reminiscences." *Journal of the United States Cavalry Association,* Vol. 4, No. 14. Leavenworth, KS: Ketcheson & Reeves, September 1891, 276-288.

——. "A Confederate Officer's Views on 'American Practice and Foreign Theory.'" *Journal of the United States Cavalry Association,* Vol. 4, No. 13. Leavenworth, KS: Ketcheson & Reeves, June 1891, 197-203.

——. "Reminiscences of Cavalry Operations." *Southern Historical Society Papers,* Vol. 13, January-December, 1885.

Munson, John M. "Life with The Mosby Guerillas," in *The Blue and the Gray: The Story of the Civil War as Told by Participants,* edited by Henry Steele Commager. New York: The Bobbs Merrill Company, Inc., 1950.

——. *Reminiscences of a Mosby Guerrilla.* Washington, DC: Zenger Publishing Co., 1983.

Napoleon's Maxims of War. Richmond: West & Johnston, 1862.

Neese, George M. *Three Years in the Confederate Horse Artillery.* New York: The Neale Publishing Company, 1911.

Newhall, Frederick C. "The Battle of Beverly Ford," in *The Annals of the Civil War: Written by Leading Participants North and South.* Philadelphia: Times Publishing Co., 1879.

Nettleton, A. Bayard. "How the Day Was Saved at the Battle of Cedar Creek." *Glimpses of the Nation's Struggle: Papers Read Before the Minnesota Commandery of the*

Military Order of the Loyal Legion of the United States. St. Paul: St. Paul Book and Stationery Company, 1887.

Norton, Chauncey S. "The Red Neckties," or History of the Fifteenth New York Volunteer Cavalry. Ithica, NY: Journal Book and Job Printing House, 1891.

Oakey, Daniel. History of the Second Massachusetts Regiment of Infantry. Beverly Ford. A Paper Read at the Officers' Reunion in Boston, May 12, 1884. Boston: Geo. H. Ellis, Printer, 1884.

Oates, William C. "Battle on the Right Flank." Southern Historical Society Papers, Vol 6, July-December, 1878.

Opie, John N. A Rebel Cavalryman with Lee, Stuart and Jackson. Chicago: W. B. Conkey Company, 1899.

Page, Charles A. Letters of a War Correspondent. Boston: L. C. Page and Company, 1899.

Parsons, Henry C. "Farnsworth Charge and Death," in Battles and Leaders of the Civil War, edited by Robert U. Johnson and Clarence C. Buel. 4 vols. New York: Century Publishing Co., 1884-89.

Patton, George S. War as I Knew It. Boston: Houghton Mifflin Company, 1947.

Perry, Bliss. Life and Letters of Henry Lee Higginson, Vol. 1. Boston: The Atlantic Monthly Press, 1921.

Perry, Leslie J. "A Shock to General Sheridan," The Century Magazine, Vol. 52, No. 4, August 1896.

Pickerill, W. N. History of the Third Indiana Cavalry. Indianapolis: Aetna Printing Co., 1906.

Pleasonton, Alfred. "The Campaign of Gettysburg." The Annals of the Civil War. Written by Leading Participants North and South. Philadelphia: Times Publishing Co., 1879.

Pope, John. "The Second Battle of Bull Run," in Battles and Leaders of the Civil War, edited by Robert U. Johnson and Clarence C. Buel. 4 vols. New York: Century Publishing Co., 1884-89.

Porter, Fitz John. "The Battle of Gaines's Mill and Its Preliminaries." The Century Magazine, Vol. 30, Issue 2, June 1885.

Porter, Horace. Campaigning with Grant. New York: The Century Co., 1897.

Powell, William H. "The Battle of the Petersburg Crater," in Battles and Leaders of the Civil War, edited by Robert U. Johnson and Clarence C. Buel. 4 vols. NY: Century Publishing Co., 1884-89.

Preston, Noble D. "The Cavalry Raid to Richmond, May, 1864." Military Essays and Recollections.

Pennsylvania Commandery of the Military Order of the Loyal Legion of the United States, 1866-1890, compiled by Michael A. Cavanaugh. Volume I. February 1866-May 1903. Wilmington, NC: Broadfoot Publishing Co., 1995.

Price, George F. Across the Continent with the Fifth Cavalry. New York: D. Van Nostrand, 1883.

Pyne, Henry R. The History of the First New Jersey Cavalry. Trenton, NJ: J. A. Beecher, 1871.

Rea, D. B. Sketches from Hampton's Cavalry: Embracing the Principal Exploits of the Cavalry in the Campaigns of 1862 and 1863. Colombia, SC: South Carolinian Steam Press, 1864.

"Reports of Major General A. Pleasonton and Philip H. Sheridan, to the Committee on the Conduct of the War." Journal of the United States Cavalry Association, Vol. 1, No. 3. Leavenworth, KS: Ketcheson & Reeves, November 1888, 394-411.

"Retaliation: The Execution of Seven Prisoners by Col. John S. Mosby." Southern Historical Society Papers. Vol. 27, January-December, 1899.

Rhodes, Charles D. "History of the Cavalry of the Army of the Potomac." Journal of the United States Cavalry Association, Vol. 11, No. 40. Leavenworth, KS: Ketcheson & Reeves, March 1898, 3-101.

———. History of the Cavalry of the Army of the Potomac. Kansas City: Hudson-Kimberly Publishing Co., 1900.

Rice, Allen. "Eyewitness to War: Letter by Allen Rice, 6th Michigan Cavalry." America's Civil War Magazine, March 1997.

Richards, A. E. "The Monument to Mosby's Men," Southern Historical Society Papers, Vol. 27, January-December, 1899.

Robertson, John, ed. Michigan in the War: Report of the Adjutant General. Lansing, MI: W. S. George & Co., State Printers and Binders, 1882.

Robins, W. T. "Stuart's Ride Around McClellan," in Battles and Leaders of the Civil War, edited by Robert U. Johnson and Clarence C. Buel. 4 vols. New York: Century Publishing Co., 1884-89.

Rock, James L. "Foraging Around Trevilian's Station," in Personal and Historical Sketches and Facial History of and by Members of the Seventh Regiment Michigan Volunteer Cavalry 1862-1865, compiled by William O. Lee. Detroit: Ralston, 1901. 147-150.

Rockwell, A. D. Rambling Recollections: An Autobiography. New York: Paul B. Hoeber, 1920.

Rodenbough, Theophilus. F., ed. *From Everglade to Canyon with the Second Dragoons (Second United States Cavalry)*. New York: D. Van Nordstrom, 1875.

——. "Civil War Lessons." *Journal of the United States Cavalry Association*, Vol. 2, No. 5. Leavenworth, KS: Ketcheson & Reeves, June 1889, 103-123.

——. "Sheridan's Richmond Raid," in *Battles and Leaders of the Civil War*, edited by Robert U. Johnson and Clarence C. Buel. 4 vols. New York: Century Publishing Co., 1884-89.

——. "Sheridan's Trevilian Station Raid," in *Battles and Leaders of the Civil War*, edited by Robert U. Johnson and Clarence C. Buel. 4 vols. New York: Century Publishing Co., 1884-89.

——. *The Photographic History of the Civil War: The Cavalry*. New York: The Fairfax Press, 1983.

Rodenbough, Theophilus. F., and Haskin, William L., eds. *The Army of the United States: Historical Sketches of Staff and Line with Portraits of Generals-in-Chief*. New York: Maynard, Merrill, & Co., 1896.

Rosser, Thomas L. "Colonel T. L. Rosser's Report of the Fight at Aldie." *Southern Historical Society Papers*, Vol. 9, March 1881.

Royall, William L. *Some Reminiscences*. New York: The Neale Publishing Company, 1909.

Schaff, Morris. *The Battle of the Wilderness*. Boston: Houghton, Mifflin and Company, 1910.

——. *The Spirit of Old West Point, 1858-1862*. New York: Houghton, Mifflin and Company, 1907.

Schofield, John M. *Forty-Six Years in the Army*. New York: The Century Co., 1897.

Scott, John. *Partisan Life with Col. John S. Mosby*. Gaithersburg, MD: Butternut Press, 1985.

Sheridan, Philip H. *The Personal Memoirs of P. H. Sheridan*. 2 Vols. New York: C. L. Webster, 1888.

Shotwell, Albert. "Winchester," in *Personal and Historical Sketches and Facial History of and by Members of the Seventh Regiment Michigan Volunteer Cavalry 1862-1865*, compiled by William O. Lee. Detroit: Ralston, 1901, 167-169.

Smith, Harmon. "Co. F at the Battle of Trevilian's Station," in *Personal and Historical Sketches and Facial History of and by Members of the Seventh Regiment Michigan Volunteer Cavalry 1862-1865*, William O. Lee, comp. Detroit: 7th Michigan Cavalry Assoc., 1901, 229-231.

Smith, Robert S. "Personal Reminiscences—Fisher's Hill to Cedar Creek," in *From Everglade to Canyon with the Second Dragoons* compiled by Theophilus F. Rodenbough. New York: D. Van Nordstrom, 1875.

Stevens, George T. *Three Years in the Sixth Corps: A Concise Narrative of Events in the Army of the Potomac from 1861 to the Close of the Rebellion, April, 1865*. New York: Van Nostrand, Publisher, 1870.

Stevenson, James H. *"Boots and Saddles:" A History of the First Volunteer Cavalry of the War, Known as the First New York (Lincoln) Cavalry, and Also as the Sabre Regiment*. Harrisburg, PA: Patriot Publishing Company, 1879.

Styple, William B., ed. *Generals in Bronze: Interviewing the Commanders of the Civil War*. Kearny, NJ: Belle Grove Publishing, 2005.

Sutton, J. J. *History of the Second Regiment West Virginia Cavalry Volunteers During the War of the Rebellion*. Portsmouth, OH: 1892.

Swift, Eben. "General Wesley Merritt." *Journal of the United States Cavalry Association*, Vol. 21, No. 83. Leavenworth, KS: Ketcheson & Reeves, March 1911, 829-837.

——. "The Tactical Use of Cavalry." *Journal of Military Service Institution of the U. S.*, Vol. 44. Leavenworth, KS: Ketcheson & Reeves, January, March, and May 1909, 359-369.

Taylor, James E. *With Sheridan Up the Shenandoah Valley in 1864: Leaves from a Special Artist's Sketch Book and Diary*. Dayton, OH: Morningside, 1989.

Tobie, Edward P. *History of the First Maine Cavalry, 1861-1865*. Published by the First Maine Cavalry Association. Boston: Press of Emery & Hughes, 1887.

Townsend, George A. *Rustics in Rebellion: A Yankee Reporter on the Road to Richmond, 1861-65*. Chapel Hill, NC: The University of North Carolina Press, 1950.

——. "The General Torbert Memorial: A Biographical Sketch," 1880.

Tremain, Henry Edward. *The Last Hours of Sheridan's Cavalry*. New York: Bonnell, Silver and Bowers, 1904.

Trout, Robert J., ed. *Riding with Stuart: Reminiscences of an Aide-de-Camp*. Shippensburg, PA: White Mane Publishing Co., Inc., 1994.

Trowbridge, Luther S. "The Operations of the Cavalry in the Gettysburg Campaign," in *The Michigan Commandery of the Military Order of the Loyal Legion of the United States*. Dearborn, MI: Ostler Printing Company, 1888.

Viola, Herman J., ed. *The Memoirs of Charles Henry Veil: A Soldier's Recollections of the Civil War and the Arizona Territory.* New York: Orion Books, 1993.

Wells, Edward L. *Hampton and His Cavalry in '64.* Richmond: B. F. Johnson Publishing Co., 1899.

Wells, William. "Reminiscences of General Custer." Denville, VT: North Star, July 28, 1876.

"West Point in October, The Christian Union, October 17, 1877, Vol. 16." Courtesy of the Merkel Collection. *Newsletter of the Little Big Horn Associates.* Vol. 38, No. 8, October 2004.

White, M. O. to J. P Cilley, Letter of February 9, 1893. First Maine Cavalry Association. *The First Maine Bugle, Bugle Echoes.* Vol. 3, No. 2. Rockland, ME: The Tribune Co., 1893.

Whittaker, Frederick. *Volunteer Cavalry: The Lessons of the Decade, by a Volunteer Cavalryman.* New York: Printed by the author, 1871.

Wilkin, William Parker, letter to his wife, July 31, 1863. Included in *The Athens [OH] Messenger*, August 13, 1863.

Williamson, James J. *Mosby's Rangers: A Record of the Operations of the Forty-Third Battalion Virginia Cavalry, From Its Organization to the Surrender.* New York: Ralph B. Kenyon, Publisher, 1896.

Wilson, James H. *Under the Old Flag: Recollections of Military Operations in the War for the Union, the Spanish War, the Rebellion, Etc.*, 2 Vols. New York: D. Appleton and Company, 1912.

——. "General John Buford." *Journal of the United States Cavalry Association*, Vol. 1, No. 2. Leavenworth, KS: Ketcheson & Reeves, July 1888, 171-183.

Wilson, John. "Passing Mosby's Pickets," in *Personal and Historical Sketches of and By Members of the Seventh Regiment Michigan Volunteer Cavalry 1862-1865*, William Lee, comp. Detroit: Ralston, 1901, 138-141.

Wood, A. E. "The Proper Employment of Cavalry." *Journal of the United States Cavalry Association*, Vol. 4, No. 13. Leavenworth, KS: Ketcheson & Reeves, June 1891, 114-136.

SECONDARY SOURCES

Adams, M. K. *Salt Horse and Sabers: Whittaker's War-Bull Run to Appomattox, 4 Years-82 Battles.* 1st Books Library, 2003.

Alberts, Don E. *General Wesley Merritt: Brandy Station to Manila Bay.* Columbus, OH: The General's Books, 2001.

Anders, Curt. *Henry Halleck's War: A Fresh Look at Lincoln's Controversial General-in-Chief.* Carmel, IN: Guild Press of Indiana, Inc., 1999.

Andrews, J. Cutler. *The North Reports the Civil War.* Pittsburgh: University of Pittsburgh Press, 1955.

Bearss, Edwin Cole. *Encircling the Union Army: Jeb Stuart's Controversial Ride Around McClellan During the Peninsula Campaign, June, 1862.* El Dorado Hills, CA: Savas Publishing, 2013. Digital edition.

Beattie, Daniel J. "Brandy Station: A Clash of Sabers." *Association for the Preservation of Civil War Sites*, January 1998, 14-17.

Berard, A. E., ed. *Reminiscences of West Point in the Golden Time.* East Saginaw, MI: Evening News Printing and Binding House, 1886.

Bilby, Joseph G. *A Revolution in Arms: A History of the First Repeating Rifles.* Yardley, PA: Westholme Publishing, LLC, 2006.

Boatner, III, Mark Mayo. *The Civil War Dictionary.* New York: David McKay Company, Inc., 1959.

Blackman, Wilmon W. "The Capture of General Custer's Love Letters." *Yankee Magazine*, March 1969, 68-70, 104-109.

Brady, Cyrus Townsend. *Indian Fights and Fighters.* New York: McClure, Philips & Co., 1904.

Brasher, Glenn David. *The Peninsula Campaign and the Necessity of Emancipation: African Americans and the Fight for Freedom.* Chapel Hill, NC: The University of North Carolina Press, 2012.

Brennan, Patrick. "I'd Rather Die Than Be Whipped: The Battle of Yellow Tavern." *North & South Magazine*, Vol. 7, No. 4, June 2004, 56-73.

Brown, Kent Masterson. *Retreat from Gettysburg: Lee, Logistics, and the Pennsylvania Campaign.* Chapel Hill, NC: The University of North Carolina Press, 2005.

Bundy, Carol. *The Nature of Sacrifice: A Biography of Charles Russell Lowell, Jr., 1835-1864.* New York: Farrar, Straus and Giroux, 2005.

Burgess, Milton V. *David Gregg: Pennsylvania Cavalryman.* State College, PA: Nittany Valley Offset, 1984.

Calder, John C. "President George Armstrong Custer." *Research Review: The Journal of the Little Big Horn Associates*, Vol. 19, No. 1, Winter, 2005. 14-23, 31.

Carroll, John M., ed. *Custer in the Civil War, His Unfinished Memoirs*. CA: Presidio Press, 1977.

Carter, Samuel, III. *The Last Cavaliers: Confederate and Union Cavalry in the Civil War*. New York: St. Martin's Press, 1979.

Castner, Charles Schuyler. "The Saga of Brigadier General David McMurtrie Gregg." *The Historical Review of Berks County*, 1993-94.

Catton, Bruce. *The Army of the Potomac*. 3 Vols. Garden City, NY: Doubleday & Company, Inc., 1953.

Calkins, Chris M. *History and Tour Guide of Five Forks, Hatcher's Run, and Namozine Church*. Columbus: Blue and Gray Enterprises, Inc., 2003.

———. *The Appomattox Campaign: March 29-April 9, 1865*. Lynchburg, VA: Schroeder Publications, 2008, 2011, and 2015.

———. "With Shouts of Triumph and Trumpets Blowing: George Custer versus Rufus Barringer at Namozine Church, April 3, 1865." *Blue & Gray Magazine*, Vol. 7. No. 6, August 1990.

Caughey, Donald C. and Jones, Jimmy J. *The 6th United States Cavalry in the Civil War: A History and Roster*. Jefferson, NC: McFarland & Company, Inc., Publishers, 2013.

Coffey, David. *Sheridan's Lieutenants: Phil Sheridan, His Generals, and the Final Year of the Civil War*. New York: Rowman and Littlefield Publishers, Inc., 2005.

Cole, Scott C. *34th Battalion Virginia Cavalry*. Lynchburg, VA: H. E. Howard Co., 1993.

Colt, Margaretta Barton. *Defend the Valley: A Shenandoah Valley Family in the Civil War*. New York: Orion Books, 1994.

Commager, Henry Steele, ed. *The Blue and the Gray: The Story of the Civil War as Told by Participants*. New York: The Bobbs-Merrill Company, Inc., 1950.

Cosmas, Graham A. *An Army for Empire: The United States Army in the Spanish-American War*. Colombia, MS: University of Missouri Press, 1971.

Crozier, Emmet. *Yankee Reporters*. Westport, CT: Greenwood Press, Publishers, 1956.

Davis, Burke. *To Appomattox: Nine April Days, 1865*. New York: Rinehart & Co., Inc., 1959.

Davis, Julia and Niemeyer, Lucian. *Shenandoah: Daughter of the Stars*. Baton Rouge: Louisiana State University Press, 1994.

Day, Carl. "If You Want to Know…" *Greasy Grass*, Vol. 9. Published by the Custer Battlefield Historical and Museum Association, May 1993, 2-6.

Deane, Fannie Parmelee, ed. *Nicknames and Pseudonyms of Prominent People with Dates of Birth and Death*. New Philadelphia, OH: O. R. Parmelee, Publisher, 1897.

Driver, Robert J. *5th Virginia Cavalry*. Lynchburg, VA: H. E. Howard, Inc., 1997.

Eckert, Edward K. and Amato, Nicholas J., eds. *Ten Years in the Saddle: The Memoir of William Woods Averell 1851-1862*. San Rafael, CA: Presidio Press, 1978.

Edwards, William B. *Civil War Guns*. Secaucus, NJ: Castle Books, 1962.

Emerson, Edward Waldo. *Life and Letters of Charles Russell Lowell*. Boston: Houghton Mifflin Company, 1907.

Esposito, Vincent J. *The West Point Atlas of the American Wars: 1689-1900*. New York: Frederick A. Praeger, Publishers, 1959.

Fagan, Roberta E. "Custer at Front Royal: 'A Horror of the War,'" in *Custer and His Times*, Book 3, edited by Gregory J. W. Urwin. Conway, AR: University of Central Arkansas Press and the Little Big Horn Associates, 1987.

———. "Custer and the Killing of David Getz." *Little Big Horn Association Research Review*, Vol. 12, No. 2, December 1987, 17-21.

"Fairfield in the Civil War." Fairfield, PA: Fairfield Sesquicentennial Committee, 2011.

Folsom, William R. "Vermont at Gettysburg." *Vermont Historical Quarterly: A Magazine of History*, Vol. 20, No. 3, July 1952.

Foote, Shelby. *The Civil War: A Narrative*. 3 Vols. New York: Random House, Inc., 1974.

Fox, William F. *Regimental Losses in the American Civil War, 1861-1865*. Albany, NY: Albany Publishing Company, 1889.

Franks, George F., III. *Battle of Falling Waters 1863: Custer, Pettigrew, and the End of the Gettysburg Campaign*. Williamsport, MD: Privately published, 2013.

Freeman, Douglas Southall. *Lee's Lieutenants: A Study in Command,* 3 vols. New York: Charles Scribner's Sons, 1942.

Frost, Lawrence A. *General Custer's Libbie*. Seattle: Superior Publishing Company, 1976.

Gallagher, Gary W., ed. *Fighting for the Confederacy: The Personal Recollections of General Edward Porter Alexander*. Chapel Hill, NC: University of North Carolina Press, 1989.

——. *The Spotsylvania Campaign*. Chapel Hill, NC: The University of North Carolina Press, 2010.

Graham, William A. *Reno Court of Inquiry*. Harrisburg, PA, 1953.

Hagemann, E. R, ed. *Fighting Rebels and Redskins: Experiences in the Army Life of Colonel George B. Sanford*. Norman, OK: University of Oklahoma Press, 1969.

Harris, John. *The Gallant Six Hundred: A Tragedy of Obsessions*. New York: Mason & Lipscomb, Publishers, 1973.

Hatton, Robert W., ed. "Just a Little Bit of the Civil War, as Seen by W. J. Smith, Company M, 2nd O. V. Cavalry—Part I." *Ohio History*, Vol. 84, Summer 1975.

Hale, Laura Virginia. *Four Valiant Years in the Lower Shenandoah Valley, 1861-1865*. Strasburg, VA: Shenandoah Pub. House, 1968.

——. "Just a Little Bit of the Civil War, as Seen by W. J. Smith, Company M, 2nd O. V. Cavalry—Part II." *Ohio History*, Vol. 84, Summer 1975.

Heatwole, John L. *The Burning: Sheridan's Devastation of the Shenandoah Valley*. Charlottesville, VA: Rockbridge Publishing, 1998.

Herbert, T. W. "In Occupied Pennsylvania." *The Georgia Review*, Vol. 4, No. 2, Summer 1950. Athens, GA: University of Georgia Press.

Hoffman, Elliot W., ed. *A Vermont Cavalryman in War and Love: The Civil War Letters of Brevet Major General William Wells and Anna Richardson*. Lynchburg, VA: Schroeder Publications, 2007.

——. *History of the First Vermont Cavalry Volunteers in the War of the Great Rebellion*. Baltimore: Butternut and Blue, 2000.

Holbrook, Arthur. "With the Fifth Wisconsin at Williamsburg." *War Papers Read Before the Commandery of the State of Wisconsin, Military Order of the Loyal Legion of the United States*, 4 vols. (Milwaukee, WI, 1891-1914), 3:530.

Howard, Charles Raymond. *Uncle Jacob's War: An Attempt to Comprehend the Military Service of Jacob Lyman Greene*. Unpublished work, 1993.

Howard, Richard P. *Mostly Good and Competent Men: Illinois Governors, 1818-1988*. Springfield, IL: Illinois State Historical Society, 1988.

Hudgins, Garland C. and Kleese, Richard B. *Recollections of an Old Dominion Dragoon: The Civil War Experiences of Sgt. Robert S. Hudgins II Co. B, 3rd Virginia Cavalry*. Orange, VA: Publisher's Press, 1993.

Humphreys, Charles A. *Field, Camp, Hospital and Prison in the Civil War, 1863-1865*. Boston: Press of Geo. H. Ellis Co., 1918.

Hunt, H. Draper. *Dearest Father: The Civil War Letters of Lt. Frank Dickerson, a Son of Belfast, Maine*. Unity, ME: North Country Press, 1992.

Hunt, Jeffrey Wm. *Meade and Lee After Gettysburg: The Forgotten Final Stage of the Gettysburg Campaign, from Falling Waters to Culpeper Court House, July 14-31, 1863*. El Dorado Hills, CA: Savas Beatie, 2017.

Jensen, Oliver. "War Correspondent: 1864, The Sketchbooks of James E. Taylor." *American Heritage Magazine*. Vol. 31, No. 5, August-September, 1980.

Jones, Virgil Carrington. *Ranger Mosby*. Chapel Hill, NC: University of North Carolina Press, 1944.

——. *Gray Ghosts and Rebel Raiders*. Covington, GA: Morningside Books, 1973.

Kinsley, D. A. *Favor the Bold: Custer–The Civil War Years*. New York: Holt, Rinehart and Winston, 1967.

Kirshner, Ralph. *The Class of 1861: Custer, Ames, and Their Classmates After West Point*. Carbondale, IL: Southern Illinois University Press,1999.

Klement, Frank L., ed. "Edwin B. Bigelow: A Michigan Sergeant in the Civil War." September 1954. Copy on file, Park Library and Research Center, GNMP.

Kobrick, Jacob. "No Army Inspired: The Failure of Nationalism at Antebellum West Point." Alison Fisk, ed. Department of History, Villanova University, November 30, 2003.

Kraft, Louis. "George Armstrong Custer: Changing Views of an American Legend." *American History Magazine*, June 2006.

Krepps, John T. *A Strong and Sudden Onslaught: The Cavalry Action at Hanover, Pennsylvania*. Orrtanna, PA: Colecraft Industries, 2008.

Kundahl, George G., ed. *The Bravest of the Brave: The Correspondence of Stephen Dodson Ramseur*. Chapel Hill, NC: The University of North Carolina Press, 2010.

Ladd, David L. and Ladd, Audrey J., eds. "Stuart's and Gregg's Cavalry Engagement, July 3, 1863." *The Gettysburg Magazine*. Vol. 16, 95-110.

Leckie, Shirley A. *Elizabeth Bacon Custer and the Making of a Myth*. Norman, OK: University of Oklahoma Press, 1993.

Lloyd, Harlan Page. "The Battle of Waynesboro," in *The Custer Reader*, edited by Paul Andrew Hutton. Lincoln, NE: University of Nebraska Press, 1992.

Longacre, Edward G. "Clash of Cavalry at Todd's Tavern," *Civil War Times Illustrated*, Vol. 16, No. 6, October 1977, 12-21.

———. *Custer and His Wolverines: The Michigan Cavalry Brigade, 1861-1865*. Cambridge, MA: Da Capo Press, 2004.

———. *General John Buford: A Military Biography*. Cambridge, MA: Da Capo Press, 1995.

———. *Grant's Cavalryman: The Life and Wars of General James H. Wilson*. Mechanicsburg, PA: The Stackpole Company, 1972.

———. *The Cavalry at Gettysburg: A Tactical Study of Mounted Operations During the Civil War's Pivotal Campaign, 9 June-14 July, 1863*. Rutherford, NJ: Fairleigh-Dickinson University Press, 1986.

———. *Custer: The Making of a Young General*. New York, Skyhorse Publishing, 2018.

Luvaas, Jay. "Cavalry Lessons of the Civil War." *Civil War Times Illustrated*, Vol. 6, No. 9, January 1968, 20-31.

Madaus, H. Michael. "The Personal and Designating Flags of General George A. Custer, 1863-1865." *Military Collector and Historian Magazine*, Spring 1968, 2-5.

Marshall, S. L. A. *Men Against Fire: The Problem of Battle Command in Future War*. New York: William Morrow and Company, 1947.

May, George S. "Message of Governor Austin Blair to the Michigan Legislature, May 7, 1861." *Michigan and the Civil War Years, 1860-1866: A Wartime Chronicle*. Ann Arbor, MI: Michigan Civil War Centennial Observance, 1964.

McFeely, William S. *Grant: A Biography*. New York: W. W. Norton & Company, 1981.

McKinney, Joseph W. *Brandy Station, Virginia, June 9, 1863: The Largest Cavalry Battle of the Civil War*. Jefferson, NC: McFarland & Company, Inc., Publishers, 2006.

McMahon, Thomas L. "The Flag of the Fifth North Carolina, the First Southern Banner Captured in the East, Has Been Rediscovered." *America's Civil War* (May 2002), Vol. 15, No. 2, 69.

McNaughton, Daniel. "Reminiscences," in *Personal and Historical Sketches and Facial History of and by Members of the Seventh Regiment Michigan Volunteer Cavalry 1862-1865*, edited by William O. Lee. Detroit: Ralston, 1901.

McSwain, Eleanor D., ed. *Crumbling Defenses: or Memoirs and Reminiscences of John Logan Black*. Macon, GA: The J. W. Burke Co., 1960.

Merington, Marguerite, ed. *The Custer Story: The Life and Intimate Letters of General Custer and His Wife Elizabeth*. New York: The Devin-Adair Company, 1950.

Merrill, Samuel H. *The Campaigns of the First Maine and First District of Colombia Cavalry*. Portland, ME: Bailey and Noyes, 1866.

Merritt, John S., Sr. "The Forgotten Professional: A Biography of General Wesley Merritt." Quantico, VA: Marine Corps Development and Education Command, Command and Staff College, 1987.

Mewborn, Horace. "*From Mosby's Command*": *Newspaper Letters and Articles By and About John S. Mosby and His Rangers*. Baltimore: Butternut and Blue, 2005.

Milgram, James W. "The Libby Correspondence of Tattnall Paulding." *The American Philatelist*, Vol. 89, No. 12, December 1975, 1113-1135.

Millbrook, Minnie Dubbs. "A Monument to Custer," in *The Great Sioux War, 1876-1877: The Best from Montana The Magazine of Western History*, edited by Paul L. Hedren. Helena, MT: Montana Historical Society Press, 1991.

———. "Big Game Hunting with the Custers, 1869-1870." *The Kansas Historical Quarterly*, Vol. 41, No. 4, Winter 1975, 429-453.

Miller, William E. "The Cavalry Battle Near Gettysburg," in *Battles and Leaders of the Civil War*, edited by Robert U. Johnson and Clarence C. Buel. 4 Vols. New York: Century Publishing Co., 1884-89.

Miller, William J. *Decision at Tom's Brook: George Custer, Thomas Rosser, and the Joy of the Fight*. El Dorado Hills, CA: Savas Beatie, 2016.

Mills, Anson. *My Story*. Washington DC: Published by the author, 1918.

Mitchell, Frederick W. "An Irish Lieutenant of the Old Second Dragoons." *Commandery of the District of*

Columbia, Military Order of the Loyal Legion of the United States, No. 77, November 3, 1909.

Monaghan, Jay. *Custer: The Life of General George Armstrong Custer*. Lincoln, NE: University of Nebraska Press, 1959.

Morris, Jr., Roy. *Sheridan: The Life and Wars of General Phil Sheridan*. New York: Crown Publishers, Inc., 1992.

Nichols, Nick. "Development of Cavalry Tactics." *The Civil War News*, February-March, 1996, 7.

Novak, Bob. "General Custer's West Point Funeral." *Little Big Horn Associates Newsletter*, Vol. 39, No. 1, February 2005, 4-5.

O'Connor, Richard. *Sheridan, the Inevitable*. Indianapolis: Bobbs-Merrill Co., 1953.

O'Neill, Robert F. *Chasing Jeb Stuart and John Mosby: The Union Cavalry in Northern Virginia from Second Manassas to Gettysburg*. Jefferson, NC: McFarland & Company, Inc., Publishers, 2012.

O'Neill, Tom. "Two Men of Ohio: Custer and Bingham." *Little Big Horn Association's Research Review*. Vol. 8, No. 1, January 1994, 10-11.

Ovies, Adolfo. *Crossed Sabers: General George Armstrong Custer and the Shenandoah Valley Campaign*. Bloomington, IN: AuthorHouse, 2004.

Patchan, Scott C. *The Last Battle of Winchester: Phil Sheridan, Jubal Early, and the Shenandoah Valley Campaign, August 7-September 19, 1864*. El Dorado Hills, CA: Savas Beatie, 2013.

Penny, Morris M. and Laine, J. Gary. *Struggle for the Round Tops: Law's Alabama Brigade at the Battle of Gettysburg*. Colonial Heights, VA: Burd Street Press, 1999.

Petruzzi, J. David. *Alfred Pleasonton's Civil Wars*. Unpublished manuscript, 2004.

Petruzzi, J. David, and Steven A. Stanley. *The Gettysburg Campaign in Numbers and Losses: Synopses, Orders of Battls, Strengths, Casualties, and Maps, June 9 - July 14, 1863*. El Dorado Hills, CA: Savas Beatie, 2012.

Reynolds, Arlene, ed. *The Civil War Memories of Elizabeth Bacon Custer*. Austin, TX: University of Texas Press, 1994.

Rhea, Gordon C. *The Battles for Spotsylvania Court House and the Road to Yellow Tavern, May 7-12, 1864*. Baton Rouge: Louisiana State University Press, 1997.

Rogers, Larry, and Rogers, Keith. *Their Horses Climbed Trees: A Chronicle of the California 100 and Battalion in the Civil War, from San Francisco to Appomattox*. Atglen, PA: Schiffer Military History, 2001.

Rummel, III, George A. *Cavalry on the Roads to Gettysburg: Kilpatrick at Hanover and Hunterstown*. Shippensburg, PA: White Mane Books, 2000.

Ryckman, W. G. "Clash of Cavalry at Trevilians." *The Virginia Magazine of History and Biography*, Vol. 75, No. 4, October 1967, 443-458.

Scheips, Paul T. "Darkness and Light: The Interwar Years, 1865-1898." *American Military History*, Army Historical Series, Office of the Chief Military History, United States Army. Publishing date unknown.

Schiller, Laurence D. "A Taste of Northern Steel: The Evolution of Federal Cavalry Tactics, 1861-1865." *North & South Magazine*, Vol. 2, No. 2, January 1999, 30-44.

Sears, Stephen W. *George B. McClellan: The Young Napoleon*. New York: Ticknor & Fields, 1988.

———. "West Point in the Civil War," in *West Point: Two Centuries of Honor and Tradition*, edited by Robert Cowley and Thomas Guinzburg. New York: Warner Books, Inc., 2002.

Servacek, Robert A. *Custer: His Promotion in Frederick, Maryland*. Frederick, MD: Privately published, 2002.

Sherman, Caroline B., ed. "A New England Boy in the Civil War." *The New England Quarterly*. Vol. 5, No. 2, April 1932, 310-344.

Shevchuk, Paul N. "Cut to Pieces": The Cavalry Fight at Fairfield, Pennsylvania, July 3rd, 1863." *The Gettysburg Magazine*. No. 1, February 1985, 1-30.

Sifakis, Stewart. *Who Was Who in the Civil War*. New York: Facts on File Publications, 1988.

Simpson, Harold B. *Cry Comanche: The 2nd U. S. Cavalry in Texas, 1855-1861*. Hillsboro, TX: Hill Junior College Press, 1979.

Simson, J. W. *Custer and the Front Royal Executions of 1864*. Jefferson, NC: McFarland & Company, Inc., Publishers, 2009.

Slade, A. D. *A. T. A. Torbert: Southern Gentleman in Union Blue*. Dayton, OH: Morningside House, Inc., 1992.

Stackpole, Edward J. *Sheridan in the Shenandoah: Jubal Early's Nemesis.* Harrisburg, PA: The Stackpole Co., 1961.

Starr, Stephen Z. "Cold Steel: The Saber and the Union Cavalry." *Civil War History,* Vol. 11, No. 2, June 1965.

——. "Dinwiddie Court House and Five Forks: Reminiscences of Roger Hannaford, Second Ohio Volunteer Cavalry." *The Virginia Magazine of History and Biography,* Vol. 87, No. 4, October 1979.

——. *The Union Cavalry in the Civil War. From Fort Sumter to Gettysburg, 1861-1863,* Vol. 1. Baton Rouge: Louisiana State University Press, 1979.

——. *The Union Cavalry in the Civil War. The War in the East from Gettysburg to Appomattox, 1863-1865,* Vol. 2. Baton Rouge: Louisiana State University Press, 1981.

——. "Winter Quarters near Winchester, 1864-1865: Reminiscences of Roger Hannaford, Second Ohio Volunteer Cavalry." *The Virginia Magazine of History and Biography,* Vol. 86, No. 3, July 1978.

Stevens, George T. *Three Years in the Sixth Corps.* New York: D. Van Nordstrom, Publishers, 1870.

Stiles, Kenneth L. *4th Virginia Cavalry.* Lynchburg, VA: H. E. Howard, Inc., 1985.

Stonesifer, Roy P. "The Long Hard Road: Union Cavalry in the Gettysburg Campaign." Master of Arts dissertation, Pennsylvania State University, January 1959.

——. "The Union Cavalry Comes of Age." *Civil War History,* Vol. 11, No. 3, 1965, 273-284.

Stowe, Mark S. *Company B, 6th Michigan Cavalry.* Grand Rapids, MI: Published by the author, 2002.

Stricker, Mark R. "Dragoon or Cavalryman: Major General John Buford in the American Civil War." Fort Leavenworth, KS: U.S. Army Command and General Staff College, 1994.

Swank, Walbrook Davis. *Battle of Trevilian Station: The Civil War's Greatest and Bloodiest All Cavalry Battle.* Shippensburg, PA: Burd Street Press, 1994.

Sword, Wiley. "'Those Damned Michigan Spencers': Colonel Copeland's 5th Michigan Cavalry and Their Spencer Rifles." *Man at Arms Magazine,* No. 5, 1997, 23-37.

Terrell, John Upton and Walton, George. *Faint the Trumpet Sounds: The Story of Major Marcus A. Reno.* New York: The David McKay Company, 1966.

Turan, Kenneth. "Yellow Hair's Final Ride." *Time Magazine,* November 5, 1984.

Trefousse, Hans L. *Rutherford B. Hayes.* New York: Times Books, 2002.

Urwin, Gregory J. W. "Custer: The Civil War Years," in *The Custer Reader,* edited by Paul Andrew Hutton. Lincoln, NE: The University of Nebraska Press, 1992.

——. *Custer Victorious: The Civil War Battles of General George Armstrong Custer.* Lincoln, NE: University of Nebraska Press, 1983.

——. "The Look of the Boy General: The Uniforms of George Custer." *Campaigns Magazine,* May-June 1979, 4-6.

Utley, Robert M., ed. *Life in Custer's Cavalry: Diaries and Letters of Albert and Jennie Barnitz, 1867-1868.* Lincoln, NE: University of Nebraska Press, 1977.

Vosburg, Brent L. "Battle of Hanover." *America's Civil War Magazine,* January 1998, 46-52.

Warner, Ezra J. *Generals in Blue: Lives of the Union Commanders.* Baton Rouge: Louisiana State University Press, 1964.

Wellman, Manley Wade. *Rebel Boast: First at Bethel—Last at Appomattox.* New York: Henry Holt and Company, 1956.

Wert, Jeffry D. "All the Powers of Hell Were Waked to Madness." *America's Civil War Magazine.* July 2002, 42-48.

——. *Custer: The Controversial Life of George Armstrong Custer.* New York: Simon & Schuster, 1996.

——. *Gettysburg. Day Three.* New York: Simon & Schuster, 2001.

——. *Mosby's Rangers.* New York: Simon and Schuster, 1990.

——. "Old Jubilee's Last Battle." *Civil War Times Illustrated,* August 1977, 20-27.

Whittaker, Frederick. *A Popular Life of Gen. George A. Custer: Major-General of Volunteers, Brevet Major-General U. S. Army, and Lieutenant-Colonel of the Seventh U. S. Cavalry.* New York: Sheldon & Company, 1876.

Williams, Robert A. "Haw's Shop: A 'Storm of Shot and Shell.'" *Civil War Times Illustrated*, Vol. 9, No. 9, January 1971, 12-19.

Williams, T. Harry. *Hayes of the Twenty-third: The Civil War Volunteer Officer.* Lincoln, NE: University of Nebraska, 1994.

Wittenberg, Eric J. ed., *At Custer's Side: The Civil War Writings of James Harvey Kidd.* Kent, OH: Kent State University Press, Kindle edition.

——. *Gettysburg's Forgotten Cavalry Actions: Farnsworth's Charge, South Cavalry Field, and the Battle of Fairfield, July 3, 1863.* El Dorado Hills, CA: Savas Beatie, 2011.

——. *Glory Enough for All: Sheridan's Second Raid and the Battle of Trevilian Station.* Washington, DC: Brassey's, 2001.

——. "John Buford and the Hanging of Confederate Spies During the Gettysburg Campaign." *The Gettysburg Magazine*, No. 18, January 1998, 5-14.

——. *Little Phil: A Reassessment of the Civil War Leadership of Gen. Philip H. Sheridan.* Washington, DC: Potomac Books, Inc., 2002.

——. "Merritt's Regulars on South Cavalry Field: Oh, What Could Have Been." *The Gettysburg Magazine.* No. 16. 111-123.

——. *One of Custer's Wolverines: The Civil War Letters of Brevet Brigadier General James H. Kidd, 6th Michigan Cavalry.* Kent, OH: The Kent State University Press, 2000.

——. *Protecting the Flank: The Battles for Brinkerhoff's Ridge and East Cavalry Field, Battle of Gettysburg, July 2-3, 1863.* Celina, OH: Ironclad Publishing, 2002.

——. *The Battle of Brandy Station: North America's Largest Cavalry Battle.* Charleston, SC: The History Press, 2010.

——. *"The Devil's to Pay": John Buford at Gettysburg: A History and Walking Tour.* El Dorado Hills, CA: Savas Beatie, 2014.

——. *Under Custer's Command: The Civil War Journal of James Henry Avery.* Washington, DC: Brassey's, 2000.

——. *With Sheridan in the Final Campaign Against Lee.* Baton Rouge: Louisiana State University Press, 2002.

Wittenberg, Eric J., and J. David Petruzzi. *Plenty of Blame to Go Around: J.E.B. Stuart's Controversial Ride to Gettysburg.* El Dorado Hills, CA: Savas-Beatie, 2006.

Wittenberg, Eric J., Petruzzi, J. David, and Nugent, Michael F. *One Continuous Fight: The Retreat from Gettysburg and the Pursuit of Lee's Army of Northern Virginia, July 4-14, 1863.* El Dorado Hills, CA: Savas Beatie, 2008.

Wolfe, Brendan. "A Civil Occupation." *University of Virginia Magazine*, Spring 1915.

MISCELLANEOUS SOURCES

Battle of Hanover Walking Tour. Hanover Area Chamber of Commerce, Hanover PA.

"Civil War in Loudoun Valley: The Cavalry Battles of Aldie, Middleburg, and Upperville, June, 1863." National Park Service, Department of the Interior. Washington, DC: 2004.

"Manual of Instruction for the Safe Use of Reproduction Repeating Rifles in Interpretive Demonstrations." National Park Service, Department of the Interior. Washington, DC.

McCullough, Ginger, Easterbrook, Richard, and Calkins, Chris. "Maps of the Battle of Five Forks, April 1, 1865." Petersburg National Battlefield, National Park Service, Department of the Interior. Washington, DC.

WEBSITES

Chapman, James D. "Sound the Charge! Custer and the Saber Charge in the Civil War." Master's Capstone Thesis 143, 2017. http://digital commons.apus.edu/theses/143.

Gehris, Roy F. "The David McMurtrie Gregg Homepage." www.geocities.com/Heartland/Hill/7117/GenGregg.html.

Hunt-Anschütz, Arlea Exelwyrd. "What is Wyrd?" in *Cup of Wonder*, No. 5, October 2001. www.wyrdwords.vispa.com/heathenry/whatwyrd.html.

Ortner, Eric. "The Man and the Menace to the Confederacy: Christopher Spencer and his Repeating Rifle." *Civil War Courier Magazine*, May-June 1999. https://www.ortnergraphics.com/services/civil-war-firearms/spencer-repeater.html.

Palmer House, Chicago. American Oliograph Company, 1873. *The Great Chicago Fire and the Web of Memory*. www.greatchicagofire.org/queen-of-west-once-more/bricks-and-mortar.

"Psalm 39." *The Psalter. The (Online) Book of Common Prayer*. New York: The Church Hymnal Corporation. www.bcponline.org/.

"West Point, Training, and the Development of Tactics." www..usregulars.com/ USMAhome.html.

Wittenberg, Eric J. "Battle of Fairfield: Grumble Jones' Gettysburg Campaign Victory." HistoryNet. Posted September 1, 2006. www.historynet.com.

CORRESPONDENCE

German, Andrew to Adolfo Ovies. "Civil War Cavalry." August 18, 2015.s

Wittenberg, Eric to Adolfo Ovies. August 17, 2017.

Wittenberg, Eric to Adolfo Ovies. September 19, 2017.

Index

About the Author

Adolfo Ovies migrated to the United States from Cuba in 1960, making his new home in Connecticut. With Gettysburg just a hop, skip, and jump away, the ten-year-old Adolfo made his first trip to the battlefield. It turned out to be one of the most impactful moments of his young life, as the American Civil War bug bit him deeply. The roguish Errol Flynn's mesmerizing portrayal of Custer in the movie *They Died with Their Boots On* not only captured the elusive nature of Custer's flamboyant personality but provided Adolfo with an intriguing hero. This book springs from Adolfo's life-time passion for the Civil War, and Custer's role in particular. Adolfo currently resides in Miami, Florida.